THE SOCIAL WORLD OF CHILDREN'S LEARNING

Also available from Cassell:

M. Bonnett: *Children's Thinking*
C. Cullingford: *Children and Society*
C. Cullingford: *The Inner World of the School*
J. Campion: *Working with Vulnerable Young Children*
R. Jones: *The Child-School Interface*
A. Pollard: *The Social World of the Primary School*
A. Pollard: *An Introduction to Primary Educaiton*
A. Pollard and S. Tann: *Reflective Teaching in the Primary School 2nd Edition*
A. Pollard, P. Broadfoot, P. Croll, M. Osborn and D. Abbott: *Changing English Primary Schools?*
S. Roffey, T. Tarrant and K. Majors: *Young Friends*
S. Tann: *Developing Language in the Primary Classroom*

The Social World of Children's Learning

Case Studies of Pupils from Four to Seven

Andrew Pollard
with Ann Filer

CASSELL

Cassell
Wellington House
125 Strand
London WC2R 0BB

215 Park Avenue South
New York
NY 10003

First published 1996

British Library Cataloguing-in-Publication Data
A catalogue record for this book is available from the British Library.

ISBN 0-304-32639-9 (hardback)
      0-304-32641-0 (paperback)

Typeset by Action Typesetting Limited, Gloucester
Printed and bound in Great Britian by Redwood books, Trowbridge, Wiltshire

This book is dedicated to Ros.

Contents

Acknowledgements   viii
Introduction   x

Part One   **Setting the Scene**   1

    1 Questions for Enquiry   3
    2 School and Classroom Contexts   15

Part Two   **Beginning**   33

    Introduction to the Case Study Stories   35
    3 Mary's Story   39
    4 Learning, Identity and Social Relationships: an Initial Analysis   81

Part Three   **Elaborating**   99

    5 Hazel's Story   101
    6 Daniel's Story   146
    7 Sally's Story   186
    8 James' Story   225
    9 Learning, Identity and Social Relationships: Case-study
       Comparisons   267

Part Four   **Reflecting**   287

   10 On the Research Process and Validity of the Study   289
   11 On the Relevance of the Study for Parents, Teachers and Policy-
       makers   305

References   318
Author Index   323
Case-study Index of Children and Teachers   325
Analytic Subject Index   326

KEY ANALYTIC MODELS

Introduction   A simplified model of teacher/pupil classroom coping strategies   xiii
Figure 1.2   A simplified model of six questions concerning social
               influences on children's learning   14
Figure 4.3   A model of learning, identity and social setting   97
Figure 9.1   The spiral of learning, identity and career   284
Figure 11.2   A complementary model of teachers teaching and pupils learning   315

Acknowledgements

I cannot adequately express my gratitude to the children, parents, teachers and governors of the school from which case-study data is drawn in this book. Without their consistent interest and trust, the eight-year project from which this book is derived would not have been possible. It has also been a pleasure to work with them and to be allowed to struggle to understand something of their lives. I am only too aware of how difficult it is to fully represent such subtle complexities and I am particularly grateful for the constructive approach to validation of the case-studies which has been shown.

My thanks too to the University of the West of England, in particular Geoff Whitty, Len Barton, Jenny Ozga and Rob Cuthbert, for supporting this longitudinal project from its inception and to the Leverhulme Trust for very important part-funding during the last few years. Naomi Roth, Justine White and Sarah Roberts from Cassell have been tremendously helpful in bringing the project to fruition in published form.

I would like to thank Kath Henry, who worked on some of the data as part of a MEd student project and my many friends and colleagues in the Faculty of Education at UWE who have indulged my obsession with this study.

Thanks also to various other academic colleagues who have discussed aspects of the ideas contained in this book with me at various times. These include Dorothy Abbott, Neville Bennett, Alan Blyth, Patricia Broadfoot, Bob Burgess, Jim Campbell, Paul Croll, Harry Daniels, Sarah Delamont, Charles Desforges, Mary Jane Drummond, Martyn Hammersley, Martin Hughes, Margaret Jackson, David James, Ian Menter, Yolande Muschamp, Jennifer Nias, Marilyn Osborn, Pat Triggs, Mike Wallace and Peter Woods.

I am delighted to acknowledge the contribution of Ann Filer to the full longitudinal project from which this book is drawn. She joined me for the last three years of data-gathering and has been an excellent collaborator. We have been able to interrogate data gathered by each other and push forward attempts to identify patterns, analyse trends and generate theory. Although Ann should not be held responsible for either the data or text of this first book, she has played an important role in shaping the presentation of the project as a whole. Her major contribution will be seen in the second book, on pupil careers, which we have co-authored and which draws on the full seven years of data which we have gathered.

The analysis and production of *The Social World of Children's Learning* could not have been sustained without the dedicated work of my excellent secretarial colleagues at UWE. The personnel in the research office have changed over the years, but I would particularly like to thank Sarah Butler, Jacquie Harrison and Jenny Wills for their work on, and interest in, this project. It has been a pleasure working with them.

I am grateful to several authors and/or publishers for permission to reproduce various figures, the originals of which were first published elsewhere: Neville Bennett and Falmer Press for Figure 11.1, first published in Delamont, S. (ed.) (1987) *The Primary School Teacher*; Methuen & Co. for Figure 1.1, first published in Bruner, J. and Haste, H. (eds) (1987) *Making Sense*; Falmer Press for Figure 4.1, first published in Pollard, A. (ed.) (1987) *Children and their Primary Schools*.

Finally, I want to thank my wife, Ros, to whom this book is dedicated. As a primary-school headteacher she provides me with constant staff-development and we have struggled together, as parents, with many of the issues which are raised in the book. Above all though, her contribution to this book has been intellectual – posing questions, providing constructive critique and discussing the major issues. As I have said before, most of my best ideas are really *our* ideas.

Despite all this support and advice, I alone am responsible for the final text.

Bristol, January 1995   Andrew Pollard

Introduction

SOME STARTING POINTS

How do young children become effective classroom learners? How do social factors, such as family life, friendships with other children and relationships with teachers, influence the fulfilment of children's learning potential? Are policy-makers justified in focusing on curriculum and assessment to 'improve educational standards', or is this out of balance and failing to recognize the range of personal and interpersonal factors which affect learning and development?

These are some of the questions with which I began the study which is reported in this book. It had its origins in the mid-1980s when the education systems of England and Wales faced a growing critique on many fronts, including those of the curriculum, assessment, management and systems of accountability. My intuitive response, as a former primary school teacher through the 1970s and as a parent of two young children, was that some very important points were being missed. In particular, I felt that there was very little understanding of the personal and interpersonal nature of the learning of young children or of the importance of the social contexts in which learning takes place. Such issues have always been rather subtle, ephemeral and hard to document but I believed that they were particularly important. Whilst the new educational policies of the British government might have provided an enabling framework in England, they also had the potential to cause considerable damage in classrooms, particularly since they appeared to be crudely driven by the ideologies of 'New Right' politicians with very little appreciation of classroom conditions, of learning processes or of the motivational issues which I believed to be so important to work with young children. I wanted to investigate the social factors in play.

RESEARCH DESIGN AND METHOD

I thus designed a research programme in which I hoped to identify and trace the major social influences on children's approach to classroom learning. I opted for detailed study of a small number of children over time, so that the development of their learning could be tracked with particular reference to the basic curriculum, and I decided to collect a wide range of different types of data so that I could construct an understanding of the life of each child as a whole. As well as seeing the children as 'pupils' within their class-rooms, I wanted to understand them as individuals, by studying their biographies and the social influences on their lives and personal identities. This type of detailed, wide-ranging and sustained case-study work, using qualitative data and with an exploratory intention, is a longitudinal form of *ethnography* – the classic research approach of anthropologists which has been adopted by sociologists to study the perspectives, inter-action and cultures of people in context (see Chapter 10 for full details).

I initially planned to work in *two* case-study schools, thinking that a comparison of experiences and provision for children growing up in contrastive socio-economic circum-stances would be particularly interesting. Thus, in September 1987, using the time which was made available to me by the University of the West of England (formerly Bristol Polytechnic) as a Reader in Primary Education, I started work with a small cohort of just ten children as they began school in an England primary school serving a middle-class community. Soon after, I heard that my proposal to a research council for funding of an inner-city case-study had been unsuccessful and the research thus continued in just one school.

The children, five boys and five girls, were four years old. In keeping with the main aim of the study, I particularly focused on the social factors which were likely to influence the children's stance, perspectives and strategies regarding learning. Data were thus collected from parents about family life, sibing relationships and the chil-dren's emergent identities; from peers and playground contexts concerning peer-group relationships; and form teachers with regard to classroom behaviour and academic achievements. There was also regular classroom observation to document the progres-sion of organization, activity structures and routine tasks in each class, and, of course, there was a great deal of discussion with the children to record their perceptions and responses to new experiences.

The study continued for seven years until July 1994, when the children left school at the age of eleven. By then, one child had dropped out of the study and two others had moved to different local schools. From June 1991 the Leverhulme Trust began to fund Ann Filer as a co-researcher and we began to work together on a second major theme, that of 'pupil career', which we began to see as unfolding through primary school as a product of successive cycles of learning, each with an influence on identity. Of course, the original theme of social influences on children's approaches to learning remained, and this, indeed, is the subject of this book. In the book, I focus on the social influences on the learning of five of the children during their first *three years* at their primary school. The extension and elaboration of this analysis to consider pupil careers is the subject of a companion book (Pollard and Filer, in press) which traces the development of the identities and strategies of four other children through the whole *seven years* of their primary school experiences. Both books are constructed around case-study 'stories' of individual children and, of course, there are strong interconnections among the char-acters who feature in each book. The anonymity of the individuals who participated is protected by the use of pseudonyms and, in some cases, by the judicious alteration of some personal and contextual information.

A more complete account of the research design, methods for data-gathering, analysis, ethical framework and dissemination strategy which underpinned this study is offered in

Chapter 10 and, for those who are interested in how the research was carried out or in assessing its validity, that chapter can be read at any point in the book.

THEORY

There is always some sort of theory, implicit or explicit, underlying social research and this study is no exception. From the start of the study, as indicated above, I wanted to investigate social influences on children's learning and, in the first place, it seemed appropriate to build on my earlier *symbolic interactionist* analysis of teacher and pupil perspectives and of classroom processes. This had been published in a book called *The Social World of the Primary School* (first published in 1985 with a second edition in press). I attempted a succinct explanation of symbolic interactionism in that book as follows:

> Symbolic interactionism is founded on the belief that people 'act' on the basis of meanings and understandings which they develop through interaction with others. Human action is thus seen as having a social basis rather than deriving, for example, from instinct or genetics. Through symbolic interaction, be it verbal or non-verbal, individuals are thought to develop a concept of 'self' as they interpret the responses of other people to their own actions. Although the sense of self is first developed in childhood, interactionists argue that is is continually refined in later life and that it provides a basis for thought and behaviour. (Pollard, 1985a, x)

We can see here the importance which is placed on children's sense of 'self' and identity and this, indeed, is a very strong theme of the present book.

In *The Social World of the Primary School* I generated a model of pupil and teacher 'coping strategies'. This model represents processes of classroom interaction and suggests that the negotiation of rules and understandings produces a 'working consensus' through which classroom relationships and classroom order are established and maintained. Stripped of its complexity, the figure on page xiii represents the major elements of the analysis, with socially derived role expectations and the unique biography of the teacher and each pupil contributing to the process of interaction.

The present book can be seen as an attempt to extend and deepen the analysis which was provided by *The Social World of the Primary School*. It is an extension because of its specific focus on *learning*, a topic which was only tangential to the previous focus on classroom relationships. It deepens the previous work because it provides a very detailed study of just a part of the earlier model – that of children's biographies and their management of identity is enacting the pupil role in school.

Notwithstanding the existence of this previous work, a more developed framework for thinking about learning was also needed and for this I turned to a psychological approach which is known as *social constructivism*. The emphasis of social constructivism is on the ways in which learning is influenced by culture and by interaction with others. Certainly, individual learners are seen as being active in such processes, constructing understanding and 'making sense' of new experiences and challenges. However, there are also many social influences such as the cultural resources on which a learner can draw and the forms of support, explanation or instruction which they receive from others. For example, in the case of school pupils, gender, ethnicity and social class are likely to have a considerable influence on cultural resources, whilst their relationships with parents,

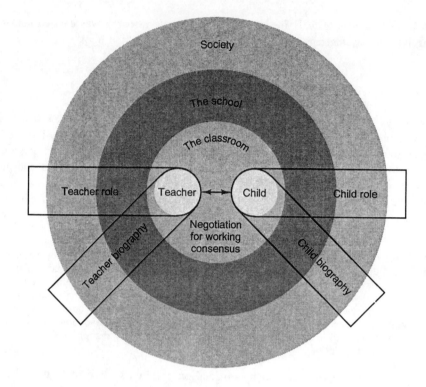

A simplified model of teacher/pupil classroom coping strategies (derived from Pollard 1985a, Figure 7.4)

siblings, peers and teachers will affect the types of support which is received as new learning challenges are encountered.

I felt that the theoretical approaches of symbolic interactionism and social constructivism were complementary. They each share a fundamental assumption that people are active and make decisions on the basis of meanings. However, whilst social constructivists provide insights on the processes through which people come to 'make sense' in particular social and cultural situations, symbolic interactionists promise to provide more detailed and incisive accounts of the contexts themselves.

Symbolic interactionism and social constructivism thus provided the two overarching theoretical frameworks from which the work reported in this book has been derived. It is essentially a sociological analysis of influences on learning processes and is intended to complement the work of psychologists, biologists and other educationalists who with their own particular expertise, continue to enquire into the complexities of children's thinking.

THE STRUCTURE OF THE BOOK

The substantive focus of this book comprises five detailed case-study stories of children's interaction, development and learning in the contexts of home, playground and classroom. These case-studies can be read independently. However, the text before and after them is intended to structure and illuminate that reading. It introduces themes and draws out implications for policy and practice. It also represents my analytical attempt to abstract and theorize the factors and processes which influenced the children's lives and their learning stance.

Part One: Setting the Scene

The book begins with an orientation to the major issues with which it is concerned and to the social context in which the research was conducted. Chapter 1 is particularly important, positioning the study in terms of related academic work and, most importantly, in suggesting six basic questions – *where, when, who, what, how* and *why* – which may be used by the reader to engage actively with the child case-studies. Chapter 2 introduces the city and community which Greenside Primary School served, and describes the school, teacher and classroom contexts.

Part Two: Beginning

In Chapter 3 an initial case-study story is provided in relation to one child, Mary. The contexts, events and social relationships which affected her learning and development are described, year-by-year and in a structured way for the settings and relationships of home, playground and classroom. Chapter 4 then provides an analytical commentary on Mary's story, using and developing the six questions which were first raised in Chapter 1.

Part Three: Elaborating

Part Three extends the analysis by making a comparative method possible. Thus the first four chapters present the learning stories of Hazel, Daniel, Sally and James, through the first three years of their schooling. Again, coverage of each school year for each child has the same basic structure, so that is is possible for specific comparisons to be made of experiences, relationships and outcomes for different children or of the same child over time. However, responding to word-length constraints, some pupil-years are relatively condensed whilst others have more extensive textual accounts. All case studies have summarizing matrices for each pupil-year which are particularly useful for comparative purposes.

Chapter 9 is based on 'case-study comparisons' and, in this way, it builds on the analyical development which accumulates through Chapter 1 and Chapter 4. It provides the final representation in this study of the major social factors which are at play within the pupil stories of learning.

Part Four: Reflecting

Chapter 10 provides an opportunity to describe and reflect on the research design and the methods which were used for gathering data and for analysis. Important ethical issues are also considered here and the overall validity of the study is assessed. Finally,

Chapter 11 addresses the relevance of the book by revisiting the three 'starting points' which were posed at the beginning of this introduction. Implications of the study for parents, teachers and policy-makers are suggested.

HOW TO USE THE BOOK

The pupil case-studies are intended to stimulate reflection, comparison and discussion of the past and present experiences of readers as children, pupils, parents and teachers. With that in mind, they have been presented in a holistic, descriptive and structured way, so that readers will be able to begin to generate plausible personal interpretations which may be set alongside those contained in the more analytical chapters of the book. In respect of the latter, key questions are suggested in Chapter 1, extended in Chapter 4, further elaborated in Chapter 9 and their implications are discussed in Chapter 11. These chapters could be read successively or with the planned interpolation of the extensive case-study material. Alternatively, perhaps the children's experiences in different school-years could be compared and, and for this purpose, the Reception year of each child is described in particular detail. Whatever strategy is adopted, the book is meant to be read *actively, cumulatively and with an element of intuitive projection* as an understanding of the lives and learning of the children is constructed by the reader.

Part 1

Setting the Scene

Chapter 1

Questions for Enquiry

1.1 INTRODUCTION

This book focuses attention on the ways in which, as young children grow up, they learn and make their way through a succession of new situations and experiences. Whilst adults may hope to provide security and opportunity within the social settings which are created in homes, classrooms and playgrounds, such contexts also often contain challenges and threats which young children have to negotiate. As children develop, perfect or struggle with their strategies for coping with such situations, so they learn about other people, about themselves and about life.

Jerome Bruner has characterized this learning in action as a form of 'praxis'.

> Social understanding always begins as praxis in particular contexts in which the child is a protagonist – an agent, a victim, an accomplice.
> (Bruner, 1990: 85)

In the book we thus have an illustration of the ways in which, through praxis, children progressively learn both about themselves and about how to accomplish the curriculum of early primary schooling. As we will see, the pupils' actions as 'agent, victim and accomplice' are readily apparent in the children's stories.

In the first part of this chapter I highlight some features of the theoretical framework which underpins the book and relate it to some of the other research in this rapidly expanding field. This is important as a way of positioning the study and, in particular, I will suggest that the book represents an application of Vygotsky's social constructivism and a sociological complement to the existing strengths of psychology in studies of children's learning.

In the second part of the chapter I introduce six simple questions which can be posed when engaging with the case-study 'stories' of children's social relationships and learning, which make up the core of this book. These questions are intended to begin to offer you, as a reader, a type of analytical tool-kit in support of the invitation to engage actively with the texts of the case-study stories.

1.2 POSITIONING THE STUDY

A review of the sociology of primary schooling and of the psychology of young children's learning since 1970 or so reveals a curious picture. On the one hand, sociologists, in one way or another, maintained their focus on issues of social differentiation. Certainly the emphasis of the 1980s and 1990s developed from that of social class to embrace issues of ethnicity (e.g.: Troyna and Hatcher, 1991; Wright, 1992), gender (e.g.: Evans, 1988; Thorne, 1993) and special educational needs (e.g.: Croll and Moses, 1985; Wolfendale 1992), and theoretical refinements accumulated too (e.g.: Walkerdine, 1988; Daniels, 1993; Davies 1989, 1993). However, the overriding impression left by work such as Sharp and Green (1975), King (1978), Pollard (1985a), Hartley (1985), Lubeck (1985), King (1989), is that *learning processes* were seen as, at best, tangential to issues such as typification, group formation and the consequences of social differentiation. Returning even earlier reveals a similar story, as is illustrated by the way in which Dreeben's *On What is Learned in School* (1968) concerns itself with the socialization of children into social norms but makes no attempt to address the sociological factors which influence the ways in which children approach learning tasks.

In the child psychology of the 1970s, sociologists' focus on social differentiation was matched by the naive individualism of many educational adaptions of Piaget's work (e.g. 1926, 1950, 1951). His research was directed, in an overarching sense, towards the study of 'genetic epistemology' and the route towards this analysis was through detailed studies of children's thinking and behaviour. Careful development and use of clinical methods over many years enabled Piaget to generate a model of learning processes based on the interaction between individuals and their environments and involving development through successive stages of equilibration, each of which was taken to be associated with particular capacities and ways of thinking. This model was powerfully adopted by primary-school teachers in England and Wales in the decades following the Plowden Report (CACE, 1967) and was used as a professional legitimation for the maintainance of 'child-centred' commitments (Ashton *et al.*, 1975; Broadfoot and Osborn, 1988), even when classroom realization turned out to be extremely difficult (Galton *et al.*, 1980; Pollard *et al.*, 1994). However, Piaget's ideas were incisively critiqued by psychologists in the late 1970s (e.g. Donaldson, 1978) and views of children's learning were increasingly modified by the gradual emergence of a new paradigm – 'social constructivism' (Bruner, 1986; Wood, 1988; Tharp and Gallimore, 1988).

Thus, the previously dominant Piagetian model, which implicitly conceptualized children as *individual* 'active scientists' (Bruner and Haste, 1986) with very little appreciation of the social contexts in which learning takes place, began to be superseded by an image of children as *social* beings who construct understandings and learn from social interaction which occurs within specific socio-cultural settings. Thus, even from birth, children are seen as intelligent social actors who, although their skills, understanding and knowledge base may be limited in absolute terms, are capable in many ways (Dunn, 1988). Similarly, sophisticated processes of 'intellectual search' through the use of language have been identified in nursery-age children (Tizard and Hughes, 1984) as have children's capacities to develop sophisticated forms of representation for meaning and understanding (Athey, 1990; Nutbrown, 1994).

This book draws on social constructivist psychology for its consideration of learning. The approach derives from the original work of the Russian psychologist, Vygotsky (1962,

1978) and from his studies of the relatedness of thought, language and culture which were conducted in the 1930s. This 'socio-cultural' theory suggests that children acquire the socially constructed psychological concepts, language and patterns of action which are available to them within their culture. These are then superimposed on organic, physiological development to form a 'single line of socio-biological formation of the child's personality' (Lee, 1985). In a sense, of course, the learning spiral which has been introduced in this book (Figure 9.1, page 284) can be seen as an attempt to describe part of this 'line of socio-biological formation'. The socio-cultural contexts in which children grow up vary considerably, for instance from Greenside in Southern England as in this book, inner-city Glasgow (Grant, 1989), small rural towns in the USA (Heath, 1983) or the diversity of Australian communities (Goodnow and Burns, 1985). In any event, social constructivist psychology suggests that the concepts, language and signs of the cultural context structure children's thinking and become internalized as 'voices of the mind' (Wertsch, 1991). They thus mediate action and new learning.

This socio-cultural psychology represents a huge advance in studies of children's learning because it invites attempts to identify and develop the complementary insights of psychology and sociology.

Most of the sociological analysis in this book has been underpinned by symbolic inter-actionist theory because of the strength of the approach in analysing how people relate together within social contexts and for its account of how children develop a sense of identity. In *Mind, Self and Society* (1934), G. H. Mead argued that people interact together on the basis of meanings. These meanings and understandings are generated through shared experiences and negotiation, become socially patterned and are sustained through cultures. Among the meanings generated over time through interaction with others are understandings of oneself. Each individual thus develops a sense of identity, a 'self', and this awareness influences the ways in which he or she acts with other people.

Language played a key role in the work of both Mead and Vygotsky. They emphasized that its use, in whatever form, draws on the concepts and ideas of the culture in which an individual lives. Language can thus be seen as a precursor to consciousness and action, but it is mediated by social and cultural meaning. As Vygotsky put it:

> Human learning presupposes a specific social nature and a process by which children grow into the intellectual life of those around them. (1978: 88)

One integrative way of representing and thinking about the factors which affect learning is to envisage three domains of influence: the intra-individual, the inter-personal and the socio-historical.

The intra-individual domain   is the traditional province of cognitive psychologists and neuro-biologists who study the ways in which individuals develop intellectual capacities within the brain, assimilate experiences and construct understanding. A particularly comprehensive account of work in this area is that of Meadows (1993) who reviews a wide range of research on children's cognitive skills and knowledge, studies of 'intelligence' and Piagetian, information-processing and Vygotskian models of cognition as well as the considerable flow of recent work on neurological aspects of brain functioning and genetic development.

The inter-personal domain   concerns social interaction in which meanings are negotiated and through which cultural norms and social conventions are learned. Such processes are studied, for instance, by symbolic interactionist sociologists and by social psychologists. Work such as Woods (1983), Mandell (1984) and Pollard (1985a) and this book itself are good examples of the sociological approach. A particularly good example of social psychological work is Dunn's study (1988) which documents how babies learn through interaction with their mothers. Jerome Bruner's book, *Acts of Meaning* (1990), is also of this type. In it, Bruner draws on a wide range of social and psychological research to argue that cognitive psychology has become fixated on information-processing models and on work within the intra-individual domain. He advocates a new form of 'cultural psychology'.

The socio-historical domain addresses the wider context in which learning takes place, its origins and the circumstances of the learner. Consideration of this socio-historical domain calls for forms of social, economic and political analysis which are beyond the reach of social constructivism and symbolic interactionism. However, socio-historical factors are important because the learning challenges, learning resources and learning contexts for children of different gender, ethnicity and social class groups vary enormously, depending on social, cultural, economic and political factors. Differences in socio-cultural and politico-economic contexts thus profoundly influence children's learning and, indeed, the ways in which they view themselves. Similarly, the curriculum to which pupils are expected to respond, the resources made available for education and the legal structures within which schools must work can each be seen as products of particular political developments which need to be located historically, geographically and in terms of associated interest groups and ideologies (Green, 1990, Dale, 1989).

In this book, socio-historical factors are described briefly in sections 2.2, 4.2 and 9.2. These enable the case-study school, community, families and children to be contextualized in the wider cultural, economic and policy context. Michael Apple (1986) underlines the importance of this argument:

> We do not confront abstract 'learners' in schools. Instead, we see specific classed, raced and gendered subjects, people whose biographies are intimately linked to the economic, political and ideological trajectories of their families and communities, to the political economies of their neighbourhoods. (1986: 5).

Overall then, this framework suggests that intra-individual learning, the traditional domain of psychologists, cannot really be understood without reference to both interpersonal experiences and socio-historical circumstances. These call for sociological contributions.

Helen Haste (1984) has provided a model of the relationship between the intra-individual, interpersonal and the socio-historical which I have elaborated in Figure 1.1.

There is, arguably, still a long way to go in the development of working relationships, theoretical development, empirical research and analytical tools before psychologists and sociologists who are concerned with children's learning will be able to take on the full implications of Vygotsky's inspiration, as reflected in Haste's framework and Apple's suggestion. However, there is now a growing consensus about the inter-relatedness of social and psychological factors (Daniels, 1993; Moll, 1990) and I would argue that this is underpinned, not just by theory and empirical research, but also by the common-sense and lived experiences of millions of children, teachers and parents.

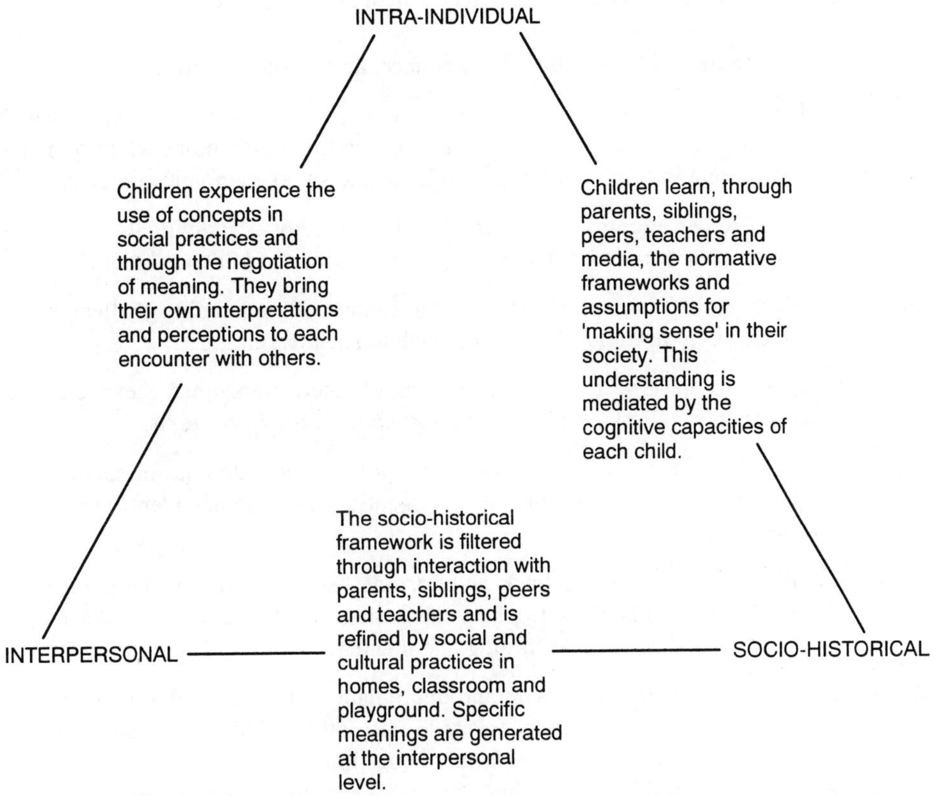

INTRA-INDIVIDUAL

Children experience the use of concepts in social practices and through the negotiation of meaning. They bring their own interpretations and perceptions to each encounter with others.

Children learn, through parents, siblings, peers, teachers and media, the normative frameworks and assumptions for 'making sense' in their society. This understanding is mediated by the cognitive capacities of each child.

The socio-historical framework is filtered through interaction with parents, siblings, peers and teachers and is refined by social and cultural practices in homes, classroom and playground. Specific meanings are generated at the interpersonal level.

INTERPERSONAL ——————————— SOCIO-HISTORICAL

Figure 1.1 *A model of the relationship between intra-individual, interpersonal and the socio-historical factors (following Haste, 1987)*

Of course, this book represents one contribution to this growing body of work and is positioned within it. Focused on the interpersonal domain, it began from the proposition that it would be worthwhile to explore the potential for linking social constructivist psychology and symbolic interactionist sociology through a longitudinal study of children's learning and development in a primary school. The study thus sought to build on the basic assumption, shared by both approaches, that people are active and make decisions on the basis of meanings. However, whilst social constructivist work had begun to identify the processes by which people 'make sense' in social situations, symbolic interactionist studies promised to provide more detailed and incisive accounts of the dynamics and constraints of the contexts in which learning takes place. The two approaches seemed to be complementary and, on testing the proposition, this book, and its particular analysis of interpersonal relationships and learning, is the result. Of course, as is appropriate, the book both recognizes and articulates with intra-individual issues and socio-historical factors but no claims are made for completeness in those terms.

1.3   QUESTIONS FOR ENQUIRY

In one sense, the key questions are deceptively straightforward but, if as a reader you do commit yourself to an active engagement with them, they should lead you towards the generation of your own interpretation of the data which are presented.

The questions are theoretically informed. For instance, among other things:

Question 1.   *Where?* and *When?* highlight the significance of the social contexts in which learning takes place. They invite a consideration of the home, classroom and playground in relation to wider political and socio-economic contexts.

Question 2.   *Who?* draws attention to the children of the study as individuals, and to the parents, teachers, peers and siblings who variously influenced them.

Question 3.   *What?* calls for a consideration of the content of the learning challenges that the children face and of their approach to such learning.

Question 4.   *How?* suggests a focus on processes of interaction, on the expectations, constraints and opportunities within specific learning contexts.

Question 5.   *What?* then prompts a review of the story and the outcomes of each child's story in terms of learning achievements, social status, identity and self esteem.

Question 6.   *Why?* asks us to stand back and consider explanations for the patterns of perspectives and interactions in the stories of each child, and the consequences for that child's learning and identity.

Of course, such questions interlock with and interpolate each other so that to attempt to answer one will immediately make it necessary to pose others. This is the nature of any qualitative enquiry and one has to accept a spiral of questioning in which, hopefully, understanding accumulates as a result of successive attempts to identify patterns and to construct interpretations.

Indeed, the structure of this book reflects that cumulative, spiralling process and these questions will be revisited and developed further in Chapter 4 and again in Chapter 9. In this way the theoretical model deriving from ethnographic procedures will be elaborated with a gradual deepening of the analysis and a strengthening of the extent of comparisons across child cases. The questions which are discussed below thus constitute a kind of 'tool-kit' for enquiry. Whilst they can be used as simple tools, their use can also be progressively refined and, as understanding deepens, they may be deployed in more sophisticated ways.

We will start at a simple, but no less fundamental, level of application.

Where and when is learning taking place?

Answers to this question will begin to provide an understanding of the influence of social contexts on action and, more specifically, on learning. In terms of Figure 1.1, these are 'socio-historical' issues.

We can identify two ways in which the question, 'where?', is important. First, there is the issue of the location of the case study at the levels of community, region and country. This has significance because of the social, cultural, political and economic circumstances within which the lives of the people who have been studied have been set. For instance, one important factor is the fact that the study was set in England, where many children start their official schooling in the year in which they become five – a very young age by international standards. Whilst restrictions on space and issues of confidentiality prevent me from giving full details of the location of the school and the socio-economic circumstances of the community, basic information is provided in Chapter 2.

At a more detailed level, the study has focused on three contexts in which children interact with others – the home, the classroom and the playground. As we shall see, each of these settings has specific characteristics with socially constructed rules and expectations guiding behaviour within them. Those of the classroom tend to be more constraining than those of the home or the playground but each is important in structuring children's experiences.

The timing and sequencing of events is another aspect of social context. Again there is the historical relationship of the case study to developments elsewhere within its community, region and country. For instance, it is important to note that this study took place over a period in which English social and economic development took a particular form as a result of the policies of Conservative governments. This affected the region, community and families, and national education policies underwent unusually rapid change with a particular impact on teachers. The teachers, parents and children in the study lived *through* those changes and experienced them sequentially. They thus contributed to the biography and identity of each individual.

In a longitudinal study such as this, it is also appropriate to compare the children's development and progress year by year as they pass through the care of successive teachers, and this is a particularly interesting line of enquiry. However, it is also complicated by the other developments within the school and by the successive phases in the teachers' lives, and these are described in Chapter 2.

'Who' is learning?

We can also ask about the children themselves. Who are they? or, rather, How do they see themselves as they strive to fulfil their individual potential within the social context in which they live? This brings us to the core issue of 'identity'.

To understand identity, we must pay particular attention to the 'significant others' in each child's life; to those who interact with them and influence the ways in which they see themselves. Data have thus been gathered from parents, siblings, peers and teachers and are presented in detail in the case-study stories of each child's learning.

Every child also has both physical and intellectual potential which, over the primary school years, continue the particularly formative and developmental stages which began at birth. Whether it is through the growth of new teeth or a sudden ability to understand a new scientific concept, the gradual realization of physical and intellectual potential rolls forward to influence self-confidence. In terms of Figure 1.1, physical and intellectual capability are 'intra-personal' factors and are the areas in which psychologists and biologists have made their well-established contributions to studies of child development and learning.

Identity is also very much influenced by factors such as gender, social class and ethnicity, each of which is associated with particular cultural and material resources and with particular patterns of social expectation which impinge on children through their relationships with others. Age, status and position, within the family, classroom and playground, are also particularly important for the developing sense of identity of very young children.

What is to be learned?

This is a wide-ranging and substantial question about the learning that young children accomplish as they grow up in home, classroom and playground settings. What are the major learning challenges which young children face and how do they respond?

At home, for instance, what happens when a young child wonders about major issues such as, 'Where do babies come from?', 'What happens when we die?' or even, 'Why the moon follows us home?'. Or, more mudanely, when he or she is confronted with challenges such as learning to tie laces, be polite to others, swim, ride a bike and to leave home for the world of school? Each child also has to develop a place within the family in relation to his or her siblings which, for some, can be stressful and competitive.

In the classroom, each child has first to learn a role as a pupil – for instance, to cope with classroom rules and conventions, to answer his or her name at registration, to sit cross-legged on the carpet and to listen to the teacher. Then, as pupils, children must respond to the curricular tasks which they are set. In English infant schools, this is likely to include large amounts of work on the core curriculum – perhaps 35 per cent of time spent on English, 15 per cent on maths and 8 per cent on science – each of which often develops within characteristic patterns of tasks and procedures.

Within the playground, we might study the learning which is involved in maintaining friendships and peer relationships. Reciprocity, a foundation for friendship, requires learning about the social and cultural expectations and needs of others, whether this is manifested in knowledge of the latest 'craze', physical skills, the rules of playtime games or how to manage falling 'in' and 'out' with friends.

In close association with these issues concerning the *content* of new learning challenges, we also need to consider the *perspectives* of children about learning and the ways in which they respond to particular challenges. Issues of interest and motivation are particularly important. For instance, a child is likely to view self-directed learning through play quite differently from practising word recognition or memorizing spellings in response to a task which has been set at school.

There are also the issues, central to the focus of this book, of each child's 'learning stance' and of the strategies which he or she is able to deploy. By *learning stance*, I refer to the characteristic approach which individual children adopt when confronted by a new learning challenge. Obviously a lot will depend on the content of the specific challenge and the context in which it is faced but there are also likely to be patterns and tendencies in approach. How self-confident do particular children tend to be? Do they feel the need to assert personal control in a learning situation or will they conform to the wishes of others? How are they motivated towards new learning? A child's learning stance is clearly linked to their sense of identity and to the self-confidence which they generate from available cultural resources, social expectations and personal awareness of potential. Whatever the initial stance of a learner, he or she must then deploy specific *strategies* in new learning situations. The range of strategies available to individual children will vary, with some being confident to make judgements and vary their approach to tasks, whilst others will need guidance and encouragment to move from tried and tested routines.

How supportive is the specific learning context?

In the settings of home, playground or classroom there are specific contextual factors which condition the ways in which a child's learning stance and strategies are enacted. This brings us back to the ways in which social expectations and taken-for-granted rules influence behaviour.

There are many examples of this. For instance, in the context of many white English middle-class families such as those in this study, social expectations are perhaps at their most structured at set-meals, such as Sunday lunch, particularly when visitors are present. The same phenomenon occurs in playgrounds when children assert the overt and tacit rules of games, such as 'tig' or 'What's the time Mr Wolf?'. Of course, there are also many times when actions are far less constrained, when family or peer expectation takes a more relaxed form, allowing more scope for individual action. The same is true for classroom life and, indeed, this was one of the main topics within my earlier book, *The Social World of the Primary School* (1985a). Within that book the concept of 'rule frame' was introduced to describe the nature of the rules-in-play in any particular situation or phase of a teaching session. These derive from the gradual negotiation of understandings about behaviour which routinely takes place between the teacher and pupils. Thus a teacher's introduction to a lesson is usually more tightly framed and controlled than the mid-phase of a session in which children may disperse to engage in various tasks or activities. Similarly, within the homes in this study, there were contrasts such as the common tensions of breakfast-times and getting ready for school and the relative relaxation of going for walks or bath-times. Quite different rules and expectations about interaction frame such occasions and these condition the way in which each phase may enable learning.

Of course, the nature of negotiation within the interactions of children and others varies in different settings and there is always an element of this which is concerned with the exercise of power. In general, adults have the power to initiate, assert, maintain and change rules, whilst children must comply, adapt, mediate or resist. Many teachers and parents, for most of the time and in most settings, act sensitively towards young children so that there is an element of negotiation and legitimacy in the social expectations and rules which are applied in particular situations. Sometimes this is not the case, there is less legitimacy and the children may well become unhappy or believe that they have been treated 'unfairly'.

This is important because of the impact of the social setting on learning, for only a child with an exceptionally confident learning stance is likely to take any chances within a context in which risks and costs of failure are high. In some classrooms, children may thus 'keep their heads down' and the same may be true in some families or playground situations, perhaps where sibling or peer rivalry creates a risk to status or dignity. With our focus on learning processes, we thus need to consider the *opportunities and risks* which exist for each child to learn within different social settings – the context of power relations and social expectations within which he or she must act and adapt. Some situations may be low key and feel safe, in which the child can feel secure to 'give it a try'. In the case of others, the stakes may be higher and a child's self-esteem may be vulnerable to public critique from siblings, parents, peers or their teacher.

The question, 'How supportive is the specific learning context?', also suggests a focus on *the quality of the teaching and assistance* which a child receives in different settings. Social constructivist psychology offers a clear analysis of the importance for learning of the guidance and instruction of more skilled or knowledgeable others. Whether support is provided by parents or teachers, siblings or peers, the principle is the same; that children's learning benefits from the 'scaffolding' of their understanding so that it can be extended across the next step in their development. This process is as applicable to learning to blow bubbles in the bath or riding a bike as it is to learning to spell or solve sums, or to do handstands or play hop-scotch. Such arguments derive from Vygotsky's work (1978) and we will revisit them in more detail later in the book.

From this perspective, the *ways* in which adults or other children teach or assist a child's understanding are seen to be of paramount importance. There are affective as well as cognitive aspects of this for it is often necessary to provide young children with a stable emotional framework as well as intellectual challenge. We thus find parents and teachers worrying that a child is 'upset and distracted' when he or she falls out with friends and we can appreciate the emphasis which is placed on children being 'happy and settled'. This however, though a necessary foundation for learning, is unlikely to be enough without a consistent and well-matched input of instruction and support for intellectual growth. This is likely to be found in discussions, questions, advice and other forms of constructive interaction with children which clarify, build on, extend or challenge their ideas. Thus we have the concern with the quality of the teaching and assistance in learning which is available to each child in the home, playground and, in particular, the classroom.

What are the outcomes?

For the purpose of this book, the first and most obvious outcome concerns the *achievement* of intended learning goals. These may vary from the official curricular aims which are set by teachers as a result of school or national curriculum policy, through to the challenges which are presented as part of peer activities in the playground and the new learning experiences which confront each child as he or she grows up within the family at home. Learning thus produces relatively overt yardsticks of attainment, whether the child is learning letter formation in handwriting or about number bonds, how to skip or to play 'Thundercats' properly or how to hold their own in family conversation or to swim. What then has been achieved? What is the new level of attainment? What can the child now do and understand?

Such questions are of particular importance because, beyond issues of explicit achievement and of the new forms of action which become possible, lie associated consequences for the ways in which child learners perceive themselves and are perceived by others. The key concepts here are self-esteem and social status.

Self-esteem is likely to rise as achievements are made. Maturational 'achievements', such as having birthdays, losing teeth or just becoming taller, are often marked with particular pleasure by young children as they see themselves 'growing up', but many more attainments are accomplished in the home, playground and classroom as children face new experiences and challenges. The classroom setting is, of course, particularly important because it is the source of official educational judgements, whilst the home setting offers the support, or otherwise, of parents – the crucial 'significant others'.

Regarding *social status*, the prominence which is attributed to the child by others, it is arguably relationships within peer groups which are of most significance to children. For many children, peer group membership is both a source of great enjoyment in play and a source of solidarity in facing the challenges which are presented by adults. In such circumstances, some children lead whilst others follow and high status may well be associated with popularity, style and achievement in facilitating 'good fun'. On the other hand, peer-group cultures can also be exclusive and reject children from membership if they are unable to conform to group norms. Thus, if a child's learning and performance regarding peer expectations is deficient, their social status is likely to be low – with a consequent roll-forward effect on their sense of self-esteem and of personal identity.

Thus the process is brought full circle and we return to the first question, *'Who' is learning?*. Such cycles represent the process of learning in a social context, with the effects of social relationships and learning achievements accumulating over time to contribute to the formation of identity. In the case of very young children, it is particularly necessary to monitor the ways in which patterns of adaption and achievement evolve or stabilize in response to changing social circumstances. This brings us to the sixth and final question.

Why do social factors influence children's approach to learning?

Posing this summarizing question begins the process of seeking explanations for the patterns of perspectives, interaction and consequence which may be found within each child's case-study story. It is an opportunity to hypothesize, speculate and generate theories which can represent the patterns which exist within the accounts.

Points of particular interest are likely to be the ways in which processes repeat themselves so that experience accumulates recursively. Thus the learning outcomes of one episode feed into the self-confidence and sense of identity which the child then embodies. In due course, this is presented at the next learning episode through his or her learning stance.

As you read the children's stories within this book, interconnections between relevant factors may sometimes seem relatively clear, but in other cases it may be difficult to derive from the text all the nuances of perspective and interaction which would enable a reader to confirm a judgement. A sounding board here can legitimately be your other experience – after all, we have all grown up as young children and have residual memories of our experiences; some readers may be parents who can recall events in family life which strike a chord with those described in this book and some will be teachers or student teachers who can review the material from the perspective of their classroom experience. These experiences, whether singular or overlapping, provide a form of 'subsidiary awareness' (Polanyi, 1958) when engaging with the text. They are an interpretive resource which may enable you to empathize and understand the complex web of lives of the people in these stories.

1.4   CONCLUSION

We thus have a set of questions which, taken as a whole, highlight the centrality of understanding the interaction of social contexts and individuals as they face learning challenges.

These six questions can be represented in a simple model, which, in due course, will be elaborated in both Chapter 4 and Chapter 9.

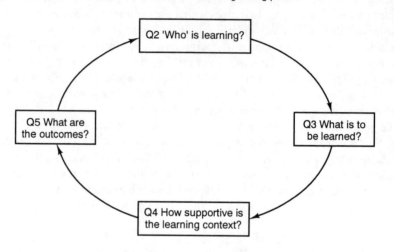

Q1 When and where is learning taking place?

Q2 'Who' is learning?

Q5 What are the outcomes?

Q3 What is to be learned?

Q4 How supportive is the learning context?

Q6 Why do social factors influence children's approach to learning?

Figure 1.2   *A simplified model of six questions concerning social influences on children's learning.*

Posing such questions may be seen as setting an unusual challenge to readers. However, it is in the nature of this study that multiple interpretations of the case-study stories of children's learning are possible and that empathic engagement with the lives of those studied is necessary for understanding. The six questions offer initial guidance in this and, in Chapter 4 and Chapter 9, the analysis will be elaborated. Thus, from the uncertainties and doubts

of early answers, the book should scaffold the development of more coherent and sophisticated interpretations.

This whole struggle to 'make sense' of our own and other people's lives is an intrinsic part of human behaviour and is thus something which we all do all the time. Needless to say, adults' interpretations often have profound implications for children, as you will see from the case-studies. As a reader of this book, you have an opportunity to reflect on processes and consequences of constructing understandings about children – both within these stories or, indeed, your own.

We move now, in Chapter 2, to consider the school and classroom contexts in which the lives of the children in this study were played out. Then, in Part Two, Beginning, we start the first example case study with the story of Mary, her learning, identity and social relationships.

Chapter 2

School and Classroom Contexts

2.1 INTRODUCTION

In this chapter, I move through successive layers of the context which, in one way or another, structured the lives of the children in this study. From the level of the national English economy and Conservative government policies, I consider the city of Easthampton, its suburb of Greenside and its primary school, before focusing on the specific teachers whose classrooms the children experienced.

The purpose of this, prior to consideration of the children's stories in detail, is to demonstrate the ways in which their biographies are related to time, place and social position. This cannot be done in great detail, but I want to at least outline the historical intersection of the biographies of many other individuals and the legacy of a range of social, cultural, political and economic processes as they influenced these educational experiences.

The focus here is on the school and the classrooms. Discussion of the two other important contexts, the home and the playground, are provided within the 'learning stories' of Part 2. This takes the form of an introduction to each family and specific discussion of the influence of peer culture and friendships on each case-study child.

2.2 BEYOND THE SCHOOL

The national context

The research which is reported in this book was carried out in England between September 1987 and July 1990 – the later years of Mrs Thatcher's premiership and between the General Elections of 1987 and 1992.

The years since 1979 had seen a generally supportive climate for business and the middle classes with particularly favourable tax policies. House prices rose dramatically during the late 1980s, creating a boom in confidence which even managed to survive the 1989 rise in interest rates to 15 per cent, with its consequent knock-on effect on mortgages. Over the same period, trade unions were in retreat following new legislation and the defeat of the miners in 1984, national unemployment levels were high and, in association, poverty deep-ened for many families. The Labour Party suffered four election defeats in a row and the gap between rich and poor grew.

Regarding education policy, a period of debate and critique of the early 1980s led to the summer 1987 publication of a 'Consultation Document' (DES/WO, 1987) setting out the principles on which legislation for a new national curriculum and assessment system would be based. This emphasized the raising of standards of pupil attainment by:

> ensuring that all pupils study a broad and balanced range of subjects; setting clear objectives for what children should be able to achieve; ensure that all pupils have access to the same curriculum and programmes of study; checking on progress towards these objectives; enabling schools to be more accountable. (edited from DES/WO1987: 8-9)

The Education Reform Act itself was passed in 1988 and the National Curriculum was introduced from the autumn of 1989. The first subjects to be specified were English, math-ematics and science but other subjects were introduced over the following two years, together with new forms of 'teacher assessment' and, in 1991, standardized assessment (SATs) for 7-year-olds.

Easthampton and its Local Education Authority

Easthampton was a city in the South of England of about one million citizens. It had a diversified industrial base and a long history. There were a significant number of high-technology manufacturing and financial companies in the area and these were gradually taking over the employment role which had formerly been filled by more traditional manu-facturing. Given its geographical location, the city had great hopes of expansion from the growing trade with European countries. It was a centre for its region with extensive provi-sion for shopping, exhibitions, libraries, sport, cinema, theatre, concerts and other forms of entertainment.

The south of the city, in which Greenside was located, was generally more affluent than the north and many new companies had chosen to locate nearby. There were some very smart residential areas in central Easthampton with Georgian and Victorian housing predominating. The between-wars expansion of suburbs, such as Greenside, had also provided many homes and these tended to be ringed on the outer boundaries of the city by large post-war estates of council housing. On these, and in some specific inner-city areas, unemployment and poverty levels were particularly high.

The Local Education Authority had had a very good reputation but during the 1980s it was challenged by successive rounds of financial cut-backs, new national requirements to implement and a lack of stable political control. From the perspective of many head-teachers, its policies were usually well meaning but there were often problems at the point of implementation. One particular decision which had been taken some years earlier was that there should be no state secondary school in Greenside itself.

The Local Education Authority assigned advisors to each school. At Greenside, the LEA's two senior primary advisors took a particular interest following the appointment of the new headteacher. The 'early years' specialist was instrumental in supporting the head-teacher in introducing more active forms of teaching and learning into the school, including an approach to a 'negotiated curriculum'. The 'junior years' specialist was particularly interested in curriculum planning and design, and he worked with the headteacher to develop and pilot new strategies for the school. In both cases, work which was done at Greenside Primary was subsequently disseminated to schools across the LEA through booklets and contributions to in-service courses. As the National Curriculum began to be introduced, Mrs Davison, the headteacher, was one of those involved in helping the LEA to create a constructive response in terms of curriculum planning and development.

The suburb of Greenside

Greenside was a well-established residential area which had a high social status in Easthampton. It had existed as a free-standing village just outside the city from medieval times, with St John's Church providing its focal point. The first significant expansion had been of Victorian residential housing in the mid-1800s and the area then developed further as a suburb of Easthampton in the 1920s and 1930s. There had been only minor post-war in-filling.

The 1981 census showed that 70 per cent of Greenside's houses were privately owned, with small, peripheral areas of council housing making up 21 per cent of households. The remaining households were mainly flats accommodating nurses from a local teaching hospital. Most houses and gardens were relatively large and there were several areas of woodland and green space nearby. The Census returns of 1981 and 1991 show relatively low levels of unemployment in Greenside, an average of 4.5 per cent.

The church remained important to many families in the community, with the church hall providing facilities for a Mums' and Toddlers' Group, a playgroup, Scouts, Cubs, Beavers, Guides and Brownies, Young Crusader's Club (known as 'Cru Club'), a choir, music groups and bell-ringing. Sunday services, of which there were four, were relatively well attended. A parish magazine and weekly news sheet were produced and circulated around Greenside and the vicar chaired the Greenside Primary School governors.

There was a cluster of small shops for local needs, though weekly shopping trips by car to nearby supermarkets was a well-established routine for most Greenside families.

Families in Greenside

The majority of families in the area were white, middle class and relatively well off, with fathers working in senior positions in business or the professions. A high proportion of mothers with young children dedicated themselves to child care and many were active in supporting associated voluntary services such as the playgroup. The fathers of such young families, like several in this study, were often at a stage of having to establish themselves in their businesses and companies and they consequently worked very long hours away from home. There was also a significant proportion of older residents, many of whom were active in church affairs, the Greenside Residents' Association or the wider affairs of Easthampton.

The majority of families of Greenside flourished during the 1980s, with rising real incomes and prosperity. Many of the families sent their children to private schools for their secondary education, feeling that there was no appropriate state provision since the nearest comprehensive school primarily served a large estate of council houses. For many of these families, the competition of the modern world meant that one had to buy the best for one's children and they felt that this was to be found in the private sector. The most prestigious of the local independent schools, King Edward's College, had a tough entrance exam, whilst entrance to Easthampton College was a little easier. Those parents using state-maintained schools were able to use buses to transport their children to Halberton Grammar School (in fact a comprehensive school) or to other secondary schools outside the city. Greenside had a history of providing solid support for the Conservative Party at elections.

Within this general characterization of Greenside families, it is possible to detect at least two major groups which, following Bernstein (1975) I will call the 'traditional' and the 'new' middle class. Whilst both were likely to be concerned about their children's educational achievements, distinct patterns in their priorities could be distinguished. Some families laid great store on children learning to think independently and acquiring new skills at school and were very concerned that they should feel 'happy' at school. I will term these 'new middle-class' families, in contrast to the 'traditional middle-class' families who asserted the prime importance of 'standards' and overt achievements. These positions had considerable implications for parental views of Greenside Primary School.

2.3   GREENSIDE PRIMARY SCHOOL

Some circumstances

The original Greenside elementary school opened in 1899 but transferred to its new buildings in 1963. These were single storey and made of brick. From a good-sized hall, two corridors led to eight relatively spacious classrooms, each with large windows. These classrooms in turn opened externally on to playgrounds for the infants and the juniors. Beyond the junior playground was an extensive playing field. Over the period of study, the school had a planned admission limit of 45 children and numbers on roll were between 290 and 320. There were 10 classes and this required the use of prefabricated classrooms on the site to supplement the internal accommodation.

In addition to the resources made available from the Local Education Authority, the school benefited from the strong fund-raising capacity of the parents. For instance, in 1987/88 a sponsorship event for science equipment raised £750 and the Summer Fair produced over £1000 in profits. The result, over the years, was that the school was very well equipped.

The headteacher between 1965 and 1985 had been Mr Evans. Mr Evans had very established views on curriculum, pedagogy, assessment and school management. Some illustrative features of this during his period of headship were the allocation of the pupils to 'houses' with competitions for various sporting cups, the explicit half-yearly testing and written reporting to parents of children's reading age, spelling performance, mathematical computation skills and knowledge of 'tables', and the coaching of particular groups of older children to pass entrance examinations for various local private schools. Mr Evans was much respected in the local community and by his staff, to whom he afforded a great deal of classroom autonomy. As one teacher put it:

Mr Evans was a gentleman, and he left you alone to get on with your teaching.
(Mrs Powell, February 1988)

Many parents in Greenside appreciated the traditional education which was provided and the school had been popular and well subscribed for many years.

Mrs Davison, the headteacher

The headteacher throughout this study, Mrs Davison, had been at the school for four terms at the start of the research and was introducing significant changes from its previous organization and practices. She had been appointed with the strong support of the governors and with a recognition that it was necessary, as she put it, to 'develop the school' from its 'extremely traditional ways of doing things'.

Greenside was Mrs Davison's second headship and she was confident and purposeful. She particularly believed in the encouragement of active learning and in a curriculum which was negotiated with pupils. She wanted to create a situation in which curriculum and pedagogy were consistent with these aims across the whole school.

Change, development and conflict

The first few years of Mrs Davison's headship at Greenside were rather difficult, for she found a school in which the staff were both used to having considerable classroom autonomy and were relatively confident in their own, broadly traditional, approaches to teaching. Mrs Davison had the formal endorsement of the governors and the active support of the Local Education Authority advisors. Working with both groups, she began to implement new policies – limiting the 'house' system to sports competition and withdrawing its use for academic attainments and for behaviour; ending pupil preparation for entry exams at private schools; redesigning the reports to parents so that they were more formative; introducing new procedures for curriculum planning and encouraging teachers to experiment with new approaches to teaching which would increase the active involvement of the children. There was a degree of conflict amongst school staff about such changes but, over time, staff turnover made it possible to implement new developments with increasing consistency across the school.

One particular initiative was the introduction of a 'negotiated curriculum'. The central proposition put by Mrs Davison was that children can be taught to think and improve their learning, and thus their life-chances, through their active and explicit involvement with the curriculum and learning process. A key feature of this was seen as a cycle of activities in which children 'plan, do and review'. Thus, guided by their teacher, the children would be encouraged to select an activity and give reasons for that selection, to engage with it and, later, to take stock of what they had experienced or achieved. This approach was introduced into the school in 1987.

A few years later the school was attracting staff who wished to work in this way and, in addition, had become something of a 'show school' for the approach.

On the other hand, the headteacher also encountered considerable resistance from some articulate parents who felt that the new developments were 'too progressive' and that the school had 'gone down dreadfully'. The record of a meeting of the school governors with parents, held in July 1987, gives a flavour of the issues. Among the questions raised were: What was being done to maintain standards? Were the teachers happy about having mixed age classes? What influence could parents have on the curriculum and direction of the school? What was being done about the concern that children from the school should be able to pass an independent school entrance exam? Were the numbers of children attending the school falling? These questions were answered by Mrs Davison and her staff and were countered by other parents who claimed that the new approach was a better preparation for the new GCSE exams than the old would have been; that independent schools did not want children who had been 'crammed' and, from the parent of a new child, that the school was '100 per cent better' than their previous school. The chair of governors maintained that:

> the school is not in business to prepare children for independent school entrance exams, but rather to provide a good, broad-based education. . . . A new head was bound to look at the school and bring fresh ideas and the governors are convinced that all changes have been made for good educational reasons.
> (Minutes of a meeting of governors and parents, July 1987)

In fact enrolment in 1987 and 1988 was significantly down, with some children additionally being moved to attend other schools which were deemed to be 'more traditional'. As one of the parents put it:

> I think the introduction of the 'negotiated curriculum' came with a lot of suspicion and I think maybe a lot of parents thought we were the only school that was doing it and that their children were going to be used as guinea pigs. It was a bit like mass hysteria really. It starts with one or two parents and then other parents get worried about it.
> (Mrs Gordon, parent interview, July 1988)

Another parent felt that the approach was simply inappropriate for Greenside children:

> From what I understand, the new system is not aimed at children who really have access to quite a bit of information at home, books and toys to play with that they can use experimentally. It's really aimed at children who come from more, probably deprived backgrounds, who do not have the facilities at home that our children have. And that it would probably benefit children from deprived areas, inner city areas, who are not getting anything like the scope that these kids have. I mean, most people round here can provide their children with a fairly comprehensive life-style, they take them to places, they show them things, they read to them, they buy them the sort of toys that they can use their imaginations with.
> (Mrs Jarrett, parent interview, March 1988)

By 1989, numbers attending the school started to rise again. However, the composition of this enrolment was somewhat different in that it now included a significant number of children from Damibrook, a council estate just outside Greenside for whom, formerly, the pressure on places had made enrolment impossible. Many Greenside parents who wanted a 'traditional' education sent their children to a different primary school in another residential area not far away. Greenside Primary School was 'not the same as it once was', but parental support was again much more consistent.

Assimilation, adaption and the National Curriculum

The introduction of the National Curriculum in 1989 was, in many ways a great help to Mrs Davison in moving the school forward, in developing more consistent practices amongst her staff and in enhancing the role of curriculum coordinators. Indeed, it was very clear to all staff that greater coordination was going to be necessary to guarantee the content, coherence and progression of the National Curriculum across the whole school. Mrs Davison's responsibility in managing that process was thus clearly legitimized.

With the support of her governors, Mrs Davison's initial strategy was to assimilate the new National Curriculum requirements into the procedures for negotiating the curriculum which had been developing over the past few years. She was very clear that 'the National Curriculum should not dictate' and that the school should not feel obliged to narrow the breadth of its existing provision. Thus, over the period of the research reported in this book, the main procedure used in curriculum planning remained the web diagram, produced and published to parents as the joint product of children and teachers in negotiation. This process moved in stages, from a first discussion amongst teachers regarding the foci (or 'bias') for topic coverage and regarding issues such as continuity and progression, to more detailed discussions among children within each class and back to a whole school level again for final ratification of details. From September 1989, National Curriculum attainment targets were identified and recorded before publication of the web diagram for each class. Figure 2.1, below, illustrates and represents the curriculum received by the children in this study during the Summer Term of their Year 2.

In summary, Greenside Primary School underwent a period of rapid and somewhat painful change in the mid-to-late 1980s, and, as we shall see, this had some effect on the perceptions of the parents and the experiences of the children who feature in this research. The educational philosophy of the headteacher was principled, coherent, supported by Governors and skilfully implemented – but it did not sit comfortably with the more traditional expectations of many Greenside families. However, in the words of an LEA advisor, it was 'a very well managed school with good resources' and Mrs Davison was extremely resilient. The result was a school which many visiting teachers and educationalists regarded as being exceptional. When the National Curriculum was introduced, the school was in a good position to assimilate its demands.

2.4 THE CLASSROOM TEACHERS

This section will provide something of a reference point for later chapters as the stories of the five individual children are told, for it is only here that the biography, educational philosophy and classroom practice of the Reception, Year 1 and Year 2 teachers are set out as integrated wholes. In fact, one child, Daniel, was taught by a fourth teacher in 1989/90, since the cohort was split in its Year 2. This teacher's practice is described briefly in Chapter 6 and in more detail in the companion volume (Pollard and Filer, in press).

Providing such an overview is difficult, for it requires the compression and communication of a very considerable amount of information about each of the teachers and their classrooms, and the most important methodological issues are discussed in Chapter 10. Within this chapter, each account describes the teacher's basic biography and educational philosophy, her relationship with the headteacher and views of changes in the school and, more widely, her classroom organization and relationships with the children.

Mrs Powell and her Reception Class in 1987–88

Mrs Powell was a very experienced Reception class teacher who had worked at the school for many years. She was very warm and caring towards the children and was greatly respected by most parents.

Mrs Powell had been a skilled exponent of what had once been a conventional way of organizing an infant classroom – 'work' in the morning and 'play' in the afternoon. However, in the context of the new 'negotiated curriculum' being introduced to Greenside Primary School, she had had to change:

> I used to be what they called one of those awful formal teachers. What I considered to be 'work things', I did in the morning. In the afternoon I had the sand and the construction and the home corner and odds and ends of reading and things like that. I always found it easier to work like that and all the creative activities we did in the afternoon as well. If I wanted to have something special in the way of creative activity I could spend time with that. What I found difficult with the integrated day, because I've tried it several times in the past, is really being able to concentrate on something really mucky, and you get covered in paint and glue, and then suddenly somebody wants you to write a sentence or something and you're in no fit state to do it. So I always went back to my former way of doing it after trying the new. . . . It was much less stressful and I always knew exactly what children were doing.
> (Mrs Powell, teacher interview, September 1987, Reception)

Mrs Powell's position at the time of the study reflected some struggle and conflict over the new headteacher's views. She compromised between her established practices and the newly favoured forms of classroom organization:

> This year I have not been so upset by the negotiated curriculum influence because I had some way of going with it which allowed me still to do quite a lot of what I really wanted to do.
> (Mrs Powell, teacher interview, September 1987, Reception)

Mrs Powell's system for introducing active learning and a negotiated curriculum was based around the identification of five groups of children, named by colours, and each receiving special attention on one day of the week. This was combined with the organization of the classroom environment into bays and areas for different activities. Each child had a colour-coded card denoting their group membership and each classroom area had a limited number of 'pockets' in which children could place their card when they were working or using the area. Some choice could thus be provided whilst overcrowding was controlled.

Use of areas and resources were allocated through the 'plan-do-review' system supported by the negotiated curriculum policy. Thus at the beginning of each day, a different colour group would have the opportunity to 'plan' first. Each child would take their card and 'book in' to a particular area – sand, construction, home corner, writing etc.

Mrs Powell would instruct some other groups to 'work with her' and would usually work on maths or English activities with them, using two centrally placed, larger tables. This could be justified within the negotiated curriculum system which Mrs Powell had adopted, but it was also a means of restoring the relatively straightforward teaching groups which she favoured. In this way she was able to continue to set the routine tasks which she felt were so important for learning the 'basics'. The remaining groups would 'plan' their choice of classroom activities using the card-booking and allocation system.

Through the day, different groups would be called out for groupwork with Mrs Powell whilst others would be allowed to 'plan', and, in so doing, choose from the other activities in the classroom.

Towards the end of the day there would be a 'review time' at which the children would sit on the carpet and members of the 'planning group' would report on their activities. As we can see below, this would normally lead to questions and discussion.

Mrs Powell's teaching skills are well illustrated in the following brief episode observed at a 'review time'. She structured and restructured the situation as she protected the flow and focus of the activity from Mary's crying and from a dispute between Sarah and Sally. At the same time she encouraged the children who were 'reviewing' and was alert to learning opportunities for the rest of the class. Her 'reprimands' were incorporative and not judgmental.

> After playtime: The children sit on the carpet and have 'review time'.
> Mary has bumped her head at playtime and is crying. She sits very close to Mrs Powell.
> Successive children come to the front to review their work. Daniel and Alec show a model aeroplane which they have made from Mobilo. It 'transforms' into a caravan.
> Harriet comes up to show a painting but she is very reticent. The class gets fidgety as Mrs Powell both encourages Harriet and tries to retain the attention of the class ... but Mary makes occasional sobbing noises.
>
> Mrs Powell: We all feel sorry for you, but there's no need to make that noise.
> Mrs Powell then hugs Mary.
> Mrs Powell moves to support Harriet in explaining her picture and then lets her return to her seat on the carpet.
>
> Mrs Powell: Right, can I see everyone's face now and can everyone sit .... on your bottoms?
> There is a pause, and Mrs Powell looks and waits, her gaze silently asserting her request. The children comply. It is Andrew's turn to review.
>
> Andrew: I've made a bomb carrier with 28 wheels.
> Mrs Powell: Oh, that's interesting.
> This is a more qualified response than usual, as Mrs Powell does not approve of bombs.
> Mrs Powell: If there are 14 wheels on this side, how many on the other side?
> Andrew: Fourteen.
> Mrs Powell: Good, I can't catch you out on that one.
> Sarah interrupts ...
> Sarah: Sally was going like that *(indicates putting finger in someone's ear)*.
> Sally: Because she was doing this *(indicates pulling her jumper)*.
> Mrs Powell: Well, just ask her to stop. Don't put your fingers by someone's ears. Now, let's count the wheels all together.
> The children count to 28 in unison.
> (Fieldnotes, March 1988, Reception)

Summary

Mrs Powell was thus a calm, warm and experienced teacher, only partially committed to new developments in the school but with a positive manner with the children. It seemed appropriate that, when she retired, the parents gave her a 'Mother Teddy Bear' badge.

We now turn to a consideration of the biography, perspectives and strategies of Miss Scott, the teacher by whom all the children were taught in Year 1, the year in which they became six years old.

Miss Scott and her Year 1 class in 1988–89

In 1988–89 when the target children were in her class, Miss Scott, a teacher in her mid to late 40s, was under a considerable degree of stress. It is hard to do justice to the complexities of her feelings and position in the school and to be fully appreciative of her perspective. However, there were tensions, which Miss Scott recognized, between how she felt about herself and how she was seen by others; between her beliefs about infant school education and how she actually taught during the year in question and between her judgements about her future and her view of what might have been. This situation was complicated by changes within the school and by the new requirements of the National Curriculum. In fact, Miss Scott eventually took early retirement from teaching on medical grounds.

These tensions were manifest in her relationships with Mrs Davison, the headteacher, and in her severe misgivings about what she saw as the 'interfering criticisms' of some parents, particularly concerning her teaching of reading. In both cases, Miss Scott felt angry, hurt and indignant.

Miss Scott had spent the early part of her career in schools in the Midlands, where she felt that she had established her professionalism. She had then moved to a school in Easthampton and, in the late 1970s, had been redeployed to Greenside Primary School because of the falling number of pupils on roll in her previous school. Both she, the head and governors of Greenside had tried to resist the redeployment, but the LEA had forced it through. As she put it in interview:

> I was redeployed much to my disgust and horror, and it totally deflated me. It really knocked me sideways. I was the scapegoat that was pushed out. ... I am a conscientious teacher, or I was, up to that point. Well, I still am, its just that .... I feel a bit embittered by it.
> (Miss Scott, teacher interview, July 1988, Year 1)

However, Miss Scott had gradually settled into Greenside and was able, as she put it, to 'just work my own way'.

The arrival of the new headteacher produced more difficulties for Miss Scott. On the one hand, Mrs Davison's ideas for the new whole-school development of forms of practice based on a 'negotiated curriculum' were a challenge to Miss Scott's autonomy. On the other hand, Miss Scott was not fully appreciative of the growing pressures on headteachers which derived from the new national policy of Local Management of Schools or of the implications of the new National Curriculum on schools. She thus resented some of the changes which she saw within the school, many of which came as blows to her professional pride as her skills of classroom organization were increasingly questioned. Miss Scott felt particularly upset by what she saw as Mrs Davison's autocratic managerial style and by the promotion of Greenside's head of infants to a headship. The latter event, of course, made it necessary for Mrs Davison to appoint a new head of infants, Mrs White, to whom Miss Scott was accountable.

During 1988/89, the year in which the target children passed through Miss Scott's class, the tensions described above were beginning to come to a head. Miss Scott, prone by her own account to becoming upset and depressed, began to act in her classroom in ways which were really against her better judgement. Aspects of her professional philosophy and of her frustrations were conveyed in interview and are presented immediately below.

> I try to teach each child as an individual ... and I take things slowly, because the infant years cannot be gone over again and they have to have this firm foundation. I would stick by that totally. ... I think the most important things are language skills and that is my first priority alongside the social training. ... I get very fond of the children too.
>
> I can't go on much longer here. I know it doesn't sound as if I care about the children some-times, but I do. I really care deeply about them, but nobody recognizes it.
> (Miss Scott, teacher interview, July 1988, Year 1)

Unfortunately, the classroom practice which the children experienced in Miss Scott's classroom, did not always reflect her personal commitment. A particular problem was that of classroom organization and this was something which Miss Scott recognized. She explained before the study began,

> I will have to be organised. .... I know, if I don't do something perfectly, it is sometimes a bit of a shambles. Because I'm an experienced teacher, I don't necessarily seem to get myself totally organised. But I've had better organisation in the class in other schools. Now, because it is expected of me, I probably don't do it deliberately. ...
>
> My one fault, I would say, is that I get on the defensive and that brings out the worst in me, ... not with the children particularly, though sometimes.
>
> (Miss Scott, teacher interview, July 1988, Year 1)

When Miss Scott's teaching sessions caused difficulties because of organizational problems, they tended to move through three stages. First, Miss Scott might be slow to begin and uncertain in her aims for the children. Practical details, such as having enough paint ready for painting, sometimes caused problems. At the second stage, the children would have moved to a variety of activities and Miss Scott would hear readers. The consequences which were likely to flow from weak initial organization, familiar enough to many teachers, then began to occur. The other children, if not focused and motivated, sometimes become distracted. Towards the end of such a session, the third stage, some children would come to ask for clarification or to show 'finished' work. It would then become apparent that not all the children had understood the original tasks. Meanwhile, overall noise levels tended to rise by this stage and time pressures, such as the bell for playtime or lunchtime, became worrying. In re-establishing control of the class Miss Scott would assert her authority loudly and strongly, so that the children thought of her as 'often getting very cross'. On such occasions, the children wre frightened of her.

On the other hand, Miss Scott took a great interest in some children. Extracts from her records of one child, Gareth, illustrate her sympathy and skill in helping a child who had something of a reputation amongst the teachers for 'being difficult'. Over the year there was a successful process of development in the relationship between Miss Scott and Gareth and, with her support, he made considerable progress in his reading and other learning.

November 1988

Everyone knows Gareth and his reputation has come before him. Attention seeking, energetic and often lacking self control, the first few weeks of term were difficult. I was determined to win and let him know who is boss! He was keen to find out the boundaries of good/bad behaviour – needed firm handling, praise when working hard and disapproval when really trying! Everybody blames him – but some days he is busy and then he spoils everything by some silly extrovert attention seeking.

December 1988

I had to see Gareth's mother about his behaviour having said I would do so if he misbehaved again. Mother came in, anticipating the worst, on the defensive, saying Gareth was being blamed again and that he was being made a scapegoat. I reasoned with her, that I was wanting Gareth to show me his best behaviour and that his reputation last year was not affecting my judgement.

January 1989

Gareth is in fact more open than his older brothers and sisters, and I do not find him so devious. He just doesn't seem to be able to control himself when he wants to be the centre of attention.

February 1989

His general behaviour has been improving steadily in the classroom and it appears he has these lapses outside the classroom to bring attention to himself. ... Being an intelligent child, one can reason with him.

May 1989
Gareth settles to work well, being often well motivated and eager. He enjoys working on his own and can produce thoughtful, well-planned work. Similarly works carefully at maths and all structured activities. He brings his imaginative thought to all activities but his exuberant energy can occasionally get the better of him, though he is more in control of himself than he was. He is quieter, more thoughtful, more aware of others. He is tolerated by his peers. The younger ones are still a little in awe of him. He is a loner in many ways.

July 1989
More in control of himself and his exuberant moods, but still a lively energy. Still inclined to draw attention to himself – often through silly behaviour. ... His good intentions do become lost or rather forgotten in the heat of the moment when his energy gets the better of him. Visibly concerned when reprimanded – soon forgotten. Praising him for his good behaviour, contrasting it with his bad behaviour, does have an effect. But he is gaining in self control and more able to put his lively personality and energy to positive use.
(Miss Scott, teacher records, Year 1)

Summary

As we have seen, during the particular year in which the children in this study passed through her classroom, Miss Scott was facing personal and professional challenges which had a detrimental effect on her practice and on her relationship with the children. Although she was skilled and successful in her work with some children, in classroom sessions she tended to alternate assertiveness with indecision and was vulnerable to swings of mood. Many children developed very cautious, defensive strategies towards her.

In the autumn of 1989 the cohort of children in the study were split into two Year 2 classes. Four of the five who feature in this book attended Miss George's class but Daniel, one of the older children, went into Miss Sage's class. Miss Sage's perspectives and practices are described both within Daniel's case study (Chapter 6) and in the companion volume (Pollard and Filer, in press). For now though, we move to consider Miss George and her classroom practice.

Miss George and her Year 2 class in 1989–90

Miss George was a very young teacher for whom the post at Greenside was her first appointment in teaching. Having just qualified with a B.Ed. from a polytechnic, she was appointed very late in the summer of 1989 having impressed the interviewing panel with her warmth and enthusiasm.

Miss George had been educated in private schools but, during her teacher-training course, had begun to see some limitations of her own schooling. Thus, although she was not very experienced or confident, she was committed to principles of active learning. Looking back at her interview for the job, she explained:

I didn't know anything about the negotiated curriculum, but I was always interested in it because I like the idea of children being independent.
I think ... I was educated to sit and listen and do as I was told, so at my college, when we had a workshop or something and we were expected to get on our feet and talk to the people, I found it very uncomfortable. So I've always been interested in making children as independent as possible. ... I think that deep down I'm probably just rejecting what I had ... the system I came through, because I went to private school and I passed the scholarship to public school.

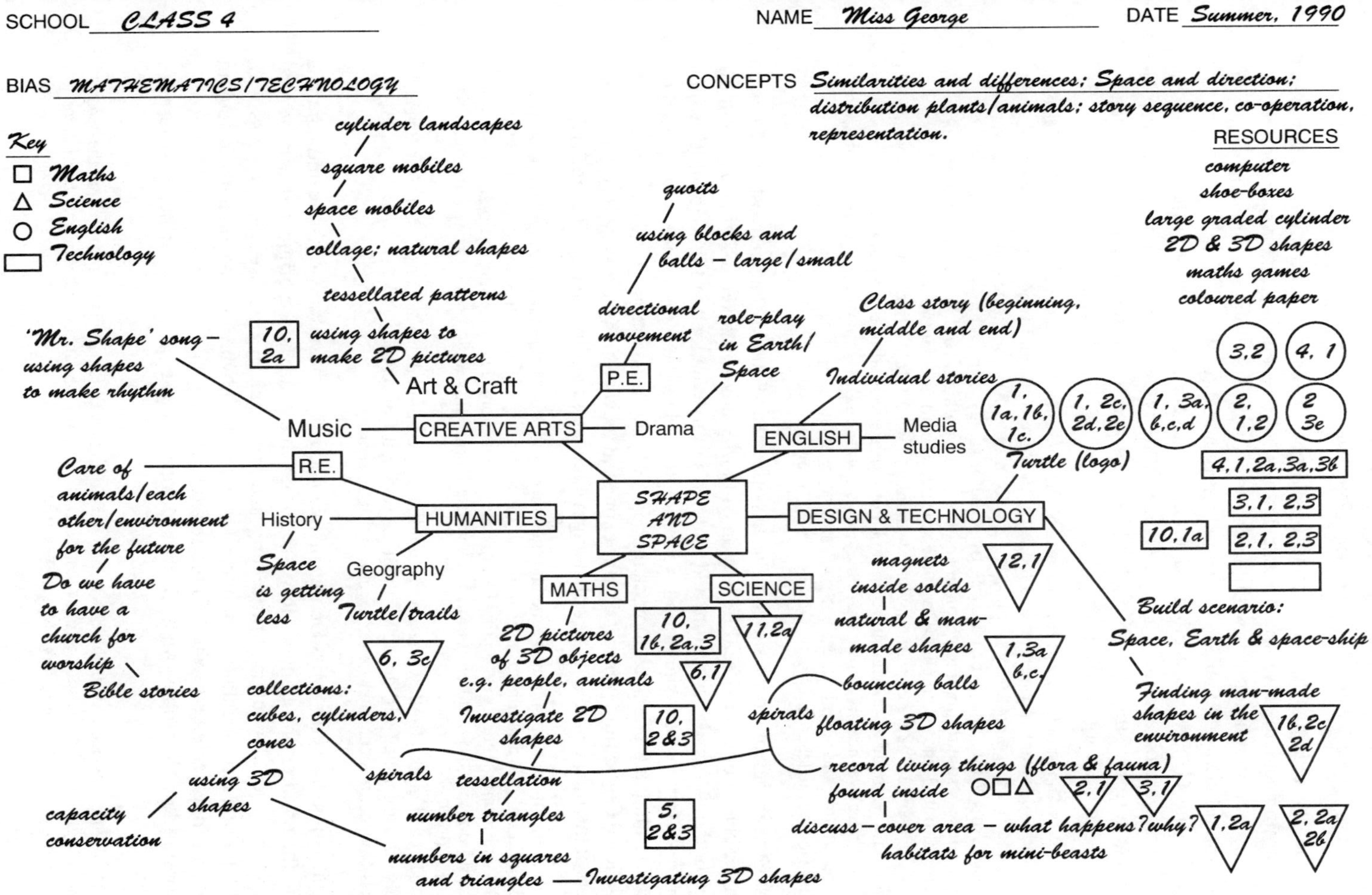

SCHOOL _CLASS 4_   NAME _Miss George_   DATE _Summer, 1990_

BIAS _MATHEMATICS/TECHNOLOGY_

CONCEPTS _Similarities and differences; Space and direction;_
distribution plants/animals; story sequence, co-operation,
representation.

Key
□ Maths
△ Science
○ English
▭ Technology

RESOURCES
computer
shoe-boxes
large graded cylinder
2D & 3D shapes
maths games
coloured paper

cylinder landscapes
square mobiles
space mobiles
collage: natural shapes
tessellated patterns

goats
using blocks and
balls — large/small

directional
movement

role-play
in Earth/
Space

Class story (beginning,
middle and end)

Individual stories

Media
studies

○ 3, 2
○ 4, 1
○ 1, 1a, 1b, 1c
○ 1, 2c, 2d, 2e
○ 1, 3a, b, c, d
○ 2, 1, 2
○ 2, 3e

Turtle (logo)

▭ 4.1, 2a, 3a, 3b
▭ 3.1, 2.3
▭ 2.1, 2.3
▭ 10.1a
▭

Build scenario:

Space, Earth & space-ship

'Mr. Shape' song —
using shapes
to make rhythm

using shapes to
make 2D pictures

Art & Craft

□ 10,
2a

Music

CREATIVE ARTS

P.E.

Drama

ENGLISH

SHAPE
AND
SPACE

DESIGN & TECHNOLOGY

△ 12.1

magnets
inside solids
natural & man-
made shapes

bouncing balls

spirals floating 3D shapes

△ 1.3a,
b, c.

record living things (flora & fauna)
found inside ○□△

Finding man-made
shapes in the
environment

△ 16.2c,
2d

discuss — cover area — what happens? why?
habitats for mini-beasts

Care of
animals/each
other/environment
for the future

Do we have
a church for
worship

Bible stories

R.E.

History

HUMANITIES

Geography

Space
is getting
less

Turtle/trails

△ 6, 3c

SCIENCE

△ 11.2a

MATHS

2D pictures
of 3D objects
e.g. people, animals

Investigate 2D
shapes

spirals   tessellation

number triangles

numbers in squares
and triangles

△ 10,
1a, 2a, 3

□ 10,
2 & 3

△ 6.1

□ 5,
2 & 3

△ 2.1, 3.1

△ 2.2a,
2d

△ 2.2a,
2b

△ 1.2a

collections:
cubes, cylinders,
cones

using 3D
shapes

Investigating 3D shapes

capacity
conservation

Figure 2.1 A Year 2 topic web emphasizing mathematics and technology by Miss George (Attainment targets for four National Curriculum subjects are indicated within their appropriate symbol).

> But when I took this job my boyfriend kept telling me about a private school which had a job going, because he was very anxious for me to take it. But I was very happy here. So I don't really know ... , but deep down, I think it's a rejection of what I knew.
> (Miss George, teacher interview, November 1989, Year 2)

Miss George regarded her appointment to Greenside as an opportunity to learn about active learning and to develop her teaching skills. She emphasized the importance of developing a close relationship with the children though, in doing so, she was concerned that she should always be able to maintain control and discipline.

Clearly Miss George's educational approach was very consistent with that of the head-teacher, Mrs Davison and, in making a somewhat nervous start to her teaching career, she felt able to turn for support both to Mrs Davison and to the recently appointed head of infants. As Miss George explained:

> When I was appointed it was after the end of the Summer Term, and so I came in the week before school started and went in and looked at the bare walls and I thought ... My bottom lip was going, I was going to cry. I think Mrs Davison must have seen the danger signals so she 'phoned Mrs White and, when I came over the next day, Mrs White had a chat with me – because it was so intimidating going in and there was nothing. And Mrs Davison kept saying, 'Well, get out all the equipment. Go to the stock cupboard and get the things you need.'
> They came and helped. I explained what I wanted and what I didn't like and they made sugges-tions and we moved all the furniture around. Perhaps there is a better way to use the space but at least I've got a nice area now where they can sit with puzzles or draw. It's a bit thin on space for the art area and science area, but you can't get it all in.
> (Miss George, teacher interview, October 1989, Year 2)

Miss George welcomed the support she was offered and quickly began to establish herself within her classroom. The Local Education Authority advisor talked to her about the intro-duction of the National Curriculum and told her 'not to even look or think about it', which, in her first few weeks she found very helpful. However, Greenside's whole-school curriculum planning practices soon caught up with her as adaptions to take account of the new National Curriculum were made. She expressed views which were very common among teachers at the time concerning her planning, which we saw illustrated by Figure 2.1:

> It just seems to take up so much time and then there's the extra care taken doing the topic work and putting all the attainment targets in and preparing a list of activities and deciding a list of skills and attainment targets again. Every time I went home, never mind the planning I was going to do with the children tomorrow, because I'd got this topic planning to finish and this list of activities.
> And you'd think, 'Well, where do the children come in to all this?' I sort of hope that even-tually all the hoo-hah will die down about the National Curriculum.
> (Miss George, teacher interview, November 1989, Year 2)

Despite such pressures, Miss George maintained her enthusiasm, work-rate and commit-ment to the children throughout the year. During this year she experimented with several different classroom layouts and procedures and she regularly discussed her progress with Mrs White. She also maintained an interest in the ways in which the negotiated curriculum was being implemented elsewhere in the school

Regarding her classroom, Miss George expressed clear priorities for her first term of teaching:

> My main thing has been to get the classroom working, to establish a relationship and get the orga-nization right and I've started getting records ready so that I can check whether I've been there.
> (Miss George, teacher interview, November 1989, Year 2)

In organizational terms, she set out the furniture in her classroom to create a number of different areas for different activities and she organized her thirty-three pupils into five groups which were 'loosely based on ability' as interpreted from reading book levels. She used these groups for teaching purposes but, more importantly, she found it helpful to be able to name groups of children for dismissal and other control purposes.

Miss George experimented with various forms of 'planning sheet' in which each child would plan their curriculum tasks and activities on a daily basis and within her overall curriculum plan for the class. She quickly experienced the challenge of ensuring a balanced curriculum and the skill of children in subverting such systems:

> On the first planning sheet where they had a column and they ticked, they put a mark in if they were going for it and ticked it off when they'd done it. And the idea was that they can't go back to it until they've done everything, so they are getting a balanced curriculum.
>
> But I found that the ones who'd learned how to work the system were going tick, tick, tick, with no thought, to make sure that they get to whatever they want to do first.
>
> So that's why with the most able group I started them on the daily planning sheet where they actually have to say what area they are going to go into, what they're going to use and what they're going to do. So they actually have to sit down and think. Imagine bringing that out of them, it's like getting blood out of a stone .... Well, I think, initially, it's because they're just not into it, I think that's the main problem.
> (Miss George, teacher interview, November 1989, Year 2)

Miss George persisted with the development of her planning and group systems through the year and, as her teaching skills and awareness improved, she began to be able to sustain them effectively.

Miss George expected to enjoy working with the children in her class and she attempted to maintain a calm and constructive demeanour in her interaction with them. On the question of discipline, of which she was very aware, she attempted to be calm and firm whilst also identifying *with* the children. An Autumn Term fieldnote illustrates her use of a well-established strategy for gaining attention and the way in which she enlisted the children's support by *sharing* her problem with them.

> Miss George: Children. Stop what you are doing please.
> Miss George holds her hands in the air, indicating that the children should stop what they are doing and copy her.
> Miss George: Children, we have got a bit noisy. I don't think we'll hear the bell when it goes, so can we try to keep a bit quieter please?
> Kirsty: Shall we put our hand up if we hear it?
> Miss George: That's a good idea – you do that.
> (Fieldnotes, October 1989, Year 2)

A warm rapport and a growing range of teaching skills continued to develop during the year. Miss George came to know the children well and often shared information about her own life with them.

She also became proficient at structuring events so that she both maintained class control and achieved her educational objectives. The example below, recorded just before a lunchtime, illustrates this:

> Miss George gives the children a warning about it being 'nearly tidying-up time'. A few minutes later she calls their attention and they all raise their hands above their heads and quieten. She calmly gives instructions to tidy up. The children begin to put their things away.
>
> Miss George moves to sit in her place on the carpet and the children begin to assemble. She chases up some stragglers, giving firm and precise instructions to some children. She begins to

count out loud in tens, cueing a routine in which everyone must be on the carpet and ready by the time 'one hundred' is reached.

All: Ten, twenty, thirty. ....

There is a flurry of activity and, by 'one hundred' the class is ready. Adele is invited to read the book which she has been writing.

Adele: It's called, 'My cat book'.

Miss George: What have you put on the *cover*?

Adele: The picture.

Miss George: So that's the *cover* of the book. Good. ... and you've put the date, so we'll know exactly *when* you've done it.

Adele reads: The cat is a white cat. The cat is a black cat. The cat is a peach cat. The cat is a brown cat.

Miss George: Good, you have written lots of sentences about your cat. Your picture looks like my little cat called 'Socks'.

The children laugh.

Miss George: What have you put on the back?

Adele: The price.

Miss George: *(To the other children)* So if you want to buy the book, you'll have to have 99 pence.

Adele: And I've put a little flower on the back so that it looks like you get on a card.

Miss George: That's very good. Right, now who can help? I wonder if anyone can help Adele to spell 'peach'?

Children strive with their hands up to be chosen 'to help'. Those selected offer letters but they do not get far with the spelling.

Miss George: Let's stop a minute and think of other words which sound like 'peach', and then we can see how to spell them.

Children make suggestions of words and Miss George receives and, where appropriate, confirms them. She starts to write words which sound like 'peach' onto a sheet of paper which she displays.

Miss George: Reach, teach, bleach, leach ... and one more ... .

Greg: Beach.

Miss George: Oh, that's what I was thinking of. Well done. So we spell 'peach', 'p', 'e', 'a', 'c', 'h', ... like this *(she demonstrates)*. Well done everyone. Now, we must put it away because it is nearly lunchtime.

(Fieldnotes, January 1990, Year 2)

The most important aspect of the episode above is the positive relationship between the teacher and pupils which is indicated. Miss George tended to be both incorporative and supportive, she asked, 'How can we help?' rather than, 'Can anyone see what is wrong?'. It also shows something of her evolving teaching skills both in terms of control and instruction. Regarding the latter it is the change in her strategy of eliciting responses about the spelling of 'peach' that is noteworthy. She realized that the individual letter approach was not working and switched to reminding the children of word patterns in spelling.

As the year progressed, these approaches produced a growth in self-confidence and progress in learning achievements amongst many children. This was extremely exciting for Miss George who was, of course, experiencing the progress of her first class of children. She particularly noted the progress of one of the slower children:

> Since I did away with the boxes, the reading boxes, ... Sophie, who was one at the bottom end, suddenly started picking books which had been in the hardest box and actually managing them. ..... . It's amazing. I just can't believe that they've improved so much because suddenly they're reading what they want to read even if they find it hard to start with.
>
> (Miss George, teacher interview, May 1990, Year 2)

Miss George took a great deal of pleasure in the progress and achievements of the children and probably identified with them rather more than an experienced teacher would have deemed wise. At the end of the year, she was quite emotionally upset that they would no longer be in her class.

However, at the end of the year Miss George was also more aware of the scope for work evasion provided by relatively individualized systems for allocating classroom tasks. Indeed, in the Summer Term of 1990 she tightened her classroom organization and made a concerted effort to ensure that the children both balanced their curriculum and completed all required tasks.

Summary

As a probationary teacher, Miss George had a great deal to learn when she began but was also exceptionally enthusiastic, hard-working and committed to the children. She was idealistic and invested a lot of her 'self' in her teaching and in her relationships with the children. However, she was constantly aware of the importance of discipline and, over the year, became more effective at monitoring children's completion of work tasks.

2.5   CONCLUSION

This chapter has located Greenside Primary School and the period of study within its wider social context and traced the phases of its internal leadership and development which were taking place at the time of the study. Additionally, it has described the biography, educational philosophy and pedagogy of the three teachers who feature most strongly in the 'learning story' case studies. The web of teacher biography, belief, experience and practices, as described above for Mrs Powell, Miss Scott and Miss George, is of great complexity and it is not possible to do full justice here to any of the three cases. However, for the purposes of this analysis, my aim has been to identify the most relevant dimensions which bear on the children's classroom experiences.

In analytical terms, each classroom represented a socio-political system in which the power and authority of the teacher was used to initiate, structure and maintain a social system of expectations, conventions and rules. Unfortunately, because of the particular circumstances, values and practices of each teacher, there was a relatively low degree of consistency in the expectations which were made of these children as they moved from class to class.

This chapter has primarily focused on the school and classroom contexts, providing geographical, historical, biographical and professional reference points. Of the two other major contexts studied – the home and the playground – accounts of each family will be found in each child's 'learning story'. Discussion of the influence of families and of peer groups and peer friendships also permeates the case studies. Issues relating to both contexts will also be highlighted in Chapter 4 and Chapter 9.

Part 2

Beginning

Introduction to the Case Study Stories

In total, there are five child case-study 'learning stories' in Parts Two and Three of this book. Although these are extensive and detailed, they are also summary accounts of the cases and only a small proportion of the actual data which have been gathered can be reproduced.

Four summarizing and representational devices have been used to provide concise overviews of the data-sets, and these are introduced below.

DIAGRAMS REPRESENTING THE 'STRUCTURAL POSITION' OF CASE-STUDY PUPILS WITHIN EACH CLASS

The first figure within the *Introduction* of each case study represents what I have called the 'structural position' within the classroom of each child in relation to his or her peers (see, for instance, Figure 3.1, on page 39, in relation to Mary). For each pupil-year, these diagrams show the size of the class, the age of the case study pupil and his or her position within a rank ordering of pupil attainment in maths and literacy.

Representation of these four variables is particularly interesting when compared over the three years of Key Stage 1. However, whilst class size and pupil age are categoric data, the ranking of pupils in terms of literacy and mathematical attainment is based on judgements made by an experienced infant teacher, Kath Henry, and Andrew Pollard. Kath Henry focused an eight-month project on an analysis of pupil documents, reports to parents and teachers' official and unofficial records for each of the three years to produce rank orderings for each class. Whilst these data cannot be regarded as categoric, they are usefully indicative of the case-study pupils' attainment in terms of the relative attainment of other children.

A note on the variations in age in relation to other pupils may also be helpful. With 1.5 forms of entry to Greenwide Primary School each year, the pupil composition of each class normally varied year by year. Children were allocated to classes strictly on the basis of age, and would be among the older or younger depending on where the 'cut' happened to fall.

YEAR-BY-YEAR MATRICES

The story within each case study has been summarized as a matrix for each year (see, for example, page 51). These matrices represent relationships for each child in the three major social settings of home, playground and classroom and outcomes in terms of the two key issues of identity and learning. The basic structure of each matrix for each year is illustrated below:

Family Relationships	Peer-group Relationships	Teacher Relationships	Identity	Learning

The basic structure of each year-by-year matrix

VARIATIONS IN CASE-STUDY DETAIL

For reasons of space it has not been possible to publish in full all of the data which underpin the fifteen year-by-year matrices which are contained in this book, though an attempt to maintain holism has been made. Each pupil-year is discussed either in 'extended' or in 'shorter' form, as indicated below.

	Reception	Year 1	Year 2
Chapter 4, Mary's story	Extended	Extended	Extended
Chapter 5, Hazel's story	Extended	Extended	Shorter
Chapter 6, Daniel's story	Extended	Shorter	Shorter
Chapter 7, Sally's story	Extended	Shorter	Extended
Chapter 8, James' story	Extended	Shorter	Shorter

Variations in case-study detail

As can be seen from the table above, extended texts have been provided for all children for the Reception Year and for all three of Mary's years in Key Stage 1. Mary's story was focused on in this way because, in some senses, it was relatively straightforward. Extended text comparisons are also possible for two children in each of Year 1 and Year 2. Despite these variations, comparisons across years and settings both within and between cases can easily be made because of the identical structure of all texts and summarizing matrices. Shorter texts highlight major patterns and new developments in the children's experiences, within the space available.

CASE-STUDY OVERVIEWS

Case-study overviews are used to conclude each case and to summarize patterns of relationship between the child, parents, peers and teachers. Particular use is made of a triadic representation as illustrated below.

The *social context* within which each child interacts and learns is represented by the outer triangle. Thus parent/teacher, parent/peer and teacher/peer relationships are developed around each child and create situations to which he or she can contribute. Importantly however, these are also the social contexts within which he or she must establish his or her identity and cope.

The *dynamic relationship* between each child's self and identity with his or her parents and siblings, peers and teachers is represented by the inner star. This summarizes the particular pattern of relationships between the individual child, with his or her evolving sense of identity, as it is enacted and developed through interaction in home, playground and classroom. The first of these triadic case-study overviews, for Mary, is on page 80.

Having clarified the origin and purposes of these summarizing devices, we can now move directly to the story of Mary and her learning.

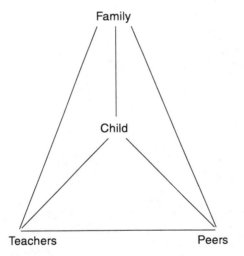

The triadic overview of each child's case study story

Chapter 3

Mary's Story

3.1 MARY, AN INTRODUCTION

Mary's case study provides an excellent illustration of a child's strategic adaptation through different settings over time. Mary's relationships with her older brothers and identification with her mother influenced her initial aspiration to be 'a good girl', but as she became more experienced and developed in maturity, she drew on a wider range of cultural resources

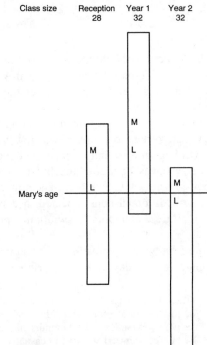

Figure 3.1 *Mary's structural position: age and relative attainment at literacy and maths in Reception, Year 1 and Year 2 classes (for an explanation of this figure see page 35)*

including those of peer culture. Would she then become more self-assertive and confident at home and in school? How might this affect her relationship with her brothers, mother and teachers and what effect would these developments have on her learning strategies?

In Figure 3.1, Mary's age and attainment in maths and literacy are shown in relation to other children in her Reception, Year 1 and Year 2 classes.

The pattern of Mary's structural position within her three Key Stage 1 classes was very similar to that of her friend, Sally (see Chapter 7). Mary was only a few weeks younger than Sally and, in academic terms, she performed at a very commendable level in relation to her peers. As we will see, in her Year 2, when she was one of the older pupils, she had a particular surge of self-confidence. However, there were important differences between Mary's structural position and that of Sally. In literacy, Mary tended to be a little behind Sally but this relative position was consistent enough to be a source of mild frustration and competition in terms of reading books and story writing. In mathematics, Mary performed ahead of Sally in Reception, dropped back in Year 1 and then moved ahead again in Year 2. How would this pattern affect her sense of self-esteem and her attitudes to learning?

3.2 MARY'S FAMILY

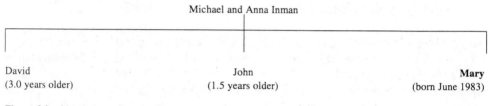

Figure 3.2 *Mary's immediate family*

At the beginning of this study, in September 1987, Mary was just four years and three months old, having been admitted to Greenside into the school year in which she became five. As the family tree above shows, she was the third child in her family and with two older brothers, John and David.

Mary's father, Michael, was a chartered surveyor. He was building up his own business when the study began and, since he often worked long hours, was not interviewed as part of this study. Mary's mother, Anna, was beginning to build up her paid work after a period of exclusive commitment to child-care. She was a qualified teacher and taught music, part-time, in a local comprehensive school. She also did some book-keeping for her husband.

The family lived in a modern, three-bedroomed house located in a very pleasant and secluded site of ten houses. Some facilities, including a swimming pool, were shared between the households.

As a young baby, Mary had suffered from what was diagnosed as an immature digestive system and had 'just screamed the place down, day and night'. However, as Mrs Inman explained:

> That came right at about six months and that was it. Absolutely no problems. She always slept, so it was easy. She didn't ever crawl. She just shuffled around and didn't walk until she was 14 months, which was very different to John who was walking at 10 months and was dreadful. He was into everything. He hurt himself; he bumped himself; he was in casualty – but Mary was very self-protective. She never put herself in a dangerous situation even at that age. She didn't walk until she could walk well and she never climbed out of her cot or climbed out of the high

chair – which the boys were doing at six months – so she never really hurt herself or put herself in danger.
(Mrs Inman, parent interview, March 1988, Reception)

Looking back, her mother interpreted Mary's behaviour as a baby as showing signs of the same strategies which she was later to adopt in school.

Mary's parents aimed to provide a secure and happy home for their children and wanted them to do well in life. However, there was a difference of emphasis between them regarding the importance of educational experiences. As Mary's mother put it:

> My husband places quite a store on academic success. He had a very academic upbringing and I think he sees success in those terms, but I try to be more liberal than that. ... But I still think that it is very important that, whatever they do, they do jolly well. We do have these discussions.

In relation to one of her sons, she went on:

> It doesn't matter if he hasn't got 15 'A' levels, but if he wants to be a film cameraman, I want him to be a damned good one, you know. I feel quite relaxed about it really, but you always want to do the best for them don't you. ... I would like them to have lots of experiences and travel, just to be good happy kids really.
> (Mrs Inman, parent interview, March 1988, Reception)

On approaches to bringing the children up, Mrs Inman explained being 'quite rigid about honesty and right and wrong' and of 'putting quite a store' on manners and being polite. As she said:

> I am prepared to have big issues with them now and I am prepared to sort of 'win' over bedtime, and telly, and manners and lying, and things like that. I don't know whether I'm right or wrong, but I believe that is my investment for their future. So perhaps I am quite strict on some things, but I am quite easy-going really.
> (Mrs Inman, parent interview, March 1988, Reception)

The diary entries for the period certainly confirm these accounts. Regarding family activities, a wide range of family events is catalogued, from games to excursions and there were often references to swimming in the pool.

3.3   MARY IN HER RECEPTION YEAR

Mary, Reception, relationships with parents at home

Mary had a close and warm relationship with her mother who provided a constant sounding board and source of advice, support and security for Mary as she encountered and overcame new experiences. A flavour of this is conveyed below, in an except from Mrs Inman's diary:

> Bath time – a bit late as I was making John's birthday cake. Mary was very chatty about school and her friends – we discussed how to pronounce words properly and in a babyish way – she said some of her friends say 'muggle' instead of 'muddle', plus other examples. She told me she had a nose bleed at school and had to see a teacher whose name she couldn't remember. She washed herself, undressed herself and I got her out and dried her. She also told me she had had PE and had really enjoyed going on the apparatus.
> After her bath we did her book and word tin which she did well, then I took her up to bed.

She went without protest, snuggled down and went to sleep 7.30 – Michael got in after Mary was in bed.
(Mrs Inman, parent diary, February 1988, Reception)

Here we can see an example of Mary's mother scaffolding her understanding regarding pronunciation and supporting her early work on reading. Mary's father, though less often available, would also help Mary in tackling new challenges. The example below, of learning to tie shoe laces, occurred when Mary was only just four years old but it clearly reveals her determination to learn following the achievement of one of her friends.

Recently Michael taught Mary to tie her own shoelaces. She had seen that Sarah could do it and wanted to learn. They sat down together with a lace threaded in a piece of card and she learned in about ten minutes. She practised and practised, was determined to master it, and was absolutely delighted when she did.
(Mrs Inman, parent diary, November 1988, Reception)

Mary, Reception, relationships with siblings at home

As the youngest of three children and as a girl with two older brothers it is perhaps not surprising to find that Mary's relationship with her brothers was occasionally characterized by tension. Her mother's diary entry in the middle of Mary's Reception year illustrates the way in which this was interwoven into everyday, routine events:

The children and Michael sit round a breakfast bar and have breakfast together. They choose what they want, either cereals or toast, and help themselves. Mary and John had an argument over the sugar. John wouldn't pass it until Mary said 'please'. Mary started crying and then the boys started teasing her so she over reacted and got more upset. She was chivvied out of it by Michael and myself and everyone was told to get on with their breakfast.
(Mrs Inman, diary entry, February 1988, Reception)

However, tension between the boys and Mary seemed to develop into a more intense, and explicitly gendered, phase in the summer. Mrs Inman commented in interview:

Over this year she has started to develop a real love/hate relationship with David the eldest. There is a three year gap and they have been at each other's throats just recently. That hadn't happened before and it is on a sexist theme as well. He will say, 'oh you smelly girl, you fat pig' or something, and she will say 'I'm not a smelly girl'. 'I hate girls' says David, and even nasty things like 'I wish you were dead' and she says 'I wish you were as well'. It is very verbal, but this sort of squabbling has really started to develop.
(Mrs Inman, parent interview, July 1988, Reception)

Of course, such squabbling had much longer origins and was also associated with characteristic strategies which the children tended to adopt in their interactions together and with their parents. This was encapsulated by her mother as follows:

She plays the same little role, the good little girl, ... and those naughty little boys are out in the garden covering themselves with mud, and she is 'Goody-Two-Shoes'. It obviously works quite well.
  She really is eager to please, unlike the boys who are sometimes really as naughty as can possibly be. She doesn't usually do that. She doesn't like to rock the boat very much and she doesn't like to be told off.
(Mrs Inman, parent interview, March 1988, Reception)

Mary, in other words, sought, on most occasions, to be 'good'. She did not want to get into trouble. On the other hand, such was her position in relation to her brothers that she was concerned to protect her interests and, on occasion, was quite prepared to stand her ground, even when a degree of conflict resulted.

Mary, Reception, relationships among friends and in the playground

Mary quickly developed school friendships, partly based on children she had known at playgroup. One of her particular friends was Amy, and for her, the honour of 'coming to tea' was often afforded. As her mother explained:

> She wanted Amy to come to tea so after much pleading and persuasion I said Amy could come. They played really well together with a lot of giggling, shrieks of laughter and general silliness. They were both wearing nighties at one stage over their uniforms. Tea was a giggly affair and they were really winding each other up and telling silly jokes etc. After tea I made them play outside – it being a glorious evening. They put wellingtons on and waded up and down the stream. They seemed to get on really well and were great buddies when Amy's mother called – they kept calling out goodbye to each other and 'see you tomorrow' etc.
> (Mrs Inman, parent diary, June 1988, Reception)

However, throughout the year there was also a degree of falling 'in' and 'out' of friendship, particularly among a small group of girls: Mary, Sally and Amy.

> Quite often if Sally or Amy is here they play very nicely and then there will be a blow up and 'I'm not her friend any more, she is not playing the game I want to play, she is not doing it right'. This, that and the other – very much so. Those particular girls who are sort of best friends and are important to her but there is a lot of rivalry between them.
> (Mrs Inman, parent interview, July 1988, Reception)

Such peer rivalry was also regularly observed in the school playground but, in that setting, the boys provided a constant source of threat, and thus a countervailing source of solidarity for the girls. As Sally, Mary and Amy explained to me:

Sally:	We like 'My Little Pony galloping'.
AP:	What do you do?
Sally:	*(demonstrates with a hopping motion)*
Amy:	No!
Sally:	You do!
AP:	Amy, you show us first and then Sally can after.
Amy:	You hold onto the reins and *(she demonstrates galloping around)*. That's how you play.
Sally:	Sometimes I play it, but a different one. But me and Mary has to do it together, don't we? We have to go holding hands and ... *(they demonstrate)*.
Sally:	Sometimes we have a race.
AP:	What, all of you?
All:	Yes! *(with great excitement and galloping noises)*
AP:	When you do that game, do the boys come and play with you?
All:	NO!
Mary:	We don't want to play with them.
Amy:	We say, 'Who wants to play with the boys?'
Sally:	*(Chanting)* Gall-op-ing, no boys!
All:	*(Chanting)* Who wants to play?
	Racing ... .
	No boys ... .

AP:	When you are singing your rhymes and playing, what do the boys think about it?
Sally:	They keep walking about our games. They go in our games and when we're playing, they join in and so we go to play something else.
Amy:	Well, when the boys, when all of us three are playing our games, the boys go, 'Oh, what a meanie, meanie, meanie, meanie girls' and they say, 'Oh, you idiots!'
AP:	What do you do?
Amy:	We just ignore them. We just go. We just laugh at them.

(Sally, Amy and Mary in interview on playtime video, June 1988)

Thus, whatever Mary's relationships with her brothers, she derived significant support from her peers and from her experiences of gender relations in the playground. At the same time though, there were some genuine rivalries among her schoolfriends and she took careful note of their learning achievements and experiences both inside and outside school.

Mary, Reception, relationships with Mrs Powell in the classroom

Mary's teacher in her Reception class was a very experienced teacher of infants who had a calm and organized approach to teaching and a warm but firm relationship with the children. Mary settled into the classroom with few problems. As she encountered new learning challenges, Mary tried hard, seeking to please as she did at home. She normally found Mrs Powell appreciative of her efforts. For instance, a fieldnote records Mary seated at a table where a small group of children are working on 'sounds and letter writing':

> She shows Mrs Powell her attempt at writing the letter 'a', which had been started in the incorrect place. Mrs Powell guides her hand in tracing the pencil over the letter correctly. Mary tries again whilst Mrs Powell turns to other children.
>   Mary shows her new attempt.
>
> | Mrs Powell: | 'Oh Mary, that's lovely. I couldn't do that *any* better myself. Do you put your thinking cap on when you do your writing? |
> | Mary: | Yes. |
> | Mrs Powell: | Well done, good girl. |
>
> (Classroom fieldnote, January 1988, Reception)

This is a good example of Mrs Powell's pedagogy. The task might be seen as being relatively routinized and decontextualized, but the atmosphere in the class and the teacher–pupil relationship was caring and supportive and children were encouraged to 'have a go'.

Mary's rivalry with some of her peers was nevertheless clear. This was particularly so with regard to Sally, whom we will meet in Chapter 7 and whose parents worked in the school. A fieldnote recorded both Sally making much of the limelight afforded by a 'review time' and Mary's response:

> The children gather on the carpet around Mrs Powell for 'Review Time'. This is the routine phase of the day in which they explain to the class what they did, following their 'planning'. Mrs Powell records what they say. It is Sally's turn to do her review.
>   Sally moves to the front and begins by getting Mrs Powell to tie up her laces. Then, facing the class, she clears her throat and begins, at dictation speed:
>
> | Sally: | I played in the home corner and me and Mary done some fancy dancing and I played birthdays. In the game I was thirty. |
> | Mrs Powell: | Sally's Mum is thirty today. |

Sally smiles.

Sally: And I put glitter on my face and I done some dancing with Mary and it was a dance what we did yesterday and I saw a tree out of the window.

Mrs Powell: I think you're making it up now, so that I will have to write it down for a long time ... so we'll stop there!

Sally grins and Mary moves forward to take her place.

Mary: We played in the home corner and we played dancing and as we spinned my hat kept on getting off. Then we played in the book corner.

Mrs Powell: What book did you read Mary?

Mary: Um ... I'll go and get it.

Mary returns with *three* books.

Mrs Powell: *(Laughing)* She goes off for one and comes back with three! Which one will you choose?

Mary: *(Under her breath)* The long one.

Mary assesses the longest and chooses 'Mr Meebles'. She spends some minutes discussing it with Mrs Powell who then has to break off to reprimand a child for not paying attention. In fact, several children are getting fidgety. As she returns her attention to Mary, Mary proffers another book to talk about.

Mrs Powell: No, I don't think we've got time now.

(Classroom fieldnote, June 1988, Reception)

Mary, Reception, progress in classroom learning

Mary had a very satisfactory year and both her teacher and parents were pleased with her learning and development. Having settled quickly into the security of the classroom routines, she made particularly good progress in the first half of the year. For instance, Document 3.1, from September 1987, shows one of Mary's first attempts at the 'picture and writing' task which she was to experience almost daily over the year. In this approach to learning to write, children began with a picture using crayons and were then asked to 'write over' a statement which was written on their behalf by their teacher. In so doing, they practised hand–eye coordination and a variety of writing skills whilst at the same time having a modest element of 'choice' in the focus of their work. Document 3.1 shows a very common early child representation of the human figure and Mary's attempts to both 'write over' and 'write under' her teacher's writing as she expressed her ballet experience.

Five weeks later Mary had made very considerable progress, as Document 3.2 shows. The drawing, in particular, is far more sophisticated and earned Mrs Powell's praise. Once again, the topic relates directly to Mary's experience.

Early in the new year Mary's writing also started to become more controlled, Document 3.3. She was being encouraged for her 'neatness' and her writing was on an imaginative topic.

Over her first six months then, Mary's development in drawing and in writing were excellent and she was beginning to use the task to express herself. The simplicity and predictability of the task combined with regular, sympathetic instruction from Mrs Powell seemed to suit her.

The maths tasks which Mrs Powell set were also fairly routine and often involved the use of work-sheets which she made. Documents 3.4 and 3.5 illustrate two of these, as they were completed by Mary.

Document 3.1   *Mary, picture and writing on 'doing ballet', September 1987, Reception*

As the year went on, Mrs Powell provided Mrs Inman with a steady flow of informal feedback about Mary's progress when she came to deliver and collect Mary from school. Mrs Powell's official reports were also rounded and very positive. She wrote:

> Mary is keen to talk about her experiences, to tell stories and to make up songs. She will attempt to write on her own and spells a few words. She is keen to read and reads with expression. Mary enjoys practical maths and number work. She works well and has made good progress with no trouble with the concepts considered up to now.
>
> Mary takes an interest in all class activities and often has something of interest to contribute to class discussions. Mary is keen to try creative activities and concentrates well, with pleasing results. Her drawings are good and she makes good use of colour.
>
> Mary is a happy, sociable girl, joining in all class activities happily.
>
> (Edited from two class teachers' official reports to parents, spring and summer 1988, Reception)

Progress in learning to read was particularly important to Mr and Mrs Inman and they recognized the considerable efforts Mary made:

> She is very positive [about her word tin], she likes to do it and she likes success. She likes to get it right, she will battle on a bit with her word tin, if there is a word she doesn't know. I can see her now, trying to learn it afterwards, to herself. She does try very hard to learn it, so she is very positive. No problems there.
>
> (Mrs Inman, parent interview, July 1988, Reception)

lovely!

I went to my
I Wen t o My
Grandma's and when
Grandmas and When
I was at my
I Wa at My
Grandma's I was sick.
Grandmas I Was Sick

Document 3.2 *Mary, picture and writing on being sick at Grandma's, November, 1987, Reception*

This is mummy Bear snoring
so daddy Bear cannot get
to sleep.

Document 3.3   *Mary, picture and writing on 'mummy Bear snoring', January 1988, Reception*

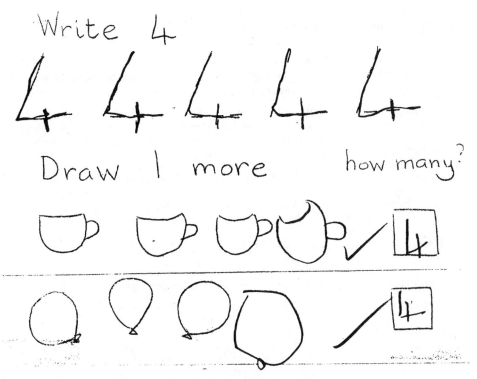

Write 4

Draw 1 more   how many?

Document 3.4 *Mary, sample of number task, October 1987, Reception*

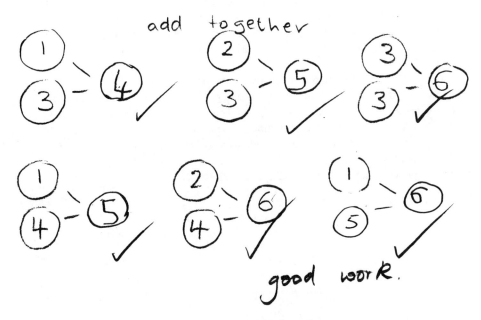

add together

good work.

Document 3.5 *Mary, number task on addition, March 1988, Reception*

Identity and learning in the Reception year

In the context of the combination of support from her mother and rivalry with her brothers, we can see that Mary became increasingly confirmed in her gender identity and in a competitive approach to life. As her mother commented at the end of the Reception year:

> She sometimes says things like 'I am glad I am not a boy. They are horrible, they have short hair and get dirty' etc., etc. She also gets on well with them at times and enjoys a good giggle with them – for example at jokes and rude words. She definitely uses her femininity and asks them to do things for her and to help her. I think she sees herself as having to keep up appearances she likes her hair done a certain way and she is clothes conscious. She also loves jewellery, perfume, make-up, etc. She looks up to her brothers especially when she sees them doing things she would not do herself – i.e. stunt riding on their bikes or climbing trees. She identifies very much with other females (of any age – from babies to great grandmother). Mary is quite competitive – again within her own peer group. She knows who can read ahead of her at school and who can do what.
> (Mrs Inman, parent diary, June 1988, Reception)

In terms of school, Mary's mother saw the year as a whole as a period during which Mary's confidence and learning achievements had steadily developed.

> She loves school and that hasn't wavered really. She is very positive about school. It has been a delightful year at school for her. Her whole experience of school is positive. I think she feels very much part of the class group.
> Well learning. ... I am trying to think back a year now, obviously physical things like she couldn't do her buckles up, she couldn't skip – she has learnt a lot of new things.
> (Mrs Inman, parent interview, July 1988, Reception)

Mary's Reception year was thus one in which, in coming to terms with starting school, she had the benefit of two very stable sources of caring support in her mother and her class teacher. And yet, in both domestic and school contexts, Mary felt some vulnerability with regard to her siblings and peers.

At home, the 'love/hate relationship' with her older brothers increased her identification with her mother and caused her to evolve a variety of strategies by which she could protect and promote her interests.

In school, Mary was challenged by many of the new learning tasks which she experienced. However, she found peer support from older children who, at this particular point in their school careers, were more self-confident and achieving at relatively higher levels. With Mrs Powell's calm and consistent support, Mary gradually developed the determination and self-confidence to work at tasks, such as those associated with reading, even when success did not come easily.

Matrix 3.1 provides a summary of Mary's Reception year as a whole.

Matrix 3.1 *Mary's Reception Year, a summary matrix*

Family relationships	Peer-group relationships	Teacher relationships	Identity	Learning
Close rapport with mother, including discussion and active support regarding new experiences and learning.	Very close friendships with Amy and Sally continue from playgroup.	Develops trusting and warm relationship with Mrs Powell.	Presents herself at home as a 'Goody-Two-Shoes', in contrast to noisy, naughty boys.	Uses mother as a source of information and explanation who can scaffold her understanding.
Love/hate relationship with older brothers. Occasional squabbling and teasing about being a girl.	Reciprocal play and visits 'to tea'.	Average age for children in her class.	Thinks boys are 'horrible' but also looks up to her brothers.	Settles well at school and is positive about work even when, as with reading, she found it difficult. Makes persistent efforts with her 'word tin'.
Likes traditional girls' activities	Gendered play in school playground and some solidarity against intrusive boys.	Mary conscientiously applies herself to school-work.	Very aware of herself as a girl and is concerned about her appearance.	Begins to use routine picture and writing tasks to review her experiences and express herself imaginatively.
Is 'eager to please' parents and tries to avoid trouble	Occasional falling 'in' and 'out' with friends.	Described as 'kind and friendly' by Mrs Powell.	Interest in all school activities. Happy and sociable.	Likes to get things correct.
	Some rivalry over school-work – especially with Sally.	Attentive to Mrs Powell and likes to receive her attention and praise.	Is competitive and aware of others' progress. Wishes to do well at school compared with peers and brothers.	Makes good progress in writing and reading. Understands concepts in maths.

3.4 MARY IN HER YEAR 1

Mary, Year 1, relationships with parents at home

The close rapport between Mary and her mother continued during the year, with discussions being initiated by Mary's questions being commonplace, particularly at unpressured times spent together. For instance:

> I put Mary in the bath and she was talking about whether 'Farmer Christmas' as she calls him visits Ethiopians and whether the children want toys or food. We thought he probably did and they had a little of both!
> (Mrs Inman, parent diary, October 1988, Year 1)

Document 3.6 is a coloured drawing by Mary which was produced as a present for her mother. It was drawn whilst Mary was staying with an aunt.

Document 3.6 *Mary's picture for Mummy, July 1989, Year 1*

Mrs Inman continued to provide Mary with guidance as her mother and with support as one female to another, in contrast to the 'maleness' of the boys. This, and some aspects of routine family life, are conveyed by another diary entry relating to Sunday morning activities:

> We were fairly pushed this morning as the boys had to be at the Rugby Club by 10.00 a.m. I asked them all to get dressed which started Mary off making a huge fuss as she didn't want to wear her dungarees. She didn't know what she *did* want to wear, just that she made a fuss about the clothes I put out. Her fuss was largely ignored by everyone and she sulked in her bedroom. Eventually she appeared dressed in her dungarees and looking really nice and trendy. We all said she looked nice but she said she didn't care. However, she looked pleased. The boys then started calling her a smelly cow pat and laughing – she totally ignored them. We all went to the

rugby and watched the boys play. Mary was fairly bored and kept asking when we were going so I took her for a walk around the fields and we eventually met some girls who were looking at some horses in the next field. Mary made friends with them and stayed with them for the rest of the morning. We had a drink after the matches and lunch at the club. Mary enjoys this aspect of rugby.
(Mrs Inman, parent diary, October 1988, Year 1)

Mary continued to achieve new milestones in her physical development. For instance, at swimming she jumped and dived with increasing confidence. Her mother reported:

We were amazed at how well she could swim and breathe with John's goggles and snorkel on. She was very pleased with herself and didn't want the swim to end.
(Mrs Inman, parent diary, October 1988, Year 1)

Mary also began to feel able to set aside some previously important sources of security, such as her 'blanker'. She had slept with and felt comforted by this blanket since infancy but in the autumn of 1988 Mary told her mother that she 'didn't need it any more'.

Mary, Year 1, relationships with siblings at home

Relationships between Mary and her two brothers continued to be somewhat strained at times, with Mary appearing to provide a particular source of amusement for David, her older brother who was eight years old at the time. For instance:

At breakfast time David was making fun of Mary's hair which kept falling in her face and she was getting annoyed, so I told David that he either stopped or went to get her a clip as it was just winding Mary up which in turn was making me cross.
(Mrs Inman, parent diary, October 1988, Year 1)

However, Mrs Inman was beginning to call upon the children to resolve their own conflicts and encouraging Mary to develop ways of defending her own interests. Nevertheless, one of Mary's tactics, screaming loudly, was beginning to lose its credibility with her mother.

Once home I ran a bath and told the children I must do some cooking but to get on sensibly etc. After about 10 minutes there was a terrible row going on and the boys were winding up Mary who was screaming. I was pretty cross – particularly with David as he was responsible and should know better. I also told Mary off for screaming instead of getting out of the bath and getting on with things.
(Mrs Inman, parent diary, October 1988, Year 1)

Despite Mary's screaming strategy, she was nevertheless increasingly encouraged to 'stick up for herself'. This reflected the perception that Mary was now capable of defending herself and even of initiating incidents.

She sticks up for herself a lot more now and often gives as good as she gets.
(Mrs Inman, parent diary, October 1988, Year 1)

In terms of favoured play activities, Mary was very influenced by her gender and by the distinction which it offered her compared to her brothers. Her mother commented:

She still plays with dolls, *loves* make up and dressing up and wearing my shoes. She is not particularly interested in playing outside with her brothers, she doesn't skateboard or play football, cricket or darts with them. She prefers to ride her bike, skip or do handstands. She has recently learnt to 'flirt' with John and David's friends and will play chase or tickle.
(Mrs Inman, parent diary, June 1989, Year 1)

Two major features of Mary's development within her family can thus be identified. First, are the achievements which she made as she developed physically and had new experiences. Second, there is the extension of her gendered identity and related strategies. In relation to her brothers, she was no longer referred to as 'Goody-Two-Shoes' but could now 'give as good as she gets'. As an increasingly competent five-year-old, Mary was trying to assert herself and, in relation to her brothers, drew considerable strength from her identification with her mother.

Mary, Year 1, relationships among friends and in the playground

When Mary moved to her Year 1 class, she lost Amy, but her other close friends moved with her. Friendships of the Reception year thus continued and deepened in her new class, with Mary, Sarah and Sally becoming almost inseparable. As video recordings taken at the time show, there were also considerable continuities in the types of play. These remained patterned by gender-based expectations and cultures but were perhaps emboldened by the fact that the children were no longer the youngest in the Infant playground. Fieldnotes and interview records reflect some of these activities:

> In the playground Harriet and Hazel are playing hopscotch up and down, using the paving to delineate the squares. Mary and Sally are playing at 'horses'. The skip along, taking it in turns to 'ride' by holding the back of the other's coat.
> (Fieldnote, February 1989, Year 1)

> Sally, Harriet and Mary are playing at magic – a game they've invented called 'Abracadabra'. Sally uses a lip-salve as a magic potion. Mary goes to get her 'magic ribbon' and they chant and dance together.
> (Fieldnote, March 1988, Year 1)

> AP: What sorts of things do you like doing in the playground?
> Mary: Mums and Dads. You get a Mummy and get a Daddy and get a Baby. Sarah is usually the Baby and Sally is usually the Mummy.
> Sally: We like Hokey Cokey, Farmer's in his Den, skipping, Mr Wolf and that sort of thing too.
> (Group interview with Mary, Sally and Sarah, April 1989, Year 1)

Although the range of Mary's friendships broadened over the year, the particular strength of the friendship between Mary, Sally and Sarah remained. As Sally once put it:

> Sally: We like playing together all the time.
> (Group interview with Mary, Sally and Sarah, April 1989, Year 1)

The closeness of these relationships was founded on shared activities and reinforced by frequent visits to each other's homes for tea. Sally and Mary also shared a particular enjoyment and talent for dancing which they developed at ballet classes on Saturday mornings. They could talk at great length about the tap, modern and ballet steps and dances which they were learning and would demonstrate these to friends in the playground.

Interestingly, during the year this friendship also provided the foundation of a form of solidarity through which the girls coped with the perceived possible threat of their teacher. They would, for example, exchange glances in teacher-led classroom sessions and were often supportive of each other if one of the group of friends were 'in trouble'. A playground rhyme of the time was sung to me by Sally and Mary:

Teacher, teacher, I declare,
I can see your underwear.
Is it black or is it white?
Oh my God, it's dynamite.
(Fieldnotes, May 1989, Year 1)

At the same time however, Mary and her group of friends remained competitive. They often vied to choose a next game, to decide on roles or on how an activity should develop. Mary described this in terms of her friends 'being bossy'.

AP: Which of your friends are a bit bossy sometimes?
Mary: Sally. All my friends really.
AP: Are they? And what do you feel when they are a bit bossy?
Mary: I start to cry. I really feel sad.
AP: Do you? But they're not bossy for long are they?
Mary: Yes, sometimes. Then when I go away from them they follow me and I don't like it. And I say 'don't follow me then' and they say 'Yes'.
AP: And then they make friends with you again, don't they?
Mary: Yes, usually they do.
(Photo interview, November 1988, Year 1)

Mary thus retained her close friends. They were a source of enjoyment and support throughout Year 1, but they were also a source of rivalry.

Mary, Year 1, relationships with Miss Scott in the classroom

Mary's new teacher, Miss Scott, was an experienced teacher who had clear educational views which might broadly be described as 'child-centred'. She was well known to the parents of the school and had a generally positive reputation for being a bit strict but for knowing the children well and ensuring that they achieved good progress in basic subjects.

However, as we saw in Chapter 2, at the time when Mary entered her class Miss Scott was rather unsettled both personally and professionally. Of course, there was a great deal of stress amongst many teachers in the late 1980s as the impact of public critique and government reforms came to be felt, and these factors certainly affected Miss Scott. She also felt unsettled by new school policies concerning whole-school curriculum planning, by the promotion of classroom practices involving active negotiation with children and by some other curricular innovations. Miss Scott became increasingly stressed and prone to swings of mood during the year. Sometimes she acted towards the children in ways which, being rather harsh or sarcastic, were against her own better judgement. In the following year, when Mary had moved on, Miss Scott retired from teaching.

Nevertheless, Mary's classmates all had to find ways of coping with the challenges of life in Miss Scott's classroom, the key characteristic of which was her relative unpredictability. Not surprisingly, many of the children were wary of her.

Mary was initially positive about her entry to Miss Scott's class. As her mother put it:

Both John and David had been in her class and she saw it as growing up.
(Mrs Inman, parent interview, November 1988, Year 1)

However, in the autumn of 1988, Mary almost immediately noted that 'Miss Scott is more bossy than Mrs Powell' and became aware that she was among the youngest in the class. Her initial strategy for coping in her new classroom was simply to keep her head down and 'be good'. For instance, fieldnotes often recorded Mary watching and listening intently to gather information on the tasks which she should undertake, even when, as we shall see, such instructions might not always have been offered with great clarity. Sometimes, when this strategy proved impossible, Mary did not know what to do and felt unable to take the risk of making a start and doing it wrong.

Mary explained the circumstances in which she, or other children, might resort to crying if her 'being good' strategy was not working:

AP:	What do you do if you are doing some maths, if you are not sure what to do? Or if you come to something really hard?
Mary:	Some people cry.
AP:	Do they?
Mary:	Sometimes I cry.
AP:	Do you? What happens when you cry?
Mary:	Miss Scott helps you a bit and things like that.
AP:	Is it best to cry, or, ... I mean, why don't you just go and ask her what to do before you cry?
Mary:	Sometimes ... she doesn't get cross. But sometimes you cry because you are a bit worried, and you think she'll tell you off. Do you know, when other people cry, you feel like you could cry, don't you? That's what I think.
AP:	Have you been told off at all?
Mary:	Not much.
AP:	How do you manage to be good?
Mary:	I just ask her things and I say, 'Can I do my writing?' and things like that.

(Mary, pupil interview, November 1988, Year 1)

Sometimes the 'being good' strategy had some odd effects, such as Mary's reinterpretation of completed work to bring it into line with Miss Scott's perception. For instance, looking through one of her books in mid-November, just after Bonfire Night, Mary commented:

That's a picture of me and Mummy. And Miss Scott thought they was a bonfire things, but they're supposed to be flowers. She said, 'Why don't you put nice things in the sky?' So I made them into things ... but they were really flowers.
(Mary, pupil interview, November 1988, Year 1)

However, the strategy had the desired effect of normally placing Mary and her friends well out of the line of vulnerability in the classroom. Thus a fieldnote recorded:

When I came in today, Mary and Sally were together and approached Miss Scott saying: 'What can we do to help?' Miss Scott said to me: 'They're so good, those girls.'
(Fieldnote, February 1988, Year 1)

Mary also developed other defensive strategies during the year, including mood detection and simple evasion. As she put it:

You can recognise Miss Scott's face if she's going to get cross. She stands like this (arms akimbo). She shouts really loud and she gets *so* angry. We keep quiet and sometimes, if I want to get out the way of it, I ask to go to the toilet.
    The supply teacher is much nicer. She doesn't say 'Shhh' all the time. She doesn't tell us to put our hands behind our back all the time ... 'cos it hurts, and it's really horrid.
(Mary, pupil interview, May 1989, Year 1)

The stakes were certainly high, with some critical incidents making a particularly strong impression. Again in group interview, Mary commented:

Miss Scott ..., she told Luke off because his work was no good and tore his book up and he had

to start all over again and he cried.
(Mary, pupil interview, May 1989, Year 1)

Once settled and sure of herself, Mary nevertheless did enjoy engagement with new learning challenges. She understood and accepted the need to 'work hard'.

It's really fun doing work because you can sort of .... if you do work all the time and try and try and try you really work hard and you really get, you'll do it really well, won't you, and it'll be really br .... good. You could be really good at it and things like that.
(Mary, pupil interview, June 1989, Year 1)

By the end of the year, Mary's confidence in coping with the classroom grew and, as we saw earlier with the playground rhyme, she was able to generate a partial critique and regain some of her own dignity. As her mother explained:

'Mary just calls Miss Scott a nickname, which is a bit cheeky – 'Old Sagbags'. I don't know whether that's because David says it, and she just repeats it, not even in a derogatory sense. It's like a joke and she giggles.
(Mrs Inman, parent interview, June 1989, Year 1)

But Mrs Inman was never really fully aware of the degree of threat felt by Mary during the year. Perhaps this was because Mary expected to have to cope with the class – after all, both her brothers had passed through Miss Scott's classroom in the past – and she did not show overt signs of great anxiety. However, a degree of unease was indicated for, as her mother reported:

Just occasionally she'll say, 'Oh Mummy, you come in because Miss Scott will tell me off if ... I haven't got the right dinner money', or something really trivial like that. 'Oh, *you* tell Miss Scott.' She does have that little bit of wariness.
(Mrs Inman, parent interview, June 1989)

In terms of Mary's stance regarding learning, her concern to avoid errors of any kind undoubtedly had an impact. In particular, she became very dependent on other people or on resources for affirming her intentions or for giving her vital spellings or other support. The following extracts from fieldnotes and interviews illustrate this:

Mary is writing a story. She asks me: 'How do you spell "pattern"?' I suggest that she begins by trying to spell 'pat'. She looks at me, pauses, ... and says to Harriet: 'How do you spell "pattern"?' Harriet tells her and she writes it into her book.
(Fieldnote, June 1989, Year 1)

AP: What do you think about your work at school?
Mary: Maths is easy for me and sometimes writing is a bit hard, 'cos there's lots of things you could do and you can think what to choose. Word cards help us a bit and the word books help us.
AP: Do you like learning new things?
Mary: I like it. If it's difficult, we just ask the teacher. If the teacher is busy, we just wait.
(Pupil interview, April 1989, Year 1)

Mrs Inman commented on my early report of such observations in ways which remind us both that Mary's strategy in the classroom built on what, in the previous year, had been described as a 'Goody-Two-Shoes' approach at home and that she was still just five years old:

Mrs Inman: I suppose it is fairly typical of Mary, she is always checking things out I feel. She will come to me and say this or that or so and so, and I will say one thing or the other and she will trot off – she does that a lot.

| AP: | Yes, checking that she is doing things correctly.... |
| Mrs Inman: | Yes. I was just thinking and she still comes for a lot more cuddles than the boys. If I am sitting down she will come and sit on my lap and the same with Michael. If there is a spare lap going she will come and sit on it, you know, she is still at that stage. She likes to watch television curled up and secure, but she still is only little, isn't she? |

(Mrs Inman, parent interview, November 1988, Year 1)

It is important here to recall the element of rivalry between the children which existed in the Reception year and in the interpersonal relations of even close friends. Fieldnotes record several extensive examples of this and, occasionally, it could threaten Mary's strategy of seeking support from others. After all, dependency is only viable if you have people available on whom you can depend. An example of this derives from a classroom episode recorded in the middle of the year:

> Mary comes up to me, rather unsure of herself. She had 'planned' to do 'shopping' (a maths activity) as her first task of the day but she had been taking the register to the office and had missed Miss Scott's explanation of what to do. She did not want to join the other children doing the task: 'If I go over there, Sally and Louise will tease me,' she says.
>
> Mary is quite clear that she cannot join the other children and that she cannot discuss the task with Miss Scott. She reported that Miss Scott had told her: 'Just get on with your first thing'.
>
> I suggest that, since she is not sure how to do her 'first thing', she should switch to her 'second thing'.
>
> To do this, she returns to her planning sheet and changes her plan using her rubber. Then she says: 'But I don't want to make a post-office van' (the second set task), there's nothing to do that I want to do'.
>
> I suggest that she goes to see what the group working on post-office vans are doing and that Miss Scott won't mind. Mary joins Harriet and Sarah.
>
> Mary soon returns to say that Sarah won't share.
>
> The bell goes for playtime and, with some relief, Mary goes into the playground.
>
> (Fieldnotes, January 1989, Year 1)

This question of rivalry between the children remained an important feature of the class. Most children were aware of their relative positions in terms of maths work and reading books, and this was particularly so for Mary and her friends. For instance, when asked at an early point in the year to explain the reading system Mary commented:

> The boxes mean you've got to choose one. When you've read one, if you can't read it very well you have it again. Then if you can read it just OK, you go away and get it on your own. But if you can read it very well, you go on to the next stage. You might ... . One day I'd go on to there, then Hippo, and then things like that ... . My friends are on Alligator box, Cat, Teddy Bear and like that.
>
> (Mary, photo interview, November 1988, Year 1)

An experienced supply teacher, providing an external view, commented:

> There's a lot of tension among the children – particularly the girls, Sarah, Mary, Lizzie, Clare. Is it competition? Sally, she's the dominant force in the class. She's bright and everyone wants to be with her.
>
> (Fieldnote, May 1989, Year 1)

That Sally was identified in this way is significant, Sally being Mary's main competitive rival as well as her best friend. In particular, Sally had taken to reading with great verve and moved quickly through the school scheme of books. At the same time, however, Mary had encountered some difficulties with her reading and had had to work hard to achieve progress.

Mary, Year 1, progress in classroom learning

At the start of her Year 1 Mary had been reluctant to attempt to learn her 'words' and read her reading book at home. In interview, Mrs Inman speculated about the cause of the problem.

> Probably, to begin with, I think Sally's success had a very negative effect because Mary just knew that she couldn't read properly – and she couldn't understand why Sally could. Possibly that might have been one of the reasons she didn't want to get her books out to start with, I don't know, I am only guessing. They went in to Miss Scott's hand in hand as it were, having seen each other a little in the holidays, and that was her main friend. Sally was off like a rocket, she knows the school, she has access to everything, she is very confident, she knows what is going on, she knows the staff. But Mary takes terrific comfort from the fact that she is bigger and stronger. Yes, I forgot to mention that. She rather likes being big for her age. Sally is only little, and she does actually mention it so perhaps there is something in it. She is in clothes size 6 and Sally is smaller.
> (Mrs Inman, parent interview, November 1988, Year 1)

After a short period Mrs Inman had become sufficiently concerned about Mary's progress to ask to see Miss Scott. As she explained:

> I was disappointed with her progress after she had been back at school for a few weeks. This is because I had been told (and also thought) that she was bright, interested and her attitude was just right and she should 'take off' with her reading at any time and it just hadn't happened. I also noticed a lot of her friends were reading really quite well so I was wondering why it hadn't happened with Mary. I went to see Miss Scott to talk about this. Anyway her progress has been a lot better recently and she seems to be more interested again. I try to be relaxed and supportive and quite enjoy doing the books with her.
> (Mrs Inman, parent diary, October 1988, Year 1)

A somewhat stormy encounter between Mrs Inman and Miss Scott took place, with Miss Scott believing that Mrs Inman was making Mary over-anxious. Nevertheless, following their discussion Mary received a steady stream of books to take home and more attention at school. However, Mrs Inman was never entirely satisfied and it was clear that reading remained a high-stakes activity for Mary.

Throughout the year, Mr and Mrs Inman worked hard with Mary to support her reading and Mary remained determined to master the skill. For example:

> We watched a bit of television together then Mary did her reading book. She tried really hard and read quite well though asked me to read some pages when she had finished. She really enjoys the pictures and enjoys talking about the book, in fact she would stop and chat about every sentence if I let her. She still reads some words backwards – saw/was, off/for, but she is remembering new words better from page to page. She still has trouble with 'with, when, went' but is *beginning* to sound out words, e.g.: got, get, go and she gets then right generally.
> (Mrs Inman, diary entry, October 1988, Year 1)

Mary herself also took learning to read very seriously indeed and was clearly very aware of her relative position:

AP:	When you do your reading, what do you think?
Mary:	I think I read it really well and sometimes I don't, I read it again.
AP:	You're working really hard with your reading, aren't you?
Mary:	Well, I try to do.
AP:	Do you think your reading has got better recently?
Mary:	Yeah, but I'm in the low stage.
AP:	The low stage? But you're still working very hard.

> Mary: Some are on that one, and there, and there.
> (Photo interview, November 1988, Year 1)

Towards the end of the year, Mrs Inman recorded both progress and continued frustration, with Mary being very sensitive to her dignity when being 'helped' with reading:

> Mary enjoys poems and rhymes and loves singing. She is sometimes frustrated and cross that she doesn't read as well as her friends. She sometimes takes ages to read her school books discussing every word and picture then she gets really cross and annoyed if Michael or I pick her up on anything. It often seems a deliberate confrontation and if we *dare* to correct her she slams shut her book and flounces off to her room.
> I feel she is still a long way from reading fluently and wonder why David could read, write and spell *so* easily and John and Mary are making heavy weather of it. I feel as a parent we get no advice from teachers and just get criticism if we want our children to progress! It must be such an advantage if reading comes easily so is Mary at a disadvantage with her peers or doesn't it matter? I feel very much in the dark.
> (Mrs Inman, parent diary, June 1989, Year 1)

Regarding her writing, Mary also made hesitant, but gradual, progress. Document 3.7 shows some of her writing from September 1988 when she made an initial attempt to write using a 'magic line' to mark words she didn't know how to spell. Miss Scott completed them later.

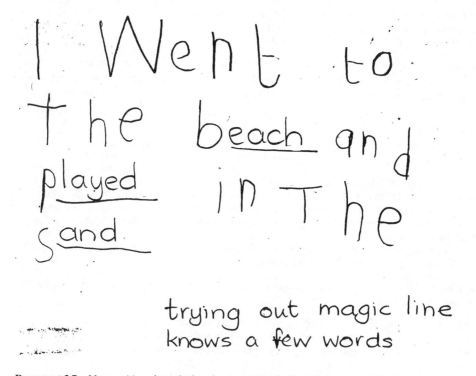

Document 3.7 *Mary, writing about the beach using a 'magic line', September 1988, Year 1*

one day I went out for a
Wawc and I saw a post offse
and) i went in and I bad yt sum
Stam ps and neve Lops
and riiting paper and boac
and I saw a postman.

Document 3.8 *Mary, writing about visiting the post office using a 'magic line', April 1989, Year 1*

By the early summer of 1989 Mary was writing rather more freely and still using the 'magic line' but it had not developed to the extent that her parents had hoped and it seemed that Mary was not using her writing to express her experiences or her imagination in quite the way that had been promised in her Reception year. Document 3.8 is a story from that period.

Overall, however, Mary's teacher, Miss Scott, was confident of Mary's learning achievements during the year and was perceptive in her comments on Mary's strategies. In her records she noted:

Mary is working well. She enjoys working with her friends and usually appears pleased with her efforts. Thoughtful and sensitive, needs praise and encouragement at times for an extra boost to her confidence. Plans her day well, fulfilling her tasks, usually with or alongside other companions. She tends to follow the ideas or suggestions of others, but takes part with interest and enthusiasm. Reliable. Likes to take her full part in all activities and share her bit of the limelight.
(Miss Scott, teacher record, May 1989, Year 1)

Regarding maths, Mrs Inman was more contented with progress and appreciated Mary's growing competence, whilst also wondering if tables should be taught.

Mary can add up numbers, count on and take away. She appears to think fairly logically and solve problems. She talks about her maths cards at school and enjoys doing them. She likes playing with a calculator. Mary doesn't understand words like divide or multiply or times ... . I feel school could bridge this gap rather than just let them work out cards. I also feel children could learn tables very easily at this age as they love repetition and chanting – they have to be learnt at some stage!
(Mrs Inman, parent diary, June 1989, Year 1)

Mary, identity and learning in Year 1

Mary's mother perceived considerable developments over her second year of formal schooling – some of which could be directly related to school, and some not. As can be seen from a selection of her diary comments below, these encompassed a wide range of skills, competencies, understandings, knowledge, independence and physical development:

> Mary has grown both physically and mentally over the year. She expresses herself much better than she did a year ago and is able to pronounce words much more clearly. She is now able to wash and dress herself without problems though I still do her hair. She is very definite about her appearance – she likes to look 'pretty' and is very proud of her hair. Mary loves ballet and asked me if she could do two extra classes and was happy to go without knowing the other girls. Sally has now joined the classes and they go together.
>
> She gets real pleasure from achieving things – she was recently chosen to sing in a school concert and also showed a sense of maturity and generosity towards Sally – who wasn't chosen. She has become more kind and understanding and philosophical about things. A friend recently said 'isn't Mary funny, she is just like a little mother fussing about things'. On occasions she talks very seriously and precisely about things – especially to adults. She is much more confident with her brothers and sticks up for herself and fights back. She tells tales about them – cries to get them into trouble and occasionally tries to 'mother' them – much to their annoyance. She has slept at friends' houses and really enjoyed it.
>
> She loves praise and responds to it. She can be quite attention seeking at times – to the point of being irritating. She does not know when to stop or is testing our limits, however, she hates us getting cross with her and gets very upset.
>
> She rarely uses her blanket now though she still keeps it in her bedroom. She was quite happy to leave it at home last time we went away for a weekend.
>
> Mary is much more able to do things physically like running, riding, swimming, all of which she does really well now.
>
> She has started to loose teeth and now has lost three – she is very proud of this.
> (Mrs Inman, parent diary, June 1989, Year 1)

At the same time however, there was an element of tension and vulnerability in the ways in which Mary approached high-stakes learning tasks, such as those associated with reading. Her mother had become very skilful at negotiating such episodes:

> Mrs Inman: I think twice before I say things (to try to help) Mary because she is quite capable of going completely mad, tearing it all up and flouncing out, so I have to be very careful not to be critical. You have to go gently, gently.
> AP: So, that's almost that you've worked out ways of being able to help her ....?
> Mrs Inman: I suppose that's true really. Definitely with the reading. I feel she's playing the game in a way. She's dominating by her behaviour, but it's required.
> AP: When she's reading, you mean?
> Mrs Inman: Yes, I know I could just, I know exactly what I could say to make her flounce off, and she knows. It's almost a challenge sometimes. 'Right', she thinks, 'if you say another word, I've had enough'. You can see it going through her mind.
> (Parent interview, July 1989, Year 1)

Clearly Mary did make considerable progress as she developed and matured during this year. Identifying strongly with her mother, she became more self-confident with regard to standing up to her brothers. At school, she faced challenges both from her teacher, in terms of interpreting and responding to tasks which were set, and from her peers, in terms of maintaining her dignity deriving from academic and other attainments. Of course, her peers represented a cultural resource for activity and 'good fun' in the playground and a source of support in coping with classroom tasks. This was particularly important because of

Mary's application at school of the strategy of 'being good' and avoiding the risks of 'being told off' and 'doing things wrong'. This was, undoubtedly her main coping strategy over the year. It enabled her to hold her position although her personal expression may have been restricted. Meanwhile, she benefited from sensitive support from her parents with the key task of learning to read. This, though knife-edging at times, was sufficient to supplement the work of Miss Scott and ensure progress.

In relation to the 'questions for enquiry' raised in Chapter 1, the case of Mary in her Year 1 offers an example of a pupil experience in which the classroom setting was not always supportive as a learning context. The key factor in this was the provision of Miss Scott whose personal difficulties had the unintended consequence of creating difficult circumstances for the children. At root, Mary and the other children, were often uncertain and sometimes frightened. Fortunately for Mary, she had support from her peers and from her parents. At home, the opportunity to learn and the quality of teaching were more specifically focused, particularly on Mary's reading. Since this was Mary's own key indicator of status and esteem, parental help and concern were harnessed to her own determination to succeed. At times though, frustration could have caused a collapse in the approach and parental sensitivity to this possibility seems to have been particularly important.

Overall, the positive achievements afforded by Mary's development and new experiences outweighed in significance the difficulties which she faced at school. Nevertheless, it is likely that the year could have been significantly less stressful and more fulfilling for her.

Matrix 3.2 summarizes the year as a whole.

Matrix 3.2 *Mary's Year 1, a summary matrix*

Family relationships	Peer-group relationships	Teacher relationships	Identity	Learning
Continued rapport, support and identification with mother.	Mary, Sarah and Sally become a threesome. Shared home visits and activities.	Amongst youngest children in her class.	Confident at home without her 'blanker' for comfort.	New physical achievements such as swimming and dance.
Strained relationships with brothers, but begins to 'stand up to them'.	Exclusively 'girls games' in playground.	Concerned by behaviour of Miss Scott. Aimed, at all costs, to avoid being told off by getting work wrong or for behaviour.	Likes to 'look pretty'. Not confident at school.	Slow start at reading and mother clashed with Miss Scott over progress. Parents important support on reading.
Exclusive 'girls play' including make-up, etc.	Occasional resentment at 'bossy friends' and Sally's easy success at reading.	Perceived by Miss Scott to be helpful, sociable but perhaps 'lacking full motivation and initiative'.	Sensitive to protect her dignity when being helped with reading at home.	Avoids all risks in learning and 'checks things out' before acting. Some restriction of personal expression.
Important support from mother over reading.	Some solidarity among friends in coping with Miss Scott.		Aware of her position 'lower' than Sally in some schoolwork.	
			Likes praise, encouragement and being told she is 'a good girl'.	Progress made across the curriculum, but Mary very aware of her continuing need to work at reading.

3.5   MARY IN HER YEAR 2

Mary, Year 2, relationships with parents at home

Throughout Mary's third year at school, she and her mother continued to elaborate a relationship that supported Mary's learning and the development of her identity on several fronts.

Mary continued to use her mother as a sounding board, her mother's responses continuing to scaffold Mary's ideas. Now, however, Mary used that support to return to and extend her ideas over increasingly long periods as she tested and worked towards new understandings.

> Mrs Inman: She does talk and think about things. Well, about Dr Who even. She'll say, 'do you think Dr Who will be alright next week? I think he will, won't he?' She'll discuss this – fact and fantasy. She will work out quite a lot with me.
> AP: Does she come back to things?
> Mrs Inman: Yes, she'll have a think and then come back with a new theory. I'm trying to think, we had a great long conversation the other day, which was all based on logical steps. I can't remember what it was now. Yes, she'll often say, "Do you think this is because of such and such?' and she'll ask questions and then she'll think about it. It surprises me how she does keep thinking about things and she doesn't let go, or they change but she'll carry on discussing them.
> (Parent interview, December 1989, Year 2)

This rapport was interwoven within and reinforced by other aspects of family life, including the element of reinforcement of gender identity. In the process, however, it is important to note the growing degree of self-confidence shown by Mary in such settings. For instance, Mrs Inman described a Sunday trip to grandparents:

> At about 10 a.m. we set off to visit Michael's parents. We had a super day, everyone enjoyed lunch then after lunch Michael, the boys and Grandpop went to sweep up leaves and build a bonfire (they have an enormous garden) and Mary, Grandma and I went to take the dog for a walk. Mary talked about ballet, the dog, she asked what 'allergic' meant. We met a few people and she was sociable and confident. Mary likes holding the lead. After our walk Mary went to play on the swing by the bonfire whilst we washed up then made tea.
> (Mrs Inman, parent diary, November 1989, Year 2)

As an indication of this growing self-confidence, we can note that, by the autumn of 1989, Mary had completely abandoned her blanket and slept with her door shut. Mary also felt sufficiently close and confident with her mother to share games which had their origin within pupil culture.

> Mary had a paper game which they had made at wet playtime and she kept asking me to pick a colour then a number then reveal something written under one of the numbers. She found it very funny when I picked something rude or silly!
> (Mrs Inman, parent, diary , November 1989, Year 2)

Overall then, Mary's mother was a secure and trusted source of support, encouragement and instruction as Mary faced new learning challenges. However, it is important to record too the ways in which she also provided solidarity in the somewhat strained encounters which Mary continued to have, from time to time, with her brothers. In the summer of 1990 I asked Mrs Inman:

> AP: How is Mary interacting with you, compared with the boys?

> Mrs Inman: She's a real buddy. She's there by my arm asking questions and talking and joining in and identifying 'we', there's a lot more 'we' and 'them'. 'Us' and 'them'. So she's very much on the side with me. And she's home more. They're off together a lot.
>
> (Parent interview, July 1990, Year 2)

Mary's gender identification was thus very strong as she approached her seventh birthday. It related to her structural position within her family as the youngest of three children and the only girl.

Mary, Year 2, relationships with siblings at home

As was implied above, relationships between Mary and her brothers continued to have their ups and downs, though there were certainly occasions when the children would play together with great enjoyment, particularly when they could participate in a shared activity. Of course, for siblings, one structural source of strength in such activities comes from the exclusion or disapproval of parents. An account of a high-spirited early evening provides an example of this:

> She then started playing a rowdy game with David and John which involved a lot of wrestling about and laughing. Michael came in shortly after and, as we were trying to talk, we asked them to play upstairs. They did this but it was still pretty noisy and lots of laughter. ... When I went upstairs to run the children's bath I found Mary and John playing in the bathroom – filling a balloon with water and having a marvellous time making a complete mess of the bathroom! I ran the bath and John got in – Mary disappeared into her bedroom. I washed John's hair and got him out and we went downstairs and David and Mary had a bath together – lots of noise and laughter coming from the bathroom.
>
> (Mrs Inman, parent diary, November 1989, Year 2)

There was, however, a continuing tension between Mary and her brothers and Mary's strategy of 'being good' seemed to be particularly challenging to David and John. They felt that she used the strategy to get away with things which would have got them into trouble. Mrs Inman explained:

> There are times when the boys really do gang up very unkindly on Mary, towards Mary. They think she is spoilt. They think she gets away with a lot. But there again, she behaves that much better than they do. And she is more willing to give in and apologise, and be better. And she is the first to back down. So she does get ... we're seen to be kinder to her in that way, I'm sure, because she doesn't push us to the absolute outer limits. I don't know why [the boys] just don't behave better. They resent the fact that she can behave better, I suppose.
>
> (Mrs Inman, parent interview, December 1989, Year 2)

Occasionally Mary would make a mistake and leave the security of her 'being good' strategy. On such occasions she was clearly aware of what she had done and took immediate steps to restore her position. Her mother reported:

> I heard David telling Mary not to play with his silver pen. I also asked her not to – but she ignored us both. Then she was horrified when she got silver ink on her arm and night-dress and the table. She *rushed* upstairs to clean it off and to avoid being told off. David helped me clean the table. Shortly after they went to bed, there was no nonsense from Mary!
>
> (Mrs Inman, parent diary, November 1989, Year 2)

By the end of the year, Mary had become more pro-active in challenging her brothers.

She started to draw on a wider range of strategies and to exploit some of the credit which she earned with her parents by, in general, 'being good'. She also benefited from some credit, given by her parents, for being the youngest and a girl.

In the summer of 1990, I asked Mrs Inman:

AP: How is Mary getting on with her brothers?

Mrs Inman: Well, much the same. They're pretty horrible to her on the whole, but then she asks for a lot of trouble and causes a lot of trouble. She'll go into their bedroom and annoy them and they'll say 'Get Out!' and she won't get out and then there's a fight. If she didn't go in, in the first place, it wouldn't happen. .... I think she handles situations quite confidently because ... she knows how far she can go and she tests that a lot. So she will instigate as much trouble as they will, but she ends up being dealt with slightly more sympathetically I suppose because she's the youngest and she's a girl and I will give in to her more.

AP: And does she play on that?

Mrs Inman: Yes, she uses that, she's very capable of manipulating that whole situation and a good scream will get somebody running. Yes, she uses that to her advantage. Sometimes it doesn't work to her advantage because she's perhaps the noisiest nowadays and she's much more dramatic. She'll flounce about and make a fuss. ... I suppose she can't compete with them physically, she can't do the things they do, or she doesn't want to, she's no desire to I suppose. But she will measure herself – actually I think perhaps she's happiest when they are all doing a similar thing and she's succeeding. Like they play monopoly and she's winning, or they are all colouring and hers is neater. That she will score points on and she'll do that quite successfully. She'll crow and she enjoys that situation. She also enjoys them being naughty. She loves that. She'll like a good old row brewing up and she'll sit there and watch it all go on and quite enjoy it, I think.

(Parent interview, July 1990, Year 2)

Here then we see Mary using her growing confidence, social skills and understanding to assert and develop her identity within the family. That she had to do this as a girl with two older brothers provided particular circumstances for Mary. However, if those circumstances presented Mary with certain challenges, there were also particular cultural resources on which she could draw. Not least of these resources was her association with other females and, in particular, the supportive disposition of her mother. Mary's particular social circumstances and her available cultural resources saw her move from struggling to stand her own ground against her brothers' teasing and sexist taunts at age five, through to the ability to instigate trouble and fight her own battles, and on to an active manipulation of the rest of the family in promoting her interests. Throughout, she made tactical use of her female identity in the assertion of her concerns, blending new, more subtle strategies with the older ones which still had the power to work for her.

Mary, Year 2, relationships among friends and in the playground

At this point in Mary's school career she was one of the oldest members of Miss George's Year 2 class. On joining the class Mary had been confident about the opportunity it would offer for making new friends and she had befriended two children new to the school whilst they settled in. Playground and classroom observations, as well as sociometric findings from the spring of 1990, showed that Mary had also retained the same basic circle of

friends at school, Sally and Sarah continuing to be particularly important to her. Her enjoyment of being with her friends led her to join 'Cru Club' (an out-of-school activities club for
young Christians).

> I met Mary after school and took her and Sally to Cru Club up at St John's Church. I don't
> think she goes for any religious reasons – just because all her friends go. Anyway she really
> enjoys the singing and activities.
> (Mrs Inman, parent diary, November 1989, Year 2)

However, by the end of the year, whilst retaining her strong desire to do things together
with her friends, Mary's growing independence was also beginning to produce a more critical appraisal of their strengths and weaknesses, seen in terms of her experience of them.
As her mother described:

> Mary asks me every night after school if someone can come to tea or whether she can go out.
> She often asks me if she can telephone her friends and now wants to go and stay the night with
> people.
>   She is much more critical of her friends and their behaviour now. She comments about them;
> eg, 'Sally is bossy' or 'Jenny is babyish' and discusses their behaviour with me. This does not
> affect her liking or disliking them, it seems purely observational.
> (Mrs Inman, parent diary, July 1990, Year 2)

Her mother saw this growing understanding of her friends as being associated with
Mary's own developing self-confidence and interpersonal skills. She explained:

> I think she has probably acquired more skills, definitely. She's much more ... if children come
> to tea, she's much more in control. She'll decide who she ... She'll ask me if I'll invite so and
> so, and then she'll control what they do.
> (Mrs Inman, parent interview, July 1990, Year 2)

Mary was also now sufficiently self-confident amongst her peers to extend this self-
assertion in informal interaction to some of the more overt forms of competition which she
had developed within the family and in other settings outside school. As Mrs Inman put it:

> Mary loves to play competitive games – cards, master mind, monopoly etc. She is always
> doing handstands and 'crab' and practising gymnastics or ballet. She loves swimming and now
> dives and jumps in – does somersaults and tricks and swims very fast – she enjoys being timed
> and racing her brothers or other children.
> (Mrs Inman, parent diary, July 1990, Year 2)

As in earlier discussions of Mary's peer relationships during Year 1, the question of the
tension between close friendship and rivalry is raised. For Mary, this was particularly acute
in her relationship with Sally. For instance, Mrs Inman saw Mary's self-confidence as
having been enhanced by her friendship with Sally, and yet, the ballet in which they both
participated was particularly important to Mary because it was something at which she felt
she excelled:

> She's had quite secure friendships over the year. She's had Sally, who in a way has brought her
> along because Sally is so confident. ... I think that's possibly helped Mary in a way.
>   I think ballet has been very, very important to her. I don't know why she does it even, but
> she does have a great degree of success from doing it and I think that's important to her. She
> does it quite well and she's always ... keen to go.
> (Mrs Inman, parent interview, July 1990, Year 2)

In the school playground Mary continued to enjoy games played with other girls and,
with them, she firmly dissociated herself from the 'not normal' games played by boys. I
talked to a group of girls, including Mary:

AP:	What sorts of things do you like doing in the playground?
All:	Clapping games, like 'Fish and Chips', swaying together, singing a song, handstand games – just normal games.
AP:	What is 'normal'?
Sally:	Not normal is football and cricket!
Mary:	I like it when we make daisy chains.

(Group interview, April 1990, Year 2)

The girls were quite explicit about some particular boys whom they particularly wanted to avoid. Sally commented:

Gary, Greg, Barney and Luke, the 'naughty boys' – we don't play with them. They spoil our game. They always play football. They always say 'we're doing that!'. They kick a football in our game and we have to kick it back otherwise they shout.
(Sally, pupil interview, April 1990, Year 2)

Despite this dislike of some of the rougher elements of boys' culture, talk of 'love' and games of 'kiss chase' were beginning to emerge in the playground. This new, flirtatious element of playground culture was to develop and increasingly be played out amongst some of the more dominant groups of girls and boys with which both Mary and Sally were associated. In *The Social World of Pupil Careers* (Pollard and Filer, in press), through the stories of other children, we track the differentiating effect of this strand of pupil culture across seven years of the children's primary schooling, together with its importance for the classroom and playground identity and status of these particular friendship groups.

Mary, Year 2, relationships with Miss George in the classroom

Mary rapidly developed a positive relationship with Miss George, the probationary teacher. Miss George was calm, warm and consistent in her relations with the children and, although she had to work at some aspects of her classroom organization over the year, Mary and the other children were trusting and open with her from the start.

For Mary, perhaps the two most important characteristics of Miss George's teaching were that she was both encouraging and patient. Given this, Mary maintained and perhaps developed her willingness to 'be good' – even to the extent of becoming, in Miss George's eyes, somewhat intrusive. As Miss George put it:

Mary always wants to be helpful. She's the sort too that always wants to hold your hand if you are walking down the corridor. Sometimes she wants to be helpful so much that she's a pain, because you're trying to explain something and she's saying, 'Can, can, can I help? Can I help?'
(Miss George, teacher interview, November 1989, Year 2)

However, Miss George's patience did hold and Mary felt an extremely close attachment to her. Not only was she aware that:

Miss George thinks I've got on well.
(Mary, pupil interview, June 1990, Year 2)

But she also felt confident:

To go to Miss George and ask her about anything and new things if I don't know how to do them.
(Mary, pupil interview, June 1990, Year 2)

Mary also became more self-confident around the school, talking to teachers and doing jobs and getting involved. The example which impressed her mother involved her in achieving an enviable role on the sweet stall at the Christmas Bazaar. Mrs Inman explained:

> Mrs Inman: She is very excited about the Christmas Bazaar. She negotiated herself to helping on the sweet stall. Off her own bat – she actually went in and asked someone if she could help. ... Sneaky really.
>
> AP: Sneaky ...?
>
> Mrs Inman: Yes, I think so, because she knew I was something to do with the organisation so she ... . She'd obviously listened to lots of conversations going on and she went up to Susan Hulme, Jessica's mum, and she said 'Can I help you on your stall Susan?' And Susan said 'Oh how nice, it's so nice of you to offer, Mary. Of course you can.' And then we thought, 'Well Susan's doing the sweets. 'I think she just thought, 'Which is the nicest one to go and help on, that'll be nice. Cunning little moo. I thought it quite clever, really.
>
> (Parent interview, December 1989, Year 2)

Overall then, Mrs Inman, in summarizing Mary's feelings towards the end of the year, said:

> She's been the happiest she's ever been with Miss George. She actually adores her. I was flattening a card which she made all on her own yesterday and she saved her pocket money, which is nothing to do with us at all. It's the sweetest thing. She's so positive towards Miss George, ... not so much about work but as a personality. She just absolutely adores her. She thinks she's terrific. I don't get much of what Miss George has said or what Miss George has thought, it's just the fact that she's been very, very happy in that class – very.
>
> (Mrs Inman, parent interview, July 1990, Year 2)

And Miss George did reciprocate wholeheartedly in this commitment by the end of the year. She concluded in her official report to Mary's parents:

> Mary is a mature and responsible member of the class. I shall miss her.
>
> (Teacher's report to parents, July 1990, Year 2)

Mary, Year 2, progress in classroom learning

One consequence of the excellent relationship which developed between Mary and Miss George was that Mary's approach to new learning challenges became more positive. She was also more willing to be openly self-critical and to work at understanding and skill development. She was particularly keen on maths but recognized her difficulties with writing. In one discussion, I asked her:

> AP: What do you think about work in school?
>
> Mary: Its fun, brilliant and good. I love maths. Reviewing is good 'cos you can stand up in front of the class and get other ideas that you can do at home. I don't like writing, 'cos I do long ones but I get muddled up when I do the editing and sometimes I get stuck on hard words.
>
> AP: Do you like learning new things?
>
> Mary: I like anything new, 'cos it's exciting. If its difficult, I listen really carefully and think hard and when she corrects it, if it's right I'm very happy and I do handstands for hip, hip, hooray!
>
> (Pupil interview with Sally, Harriet and Mary, April 1990, Year 2)

The contrast here with Mary's defensive reserve in approach to learning in the previous year could hardly be more stark. At the same time however, Mary was unsure about her progress at school, except at maths.

I ask Mary how she thinks she is getting on at school. She says she doesn't know. She feels good about doing maths, and proudly explains that she 'did five cards yesterday'. She explained:

'Miss George put me up to Level 2. My Mum thinks I'm good at maths, but I'm not so good at writing. My reading is OK, but my Mum thinks I should be on higher.'

She showed me a 'very good', written in her maths book, many pages back. The book is very neat, with pages of sums from the Peak cards.

(Fieldnote, January 1990, Year 2)

Document 3.9 provides just such an example of the maths work in which Mary took such pleasure.

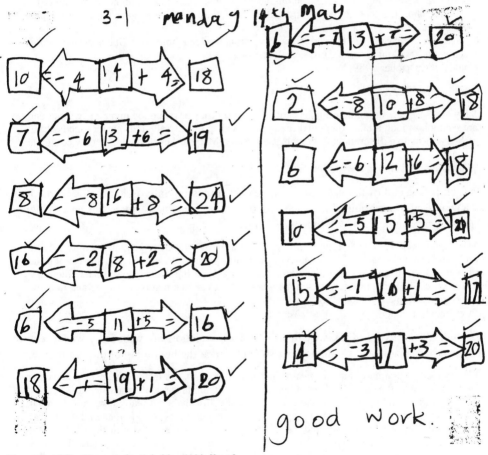

Document 3.9   *Mary, maths task, May 1990, Year 2*

Mary's progress and enjoyment in maths is significant because of the way in which it bolstered her status and self-esteem – as seen both by herself and by the other children. Her proficiency and progress were manifest in the context of the element of pupil competition which existed in the class, and this was itself made possible and reinforced by the use of the Peak Maths Scheme, with its carefully graded work cards. Such cards, of course, provided an overt measure against which the children could rank themselves. I regularly observed the effects:

> I watch the 'maths group' – James, Mary, Harriet and three others. They are seated at the maths table and are doing 'cards'.
>
> Mary is busying herself doing a card which involves addition to ten. She is confident and takes some time to help Amita. She works very fast and tells me she is on Stage 9. She now has to write out a story sum and answer the question. She speaks to me: 'I'm on Blue Stage soon'.
>
> Harriet volunteers that she is on Stage 9 too.
>
> Then Alistair says he is on Stage 8 and, turning to James remarks, 'You haven't done these cards yet!'
>
> 'Yes I have', says James, 'cos my mum's a teacher and she's got them at home.'
>
> The conversation then turned to why Barry is in a 'higher class' (he had been with this group of children the year before). Alistair thought, 'it's funny, 'cos I'm on a higher card than him,' but James said, 'It's 'cos he works harder than I do.' Harriet however, gave the correct explanation, 'I think it's 'cos he's older.'
>
> Meanwhile, Mary is still beavering away, working hard in a bold style. She is determined to reach the next colour – 'Blue cards next!', she says.
> (Fieldnotes, October 1989, Year 2)

On another occasion:

> Sally and Mary are doing their maths cards. I go over. They have a three minute egg timer and are seeing how long it takes them to do each card. As I approach Sally tells me that she is ahead of Mary. 'I'm on a different card though,' says Mary. Mary rushes through and they complete the tasks.
> (Fieldnotes, November 1989, Year 2)

In fact, by the end of the year, Mary had easily surpassed Sally in her maths work. This was a source of great pride and, as she progressed, she regularly shared her new achievements with her mother. As Mrs Inman explained:

> Mary appears to have made a lot of progress in maths. She seems to genuinely enjoy solving problems and working out sums. She can count money and work out change, she can tell the time and she is much more confident with 'technology' – using the microwave, the video, TV control, etc. She is always keen to tell me when she moves on a maths card stage and tells me she is going to 'plan' to do maths.
> (Mrs Inman, parent diary, July 1990, Year 2)

Miss George was aware of the way in which Mary's relationship with Sally was affecting her approach to maths and to literacy. As she put it in at the beginning of the summer term:

> Mary's made a dramatic improvement in her maths work. Apart from James, she's ahead of everybody else in the class. She's confident and happy with this area of the curriculum, usually completing more than the designated number of tasks. But she's not really taken off with her reading yet ... but seems to be enjoying more success in her maths. And I wondered if this was due to this rivalry between her and Sally, because she can't catch Sally in the reading and writing ... and so ... . Well, Sally is so confident and sometimes, you see, Mary is really, really jealous. Perhaps she feels she can't compete in the language stakes but she can excel at maths.
> (Miss George, teacher interview, May 1990, Year 2)

Reading and writing certainly did remain challenging areas for Mary for much of the year. Positive support from her mother continued:

> The children then had hot chocolate and Mary read some of her book to me, then some more

when she was in bed and I went to snuggle her. We discussed the story – Sleeping Beauty – at
great length.
(Mrs Inman, parent diary, November 1989, Year 2)

However, there remained the same problem as previously of Mary's concern to 'get
it right' combined with her difficulty in mastering reading quickly. Again, her mother
explained:

She doesn't particularly want to do it wrong so she'd rather not do it at all – which is something I suppose she will overcome. But I've found that with her reading she'll stop or make
something up.
(Mrs Inman, parent interview, December 1989, Year 2)

Of course, one result of Mary's insecurity at reading was that she also found writing difficult. How then, could she 'be good'? This was an acute dilemma for Mary and one which
led her both to seek help from wherever she could find it and to reduce her commitment to
writing tasks. Several instances of this were recorded in fieldnotes:

Mary is writing a story and is determined to get it 'right'. She keeps coming to me to ask how
to spell things: 'dog', 'baby'. Thinking of Miss George's emphasis on being independent, I
decline to help her.
    She asks Harriet how to spell 'car'.
(Fieldnotes, October 1989, Year 2)

Mary and James are going at their stories in a quite different way than Hazel and Harriet. One
is minimalist, to satisfy the task, reduce the risk and the time spent. The work is short and the
content is rather routine. Hazel and Harriet are more into intrinsic satisfaction – plus the glory
of length!
(Fieldnote, November 1989, Year 2)

Document 3.10 below, provides one example of such relatively minimalist work.

Tuesday 3rd April   The chick

The chick moves it's head a lot,

It had Brown eye's

It peck's the GLaSS a 'lot as weLL

I am allowed to hold the chick.

The end

Document 3.10 *Mary, writing about a classroom chick, April 1990, Year 2*

Mary, however, was immensely determined to learn to read and she both worked at it with Miss George and drew greatly on the help that was available to her from her mother. She explained to me:

> Mrs Inman: I thought she was never going to read actually ... but she'll struggle. I think if John had a book that he couldn't read, he'd throw it across the bedroom, bury it somewhere. But she will struggle on, so much so that it's quite ... 'oh, for heaven's sake Mary, can't you get one that you can read'. She'll go on and on. She'll actually do that with an argument too. She has developed ...
>
> AP: Persistence?
>
> Mrs Inman: Mmm, yes, persistence, that's the word.
>
> (Parent interview, July 1990, Year 2)

In the Summer Term Mary's persistence began to pay off and she had something of a breakthrough with her reading. As her mother explained:

> Just recently she has made great progress and seems to be well on the way to being an independent reader. She likes to read her books by herself now – this is a recent development, she usually takes them to bed with her and reads before she goes to sleep. ... She is much more aware of the world around her now that she can read – she reads signs, things on TV, school notes, packet instructions etc. etc., so again it helps understanding and self-confidence.
>
> She can still be very stubborn when corrected or if she has misunderstood or misread something – she can get quite cross and upset if she doesn't understand something.
>
> She was absolutely delighted when Miss George said she could move on to library books.
>
> Mary still loves rhymes and poems, but has recently been choosing more story type books with less pictures e.g., Milly, Molly, Mandy and Peter Pan.
>
> (Mrs Inman, parent diary, July 1990, Year 2)

However, her writing, as one would expect, still lagged somewhat behind:

> Mary still spends quite a lot of time writing. She usually writes her friends' names and telephone numbers or silly things like 'John is stupid' or that kind of thing. In fact, the things she writes haven't really changed in complexity so I find it hard to comment on her use of words or spelling. Perhaps it is because she does not know *how* to write more complicated things that prevents her from doing so. This area has not *really* shown any real development at all over the year though I do not know what she has been writing at school.
>
> (Mrs Inman, parent diary, July 1990, Year 2)

The picture which forms part of Document 3.11 and its associated writing conveys much about Mary's learning achievements during the year and the relationships which were so important to them. She is receiving her maths book from Miss George having had it marked and there are smiles all round from an assembled audience of significant other pupils, including Sally. What is more, her status on 'Library Books' in her reading is affirmed. Mary's writing conveys her meaning well enough and shows considerable development from her work earlier in the year. Her writing is, once again, a clear medium of personal expression, yet it is not altogether confident and contains a variety of idiosyncrasies. However, on this occasion, Mary wanted to communicate sufficiently to attempt difficult spellings and her version of 'excited' (itsitidind) is a triumph of both risk-taking and a logical attempt at spelling an unknown word.

As Miss George noted in her report to parents at the end of the Summer Term.

> Mary's reading has developed rapidly in recent weeks and she now chooses her reading books from the library. As a result, her written work is also improving both in content and quality. She continues to listen well and make valuable contributions at Review Time.
>
> (Miss George, teacher report to parents, summer 1990, Year 2)

On this piecher there is Richard and Barney and miss George and me and Gary and miss George is Jivig me a maths Book Book and i am 1sitidind and I have Plened maths and i am going to do it now and i was sitting next to Harriet and Sally and the miset George is Please and so am I and I'm on Lidre and i am Please

Document 3.11 *Mary, excited writing about progress in school work, July 1990, Year 2 (edited to preserve anonymity)*

Mary, Year 2, identity and learning

As we have seen above, Mary had a successful year socially and academically and made considerable strides in her last term in the infant school. She struck up a close and warm relationship with Miss George who summarized her as 'mature and responsible' and as someone she would miss when she moved out of the class at the end of the year. Mrs Inman described Mary's school experience in these terms:

> Mary has adored Miss George this year. She has been very happy at school and enjoyed all aspects of the curriculum. She is enthusiastic about school trips, sports and PE, concerts etc., etc. I feel it has been a very positive year for her.
> (Mrs Inman, parent diary, July 1990, Year 2)

In other parts of her diary entry of the late summer, Mrs Inman provided a comprehensive review of Mary's development over the year:

> Mary has grown increasingly self confident over the year. She has grown physically so is able to do more, i.e., she is taller, stronger, can cope without getting so tired. Also her mental development has meant she can also do a lot more as she is able to understand things, communicate, read and express herself better. She has gained pleasure from these developments.
>
> Mary likes to do things well and she has never really attempted to do things before she is ready – in contrast to her brothers. Therefore with these new physical and mental developments she is able to do lots more things – and do them well. She can express herself much better so is able to hold her own in an argument. She can reason and see others' point of view more clearly. She can work out and calculate things like money and tell the time which both give her more freedom: i.e. she can go and spend her pocket money, or go out to play and be back at a specific time. She can now brush her hair and bath herself and choose what she wants to wear which obviously makes her more independent. In fact she is quite keen to take more control of her life – she likes to get her own breakfast, prepare all her clothes for school and ballet and often it is Mary who reminds me about things e.g. she is going out to tea or must not forget something for school etc. etc.
>
> Mary's sense of humour and fun has developed in the last year. She is quite cheeky and mischievous and something of a mimic. She is quite confident about 'holding court' and making everyone laugh – (with her and at her)! She loves performing on stage, at school and at ballet. This year her ballet school put on a show which involved three live performances. Mary had one solo and two other dances to perform which she really enjoyed. The show was at St George's Hall and she loved getting dressed up and made up and the behind stage atmosphere. She thoroughly enjoyed performing and the applause, and the sheer 'theatre' of it all. After it all finished on the final night Mary went home in floods of tears because it had all ended. I am sure ballet has helped her self confidence as she is quite successful at it and has always been highly commended in all her exams. It is also an area personal to her i.e. her brothers have nothing to do with it so cannot encroach or steal her thunder.
>
> Mary's main areas of frustration are when she is tired and she is not allowed to do something which she wants to, i.e. stay up late to watch something on television or have a friend round. Her stock phrases in this situation are 'I hate you mummy' or 'I am leaving home to find a nicer mummy', though she is beginning to argue more rationally and question my decisions and try to compromise in a much more mature way. In fact she is trying much harder to rationalize and understand things in all spheres of life.
>
> (Mrs Inman, parent diary, July 1989, Year 2)

Altogether then, with Mary's broadening experiences and gradual achievements, came an increasing degree of both self-confidence and independence. Sometimes, mostly in the home setting, she would experiment. Mrs Inman described an incident:

> Mrs Inman: I just see the whole thing as growing up and being assertive. She tries a bit of naughty behaviour and bad language and she can be very petulant ... 'Oh it's my life. I can do what I like with it'.
>
> AP: When did that come up?
>
> Mrs Inman: Oh, this was after school the other day. Well, it does come up from time to time, and she said, 'Can we go and call on somebody or other?' and I said 'Well, we can't now'. She said 'Ah. I don't want to come home, I don't want to walk home with you, it's my life, I can do what I want, I don't want to walk home with you'. And she dragged her feet and sulked and nothing much, I could see almost laughter as well underneath it all. She was amused by her own behaviour almost. So it wasn't too awful.
>
> (Parent interview, December 1989, Year 2)

I explored with her mother the extent to which Mary was herself aware of these developments:

AP: Do you think she's actually seeing herself in a different way then?

Mrs Inman: She's started to ask questions about herself quite recently. All sorts of questions like, 'When you had David, did you know you were going to have a boy or a girl?' and about other people's families and how she sees them and how things come about basically. She's quite interested in all that now.

AP: So do you think she's taking control of her own life more ... that she can decide things, that she can ...?

Mrs Inman: Definitely, yes. How she made a decision the other day when she had one of those little 5p coins. She said, 'I'm going to save an old one for my children' and she put it in her drawer in her bedroom. I thought that's perceiving herself in many years time, which I don't think she's ever done quite so noticeably before. And she says things like 'You don't have to get married, do you? You don't have to have children?' She's asking all these sort or things.

Yes, it's much more. What she does, she negotiates bedtime more, what she wears, how she wants her hair – she's always been sort of finicky about that but even more so now. Following the fashion.

She's also asked ..., she wants to learn the piano. That's something that's come completely from her.

Also, she's told us that she'd like a desk in her bedroom and she'd like this kind of bed and not that kind of bed, so she's making choices there.

AP: ... which she wouldn't have been doing a year ago?

Mrs Inman: No, I don't think so. I think she was much more under my control. If I said, go to bed, she went to bed and if I said, wear this, she wore it, obviously up to a point. Now, she's certainly happy to make choices herself. She's not asking me to make the choices for her. She's asserting herself and negotiating with me.

(Parent interview, July 1990, Year 2)

Mary herself shared some of her pride and growing self-awareness in conversations with me:

I'm the second best in the class at maths. 'Cos I've got about three more cards till I'm on books. I will feel very pleased because my Mummy will give me something nice like a box of chocolate. She often gives me things, like for my birthday, and when I got onto 'Library' for my reading. She didn't believe me at first.

(Mary, pupil interview, June 1990, Year 2)

AP: How do you think you have got on this year at your school work?

Mary: OK. I've worked hard most of the time. I find it boring when you go to the home corner and nobody's there. Boring is when all you can do is sit there, or in the playground if there's no one to play with.

AP: And what do your parents think?

Mary: When I wasn't very high, they sort of made me work hard, like in Miss Scott's [Year 1] when I was 'Cat Box' [a relatively low reading level]. Now I'm on the top stage, that's 'Library' (*about eight other children were allowed to choose their reading from the library at this point*).

AP: What about your teacher?

Mary: Miss George thinks I've got on well.

(Pupil interview, June 1990, Year 2)

Mary then began the year, adopting her 'being good' strategy and capitalized on her understanding and capability at maths. However, in the classroom context in which she found herself and with a great deal of persistence and determination, she also gradually came to achieve higher levels of reading. Whilst, as Mrs Inman said, she had been 'very much the little girl that accepted everything that was going on,' by the end of the year she was starting to reflect on herself as a person, on her relationships with others and on her future. She was becoming increasingly independent and willing to present an identity which was very much her own.

This was reflected in her calm assurance at moving up to the juniors – a major status passage for children of this age. I asked her:

AP: What do you think it will be like in the Juniors?

Mary: The work will be a little bit harder. Like when I go to ballet. I passed my exam and it's getting a little bit harder. Like Modern is difficult. It gets a little bit harder each time. I think it is good, 'cos if you stayed on the same thing all the time it'd get really easy. It's more interesting.

(Mary, pupil interview, June 1990, Year 2)

Matrix 3.3 *Mary's Year 2, a summary matrix*

Family relationships	Peer-group relationships	Teacher relationships	Identity	Learning
Identification with mother very strong – against the boys.	Widening circle of friends – all girls.	Miss George very keen and establishes warm, relaxed atmosphere in class.	Continues to make strategic use of her female identity in defending her interests against her brothers.	Gymnastics, ballet, swimming achievements.
Continuing clashes with brothers. Began to be able to manipulate situations and relished occasions when they were told off.	Keen to be with her friends at most times, but can also be critical of them.	Amongst oldest children in the class.	Flourishes in classroom, as do many other children.	Many discussions with mother about new ideas and experiences.
Able to play many games on equal terms with family.	Enjoys board or card games as well as dolls, dressing up, etc.	Excellent rapport with Miss George – Mary 'adores her'.	Feels confident to learn 'anything new'.	Great progress in maths throughout the year.
Confident and sociable with grandparents.	Very aware of 'the naughty boys' and entertained by Sally 'in love' with James.	Given more choice over activities through use of 'planning folder'.	Particular effort and self-confidence in maths (where she outshines Sally). Especially likes using maths cards.	Some unoriginal and repetitive writing for much of the year. Reluctance to 'get things wrong'. Miss George feels Mary is less keen in writing because she cannot match Sally.
Beginning to make decisions for herself.	Practises handstands, gymnastics and ballet.	Independently negotiates way into helping a parent on the bazaar sweet stall.	Proud of progress and performance at ballet.	In reading, progresses to 'library books' as an independent reader by year end. Delighted, and her writing begins to become more expressive.
	Some resentment that Sally does very well at school and often gets singled out.		Confident in 'going up' to Junior school.	

3.6 MARY'S LEARNING AND DEVELOPMENT

Overall then, the case of Mary shows us a child who made a very sound start to school learning. Despite being only four years old on entering her Reception class, she built up her self-confidence from the foundation provided by a supportive mother and under the guidance of a caring and experienced teacher. Two other major themes are present too, that of Mary's relations with her siblings and with her peers. Her two older brothers had an important influence in causing Mary to identify increasingly closely with her mother. Female cultural resources were gradually transferred and taken up by Mary and deployed to resist the domination of her siblings. Regarding her peers, Mary experienced friendship, enjoyment and affirmative support – but this was also combined with a degree of rivalry in achievement. However, there was no real incompatibility in the direction of social influences on Mary. She sought 'to be good', willingly engaged with new learning challenges in the classroom and made progress across the curriculum.

In Mary's second year at school, Year 1, she encountered a teacher of whom she was very wary. She was extremely concerned to avoid being told off and thus to avoid getting school work wrong in any way. At the same time, she had some difficulties in learning how to read, and this became a source of anxiety for her. She was particularly helped by her mother, but her position in relation to her peers was a source of additional pressure despite the fact that she was amongst the youngest children in the class.

Year 2 was a period of greater fulfilment for Mary. She was comfortable and happy with her teacher, amongst the oldest children in the class and continued to receive support from home. Now, however, she felt able to pursue her determination to achieve and she made good progress in her reading. In maths, she found a subject in which she could excel relative to her peers, and this gave her some satisfaction. Her self-confidence grew.

As a summary, and recognizing all the dangers of generalization which that implies, the pattern across these variations is represented by Figure 3.3, the 'case-study overview'.

Figure 3.3 *Mary's case-study overview*

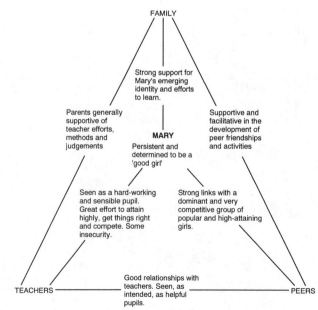

Chapter 4

Learning, Identity and Social Relationships: an Initial Analysis

4.1   INTRODUCTION

In this chapter the 'questions for enquiry' which were suggested in Chapter 1 are revisited, extended and applied in the case of Mary (Chapter 3). The analysis here is used to build up a model of the major factors which are in play in a consideration of the 'social world of children's learning' and this accumulates towards the integrative diagrammatic summary which is provided as Figure 4.3 (see p.97).

The overall argument is a product of analysis across all the case studies, but, to maximize clarity at this point in the book, the discussion is rooted in the single story of Mary's experiences and development. Four additional case studies are presented in Part Three and these lead, in Chapter 9, to the further elaboration of the analysis and of the theoretical model.

Before we begin, it is worth noting that, just as lived experiences are infinitely more complex than any social scientist can represent, so too, at another level, there is a disjunction between the multiple themes and issues which run through each of the child case-study stories contained in this book and the analysis which has been derived from them. This complexity is apparent from the richness of the voices of the participants and it opens the way to multiple interpretations of the material. Nevertheless, what follows represents my attempt to identify, order and represent the factors which have been produced by the processes of ethnographic analysis. You may well detect other themes and elaborations from your active reading of each case.

And so we can begin to reconsider each of the six basic questions.

4.2   WHERE AND WHEN DID MARY'S LEARNING TAKE PLACE?

In terms of location, as Chapter 2 described, Mary and her family lived in an established and affluent suburb of a city in the south of England. Greenside reflected many aspects of traditional English culture. People who lived there were predominantly white, middle class, well educated, conservative, successful, self-confident and relatively secure financially. The culture was one in which children were expected to 'do well' at school and in which relatively traditional forms of education were seen as important in the reproduction of social and cultural values and economic advantages. Roles for men and women were differentiated, with most fathers earning significant salaries in professional or business occupations and most mothers taking responsibility for child-care and the home or, when their children were established at school, renewing previous occupations such as secretaries or teachers. As we saw in Section 3.2, Mary's parents fitted this pattern, both being well educated and with the family economy underpinned by Mr Inman's work as a chartered surveyor. Mary's home was very comfortable, with access to a swimming pool and space for children to play both indoors and out. Mary had her own bedroom and the house was located so that visits from other children were convenient. Section 2.3 demonstrates that facilities at Mary's school, Greenside Primary, were also good, with spacious classrooms and grounds and excellent equipment.

Regarding time, we might note that Mary entered school in the late 1980s, at a time when Mrs Thatcher was well established in her premiership. Competitive and individualistic values were being strongly promoted. Teachers and schools were frequently criticized in the media both before and after the Education Reform Act 1988 and the introduction of the National Curriculum. Like most parents (Hughes *et al.*, 1994), Mr and Mrs Inman supported their local school, but their views on Mary's education (p. 41) also reflected their perception of the outside world within which she would eventually have to make her own way. Their comments on academic success, honesty, good manners and happiness are simple indicators of their aspirations for their children. They reflect Mr Inman's awareness of the future challenges which the children would face and Mrs Inman's more liberal disposition, but the particular conjunction is also of it's time.

Time is also significant in terms of the development of Mary's family. She was the third and last child thus occupying a particular structural position within the family. She grew up at a time when Mr Inman's business was increasingly established and when Mrs Inman was relatively confident in bringing up her children and contemplating her own return to work. Mary's development, as her only daughter and last link with the child-rearing phase of her life, gave her mother particular pleasure.

At Greenside Primary School, Mary's years in the infants were years of change both because of the innovations of the new headteacher, Mrs Davison, and because of the requirements of new legislation. Mary's first two teachers were concerned by these pressures and, although Mrs Powell was able to retain her 'motherly' rapport with the children, Miss Scott was severely stressed. Miss George represented a younger generation of new teachers starting their professional careers and beginning to work with the new requirements. Mary's learning thus tied into the history of the school and the biographies of her teachers. As we saw in Chapter 3, this brought her both positive and negative experiences.

4.3 'WHO' WAS MARY, IN TERMS OF HER IDENTITY?

How did Mary see herself? At the most general sociological level, what we know about Mary's gender, ethnicity, social class and social circumstances might suggest that a particular pattern of identity would be likely. However, to study the influence of identity on learning, we need to look in much more detailed ways than that, beginning with the formative influence of the 'significant others' in Mary's life.

Relationships between self and others

The relationship between the sense of self of individuals and the perceptions which other people have of them expresses the core symbolic interactionist insight about the creation of *meaning* (Mead, 1934). In this perspective, social understandings and personal identities are generated over time as people interact together. Thus, the way Mary was seen by others must be seen as an important influence on the way in which she came to view herself and, to understand Mary's identity, we need to focus on the influence of Mary's relationships with her parents, siblings, peers and teachers.

Of course, relationships between self and others are played out within social settings which reflect the particular distribution of power and social status which exists among the participants. For example, what are the dynamics among siblings in the family? Which peer becomes the leader of games in the playground and which pupils do, and do not, establish positive rapport with their class teacher? In routine social settings, such as those arising in families, playgrounds and classrooms, any potential conflicts are likely to be contained within the overt and tacit rule systems which are developed to structure and legitimate behaviour, as is described for classrooms in *The Social World of the Primary School*, Chapter 7 (Pollard, 1985a). However, as the analysis in that book makes clear, these rule systems are social creations. They are patterned by social circumstances and are maintained and reproduced as cultural resources and forms of perception, expectation and behaviour. They may be both used by, and attributed to, people occupying particular structural positions.

We can begin to apply these ideas to Mary as she sought to establish herself within her family. In one sense, her sense of identity may be seen as a reaction *against* her older brothers, but at the same time it represented an identification *with* her mother. Thus, in her Reception year, we hear of Mary being teased by her brothers and of her eagerness to be 'Goody-Two-Shoes' who is contrasted with the 'naughty little boys ... covering themselves with mud'. Tracking through the sections on sibling relationships for each year (pp. 42, 53 and 66) shows how Mary later began to 'stand up to' her brothers and, by Year 2, started to manipulate situations so that the boys might 'get into trouble'. Simultaneously, tracking the case-study data on relationships with parents (pp. 41, 52 and 65), we can see how the care-giving role of Mary's mother, which is illustrated in Reception by the discussion of a bathtime, develops through shared experiences such as waiting on the touchline of boy's rugby matches in Year 1. By Year 2 the combination of continued hustle with her brothers and identification with her mother meant that Mary had formed 'a real buddy' relationship with her mother.

Of course, there were also many other influences here and what has been described is but a fraction of the patterns of gendered behaviour which are likely to have been developing within the family throughout Mary's life. The very different role models provided by Mr and Mrs Inman were replicated among many Greenside families, in story books and through television programmes and other media so that Mary had a developing sense of female roles on which she could model herself and of female cultural and strategic resources which she could deploy.

Peer relationships provided further reinforcement, with Mary and her friends joining together in solidarity against the playground intrusion of boys whilst also replicating gendered roles through imaginative play at 'mummies and daddies' and, at times, 'kiss chase' games. The playground can, of course, be seen as a site of gendered struggle

(Clarricoates, 1987) in which boys and girls vie for space and to establish favoured activities. The usual pattern shows the relative domination of boys and Greenside was no exception. Thus each annual record of Mary and her friends (pp. 43, 53 and 67) provides evidence of some conflict. The girls' identities were progressively clarified by their increasing solidarity and identification with each other and by their rejection of many of the activities which the boys favoured.

Mary's relationship with her close friend, Sally, was particularly important in her learning at school and in the development of her identity, and can be tracked both in Mary's case study (Chapter 3) and in Sally's (Chapter 7). Their friendship began at playgroup and they moved together through the primary school. They often played and worked together at school, visited each other's homes and, of particular significance, went to dance lessons together. However, there was also rivalry between them with Mary often feeling a little put out at Sally's fairly consistent successes and self-confidence. This was particularly overt in respect of learning to read, at which Mary had to work hard, and through the leading roles which Sally held in school performances, such as Nativity plays, and in external dance events. In Year 1, Mary articulated her feeling that Sally could be 'bossy' and began to develop her own, independent stance alongside her continuing friendship. In Year 2 Mary found, in mathematics, a medium through which she could succeed at a higher level than Sally and she exploited it to the full. However, her written stories, on which she could not at the time compete, lacked comparable commitment and flair.

In terms of relationships with her teachers, Mary's Reception story (3.3) shows the trust and warmth which grew up between her and Mrs Powell with particular reinforcement by Mrs Powell of Mary's presentation of herself as 'a good girl'. In Year 1 however (3.4), Mary was extremely worried that she might be 'told off' by Miss Scott which would, of course, have undermined her perception of herself as 'a good girl'. Unfortunately though, her unwillingness to take risks was perceived by Miss Scott as showing a lack of 'full motivation and initiative'. In Miss George's class during Year 2 (3.5), the relationship was very positive and happy once again, with Mary 'adoring' Miss George, constantly striving 'to help' her in the classroom and earning a judgement as a 'mature and responsible member of the class'.

Identity, potential and resources

What seems to have been demonstrated in the previous section is Mary's transfer to school of a sense of identity as a 'good girl' which was first developed through relationships with 'significant others' within her family. Although the strategy was at risk of misinterpretation during Mary's Year 1, it continued to be reinforced within the family and also by Mary's peer group relations – after all much of the rivalry with Sally was over who could display the best symbols of 'goodness'. In Year 2 at school, Mary achieved almost complete fulfilment as a 'good girl' through new achievements and her identification with Miss George.

In a sense then, we can see the settings of home, playground and classroom as politico-cultural contexts in which interaction takes place and relationships and identities form. Such factors condition the identity which is presented and the self-confidence with which individuals act as they approach new learning challenges.

As a description of factors influencing her personal capacity to learn, this account of Mary's identity is necessary. However, it is not sufficient, as a considerable range of psychological and physiological factors could also be considered. Thus data on Mary's 'innate' personality, intellectual capacities and physical development might be called for. We know, for instance, of Mrs Inman's view that even as a baby of six months her daughter was 'self-protective' and 'would never put herself in a dangerous position' (see p. 41), but the question of whether we should attribute this disposition to 'nature' or to 'nurture' is obviously fraught with difficulty (Dunn, 1988). Yet this apparent manifestation of what might be taken for an aspect of 'personality' has an obvious resonance with Mary's later 'good girl' identity. Similar difficulties relate to any consideration of Mary's intellectual capacities. What should we attribute to her biological endowment and what to social learning? In fact, psychologists and biologists who have studied brain functioning in recent years are increasingly clear on the importance of the interaction of neurological capacities and their use in social situations and in emotional and cognitive processing (Meadows, 1993). Capacities are developed through use, particularly when children are young, and may decline if neglected. These issues are obviously extremely important, though they cannot be taken very far here, since the study was designed to focus on the social contexts and social processes of learning, rather than on intra-individual processing itself. Nevertheless, it is right to recognize that there is an important element of learning capacity which is likely to reflect a combination of the genetic make-up and the previous developmental experience of individuals. For the purpose of this analysis, I shall refer to these capacities as *potential*.

For example, in Mary's case we might note the difference in her relative engagement and success with reading and with mathematics. A range of social factors on these attainments have been described above, but it is obviously also important to recognize that a particular configuration of intellectual capacities may have enabled her to succeed in mathematics more readily than she did initially in her reading and writing. Similarly, her particular physical skills and agility enabled her to succeed at dance and gymnastics in ways which did not seem to be open to many other children.

In Mary then, we have a child whose 'potential' seemed to have been fulfilled in some important intellectual and physical areas. That fulfilment itself flowed back to support Mary's personal sense of self-confidence that she could indeed succeed in maths, and could achieve very high standards at dance and gymnastics. There is even the suggestion, from Mrs Inman, that Mary's behaviour as a baby showed the same relatively cautious disposition which was later evident in her sense of identity, though the extent to which this should be attributed to inherited 'personality' or to social learning is impossible to say. What this analysis can do, however, is to document the structures, processes and experiences through which that social learning took place and came to inform Mary's sense of identity.

A further set of factors influencing identity are associated with the *resources* which are available to individuals and which structure their lives. There are many forms of resource, but I will focus on just three – material, cultural and linguistic – and, in each case, pick out some of the ways in which they affected Mary's opportunities to learn and thus, her identity.

Mary's identity was shaped by her experiences, and these were underpinned by the material resources of her family. We might identify the comfortable house and garden in a pleasant suburb, the availability of a swimming pool in which her early athleticism developed, her subsequent access to dance lessons, the books and toys which were provided, the time of her mother before she returned to full-time employment and the range of experiences which it was possible to provide during weekend family outings and on holidays.

Mary was fortunate in these respects, as were all the children of Greenside in having a primary school which was particularly well funded.

In terms of cultural resources, Mary's gradual construction of identity particularly drew on those of her social class and gender. Simple elements of white middle-class culture were passed on to her in the home and, for example, we might identify a particular emphasis on manners and application to learning tasks. She also received a gradually widening range of experiences and participated in discussions through which the 'cultural capital' (Bourdieu and Passeron, 1977) of her parents and wider family was gradually transferred to her. Regarding gendered resources, this is very evident through Mary's identification with her mother and with her female peers. She drew on such resources to model her presentation of self, for solidarity and as a source of strategies in her relationships with males. The most overt example of the latter is in relation to Mary's evolving assertion identity vis-à-vis her brothers.

Linguistic resources are identified because of the enormous significance of language in learning, as researchers such as Dunn (1988), Wells (1986) and Tizard and Hughes (1984) have demonstrated. We will return to this theme, but for now, we simply need to note that the availability, sensitivity and skill of others in supporting a child in discussion and elaboration of his or her thinking is a vital element in learning, in reasoning and thus, in contributing to this aspect of identity.

Each of these three resources are illustrated in Mary's case by the Sunday visit to grandparents which is described on page 65. The material resources of the grandparent's home provided experiences of Sunday lunch, walking the dog in the country, collecting leaves and having a bonfire in the garden. Cultural resources and expectations were deployed through the conventions of the family meal and in the division of labour as 'Michael, the boys and Grandpop' made the bonfire whilst the females walked the dog, washed up and made tea. Linguistic resources were used and developed though the discussions which Mary had with her mother and Grandma about ballet, the dog and the meaning of 'allergic'. Such experiences were enjoyable and fulfilling for Mary and contributed to her growing sense of her security and self-confidence as a person.

Material, cultural and linguistic factors can thus be seen as elements of the social contexts in which any child must develop but also as providing resources on which a child draws in developing his or her strategies and sense of identity. Of course, the particular nature of the resources which are available to children will vary very considerably depending on their circumstances. In educational terms, the degree of consistency between the expectations of home and of school is likely to be important here, and again, Mary was relatively fortunate. The middle-class conventions of Mary's home were relatively consistent with those of the teachers at Greenside Primary School. In both settings, Mary was supported with encouragement of her attainments and the setting of high standards. Rules about behaviour were broadly similar and there was considerable overlap in expectations regarding dress, food, music and sport. For many children, of course, this is far from the case and, in such circumstances, it is possible that the material, cultural and linguistic resources which are available within the home will contribute to child identities which are much more dissonant with the expectations and values of school.

4.4   WHAT DID MARY HAVE TO LEARN?

Learning challenges

The range of learning challenges which face young children is obviously diverse but they can perhaps be most easily classified into the *experiences, relationships* and *tasks* which occur within the major settings of home, playground and classroom. Consideration of Mary's case-study story will illustrate the ways in which these contribute to intellectual and emotional development.

Tracking the home learning in Mary's story for each of the three years, we find her experiencing, thinking about and learning about things as diverse as new language (p. 41), board games, swimming, dance and the moral range of Father Christmas (p. 52), the plot of Dr Who (p. 65), marriage and having children (p. 77). The major relationships which challenged her learning were with her brothers and, to negotiate this, she observed and learned a great deal about her mother. In terms of tasks, she had to learn how to wash and dress herself, with one particular success being learning to tie her shoelaces (p. 42), how to help with relevant domestic chores and how to work with her mother on schoolwork associated with learning to read (p. 59). She developed skills, knowledge and understanding through these experiences, many of which she discussed with her mother. As has been found in other studies of young children, Mary actively maintained a process of 'intellectual search' (Tizard and Hughes, 1984) to create a better understanding of the structures, patterns and regularities in her life (Athey, 1990) and of what she might experience in the future.

In the playground Mary learned how to fulfil her role in the games and play activities which she and her friends created, whether these derived from imaginary ideas or were passed on through child culture. Relationships with friends were perhaps the greatest source of challenge to her learning, for she had to come to terms with both the 'nastiness' of some boys and the fickle nature of some of her relationships with other girls. She learned both of the reciprocity and support which friendships provided and of the times when 'bossiness' could leave her feeling alone (p. 54).

Regarding the classroom we can see how Mary's first learning challenge was simply to come to terms with the experience of being at school. She learned of the ways in which teachers run their classes and, gradually, of the ways of the school as a whole so that, by Year 2, she was confident enough to be able to be able to negotiate her way onto the Christmas Bazaar's sweet stall (p. 70). Developing an appropriate relationship with her teacher was a significant learning challenge in Mary's Reception year, but Mrs Powell did much to help the children in this regard. However, her relationship with Miss Scott was Mary's greatest classroom challenge during her Year 1 and we find her learning defensive strategies such as cross-checking interpretations, mood detection and evasion to ensure that she was not 'told off'. The year was a difficult one for Mary emotionally, and on pages 55–7 we saw her reflecting on her feelings and taking decisions on how to manage them with great sophistication. Mary's Year 2 posed few learning challenges in terms of relationships because the rapport which Miss George promoted was so consistent with the identity which Mary had already adopted. Perhaps this was one reason why Mary was so contented in that classroom, but she still had to manage her attachment to Miss George and she undoubtedly felt a great sense of loss when their year together ended. The affective aspects of Mary's learning were thus very significant to her as she moved, year-by-year, through the school.

Classroom tasks represented the ways in which the curriculum aims, planning, organization and policies of the Greenside Primary School and its teachers were manifested in terms of the curricular learning challenges which faced Mary. We saw how Mary tackled the initial stages of learning to write (pp. 45, 60 and 73) and how she struggled with determination to improve her reading (pp. 46 and 59) until she eventually made it to 'Library' (p. 74). Specific reading tasks included working on the 'word tin' and 'doing her reading book', activities which occurred at both home and school. The routine maths tasks of Mrs Powell's class had been enjoyed and this had continued with the 'maths cards' which Miss Scott favoured. By Miss George's class, Mary had fully embraced doing maths cards and saw them as a particular source of fulfilment (p. 70).

Learning stance

'Learning stance' is a term which denotes a learner's characteristic approach to learning challenges and I would argue that this is particularly influenced by an individual's sense of identity and by their interpretation of the learning challenges they face. I will identify three particular aspects of this – *motivation, self-confidence* and *strategic resources*. Together, these accumulate to give a learner a sense of control, or otherwise, in a learning situation.

Mary was highly motivated to learn and there are indications that much of her motivation was intrinsic. Consider again the learning challenges which were illustrated above. Most of these, particularly at home and in the playground, involved learning in which Mary engaged for its own sake: she wanted to develop her language; she enjoyed the thrill of physical activity; she wanted to understand some of the issues which she discussed with her mother and she loved to play with her close friends. Some educationalists argue that such intrinsic motivation makes an essential contribution to school learning and among the best illustrations of pupils' intrinsic engagement are those of Armstrong (1981), Paley (1990) and Rowland (1985). Armstrong, for instance, highlights the ways in which children 'appropriate knowledge' in the service of their own 'expressive purposes' during processes of intellectual and creative exploration in his classroom (1980: 129). Intrinsic motivation was not absent from Mary's engagement with the school curriculum, but it was not as strong as in other settings.

Mary's motivation to learn at school was particularly strong because, with complete consistency, it was expected of her by her parents, siblings, peers, teachers and, in association, by herself. The social side of her motivation was very significant with achievements denoting status and esteem in respect of both her brothers and her closest friends. In some areas, particularly her physical activities, there were also strong signs of her intrinsic motivation.

However, Mary's self-confidence varied in respect of different types of learning and in respect of the situations in which she was called upon to demonstrate her knowledge. Thus, we find her self-confidence was low where the outcome of tasks were uncertain, such as when asked to attempt spellings (p. 73), or when she felt her dignity to be threatened, such as when reading to her mother (p. 62). In the latter case, in the security of home, she might 'flounce out', whilst in the classroom her strategy was always more defensive and cautious. Gradually, as the years went by, she became more and more confident about her work in maths, both because of the low task ambiguity of maths work cards and because she was able to develop and apply her capability for reasoning. The result was that the activity became not just 'low risk' but a source of personal fulfilment.

Strategic resources and their use seem to vary a great deal with levels of confidence. For Mary at school in her Reception year, she was essentially 'responsive' to the new challenges which were presented to her. She was supported and was 'very positive' about school, but she did not behave pro-actively and the range of strategies she used was relatively narrow. Basically, Mary's strategy was to conform; she listened well, took Mrs Powell's advice and did her best to meet the requirements which were made of her. However, in her Year 1 classroom, Mary's strategies can be characterized as 'defensive'. She found that the simple range of responsive strategies was inadequate for the challenges which Miss Scott presented and she began to develop a further range designed not just to conform but to 'avoid trouble'. The threat that she perceived in the classroom, meant that it was this range of strategies on which she tended to draw, even when others might have been possible. In Year 2, Mary felt less need of general defensive strategies and began to use a wider repertoire in relation to different areas of learning. Whilst she flourished in maths, 'beavering away' at maths cards (p. 70) she also began to develop 'persistence' in her approach to her reading which, in turn, rolled through into signs of an increased willingness to take risks with spelling at the end of the year. Mrs Inman's review of Mary's learning during Year 2 (p. 76) vividly conveys the greater range of strategies which were associated with Mary's growth in self-confidence and achievement. Importantly, there are signs there too of Mary experimenting, such as her declaration to her mother that 'it is my life, I can do what I want', of her sense of her own biography and development, such as her decision to save a new 5p coin 'for her children' and discussion of marriage and of her developing skills of negotiating, such as over bedtime and clothes.

Learning stance can thus be seen as being associated, through motivation, self-confidence and strategic resources, with the degree of control which a learner is able to achieve in coping within the social settings in which new learning challenges are presented.

This brings us to a new focus, the characteristics of learning contexts themselves.

4.5 HOW SUPPORTIVE WERE THE SPECIFIC CONTEXTS IN WHICH MARY LEARNED?

This is a complex question which I shall discuss in two parts, each of which will then be applied to the case of Mary.

First, we will consider the 'opportunity to learn' which is associated with the power context, social rules and expectations which exist in different settings. Here I will draw significantly on my earlier analysis of classroom settings from *The Social World of the Primary School* (1985a).

Second, we will address the question of the 'quality of the teaching and assistance in learning' which is offered by others, such as teachers, parents and peers. This will take us into some of the detail of social constructivist thinking on teaching–learning processes and, in particular, to a discussion of Vygotsky's concept of the 'zone of proximal development' (1978).

Opportunity to learn in social settings

The Social World of the Primary School provided an analysis of the ways in which pupils and teachers cope with school life and interact together to produce taken-for-granted understandings and rules about behaviour in classrooms. This analysis is connected to the notion of developing a 'good classroom relationship' which so many primary school teachers, correctly in my view, make a priority. Following Hargreaves (1972), I termed the product of these negotiated understandings the 'working consensus'. A working consensus is important because, it defines a form of morality for classroom life based on a mutual exchange of dignity between teacher and pupils, through it the *behaviour* of both teacher and pupils is legitimated or contested. In another sense though, it also generates the social characteristics of the context in which *learning* takes place – hence its significance for us here.

Given that the working consensus is a product of negotiation between each teacher and his or her class of pupils, it is necessary to consider the various factors which condition the ways in which each individual acts. I draw particular attention to three:

Structural position:
Each individual's power, influence and capacity to take active decisions.

Interests-at-hand:
The immediate concerns of each individual in processes of interaction, given his or her goals and structural position within a particular social setting.

Strategic action:
Strategies used by individuals as a means of coping with different settings. These include conformity, negotiating and rejecting and may or may not be transferred across different settings.

Of course, teachers occupy the strongest structural position with power to initiate and direct pupils. However, pupils are by no means powerless if acting collectively and the structural position, and influence, of each will also vary depending on factors such as age, gender, achievements and status. In my earlier analysis I documented 'self' as the primary interest-at-hand of both teachers and pupils, with enabling interests for teachers of 'order' and 'instruction' and for pupils of 'peer group membership' and 'learning'. I also suggested that teacher and pupil strategies tend to mesh together, with teachers often using forms of 'routinization' which is matched by pupil strategies of 'drifting' – a suggestion which is echoed in much other classroom research (e.g. Galton, 1989).

The real underlying issue here is that of power. How do the participants in interaction make decisions? How is conformity defined and by whom? How is deviance sanctioned?

Although this analysis was developed in the context of classrooms, I believe that, in principle, it can be applied to other settings such as those of the home and playground. In all three cases we have individuals interacting together. Some have more power and influence than others but each one has a set of interests-at-hand which will inform their strategic actions as they cope with, adapt to and come to understand the situations they face. Parents are clearly the most influential within homes, and different children will vie for influence in playgrounds, but, as with teachers in classrooms, neither can normally act entirely unilaterally and each will be involved in a variable degree of negotiation with others. The result, in home and playground as well as in the classroom, is that forms of working consensus normally evolve. These embrace expectations, conventions and rules for both interpersonal behaviour and the use of power.

The contexts in which learning takes place are thus social products and must be seen as micro-political 'power contexts'. This matters enormously because, as we have seen, pupils' learning stance is highly susceptible to self-confidence and willingness to take risks. If the power context within a social setting is very prominent and a child feels vulnerable, then he or she is likely to minimize exposure and 'play safe' by opting for a tried, tested and defensive range of strategies. A more secure environment, in which a child feels at ease with the expectations and rules which frame behaviour, is likely to make experimentation possible and to encourage the risk-taking which is a necessary part of engaging with new learning challenges. The social character of different settings, in other words, has an important influence on opportunities to learn.

Thinking about Mary's opportunities to learn, it is apparent that her classroom experiences were uneven. From a steady start in the rather traditional Reception class, her time with Miss Scott was a year in which she perceived high risk within an unpredictable power context, and the extent of this was made even more apparent by the contrast with her experience and learning in the Year 2 class which followed. The playground context also varied for Mary, but was neither so tightly structured nor so official. Nevertheless, Mary seemed much more contented and open to learning when she felt a part of her friendship group rather than when they were experiencing a period of 'falling out'. Home was a source of relative stability here, with Mrs Inman mediating between Mary and her brothers and providing the key role in maintaining expectations, routines and rules. The home context was relatively secure for Mary throughout the period, and it is noticeable from Chapter 3 as a whole that she derived particular support for her school learning from home at times when she was experiencing uncertainty in the classroom.

Reviewing this overall argument, we might say that, whatever a child's potential, it is unlikely to be fulfilled if opportunities to learn within social settings inhibit the exploitation of that potential. This statement underlines what is, for me, a key point in social constructivist models of learning about *control* within learning processes. Since understanding can only be constructed in the minds of learners, it is essential that they exercise a significant degree of control of the process so that they can build on intrinsic motivation where that exists. As Galton (1989) has suggested, following Doyle (1986), we need to focus:

> on the social factors affecting pupil learning and (on) the ways in which teachers can create classroom climates which allow situations of 'high risk' and 'high ambiguity' to be coped with successfully
> (1989: 44).

However, this again is an argument about necessary but not sufficient conditions for, whatever the social context, learning will be greatly enhanced by high-quality teaching and assistance from more knowledgeable or experienced others. This brings us to the second factor in judging how supportive different learning contexts may be.

Quality of teaching and assistance in learning

The nature and quality of teaching and assistance in learning is a crucial factor and brings us directly to the skills and intentions of more knowledgeable others in supporting the development of understanding. My approach follows Vygotsky's insight that the learning which an individual can achieve alone is by no means the same as that which he or she may achieve with appropriate teaching and assistance. Each of us, he posited, has a 'zone of proximal development' (ZPD) – an area which is accessible for the next steps in our learning *if* we are appropriately guided and supported in taking those steps. The process has been described by Bruner (1986) who identifies a key role for others in 'scaffolding' the understanding of the learner across his or her ZPD. The analogy with the process of building is a very suitable one for, as with a house, the construction of understanding may well need support at various stages until it is fully formed and can stand upon its own foundations. This social constructivist approach has been clearly summarized by Wood (1988) and features strongly in my own textbook on reflective teaching (Pollard and Tann, 1993). As I have argued elsewhere (Pollard, 1992b), it is fast becoming a new conventional wisdom in its application to pedagogy, although empirical researchers are having some difficulties in identifying it.

The model on which I have settled to represent this teaching–learning process is an elaboration of Rowland's (1987) work and highlights the Vygotskian insight of the importance of a learner's understanding being scaffolded across his or her relevant zone of proximal development. With Rowland, I deploy the concept of 'reflective agent' to encapsulate the highly skilled role which calls for understanding of and empathy for the learner as well as of knowledge of that which is to be learned. Although the model has been developed with classroom contexts in mind, it is just as applicable to home settings or, with suitable amendment, to playground learning.

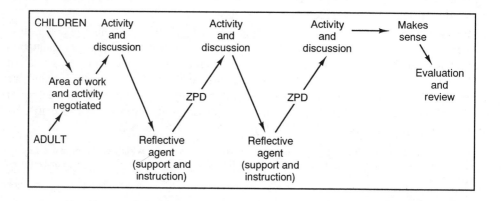

Figure 4.1 *A social constructivist model of teaching–learning processes*

The suggestion here that objectives be negotiated should be noted, for this model should not be confused with a romantic conception of an entirely open child-centredness. In the classroom, negotiation could encompass making children aware of National Curriculum requirements and discussing how these may best be satisfied. At home, the same process is likely to be applied to less formal, less structured but more particular and wide-ranging purposes. Examples in this study ranged from adult-initiated cleaning of teeth, getting on with siblings and learning to be polite, to child-initiated discussion on 'why the sky is blue' and considering life, death and Father Christmas.

There are several good examples of this teaching–learning process at work in Mary's case-study story. For instance, the beginning of Section 3.3 (p. 41) contains accounts of Mary's bathtime advice from her mother on how to say 'muddle' rather than 'muggle' and of her father teaching her to tie shoelaces. There are many more examples, particularly of Mrs Inman answering Mary's questions about new thoughts and issues which occurred to her, supporting Mary in her reading and mediating her relationship with her brothers. Often these discussions occurred in relatively quiet periods when they were together – such as walking to school, a pause in the late afternoon, getting ready for bed – times, in other words, which were low in tension and when the opportunity to learn was great. In such episodes, Mrs Inman fulfilled the role of 'reflective agent' by offering support and instruction so that Mary's thinking and understanding was extended, across her ZPD. Of course, where schoolwork was concerned, the same thing was going on within the classroom and can be found, for instance, on page 44 which records how Mrs Powell guided Mary's hand as she learned correct letter formations for her writing. Such teaching was also a part of Mary's experience in Year 1 and Year 2 but it is noticeable that the classroom accounts in Chapter 3 record less one-to-one encounters. In fact, page 56 documents an unfortunate incident which shows quite the reverse, when Miss Scott mistook Mary's picture of flowers for fireworks and the overall tone for Year 1 is of Mary, far from seeking to approach any ZPD, simply wanting to get through each day. She aimed to 'drift', with minimum risk, within the routines which Miss Scott provided. Acting as a 'reflective agent' is thus not at all easy for teachers in classrooms, given the numbers of pupils to whom they have to attend and this, of course, is one major reason for the recent recommendation that there should be more whole-class teaching (Alexander *et al.*, 1992) and interest in groupwork systems which could mitigate organizational difficulties (Bennett and Dunne, 1992; Galton and Williamson, 1992).

The model in Figure 4.1 describes a pedagogic process, a process which is dependent on a number of important factors. In particular, carrying out the role of a reflective agent effectively is dependent on accurate knowledge of each child's affective and cognitive needs and on being able to respond to them appropriately. Thus, in addition to describing the social conditions in which fruitful dialogue can take place, the model identifies the vital role of formative assessment or empathy, and the importance of having appropriate knowledge from which to offer support. In Mary's case, Mrs Powell and Miss Scott had a fund of knowledge which was related to their relatively traditional approaches to the teaching of reading, writing and maths but, it could be said, Miss George was only at the start of beginning to develop such knowledge. Thus whilst Miss George created classroom conditions in which many opportunities to learn existed, it is arguable that at this initial stage of her career the level of her own subject expertise was insufficient to capitalize on these circumstances. The children were happy, but did they learn as much as they could have done? Mary's mother was certainly the most empathic adult in her life, was probably the most able to support Mary's intrinsically motivated concerns and may have known most about her progress in reading. However, she did not have sufficient curriculum knowledge to extend Mary's learning in all of the specific ways which were expected of Mary by her teachers. In other respects though, Mrs Inman's effectiveness as a reflective agent was clearly enhanced by her sympathetic understanding of her daughter and by her own education, knowledge and cultural and linguistic resources.

In summary, I would thus suggest that there are two major elements in the judgement of how supportive a learning context is:

- *provision of a social context in which there are opportunities to learn* and in which children are enabled to exercise some control over their construction of meaning and understanding, and,
- *high-quality teaching and assistance in learning*, including effective communication, assessment and empathy and the provision of appropriate and knowledgeable support and instruction.

The nature of power relations within the learning contexts and the type of direct support for learning may be interconnected in their effects on particular children. First, a teaching–learning situation may suit a child's identity and stance in respect of a new learning challenge in *both* respects, in which context the child is likely to learn effectively with an element of both control and support. Second, however, contextual openness and the provision of suitable opportunities to learn may satisfy many children and seem to be sufficient but, without instructional challenge, support and higher expectations, it is likely to result in lost opportunities and unfulfilled potential. Third, high levels of learning challenge in a context which is highly framed and perceived as threatening may, depending on the child's identity, stance and home support, depress *or* enhance overt indicators of learning. There is a danger, in any event, that such learning will be experienced by the children as stressful and could lead to superficial achievements as children prioritize 'pleasing teacher' rather than understanding itself. Fourth, and finally, it is also possible that neither aspect is satisfied in which case learning is likely to be fitful and hesitant with a sense of lack of control producing risk avoidance and a lack of instructional support producing routinization and drift.

We can represent these four propositions diagrammatically:

	Appropriate quality of teaching and assistance	Inappropriate quality of teaching and assistance
Empowering opportunities to learn	1. Positive child feelings of control and effective learning	2. Child satisfaction but some wasted learning opportunities
Constraining opportunities to learn	3. Likely child stress, but possible learning	4. Likely child stress and defensive, unintended and superficial learning

Figure 4.2   *Four possible outcomes from learning contexts*

The application of this model to any particular learner is obviously difficult and you, as the reader, may want to form your opinions about Mary and the four other children who feature in this book. My own judgement in Mary's case is that learning at home seems mainly to have had the characteristics of the first or second combinations. Learning in her classrooms might be seen as tending towards the first combination in Reception, the third or fourth in Year 1 and the second or first in Year 2. Mary's learning in the playground context depended largely on the particular state of her relationship with her peers and, with consistent but relatively low levels of learning challenge, varied between the first or third combinations.

What though, of the results of all this? This leads us to our final question.

4.6 WHAT WERE THE OUTCOMES OF MARY'S APPROACH TO LEARNING?

There are many important learning achievements as the baby grows into the toddler, to the child, the young person, the adolescent and the adult. For instance, one constant theme of Mary's story is her growing independence in successive years, from learning to dress herself fully, to discarding her 'blanker' at night, to defining how she wanted to set up her bedroom and to thinking about her future. These experiences and achievements influenced both the way Mary was seen by others, such as her parents and siblings, and the ways in which Mary saw herself.

Such learning goes on all the time and, for any individual, is an integral element of inter-action with others and of responding to his or her environment. Indeed, such issues are addressed within all the case studies. However, I also wanted to demonstrate the particular policy relevance of the research by focusing on the specific curricular indicators of learning which are of prime concern to policy-makers, parents and teachers – those of the basic curriculum of reading, writing and number. These are 'high-stakes' areas for pupil attainment and can be described both as formal outcomes and in terms of more informal implications.

Formal learning outcomes

Formal learning outcomes in the 'basic' curriculum are, in one sense, a relatively straight-forward issue. What, at the end of the day, has actually been learned? What can, say, a child now do or understand that he or she could not manage before?

Within classrooms, following the introduction of the National Curriculum in England and Wales, the specification of curriculum aims and of summative assessment procedures were considerably developed. In fact, they were implemented in 1989, objected to, rejected, revised, re-introduced and, finally, largely accepted following teacher and parent protests in 1993 and the Dearing Review (Dearing, 1994). From the mid-1990s 'level descriptions' were deemed to represent the characteristic attainments in most subjects of children who pass through a broad sequence of achievements. Parents were to be informed of their children's progress by means of both ongoing, formative Teacher Assessment and through the completion of Standard Assessment Tasks (SATs) at the age of seven and further tests at the age of eleven. Such structured, overt and nationally comparable indica-tors of learning did not exist at Greenside Primary School at the time of this study, but the school was very unusual in providing written reports to parents for every child twice each year. Parts of these reports are drawn on in Chapter 3 to document Mary's progress in learning of the 'basic' curriculum (Alexander, 1984). They were undoubtedly important to Mr and Mrs Inman and provided a time to 'take stock' for each teacher. Reflections on each year by Mrs Inman, Mary and her teachers (pp. 50, 61 and 75) reveal the influence of achievements of many kinds and these undoubtedly affected both the perception which others had of Mary and Mary's view of herself.

For Mary though, it seems that she also paid close attention to some more immediate indices of academic progress and, in particular, the box of reading books that she was 'on' and the stage in the maths scheme which she had reached. She was also very aware of her attainments in dance, gymnastics and swimming. For her, in addition to enjoyment of such absolute standards, she monitored her position relative to her peers. Her attainment in relation to Sally was of particular significance.

This brings us to more informal learning outcomes of Mary's attainments.

Informal learning outcomes

There seem to be two major forms of informal learning outcome – those associated with *self-esteem* and those deriving from *social status*.

First, learning outcomes affect self-esteem, the way in which the learner perceives himself or herself. This may have intrinsic features – a simple pleasure at mastery, as Mary felt with her ballet and maths. Alternatively or additionally, it may also reflect the extrinsic satisfactions of achievements which are 'as good as' or 'better than' others. Self-esteem thus contributes to identity and to the self-confidence which is brought to bear when new learning challenges are faced. Mary's views of her achievements at the end of Year 2 (p. 77) provide clear evidence of this. She knew that she was 'second best in Maths', that 'Mummy will give me something nice' and that both her parents and teacher were delighted at her progress in reading. She had developed though, from being 'very much the little girl that accepted everything' into a child who now expected and welcomed the fact that 'the work will be a little bit harder' in the juniors, and declared that to be 'more interesting, 'cos if you stayed on the same thing all the time it'd get really easy'. The learning outcomes of Mary's achievements were rolling forward to affect her self-esteem, her sense of identity and her self-confidence in facing new learning challenges. Her self-perception remained, of course, very strongly influenced by gender.

Second, learning outcomes affect social status, the ways in which others perceive and act towards the learner. As we have seen, in the case of young children, particularly significant others are likely to be parents, siblings, peers and teachers, hence the wide sampling framework used for this study. Mary's social status rose as her achievements grew, though in terms of popularity among her peers Sally tended to shine throughout their passage through Key Stage 1. Similarly, winning board games at home and her athletic achievements gave Mary important social status in respect of her brothers and, in turn, fed through to influence their interaction with her and their influence on her identity.

This consideration of self-esteem and social status thus brings us back to the question with which we began, 'Who' was Mary, in terms of her identity? Such is the recursive nature of experience. The model discussed in the next section summarizes and relates the factors which have been discussed and represents the cyclical process.

4.7 WHY DID MARY'S APPROACH TO LEARNING DEVELOP AS IT DID? A THEORETICAL MODEL

The model (Figure 4.3) bears a direct relation to the 'Questions for Enquiry' which were posed in Chapter 1 and summarized in Figure 1.2, and to the text of the present chapter. It is an expression of the recursive cycle through which identity, learning challenges, learning

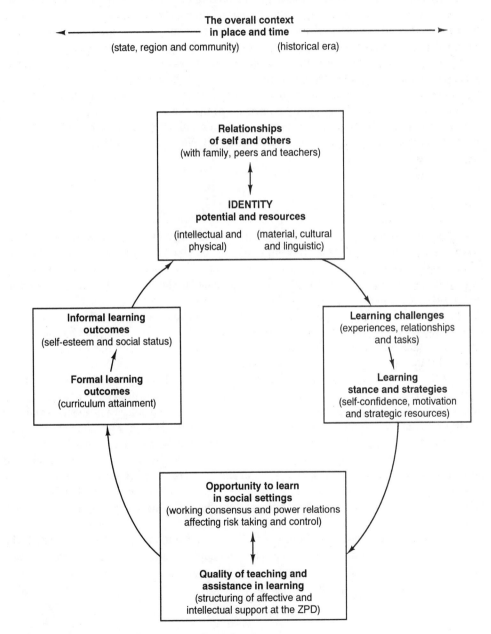

Figure 4.3 *A model of learning, identity and social setting*

contexts and learning outcomes feed into and condition each other. It is a way of abstracting the details of Mary's experiences over the three years on which we have focused and could be seen in terms of a major cycle during each year, as informing an innumerable number of cycles through which identity and learning interact and evolve together or as a something in between. Whatever the time-frame of major, minor or other cycles, the basic factors in play seem to remain the same.

So why did Mary's approach to learning develop in the way that it did? I believe that we have enough evidence from sibling and peer relationships to account for her sense of determination, and we know of the relative stability of support and modelling which was provided by her mother. From this base, Mary encountered successive teachers and her learning can be said to have ebbed and flowed in response to her adaptions and coping strategies within the conditions which they created. Happily, at the end of her Year 2, she had developed very positively with considerable achievements and growing self-confidence. If we were to track Mary's progress to the end of her primary school career we would see that this basic process continued right through to her Year 6 in 1993/4. Data of this sort will be indeed be available in Pollard and Filer (in press), *The Social World of Pupil Careers*.

4.8   CONCLUSION

In this chapter I have extended and applied the basic 'Questions for Enquiry' and I hope that Figure 4.3 provides a clear representation of the key factors and their relationships, as highlighted in this chapter. They have been considered in relation to Mary and it may be time, if you have not done so already, for you to consider your own childhood in relation to this model, or the childhood of your children, or those of your pupils. It is time to think of the process of learning as a whole. In your experience, how do logic and curiosity, reasoning and imagination, intellect and emotion, experimentation and play interact in the struggle to understand in which young children engage? And how do the social settings in which children act, facilitate or constrain their learning?

What follows, in Part Three, Elaborating, are four more detailed case studies of children learning. The uniqueness of each child comes across very strongly; Hazel and her exceptional drawings and imaginative worlds of dinosaurs and dragons; Daniel and his uncertainties as the youngest of five, his classroom bewilderment and attachment to his 'special friend'; Sally, whom we have already encountered, daughter of the school care-taker and a young child of extra-ordinary poise, achievement, self-confidence and popularity with pupils and teachers alike; and James, whose mother suffered from ME and who found himself both somewhat cut off from child culture and suffering between a considerable gap in home and school perceptions concerning his education. How then, will these children fare?

These four further case-study stories enable a comparative method though which the model represented in Figure 4.3 is elaborated and applied further. This, in due course, will be the subject of Chapter 9 and, once more, you will be able to relate that analysis to your own experiences as child, parent or teacher.

Part 3

Elaborating

Chapter 5

Hazel's Story

5.1 HAZEL, AN INTRODUCTION

In this chapter we meet Hazel who was, for one of her teachers, 'the most extraordinary child I have taught for some years'. Hazel had a creative imagination and a very independent spirit, thus a central theme of her story concerns the ways in which she coped with the classroom rules and learning requirements which were presented by her successive teachers.

Before we embark upon Hazel's story in detail, the reader is invited to consider the possibilities for the experience of such a child. How might Hazel, with her liking for immersion in her own 'dream-world', respond to the structured expectations of Mrs Powell's Reception class? How would Mrs Powell assist Hazel's learning in the face of the four-year-old's determination to fulfil her imaginative impulses through play and her withdrawal from elements of classroom life which she found threatening or incomprehensible? In previous chapters we have seen how Mary and her group of friends responded to the more volatile context of Miss Scott's Year 1 class with increased 'goodness', peer support and watchfulness. What strategies could Hazel employ, a child who was fiercely independent and relatively unconcerned about peer group norms and expectations? Indeed, what quality of teaching would Miss Scott offer to a child who was reluctant to compromise on her intentions in any setting? Similarly, we might speculate on the impact which the young and inexperienced Year 2 teacher, Miss George, would have on the learning of a child who brought to her classroom a profound wariness, a slightly devious sense of fun and distinctive drawing skills which were invariably fulfilled through representations of mythical and exotic animals.

Of course, many further factors were to be crucial to Hazel's experience of each of these classroom settings, not least the nature of Hazel's support from her parents and her relationships with her sister and peers. Each of these relationships had implications for Hazel's sense of identity, her self-esteem and for the ways in which she learned from her successive experiences within her three infant classrooms at Greenside Primary School.

Figure 5.1 provides an overview of her structural position within each class. It shows that Hazel was slightly older than average in her Reception class, among the youngest in Year 1 and one of the eldest in her Year 2 class. In each class, her attainment was weak in relation to her peers though she did significantly better at literacy than at maths. In her Year 1 however, when she was taught by Miss Scott, her literacy seems to have fallen away somewhat.

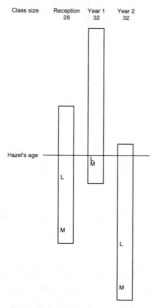

Figure 5.1 *Hazel's structural position: age and relative attainment at literacy and maths in Reception, Year 1 and Year 2 classes (for an explanation of this figure, see p. 35)*

5.2   HAZEL'S FAMILY

Hazel was a summer-born child who entered school aged four years and four months. She was the eldest of two girls in her family and her sister, Katie, was two years younger.

Mrs Farthing, Hazel's mother, had worked as a secretary before having the children, when she gave up work outside the home for a time. However, she studied to improve her qualifications (particularly in maths) so that, when Katie started school in autumn 1989, Mrs Farthing was able to begin a four-year B.Ed. degree course to become a primary school teacher. When she graduated in 1993 she did so with excellent results, particularly regarding her main subject of Art. Hazel's father, Rob, worked shifts for a high-technology engineering company throughout the period of this study. Although there were always disadvantages in the shift-work pattern which went with his job, it did enable him to play an important role in the early years of childcare and in supporting his wife during her studies. The family was close and Mr and Mrs Farthing shared a great interest in their children as they developed.

Mr and Mrs Farthing had moved from a nearby council estate into a very pleasant semi-detached house on the edge of Greenside in the early 1980s. As Mrs Farthing put it: 'It was the best we could afford. Then we had five years of DIY and babies'.

As her mother described her, Hazel had always been very determined.

> She is a very determined young lady. I don't think it is something that we've bred in her if you see what I mean, it is part of her character. Its since birth I would say. As a baby if she wanted something you knew. She was a very happy baby but very determined even then. When other babies would sit in their pushchairs when you went along Hazel was strapped in on tiptoe –

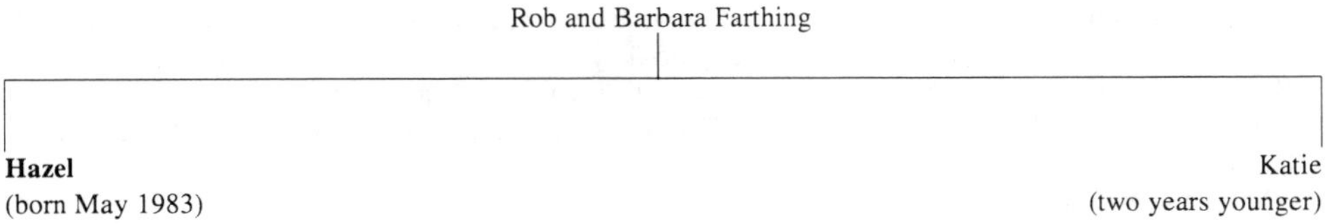

Rob and Barbara Farthing

Hazel
(born May 1983)

Katie
(two years younger)

Figure 5.2 *Hazel's immediate family*

straining ... . We used to call her Boadicea – 'let me get at them all', sort of thing. Wonderful, but ... and she is like that now I think.
(Mrs Farthing, parent interview, March 1988, Reception)

From an early age Hazel also developed a strong liking for creating imaginary worlds in which she could both play and control events. As we will see, such imaginary worlds were to be very important to Hazel as she developed through school. Later, as Katie too grew up, she was drawn into these games. Mrs Farthing explained:

From before Katie was born, Hazel would always go and play little games with odd toys and talk to them and do voices back and all that. Yes she has always done that and Katie has always joined in. I am never quite sure whether Katie has done it herself or whether she has just copied Hazel but it is something they do. Hazel likes to be top dog as well, very much so, at home with Katie.
(Mrs Farthing, parent interview, March 1988, Reception)

In terms of long-term educational aspirations Mrs Farthing explained that, although hoping for 'success', she had not forgotten her own educational experiences. She thus prioritized the happiness of their children and was very willing to take account of their wishes directly. She explained her position:

I am always encouraged when Hazel comes out with something like 'I want to be a doctor'. If I am absolutely honest, what parent doesn't hope that their child will be successful? When I really think about it, basically I want her to grow up to be a happy, stable person. I think that is paramount and anything else is, well ... .
We obviously want to offer her the best chances that we can but that doesn't necessarily mean pushing her but, to a certain extent, encouraging her and doing things like homework. I think that stems back from me because I was a lazy little so-and-so. ... If I could be out playing, I would climb out of a bedroom window rather than stay in. I can see how I behaved so perhaps I am not strict – but with schooling certainly, certain things have to be done to a certain stand-ard. But if she turns round and says, 'I really don't want to do this', then I will certainly listen and give my point of view. But I think, knowing Hazel, she will do exactly what she wants to anyway.
Basically, I think that for her to be happy in what she does is the most important thing.
(Mrs Farthing, parent interview, March 1988, Reception)

Hazel's parents were thus clear that they wanted to provide a warm, secure and under-standing environment.

The educational philosophy of Mr and Mrs Farthing was particularly close to that of the school, compared with many parents in the catchment area during the late 1980s. For instance, commenting on the time when the new headteacher, Mrs Davison, had started at Greenside Primary, Mrs Farthing said:

There was all the gossip around that – the previous headteacher believed in the three Rs and Mrs Davison seemed to be a little more lax and they weren't too sure about it. But personally I think that is not altogether a bad thing anyway. The school isn't just about three Rs, it is about helping them develop as a whole person. That's what I think anyway, so I was quite pleased with that change.

(Mrs Farthing, parent interview, March 1988, Reception)

For much of Hazel's primary school career her mother was studying education herself and also enjoying the development of her own artistic skills. Perhaps this teacher education programme provided ways of interpreting the patterns in the children's development as they grew up and, certainly, supported Hazel's desire to express her imagination.

5.3 HAZEL IN HER RECEPTION YEAR

Hazel, Reception, relationships with parents at home

Hazel's family life during her Reception year was rich and active, with Mr and Mrs Farthing being closely involved with the children. For instance, the two diary entries below record first the events of one Sunday afternoon and then Hazel's activities in general:

We have an early snack lunch and then drive out to the woods, don our wellies and go for a long muddy ramble. Great fun. Play tag. Katie gets a bit frustrated because she can't catch anyone. Hazel falls over and gets completely covered in mud. Manage to do a quick wipe down job, but ask her not to suck her fingers until she can wash her hands. This proves to be annoying for her during the car journey home. Stop off on way home and get a video, one for us and one for the girls. I prepare the girls' favourite tea, chicken stroganoff, while they watch the new Rainbow Brite cartoon video.

About 6.45 I take them upstairs for a bath and hair wash. Rob reads them a bedtime story. Girls settle down very quickly tonight as they are absolutely shattered after their long walk.

(Mrs Farthing, parent diary, February 1988, Reception)

Hazel loves to be active – she loves going to the swimming baths, riding her bike, going to the park and playing on the slides and swings etc. She also loves adult participation in games such as Tag or Hide and Seek. She and Katie can also play for hours outside collecting, making homes and feeding small creatures such as woodlice. She also seems to be interested in all forms of natural history, from collecting bits of rock to naming butterflies, going to the museum or spending hours scrutinizing different animals and fish at the zoo. She also likes to help me cook!

(Mrs Farthing, parent diary, July 1988, Reception)

Daily routines also reflected Hazel's commitment to her play, and, because of her tendency to become totally absorbed in them, posed some challenges to her mother. Mrs Farthing described one morning:

Alarm goes off. Everyone else still asleep. Start the zombie-like Monday morning routine – make breakfast, prepare lunch box etc. Katie appears first complaining about not being able to find her slippers. A few grumpy noises from upstairs and Hazel appears with a handful of toys and sets up her favourite ones around her breakfast mat. Katie does likewise and so breakfast (with friends) begins. I disappear upstairs to get washed and dressed.

Try to 'up' the pace of the morning preparations. Eventually manage to prise Hazel from toys and upstairs to get ready for school. She washes herself and brushes her teeth, but as every operation is turned into a game (lovely for her but infuriating for me) I end up practically dressing her. She can do it herself, but we wouldn't get to school before 10.00 if she was left to her own devices.

(Mrs Farthing, parent diary, February 1988, Reception)

Nevertheless, one of the characteristic features of family life for Hazel was the closeness of her parents to her. In respect of her mother, this was particularly so regarding her sense of humour and mischief. For instance, the diary records an example of mother and her four-year-old daughter sharing a joke about school procedures:

> On the way to school Hazel tells me about Mrs Powell taking the register in the morning and how when each child's name is called they have to shout out either 'packed lunch' or 'school dinners'. She starts to make jokes about the way she shouts out 'packed lunch' – very funny!
> (Mrs Farthing, parent diary, February 1988, Reception)

Hazel's independent approach to school was thus supported from an early age, with echoes back to the school experiences of her parents.

However, Hazel's parents certainly wanted her to learn effectively and they were concerned when Hazel became frustrated in some new learning situations or on some occasions when adults tried to help her. As Mrs Farthing explained:

> She likes to 'know' things. She seems to get a bit angry or frustrated when she has to learn new things that she doesn't immediately understand and I think she gets very cross about it. I think probably it makes her cross because she doesn't immediately understand what they [adults such as teachers] are thinking about. I know it is definitely a frustration for her and making a big scene is her way of reacting.
> She seems so determined. Also I look around at other children and they seem to be a lot more willing to learn a lot of the time, although I suppose they have their particular problems. But they are not this almost sort of *rigid*. She sort of says, 'I can see you want me to do something so I am actually getting cross'. It is actually a visible thing sometimes with her – you can see her muscling against it.
> The first time it came to light was at playschool. Hazel had a My Little Pony or something there. Angela [the playgroup leader] said, 'Hazel would you like to put the pony down on the tray over there while we have a story?'. Hazel ignored her to start with, and Angela said, 'Hazel, just pop the pony down for a minute,' and, 'Hazel, put the pony down please'. Angela said that she could see her building up and it became a stamping foot situation.
> In a way it was funny. But it wasn't, if you know what I mean. It was as if she felt, 'I have to defy'.
> I find that very difficult to cope with.
> (Mrs Farthing, parent interview, March 1988, Reception)

Hazel, Reception, relationships with siblings at home

Hazel's relationship with her sister Katie revealed a very common pattern of affection, rivalry and a degree of jealousy. There are, for instance, many examples of the sequence of interaction which is noted in the diary entry below:

> Hazel finishes off game with Katie. She is giving Katie a huge cuddle and telling her how much she loves her and will miss her today. I can't help smiling, are these the same little girls who were fighting and screaming at each other the day before!
> (Mrs Farthing, parent diary, February 1988, Reception)

As Mrs Farthing graphically explained this complex relationship:

> It is ever so difficult, sometimes they can get on wonderfully well together and they love each other. And Katie is an absolute hero worshipper when it comes to Hazel. She thinks she is the cat's whiskers most of the time, except when she does hurt her or something. But if Hazel is a bully towards Katie, she just can't cope with it if Katie hits her back. Then she just thinks Katie

ought to be hung, drawn and quartered for doing this to her. She would have made a wonderful Roman Emperor or something, I can just imagine her up there, thumbs down, send them all to the lions, sort of thing.

(Mrs Farthing, parent interview, July 1988, Reception)

Mrs Farthing was very aware of the similarities and differences between Hazel and Katie:

Katie is much quieter and it's much easier to sit down with a book and talk about things with her than with Hazel. Hazel is much more easily diverted, unless she is really interested in that particular thing. Katie will sit down and want to learn things. She is much easier to teach if you see what I mean, I think she will probably get on better in school in some ways. She seems to be much more happy-go-lucky than Hazel and she doesn't seem to have her moods. She doesn't appear to be jealous of Hazel particularly, unless it is just a cuddle situation where she wants to get in on it sort of thing. Hazel seems to feel things very dramatically, whereas Katie seems to be much more able to take everything with a pinch of salt.

They are completely different when they are on their own with either Rob or myself and in fact, they are wonderful. That sounds as though they are horrible together but you know what I mean. You could actually have a conversation and they behave like proper, what do I mean, 'proper people'? I mean sensible, reasonably sensible, children, and you can have conversations! When they are together, they are like little mad things around the place.

(Mrs Farthing, parent interview, March 1988, Reception)

Hazel's determination and unease when confronted by new learning tasks in which she was not greatly interested, and the influence of her relationship with Katie, is well illustrated in the following account of learning 'new words' at home. This stemmed from the practice in the Reception class of sending a book and 'word tin' home so that parents could assist their children in early reading. However, for Hazel the scenario was complicated by Katie's involvement as the younger child saw her sister striving to learn the new words. As the account shows, Hazel went from frustration with her learning, to scapegoating of Katie and then to re-establishing calm and good relationships through fantasy play. Mrs Farthing's diary described the scene:

After tea I switch off the television and encourage Hazel to fetch her book and words. Hazel, Katie and I sit down to read the book. Hazel was very tired but enjoys the book, but when it comes to her words she says, 'I don't want to do my words. I'm too tired and it's boring'.

I try to explain that it doesn't *have* to be boring, it can be fun. I try to make it into a game, with Katie trying to guess the words too. This works for a little while, but as soon as a word she is not sure about comes up she becomes very cross about it. Before I can tell her the word she unfortunately vents her anger on Katie by telling her to go away and thumping her. I shout at her for this and threaten her with no television tomorrow if she doesn't settle down. After a few protests and threats from Hazel, she eventually finishes her words.

Immediately after that she starts another pretend game. She is now 'Snap' the black and white Police horse and Katie is her 'man'. Very funny listening to their 'pretend' voices. This continues until bath time.

(Mrs Farthing, parent diary, February 1988, Reception)

Mrs Farthing thus illustrates a strongly supportive mother juggling with the challenge of managing the complex identities of her two children. With regard to Hazel, Mr and Mrs Farthing faced a particular dilemma between appreciating her creativity and imagination and being concerned about the extent of her absorption in a world of her own and her determination that seemed to be associated with it.

Hazel, Reception, relationships among friends and in the playground

Hazel's self-absorption and determination was reflected in the nature of her friendships. At home, she had the great advantage of having a friend next door, Amy, who was of the same age and in her class at school. They generally got on well together, although Hazel was a bit disdainful of some of the more traditional girls' games favoured by Amy. Mrs Farthing explained:

> They play quite a lot together. When Amy has been here for tea or whatever, if she says 'come on Hazel, let's play mums and dads and babies', Hazel sort of looks at her as if to say 'not that old rubbish' sort of thing, 'come on I want to be a horse or something'. They are not on the same wavelength in that sort of way.
> (Mrs Farthing, parent diary, July 1988, Reception)

As her mother saw it, such was Hazel's own imagination and desire to control her play that she 'seemed not to need other children terribly'.

> Hazel can relate well when playing with friends in so far as she likes to be able to 'control' the game. If she loses this 'control' she either becomes frustrated and cross or totally ignores the other person and carries on playing alone. In fact, if she is very involved especially with a 'pretend' game, she seems to be able to play happily with or without the co-operation and participation of friends. This is not to say that she does not enjoy playing with other children, she certainly does, especially if it is with a special friend or a much loved cousin.
> (Mrs Farthing, parent diary, July 1988, Reception)

At school she did not develop strong peer-group relationships, preferring to play on her own terms. It was noticeable that, although she often played with Amy and Mary, she did not particularly align with other girls. As her mother explained, her activities provided a more personal form of expression:

> Hazel knows she is a little girl and if we are playing something she will say, 'I am not so and so. I am Hazel Farthing. I am a little girl'. She knows that – but she is not a 'typical little girl', liking very pretty, pretty things, wanting to play Mummies and Daddies and playing with dolls. That is not her at all.
> She seems to like playing rough boyish games more. She loves to be running around the place and going mad.
> I think she needs this terribly. She seems to be so pent up sometimes and I think this has something to do with her not being able to sit down and concentrate. It is too much to think about when she wants to get away and do what she wants to do.
> (Mrs Farthing, parent interview, July 1988, Reception)

However, Hazel had a particularly special friendship during the year with a boy called Billy who seemed to accept his role in her games. They could often be seen playing imaginative role-play or chasing games in the playground. Towards the end of the year, when most of the children had become five years old and such declarations were in fashion among the girls, Hazel even reported to her mother that she loved Billy and intended to marry him. A little later, the declaration of affection was for a boy called Edward.

The relationship with Billy was certainly on Hazel's terms and lasted as long as she required it. However, although on the margins of the friendship networks amongst the girls, she was not completely cut off from them and from awareness, for instance, of 'kiss-chase' games.

More commonly though, Hazel would attract other children into her imaginary games – or exclude them if she saw fit. For instance, one playtime Hazel, Amy and Sarah were playing 'cows' at Hazel's instigation. Hazel was the 'Mummy cow' and shoe swapping was involved in some important part of the game to do with hooves. This attracted Mary and Sally who came across and asked to play but Hazel would not let them. 'No, its my game', she said.

Hazel was seen by other children as being unusual but amusing, and as determined in a way that could occasionally make her seem obsessive. By not offering the reciprocity which underpins most childhood friendships, Hazel placed herself on the margins of the main playground peer groups, but she seemed perfectly content with, and protective of, her independence.

Hazel, Reception, relationships with Mrs Powell in the classroom

Hazel's first schoolteacher was Mrs Powell, who, as we saw in Chapter 2, provided a steady routine for the children with plenty of work on basic skills. She was caring and her manner was calm. She was also firm.

Mrs Powell was interested by Hazel, but she did not feel that she really understood her. This uncertainty began at the start of the year and continued throughout. An incident recorded in fieldnotes during the Autumn Term illustrates Hazel's sense of vulnerability at school, but also her trust of Mrs Powell. However, Mrs Powell also revealed the difficulties which she faced in socializing Hazel into the routines and expectations of the class.

> Hazel had been looking about the classroom and not beginning her work. She played with her hair. Then she went over to Mrs Powell. They talked and Mrs Powell gave Hazel a hug. I talked to Mrs Powell afterwards and she explained that Hazel had said she was cold and she 'wanted a cuddle!'.

Mrs Powell went on:

> I haven't quite got to the bottom of her. She doesn't do what you ask her to do straight away, it's quite a struggle. It was a lot easier this morning actually but usually if I want her to do something I have to catch her about three times.
>
> If she's drawing, she'll draw face after face after face and be really interested in what she's doing then. It doesn't have to be anything to do with what you've asked her to do. She just thinks, 'I'll do this,' and gets really interested in it, ... and playing at the sand she has all the little zoo animals out and she puts them on the draining board and talks to them and has a little imaginative game with them. But she doesn't really involve anybody else. So it will be interesting to see how she turns out.
> (Fieldnotes and teacher interview, November 1987, Reception)

Later in the year Mrs Powell's view was much the same, though perhaps with a little less indulgence.

> Hazel is a strange little girl really. She'd be quite happy all day just doing whatever it is that takes her fancy at the time. She's not really relating very well to grown ups or other children at the moment.
> (Mrs Powell, teacher interview, March 1988, Reception)

Despite Mrs Powell's comments about her relationships with her peers, Hazel nevertheless very much enjoyed having fun with other children at school. One incident which illustrates this well concerned two jigsaw puzzles, one of a boy and one of a girl, which Hazel was required to complete. She completed most of the puzzles and then discovered that the pieces were interchangeable and that this attribute, if used selectively, could produce sex reversals. The result was great hilarity amongst the children sitting with her.

As Hazel faced school tasks which she disliked or did not fully understand, she was quite prepared to engage in a little routine deviance and mischief. For instance, fieldnotes of one occasion record how Hazel had been drifting around the classroom but was then issued with her writing book by Mrs Powell.

> Hazel was then expected to sit at a particular table to practise letter formation and the sound 'k'. She was resigned to this task, but certainly not pleased to be asked to do it. As she wandered towards the designated table, she began to curl the corners of her book. Mrs Powell interjected in a shocked tone, 'Hazel, Hazel, what *are* you doing?' and the classroom hushed as the children turned to see what was happening. Mrs Powell asserted: 'Hazel, that's not what you are supposed to do with your book. Open it up properly, find a clean page and start please'.
>
> Hazel, was then seated at the writing table, but was only fitfully engaged with her task. She was working alone and getting frustrated, banging her pencil, looking around, glaring and, just occasionally, forming a 'k' by writing a 'c' followed by a line down the left hand side [see Document 5.1 overleaf]. She was bored.
>
> Amongst the other children there was one boy, Damien, who was also a little distracted and was pushing his sharp pencil into a rubber. Hazel looked across, grinned and said in a very loud and teacherly voice, 'And what is Damien doing?'. It was clear that she was trying to get Damien into trouble, but, as it happened, Mrs Powell was heavily engaged elsewhere. Damien gave Hazel a hurt look and turned the damaged rubber over.
>
> Mrs Powell then approached the table and began to give Hazel a thorough explanation and demonstration of the correct way to form a 'k'. She wrote the words 'a keeper' and 'a kite' for Hazel to copy under. Hazel did this, with pictures and practised writing 'k's for a few minutes.
>
> Hazel then approached Mrs Powell and showed her book.
>
> Hazel: Can I stop now?
> Mrs Powell: Alright, you've tried hard now. I'll get you a tracing card next time and you can practise some more.
>
> Hazel moved off. She went around the classroom, looking about at the activities, sucking her fingers and with a sense of release.
> (Fieldnotes, March 1988, Reception)

By the end of the year, Mrs Powell was trying to get Hazel to come to terms with the need to concentrate on her work and in this she attempted to affirm Hazel and build her confidence whilst still being firm with her. Hazel seemed very aware of this and was particularly conscious of the pressure which was being exerted for her to complete maths and writing tasks. Just before the Parents' Evening in the Summer Term, Mrs Farthing asked Hazel what Mrs Powell would say about her. The conversation went like this:

> Hazel: Oh, Mrs Powell thinks I am lovely.
> Mrs Farthing: And what will she say about your work?
> Hazel: Ummmm ...Well, I don't like maths. I'm not very good at that. Ummmm ... I don't like writing. ... Yes, I do like writing but I don't like maths.
> (Mrs Farthing, parent diary, June 1988, Reception)

As Hazel's comments suggest, by the Summer Term, she began to see the possibilities of writing as a means of expression and she was to exploit this in later years. However, her attitude to maths was one of bored incomprehension and disinterest – for the tasks with which she was presented conveyed no meaning and made no connections for her. She was far happier thinking independently, on her own agenda. One example of this occurred when a visitor talked to her about some grass which was on a classroom display and explained that it was 'a collection of grass'. Hazel said, 'I think it's wheat'. The visitor replied that he thought wheat was bigger but that the display 'might be different *sorts* of grass'. To this Hazel confidently said, 'Well, it might be different sorts of *wheat*'. She then drifted off into the book corner to read, sucking her fingers all the time.

Mrs Powell was but the first teacher to be both fascinated and frustrated by Hazel's capabilities. In Mrs Powell's case she experienced the two feelings in almost equal measure – a

Document 5.1 *Hazel, writing and phonics exercise on 'k', March 1988, Reception*

position which was shared and appreciated by Hazel's parents. As Mrs Farthing explained:

> Mrs Powell appreciated Hazel's good qualities and her concentration and involvement in things. She said she thought Hazel had something very unique and perhaps it had to be nurtured rather than squashed. It made me think about other aspects rather than just discipline, although she does obviously have to learn that a certain amount, otherwise she won't ever learn.
> (Mrs Farthing, parent interview, March 1988, Reception)

Hazel, Reception, progress in classroom learning

Despite her reluctance to tackle learning tasks which she found difficult, Hazel did make considerable progress during the year. This was particularly so with her reading and, gradually, with her writing. Progress in maths was a rather different story. Throughout, Hazel's imagination and creativity in picture, story and play were a great source of strength and fulfilment to her. The two major influences on this progress were the various skills and strategies of her teacher and her mother. We can look at this with regard to reading, writing and maths in particular.

One of the influences on Hazel's learning to read was the routine and 'tried and tested' methods of Mrs Powell's practice. Although Mrs Powell offered a relatively safe and sympathetic environment for Hazel's early attempts to read, as we saw earlier, both the reading schemes and 'word tins' of Mrs Powell's practice were frequently a source of frustration for Hazel. One response which her mother described was:

> If Hazel is feeling tired and she comes across a word she doesn't know and I don't immediately tell her, she says, 'Oh, it's all rubbish' and throws the book on the floor.
> (Mrs Farthing, parent interview, July 1988, Reception)

However, Hazel's mother became very sensitive to this possible reaction and found ways of avoiding such responses whilst still making progress. For instance, one Sunday:

> Lazy morning. Children have their treat, eggy toast (French toast) whilst watching cartoons. Later on we read school book, Hazel doesn't want to do her words, so we read some other stories. I try to point out particular words to Hazel e.g. 'Oh look Hazel, you've got that word in your tin haven't you?' This seems to work.
> (Mrs Farthing, parent diary, February 1988, Reception)

Similarly,

> I think she tends to think of her word tin as being something she has got to do, which is unfortunate really. Sometimes I forget about that completely and I get a book out and do something different. Then I try to get her to go through the words or we make up silly sentences and things like that and play different games.
> (Mrs Farthing, parent interview, March 1988, Reception)

Towards the end of the year a new level of reading enjoyment had been achieved and another strategy for learning new words was established. We might note, in the diary account below, the pleasure (and status) which is offered to Hazel through reading to Katie, the dignity which is preserved by allowing her to take more personal control of learning words and the breadth of interest and enjoyment which is opened up by regular use of the local library.

> Hazel loves to be read stories and is very pleased with herself when she knows a book well and can read it to Katie. She seems to really love books and will happily sit down and read with me, rather than go through her word tin. We now have a new approach to the word tin. Hazel now goes through it on her own and shows me any word she doesn't know or remember. She seems to like having the responsibility of this and obviously feels less pressurized. We have joined Easthampton Library and go there about every two weeks. This is thought of as quite an outing as there are toys and puzzles to play with there as well as books to choose to take home.
> (Mrs Farthing, parent diary, July 1988, Reception)

Mrs Powell's end of year report that Hazel had made 'very steady progress' with her reading clearly reflected the joint effort of herself and Mrs Farthing. In essence, Mrs Powell provided a clear structure of goals and basic instruction at school whist Mrs Farthing mediated and complemented this provision with encouragement and strategies to support Hazel in overcoming her impatience and frustration.

In writing, it was a similar story but one in which Mrs Powell's support of Hazel was fuelled by Hazel's imagination and desire to express herself in both visual and written forms. At the start of the year Hazel was completing the standard exercise of doing a picture and then 'writing over' the caption written by her teacher. The example of Document 5.2 overleaf is from September 1987.

As Hazel became more proficient, she was required to 'write under' her teacher's words (Documents 5.3 and 5.4) and, although Hazel sometimes found this boring and did not complete the tasks, she also found that her pictures and writing were a means of expression which she could use for her own purposes. Her divergent imagination and humour became more and more apparent and her drawings were admired and praised by Mrs Powell, other children and by her parents.

Mrs Powell was thus able to officially record that Hazel's written work is 'very imaginative' although she also wrote that 'the presentation of it varies'.

Writing thus provides an example of an activity through which, in association with the progress made at reading, Mrs Powell was able to harness Hazel's imagination and concentration to achieve important developments in terms of skills and powers of expression

Perhaps this was just as well, for, as we have seen, except for in some forms of imaginative play, Hazel continued to be somewhat disconnected from the rest of the class and many of its activities throughout the year. Hazel's engagement with maths was weak, to put it mildly. In the case of this subject there was little linkage between the maths curriculum which Mrs Powell offered and the imaginative world which Hazel favoured. Maths activities often consisted of practical sorting or manipulation of apparatus to carry out simple sums or of the completion of preprinted worksheets for measurement activities. Examples of such worksheets are provided below (see Documents 5.5, 5.6 and 5.7).

Document 5.2 *Hazel, picture and writing on 'people in the car', September 1987, Reception*

Mrs Powell acknowledged that, for such exercises, it was necessary to 'sit with Hazel and do it with her'. If Hazel was left alone to do maths, the most likely outcome was either withdrawal, which would probably involve gazing about, talking, sucking fingers and playing with her hair, or a redefinition of the activity. In one classic example of the latter Hazel had been required to count some small plastic pigs which were being used as maths

The boys are going for a picnic. One is flying.

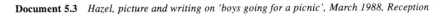

Document 5.3 *Hazel, picture and writing on 'boys going for a picnic', March 1988, Reception*

Document 5.4 *Hazel, picture and writing about 'baby dragons', May 1988, Reception*

apparatus. Mrs Powell structured the task with her and went to attend to other children. When she returned Hazel was talking to the pigs and they were all in role within a game of 'pig families'. No counting had been done.

Despite Hazel's general reluctance to talk about the subject she disliked, her parents tried to support and interest her. Mrs Farthing recounted 'the first time ever' that Hazel spoke about it:

> Yesterday she mentioned she had been doing some maths and that was the first time ever. I said, 'Oh, were you doing adding up?' and I played this little game. But she got a bit confused with large numbers like 23, thinking 2 and 3 were a larger number and I was explaining about adding them up. That was the first time really, and counting. She doesn't really discuss maths at all. (Mrs Farthing, parent interview, March 1988, Reception)

The fact that Hazel would not often talk about maths meant that it was difficult for her parents to help her. Mrs Farthing in fact, felt constrained by her own insecurity in maths,

Document 5.5   *Hazel, sample of number task, October 1987, Reception*

How many conkers

balance a roller?

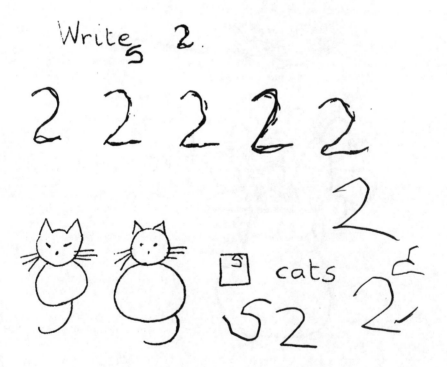

2 conkers.

Document 5.6 *Hazel, sample of weighing task, January 1988, Reception*

Write 2.

2 2 2 2 2

cats

Document 5.7 *Hazel, sample of number task, January 1988, Reception*

though the subject was one of her husband's strengths. One of the few occasions on which Hazel did talk to her parents about maths during her Reception year did result in a growth in confidence, with her mother using the same sorts of strategies which she had adopted to support Hazel's reading. However, such occasions were not common for maths. Mrs Farthing recounted:

When I went to fetch her from school I said 'Did you have a nice day?' and she said 'No – I don't want to talk about it,' ... that sort of thing. I said 'Oh, what didn't you like?'. She said, 'I hated school today'. I said, 'What did you hate about it?' and she said, 'We had horrible, horrible maths.' She comes out with things like that, 'I hate maths'.

I thought, 'Oh dear', and stepped back and didn't say anything about it for a little while until she had cooled down a bit.

I talked about it with her and we did a little bit at home – I was playing games with her, a bit like doing tables but not really. We were playing with some toys, and Katie was joining in.

Then they obviously had maths another day and either Mrs Powell or somebody had sat down with her and gone over things and she had been able to do it OK. She came home and when I said 'Did you have a good day at school?' it was, 'Yes, yes we had maths and it was lovely'. It was all right then. Then we went over it again, just a few simple sums again and I said 'Yes, you're very good, you're going to be good at maths like Daddy', (not saying that I wasn't, but just, you know ...). 'Yes I am, Mummy,' she agreed.

(Mrs Farthing, parent interview, July 1988, Reception)

Both Mrs Powell and Mrs Farthing thus attempted to support Hazel's engagement and learning in maths, though they were not successful in sustaining Hazel's interest for long.

Hazel, Reception, identity and learning in the Reception year

Perhaps the most important aspect of Hazel's identity in the Reception class was her love of play and of imaginary games into which she could herself step. A key element of Hazel's play with sister or peers was, as we saw earlier, the control which Hazel liked to exert. I asked Mrs Farthing about the relation between this control in play and control in learning. She replied:

I think it is a lot to do with Hazel's character. She is a very independent child. Last night something happened ... . I was saying, 'Come on, we have got to settle down now. Come and sit down and let's have a story,' and she said something like, 'I am going to do exactly what I want to.' It was almost a case of 'Go away, it is my life, I'll do what I want,' sort of thing. She does this all the time. I approach her a bit like approaching a time bomb at times, you know what I mean, but then again you have to lay down the law sometimes as well.

She likes to play games with other children and she is pretty easy if the game is going the way that she likes. Even if she is not in control she is quite happy about that, but if somebody wants to play something she is not interested in, if she is really enjoying the game as it was, then she gets stroppy. If she is not particularly interested in it anyway, she will just go off and do her own thing. She is not terribly worried in that respect.

I think she is going to find learning difficult in lots of ways because of this sort of antagonistic view of everything ... it is almost a case of you have to step back from Hazel rather than try to push her, because the more you push the more she rebels. I can see terrible problems as a teenager looming, you know.

I can see the same characteristics in her as a baby developing now into a child ... and that determination can stand her in good stead sometimes and it can also work against her, very much so.

It can go one of two ways next year. I must confess I am not looking forward to it in lots of ways.

(Mrs Farthing, parent interview, July 1988, Reception)

As we shall see, Mrs Farthing was right to be uneasy about Hazel's experience in her next class.

Mrs Farthing had clear views on gender and was very clear that she wanted Hazel and Katie to grow up 'as people, not just as girls'. She had been concerned about equal opportunities since her own childhood and wanted the children to fulfil themselves without discrimination. She was pleased with Hazel's stance:

> I don't think she even thinks of herself as being male or female, she just thinks of herself as being a person, and that is something I would encourage anyway.
> (Mrs Farthing, parent interview, March 1988, Reception)

Overall then, we have a picture of a four-year-old child with a strong, internal locus of control and a developed imagination which she was determined to fulfil. These two facets of her identity were beginning to have profound impact upon her learning as, through the experience of school, she encountered people and activities which required her to adjust her goals and actions. As we have seen above in the discussion of Hazel's learning progress-where her need for autonomy and her imaginative response could be harnessed to curriculum aims and processes, classroom learning took place. Where a disjunction remained, Hazel tended to reject tasks and very little learning took place.

Hazel's sense of self, her identity, arguably changed relatively little over the year. She began with a strong independence and determination and she retained these attributes at the end. Her school experience of both curriculum and peer culture confirmed that, for her, whilst enjoyment was associated with personal expression, boredom was often connected with tasks and activities which other people required of her.

Matrix 5.1 *Hazel's Reception year; a summary matrix*

Family relationships	Peer-group relationships	Teacher relationships	Identity	Learning
Close and supportive relationship between Hazel and both parents who see her strengths and weaknesses clearly.	One friend, Amy, lives next door but Hazel disdainful of many 'girls' games.	Mrs Powell interested in Hazel but also puzzled by her. Sees the positive potential in her determination and imagination but regards her as difficult to understand and to motivate.	Hazel presents a clear and very individual identity in all settings – she is independent and often absorbed in creative, imaginative play.	Considerable progress with reading, gradual with writing.
Diverse family activities.	Hazel favours self-directed play into which others may enter on her terms. Often self-sufficient within her imagined worlds.	Mrs Powell provides a routine curriculum for development of the basics – which Hazel finds boring. Towards the end of the year, Mrs Powell becomes more assertive and increasingly requires Hazel to conform.	Often seen as very 'determined' – in the playground, classroom and, since babyhood, at home.	Mrs Powell's system of reading schemes and word tin is complemented by flexible response to Hazel's needs at home.
Mrs Farthing describes Hazel's 'determined' character, its development from birth and her attempts to help Hazel adjust to others. Mrs Farthing finds Hazel difficult to manage at times.	Does not develop a circle of close friends at school.	Hazel finds ways of evading, having fun or partially withdrawing from routine classroom activities.	Hazel's play seen by other children as unusual and sometimes amusing. However, some are cautious of her.	By end of year, Hazel is reading simple books and taking great pleasure in reading to Katie.
Her imagination and sense of fun nurtured at home. Some shared amusement regarding school.	Hazel sometimes alone in class or playground.	Sometimes mischievous in class.	Play is distinct from that of mainstream girls' culture which does not interest Hazel.	Hazel finds writing boring but enjoys drawing pictures. These are praised as 'very imaginative' and Hazel begins to use the picture and writing task as a means of expression.
Affection and rivalry between Hazel and younger sister, Katie. They often play together, particularly within Hazel's imaginative play.	A special friend towards the end of year is Billy, who accepts her rules and whom Hazel says she 'loves'.	Mrs Powell fascinated but also frustrated by Hazel's capabilities and withdrawal. Considers she has qualities to be nurtured not squashed. Parents appreciative of this.		Very slow development of maths. Hazel withdraws, day dreams or converts the task into play. Maths seems to have no meaning for her and she is sometimes distressed by it.
Katie is often quieter and more compliant within the family. Hazel is sometimes annoyed by her.	Towards the end of the year, other children, especially girls, are increasingly attracted into Hazel's imaginative play, such as 'cows' and 'Mummies and Daddies'. However, Hazel still excludes them if they do not conform to her rules.	Hazel tells her parents that Mrs Powell 'thinks I'm lovely'.		Hazel is particularly keen on imaginative play in the sand or home corner.

5.4 HAZEL IN HER YEAR 1

Hazel, Year 1, relationships with parents at home

The diary entries for Year 1 vividly convey the warmth of Hazel's family life, whilst the demands and routines of everyday living continued to press. For instance:

> Rob arrives home from work earlier than usual, brings us all a drink. Children come in bed for a cuddle, end up getting up late. Bit of a rush to get both girls and myself washed and dressed in time. Hazel and Katie much too interested in playing than helping. End up shouting at them every five minutes to hurry.
> (Mrs Farthing, parent diary, October 1988, Year 1)

A family outing to a nearby zoo provided a conjunction of interests, with the children becoming fascinated by the animals and Mr and Mrs Farthing enjoying and extending the excitement of their children. As we shall see later, Hazel's capacity for visual expression of real and imagined animals developed considerably during the year and visits such as the one described below are likely to have been very important.

> In the afternoon we go out to the zoo. We start off with the Reptile House. The children are fascinated. We tell them about the different sorts of reptiles and about how some of them, such as the iguanas, look like miniature prehistoric monsters. Spend a lot of time watching the turtles swimming about and then go on to the aquarium. Both children love the section that looks like a rock pool with aesop prawns, crabs and sea anemones, although they know most of the different types of fishes. We then go on to Katie's favourite, the bats in the Nocturnal House. End up in the Elephant House watching 'Sally' eating her tea.
> Drive home, children in very good humour, making up their own stories about when 'Mr Funny' went to the zoo, something about a tarantula laughing so hard, he nearly laughed his legs off. Hazel tells Katie her favourite joke about a one-eyed dinosaur. Evening carries on a prehistoric note, by special request Rob draws various types of dinosaurs for the children. I cook tea. Decide that this half term holiday might be a good time to take children to Natural History Museum in London to show them the Dinosaur section there. I take children upstairs for their bath, hair wash and story.
> (Mrs Farthing, parent diary, October 1988, Year 1)

Hazel's parents also continued to be active in supporting Hazel as she encountered new challenges at school. They tried to empathize with Hazel's experience, to help her interpret it and to adapt herself as necessary. This was often done with a light and humorous touch. One example of this concerns Hazel's relationship with other children in the playground on an occasion when she was being teased. As Mrs Farthing explained:

> I fetch Hazel from school. Ask Hazel what sort of day she's had, 'terrible' she says. I ask her 'why?'. Apparently two or three boys in her class have been making up nicknames for her, the offending name being '*Hazel, Tazle Wazle*'. I have to stifle a laugh. Explain about sticks and stones and tell her to thank her lucky stars her name isn't Higginbottom. She thinks that this is highly amusing. Rob tells her that he was sometimes called funny names at school.
> (Mrs Farthing, parent diary, October 1988, Year 1)

Unfortunately, as we shall see, Hazel's relationship with her teacher, Miss Scott, was somewhat strained for much of the year and Mrs Farthing was particularly concerned to help Hazel find ways of developing more confidence. Mrs Farthing described one such conversation:

> Later in the morning ask Hazel about school again. What she does and does not like, she says that she likes making patterns with Multi-link bricks, but she hated doing 'writing sort of

maths'. I ask why and she says that she doesn't understand it. I ask how she feels when she doesn't understand something and she says it makes her feel cross and like crying at the same time. Suggest to her that when she doesn't understand something to ask Miss Scott to go over it again slowly so that she can try to understand. Unfortunately she seemed to think that she would be shouted at if she asked. I asked what she did then, if she didn't understand something and she was too scared to ask. She said, 'I just suck my fingers and think about something else'!
(Mrs Farthing, parent diary, October 1988, Year 1)

Mrs Farthing offered Hazel support for reading, writing and some maths. This was provided both as opportunities arose and in more specific sessions. There was always a great deal of encouragement as Mrs Farthing attempted to help Hazel come to terms with the need to apply herself to learning about number and the skills of writing. However, as she acknowledged, this was not always easy.

She likes doing the puzzle type maths but she doesn't like doing the sums ... . If I try to encourage her, like when we hair-wash on Sunday night, we also used to count a minute, 60 seconds, with the conditioner on. We all sat down the other day and we had two dice each and we were throwing dice all over the table and Hazel was counting up the numbers on the dice to see if she beat us and this sort of thing – that was quite good.

She can't seem to cope with when she goes wrong, she gets terribly upset and wants to rub it out and destroy it almost.

She has written birthday cards and things, but usually she wants me to write it out first and then copy it, she won't actually have a go.
(Mrs Farthing, parent interview, November 1988, Year 1)

Hazel's parents remained close and supportive in their relationship with her during her Year 1 and this was particularly important to Hazel in the light of the relatively poor relationship which she developed with her teacher. Indeed, whilst sharing a concern that Hazel needed to apply herself to her learning at school, there were some considerable differences in the perceptions of Miss Scott and Hazel's parents. In essence, whilst Mr and Mrs Farthing saw Hazel's imagination, humour and divergence as a source of quality, enjoyment and identity, Miss Scott, for much of the year, found such attributes hard to connect with and to understand and she was unable to draw on them within her classroom practice.

One particularly vivid example of this communication problem between Hazel and Miss Scott and of the role of Mr and Mrs Farthing, was provided by the following episode from the Autumn Term 1988. The diary records Mr Farthing spending some time at home sorting and discussing his collection of fossils and minerals with Hazel. A little later, fieldnotes of playground activities show how Hazel was collecting pebbles to form 'her own collection' which, she explained to her friends, had magical properties. It seems that this collection was then left overnight on the floor of the classroom changing area, by Hazel's coat-peg. Mrs Farthing then takes up the story:

Take Hazel to school this morning. Go inside with her, I had to start doing this with her again at the beginning of term, but would rather do this than get her upset at the beginning of the day.

As we walk in Miss Scott has just noticed a pile of stones under Hazel's peg and found out that they belong to Hazel. We both get 'ticked off' by Miss Scott. I felt five years old again, but it was quite funny. I ask Hazel, 'would she kindly refrain from bringing stones into school and getting me into trouble with *her* teacher?'.
(Mrs Farthing, parent diary, October 1988, Year 1)

Here we see one of Hazel's imaginative games having been developed from an experience at home with her father and extended in the playground with her peers. However, a connection with her teacher was not made.

Hazel, Year 1, relationships with siblings at home

Hazel's relationship with her younger sister, Katie, did not change from that of her Reception year and the pattern of affection and rivalry which was noted.

> I think Hazel is looking forward to Katie starting school in September. She's very proud that she's going to have a little sister at school. .... But she's also very jealous of her, always has been – and she really has had no reason to be.
> (Mrs Farthing, parent interview, November 1988, Year 1)

However, the differences between Hazel and Katie were now described in terms of more distinctive strategies or approaches to new situations. Mrs Farthing foresaw the consequence of these strategies as applied to school:

> Katie wants to please more, whereas Hazel wants to do what she wants to do. Katie ... will want to please the teacher, whereas Hazel, although she wants to be praised by the teacher, she will still want to do it in her own way.
> (Mrs Farthing, parent interview, November 1988, Year 1)

Mrs Farthing believed that the willingness of Katie to conform was sometimes seen as a problem by Hazel, because it undercut her own position.

> I think that gets to Hazel sometimes ... I think she looks at Katie and sees this little goodey, goodey and she just wants to flatten her. I love them both the same anyway, they're just potentially different characters.
> (Mrs Farthing, parent interview, November 1988, Year 1)

Here then we see Hazel's identity forming in relation to that of her sister. As in many families, each child was valued in her own way – but part of the distinctiveness of each developed and was defined in terms of the other.

Hazel, Year 1, relationships among friends and in the playground

The year began somewhat unfortunately for Hazel because her two closest friends were no longer in her class at school. Billy, the boy whom she had 'wanted to marry' the previous term, was older than Hazel and had been allocated to a different class. The parents of Amy, her next-door neighbour, had decided to move Amy to a nearby private school so that their paths began to diverge.

Hazel thus began the year rather alone at school and without a close friend. However, given her capacity for immersion in imaginary worlds of her own making, this was not necessarily a problem for her.

> Dinner time playtime and Hazel is alone in the playground, as she was at morning playtime. She seems perfectly happy and has collected some leaves which she carries around. She is singing 'Oh, I do like to be beside the seaside' loudly and without any regard for other children and their activities. Some give her slightly puzzled looks. Later, she comes across and drops some seeds from the sycamore tree on to my notebook as I write. 'Look, there's a spider!' she laughs and is delighted.
> (Fieldnotes, September 1988, Year 1)

> Hazel is sitting in the gutter by the edge of grass, alone. She has leaves, twigs and grass. As I approach she declares that she is 'making a bonfire.' She asks, 'Can you get a flame from rubbing twigs together?' She seems perfectly happy, though she is on her own.
> (Fieldnotes, October 1988, Year 1)

Mrs Farthing explained that, at this point of the year, Hazel 'hadn't really found any one special friend' though she would 'fit in' with other children if necessary. For instance, when Mrs Farthing went off to college Hazel sometimes walked to school with Robert and his mother.

> I drop Hazel off at Robert's house and they walk to school together. They get on but it is almost as if, I won't say a relation, but it is almost like a cousin, it is not someone special, just someone who is there that she knows if you know what I mean.
> (Mrs Farthing, parent interview, November 1988, Year 1)

However, as the year developed Hazel began to develop more friendships, particularly with other girls. This was at a time when more distinctive activities were developing between the boys and girls, with the greatest contrast being between the chasing games of the boys, which tended to dominate the space, and the skipping, role-play and gymnastic games of the girls. In this context, Hazel began to attract some girls into her imaginary games. Harriet, Nimra and Alice became particular favourites and were often seen with Hazel playing diverse variations on 'Mummies and Daddies, sisters and babies'. This game had story lines which emerged through the process of play itself and used props and personnel with great creative pragmatism.

Hazel, still regarded as a little bit odd by some children, remained vulnerable to some teasing in the playground. For instance, on one occasion in February 1989 Hazel reported that Robert had 'called her a pumpkin' and that the boys in the playground had 'tried to get her'. However, she was protected by Nimra and Alice who 'shooed the boys away'.

Happily for Hazel, these friendships developed strongly during the year. In part, this was probably because Hazel became more tolerant of other children at school and more willing to play with them on a reciprocal basis. However, some aspects of her friendships, particularly with Harriet, were also founded in the children's shared experience of Miss Scott and, increasingly, of boys. Hazel's friends were neither the high-attaining group in school terms nor the most 'popular' amongst the peer group as a whole. They thus shared a basic structural position and some common problems in coming to terms with school life. As Hazel experienced difficulties in her relationship with Miss Scott, so she found a source of support in her peers. As the boys developed games which were in a sense 'oppositional' to the girls, so the girls needed and developed their solidarity. Hazel thus began to share more experiences and to have a stronger basis for the reciprocity which underpins friendship. Mrs Farthing began to explore this in her diary and she also elaborated in interview:

> Hazel's special friends are Harriet, Nimra and Alice. I think those friendships, especially the one with Harriet, have been her saving grace, and have made life at school bearable.
> (Mrs Farthing, parent diary, July 1989, Year 1)

> Harriet and Hazel – they're very close. She comes home and talks about her. Harriet goes riding apparently and Hazel'd love to go riding and things like that. ... She goes over and sees her sometimes. Harriet has been here a couple of times.
>   It's helped Hazel to cope with the year I think, the friendships, because I think ... I think she's frightened of Miss Scott. It's almost like a camaraderie with her mates, it's a 'them and us' situation, and I think that's given her confidence having these friends.
>   She's definitely more outgoing with her friendships now. There's a few, I noticed at her party, there were people like Mary who she used to be very friendly with and she's always been to every other birthday party and I said, 'Who do you want to come? What about Mary?' and she said, 'No, she's not my friend anymore'. It wasn't that she didn't get on but she wasn't a close one. And they were nearly all girls this time. It's changing. She used to have a lot more mixture of friends. Whether or not that will change, I don't know. That's different. At one time,

she didn't give a damn about whether she played with girls or boys, but now she plays more with girls. She's beginning to treat them as different, whereas at one time she didn't care. I think perhaps she's joining the clan, with this 'boys are stupid', or whatever it is they say to each other.

I think it's a case of she wants to belong now, where she didn't care before. And I think for her own preservation in school life, she needs to belong.
(Mrs Farthing, parent interview, July 1989, Year 1)

Hazel, Year 1, relationships with Miss Scott in the classroom

Hazel found it hard to develop a relationship with Miss Scott, and vice versa.

Having inherited children from two Reception classes, one of which she regarded as 'noisy and poorly controlled', Miss Scott began the year with a conscious strategy to establish her authority and a firm routine. However, as we saw in Chapter 2, Miss Scott felt stressed and devalued in her professional role and her classroom organization and teaching style were not operating in the ways in which she would herself have wished. Her situation was thus a source of great frustration to her and unfortunately she often acted in ways which the children found unpredictable and upsetting.

From soon after the start of term, Hazel became reluctant to go to school. She was tearful and unwilling to leave her mother.

Within the classroom, Hazel showed many signs of withdrawal and a sense that this was was what was expected of her also seemed to evolve.

Miss Scott takes the register and the children have been asked to sit on the carpet. Hazel is at the rear, behind a table, and seems distracted. After the register, tasks are set for the session. Hazel watches from the periphery of the group and seems both overlooked and content.
(Fieldnotes, September 1988, Year 1)

After Service. Miss Scott is sorting out groups of children who are to plan for various activities. Hazel sits with her paper, staring about, fiddling with her hair, sucking her thumb. She is not engaged in the planning activity at all. Nimra, who is sitting next to Hazel, starts to talk to her and to explain what she has to do.
(Fieldnotes, November 1988, Year 1).

Hazel has sat with Mrs Smart (a parent helper) to get guidance in doing her planning. She then goes to the toilet and back to Mrs Smart. She has not yet done anything today. Miss Scott doesn't appear to have noticed or, perhaps, to expect anything different.
(Fieldnotes, January 1989, Year 1).

Mrs Farthing was very worried by the evolving problem of Hazel's reluctance to go to school. It was not only making Hazel unhappy but also resulting in her losing interest in continuation of the reading activities on which she and her mother had worked previously. In the middle of the Autumn term, Mrs Farthing used her diary to express her worry and confusion on what to do – and finished with reference to the children drawing with their father before bedtime:

After tea I ask Hazel what sort of a day she's had. She says, 'not very good because Miss Scott shouts' at her. I ask her, 'how does it make you feel when you are shouted at?' 'Sad', she says. 'I sometimes cry.'

I feel very confused about all this. On one hand, Hazel might be behaving badly at school and *any* teacher might shout at her, but on the other hand, she is my child and I am concerned that someone might be frightening her. I know Hazel well enough to know that shouting does not work – I've tried it often enough myself to know. Also it is different when I shout at Hazel because she knows that even when I'm cross with her that I still love her. But coming from a stranger, although I know she can be exasperating, I feel will do no good. Shouting at her will only get a negative response. I feel that is half the reason why she is disappearing into her own little world. I don't want her 'squashed', although I can appreciate that she can be a difficult child to handle. I shall have to wait and see what happens next, the whole thing might just be a bad settling-in period.

During the evening Hazel, Katie and Rob do some wonderful drawings, mainly of prehistoric animals. Rob takes them up for their bath and story while I make a start on this diary.
(Mrs Farthing, parent diary, October 1988, Year 1)

The gap in understanding between Hazel and Miss Scott was illustrated again a few days later when the children were all asked to draw the characters from the story of Billy Goats Gruff, which they had just heard. Fieldnotes record how Hazel wanted to draw a dinosaur, as she had done with her father:

Hazel wants to do a stegosaurus instead. Miss Scott tries to persuade her to do something from Billy Goats Gruff.

Hazel speaks up and says, 'I know how to do a stegosaurus. My Daddy showed me. They have prickles on their back.'

Miss Scott turns to me and says, 'This is the first time she has spoken, you realise?'

Then to Hazel, 'Why not do Billy Goats Gruff?'

Hazel sits and sulks. She tells me that she can draw 'a beautiful red and yellow dinosaur', says she would like to write a story.

She says, 'I'll write that, "the dragon lived up a mountain and came down to go to a party"'.

She begins to draw a dragon.
(Fieldnotes, October 1988, Year 1)

Here we have an example of Hazel resisting Miss Scott's request to carry out the same task as the other children and, in an act of determined independence, adapting the task to connect it with her own interests and previous experience. As we have seen, Hazel's confidence in her ability to draw a stegosaurus or a 'beautiful red and yellow dinosaur' had been developed by her parents in visits to the zoo and museums, through stories, collections of toy animals and fossils and through Hazel's own play activities and, in particular, her drawings – some later ones of which are reproduced on pages 129, 131 and 136.

Hazel's felt very uneasy about the relationship but, as one would expect from a five-year-old, almost always accepted Miss Scott's judgement – albeit reluctantly. In interview, she explained that, 'Miss Scott keeps telling me off ... because I do something wrong', (Hazel, photo-interview, November 1988, Year 1). However, she also asserted that she 'didn't mean to do things wrong' and clearly did not accept all the reprimands which she received. This was not unconnected to a form of defiance of which her mother was well aware and which Miss Scott was later to term 'stubborn'. Mrs Farthing explained:

Miss Scott said that when Hazel looks at you you know exactly what she is thinking. I said it is just as well she hasn't got the language to go with it because, I know I have seen it in other situations, she treats Miss Scott with contempt. When she sucks her fingers and she looks at her it is almost as if she is saying, 'well you might be bigger than I am and you might be the boss around here but I am not doing what you want me to do.' 'You can beat me black and blue but I am not giving in.' That's the sort of feeling that comes from her, under scowling eyebrows there.
(Mrs Farthing, parent interview, November 1988, Year 1)

Hazel developed strategies beyond that of the various types of withdrawal and defiance which have been described above. One of these was a form of evasion in which Hazel avoided presenting her work to Miss Scott for evaluation. This was made easier by Miss

Scott's practice of sitting to hear readers whilst also checking the children's work at other tasks which had been set. Having work checked was a strongly enforced rule and a queue to see Miss Scott would commonly form towards the end of a work session. Often this queue would be swelled by those children who may have encountered a difficulty and who wished to avoid risk, or, ever positioned towards the rear, by those who were using it as a form of diversion. Hazel often used this strategy.

> It is nearly 10.30 and Miss Scott sits at the reading table, hearing readers. At the same time, a queue of children begins to form to show their sounds work. They have been doing pictures of things beginning in 'c'. The queue is eight children long and Hazel is one of the last. She has done some strong, involved pictures. As I go past, she looks up, sucking her fingers and the playtime bell rings
>
> AP: Hello, what have you done then?
> Hazel: Well, cactus, cockerel, cactuses!
> AP: Very good. That's nice. Are you going to show Miss Scott?
> Hazel: No. ...
>
> Hazel looks at me as if questioning my reaction, puts her book down and slips away to play. Miss Scott still has a queue.
>
> (Fieldnotes, November 1988, Year 1).

The difficulty Miss Scott found in understanding Hazel is well illustrated by one of her records, made at about the same time as the incident above. The entry begins:

> Stubborn. Very quiet and very introverted at first. Wouldn't speak even if encouraged. Response little – stony silence. Parted from mum well (no problems, mum has a very sensible attitude and outlook). But Hazel, is a totally difficult child to assess. Two fingers stuck in her mouth. A very strong will – will not speak if she doesn't want to. Works *extremely* slowly but draws the most amazing pictures – usually dinosaurs and weird, fantastic animals. It is as if her inner thoughts are working overtime.
>
> (Teacher record, November 1988, Year 1)

Miss Scott saw Hazel as, 'the most extraordinary child I have taught for some years' (teacher interview, November 1988, Year 1), but she was not fully aware of Hazel's feelings about coming to school because Mrs Farthing, fearful of upsetting Miss Scott which she believed some other mothers had in the past, had taken a decision not to tell her directly but rather to 'appeal to her better nature' (Mrs Farthing, parent interview, November 1988, Year 1).

In this attempt to work with Miss Scott, Mrs Farthing made contact both in the Autumn Term parents' evening and early in the Spring Term to discuss Hazel's character and needs. Indeed, this did have some positive effect when Miss Scott sought out opportunities to praise Hazel's work, much to her delight.

> Hazel arrived home very happy and pleased with herself. She told us that Miss Scott said that her writing was *brilliant* today – wanted to show us how good it was by writing for quite a time that evening.
>
> (Mrs Farthing, parent diary, January 1989, Year 1)

However, a wholly positive relationship between Miss Scott and Hazel was never really formed and whilst the situation of mutual incomprehension which had formed in the autumn did not worsen during the year, it improved only slowly. Certainly Miss Scott came to appreciate Hazel's unusual abilities in drawing but she was unable to harness these talents as a means of motivating Hazel to engage in her school work. For her part, Hazel continued to evade or withdraw where she could. There was a mesh of coping strategies around mutual acceptance of low expectations. As Mrs Farthing perceived Hazel's propensity to daydream:

> It's a cut off, definitely, a cut off. ... In the school situation, it's more cut off time –'boring'. 'The teacher's talking so I'm going to go into my own world,' sort of thing.
> (Mrs Farthing, parent interview, July 1989, Year 1)

Hazel continued to express her imaginative world through drawings, as illustrated by Documents 5.8 and 5.9 below.

Document 5.8 *Hazel, drawing of creature with big ears, June 1989, Year 1*

Hazel, Year 1, progress in classroom learning

At the start of the year both Miss Scott and Mrs Farthing were concerned about Hazel's learning – Miss Scott because communication was so difficult, Mrs Farthing because Hazel seemed to be making no progress. Mrs Farthing commented on Hazel's reading at home:

> Hazel actually seemed to be going backwards for a little while, such as the words out of her word tin that she knew very well at the end of [the previous] term ... but I thought maybe that was just settling in too. It was almost as if she didn't want to know about reading.
> (Mrs Farthing, parent interview, November 1988, Year 1)

Following discussions at Parents' Evening, Miss Scott adjusted the reading programme to include more stories and Hazel started to make progress again.

Her reading is fine now. I have been reading books at home and we have just started reading big books and having chapters now. We have always had short stories. We have read, or I read, *Charlie and the Chocolate Factory* which went down wonderfully well and she has started looking at the text as I am reading saying 'that says ...' whatever it is.
(Mrs Farthing, parent interview, November 1988, Year 1)

Hazel was particularly excited when she 'moved up' to 'Teddy box' to earn the right to take home a different level of reading book. With some glee she grabbed me to make sure that I knew of this event:

> Hazel: I'll show you where Miss Scott writed, 'Teddy'.
> I'll show you where she writed, 'Teddy'.
> She thumbs through her book.
> Hazel: Teddy!

(Hazel, pupil interview, November 1988, Year 1)

As we have seen, Hazel was not disposed to talk to Miss Scott very much at all. Even when she felt more confident, she was very likely to divert the conversation away from topics which she did not wish to discuss or to subvert the conversation to focus on her own particular interests. A photo-interview which I attempted illustrates this tendency:

> AP: So your favourite is playing with the construction things, ... and then which other things do you like?
> Hazel: Drawing dragons.
> AP: What about the maths and the writing? Which of those do you prefer?
> Hazel: That's Alice.
> AP: Yes, that's Alice. Do you prefer the maths or the writing, or the writing to the maths or are you not sure?
> Hazel: *(Whispering and looking through her book)* Not sure.
> AP: That's a beautiful picture that you did there. (*Pointing to an ullustration in her book*)
> Hazel: I did fireworks.
> AP: Those are fireworks, are they?
> Hazel: There's a frog in the pond, there's me and there's my dragon.
> AP: Beautiful picture and everything ... .
> Hazel: There's my ... another dragon.
> AP: Super, isn't it?
> Hazel: And there's a bumble bee in a beehive and there's a caterpillar; more dragons and meeeeeeee!

(Photo interview, November 1988, Year 1)

However, as Hazel's relationship with Miss Scott slowly developed so too did her approach to work. As the following extracts from teacher records show, by the Summer Term Miss Scott had begun to recognize Hazel's abilities and to develop strategies for drawing her into class activities. Miss Scott wrote:

Hazel has continued to progress at her own set pace – erratic and usually slow. Usually planning and working with her friend Nimra. Hazel is an able child, can work well when she puts her mind to it ... .
She will now speak when spoken to, and occasionally offers some information independently when the mood takes her ... responding more positively in all situations she does not withdraw to herself so much, and is much more cooperative. But the strong will is there still, and she needs to be coaxed into some activities.
(Miss Scott, teacher record, May 1989, Year 1)

Document 5.9 *Hazel, drawing of dragon with head down, June 1989, Year 1*

These coaxing strategies bore some fruit, with Miss Scott becoming very aware of Hazel's untapped potential. Her official report to Mr and Mrs Farthing conveys the same elements of frustration and fascination which had been expressed a year earlier by Mrs Powell. This time though, the balance was more in terms of frustration.

Language development: Although shy and retiring in class oral situations, Hazel is becoming more responsive and will speak with encouragement. Progress in reading has been slower than anticipated, but she reads with awareness and her skill is developing. Enjoys books and will read when she wants to. Completes her writing slowly but is not lacking in skill. Her illustrations are beautiful.

Maths: Her true ability is not revealed because of her working so slowly at activities. Reveals sound understanding of the basic concepts attempted.

Project: Hazel is beginning to show more interest, but needs to be drawn into activities. Rarely completes all that she has planned, often lost in a dreamworld of her own, or spending a lot of time planning but not 'doing'. If the projects were related to Hazel's dream world of dinosaurs and fantastic animals, her contribution would be 100%.

Creative activities: Exceptional detail in drawings reveal her skill and creative abilities. Enjoys all activities in her own particular way.

Social: Hazel is shy with adults but is slowly becoming more confident. She has one or two particular friends but often prefers her own company, though this may be due to the fact that she does take so much time to complete work. Although introverted and shy, she is beginning to open out and reveal her gifted, sensitive personality – slowly.

(Miss Scott, report to parents, summer 1989, Year 1)

Interestingly, as the report shows, by the end of the year Miss Scott had begun to see the possibility of very positive qualities in Hazel – 'true abilities' in maths, 'creative ability' and a 'gifted, sensitive personality'. Indeed, the year ended on a high note with both Miss Scott and Hazel being delighted by each other during a special whole-school topic project at the end of term during which the entire interior of the school hall and corridors were converted to resemble a South American rainforest. All classrooms became creative work-shops for this environmental topic and teachers, children, parents and helpers mixed together in this single, collective mega-project. In these circumstances, Hazel came into her own, taking particular responsibility for drawing and advising other children on the wildlife. She played a key role in creating a particularly spectacular crocodile which was a prominent feature of the 'rainforest trail' which was set up for visitors.

Miss Scott began as a somewhat reluctant participant to the whole-school project but was soon drawn in. Hazel, moreover, played a key role in this because, as the workshop activities developed and the project took shape, she became increasingly eager and animated. Much to Miss Scott's delight communications between herself and Hazel opened up in a way which had not happened previously.

> 'Just look at this! Hazel's made all of it and she's really been talking more than I've ever known her.'
> (Miss Scott, fieldnote, July 1989, Year 1)

Later that year, Mrs Farthing looked back at that time:

> On the last week of the Summer Term, Hazel and Miss Scott – they did the rainforest bit and they really hit it off, both of them.
> And Hazel, I think, felt 'expressed'. She'd had this fortnight of doing exactly what she loved doing and I think Miss Scott had enjoyed it too, although I think she was glad to get back to teaching after two weeks of that, I think they were all going round like zombies the last two days, and I think they both sort of went back to school work with added zest and she actually called me in one day and said, 'Come and look at Hazel's work, it's brilliant and her writing's been good', 'Take it home and show your mum and dad', and they really got on really well and she moved up a box with her reading.
> (Mrs Farthing, parent interview, December 1989, Year 2, recalling Year 1)

Hazel's progress over the year as a whole was thus steady, at best. Whilst her reading moved on, her achievements at writing and maths were limited by her low motivation and tendency to drift or withdraw. Unfortunately the new rapport forged between Miss Scott and Hazel by the rainforest project really came too late to make any significant impact on her overall attainment.

Hazel, identity and learning in Year 1

As in her Reception year, Hazel continued to be distinguished by a combination of inde-pendence, imaginative immersion in a world of her own and determination. However, as we have seen, for most of the year the difficulties of her relationship with Miss Scott led her to become increasingly withdrawn and evasive in the classroom. Unfortunately the result was that communication with her teacher was further impaired and Hazel's level of work output was severely restricted. Mrs Farthing's strategy of 'appealing to Miss Scott's better nature' whilst also trying to support Hazel at home, contained the problem, but did not solve it. And yet there is no evidence that Hazel actually *wanted* the experiences and identity which she began to acquire during the year. Indeed, she clearly wanted to make progress with her reading and to understand her maths. This is illustrated by a conversation which she had with her mother in the Autumn Term.

> We had a conversation which was interesting in the car the other morning. ... We were just talking and I said 'You did very well doing those letters. They were very good. They were like grown up writing', and I said 'Did you enjoy doing them well?' and she said 'Yes', and I said 'Would you like to write really well?' and she said 'yes'. I said, 'Darling there is only one way and that is to practise. You can't just suddenly be good at something, you have to practise at it. ... And she said to me ... 'I would like to be very, very good. I would like to be top of the class'.
>
> (Mrs Farthing, parent interview, November 1988, Year 1)

Of course, in Hazel's case the act of withdrawal was full of meaning in its own right. For her, withdrawal from external social expectations made it possible to open up the personal imaginative worlds in which she became so immersed. She rejected the setting of the classroom in which she was powerless, could exercise little control and was regularly evaluated on tasks which she often found boring and difficult to execute. Rather, she adopted the free settings of her imagination. She became liberated. But in so doing, she generated the incomprehension of Miss Scott and reinforced the teacher's perception of her as 'stubborn'. This perception was, of course, passed on to other teachers and Hazel, though much admired for her creativity and artwork, also became known amongst the teaching staff as a particularly challenging child to teach.

As we have seen from Mary's story, many children in that class experienced difficulties in adapting to and coping with Miss Scott's practice. Compared with those who, like Mary, adopted or elaborated 'good' identities and cautious strategies, Hazel's responses to Miss Scott tended to be individual and personal. This fuelled the perception among her peers of her being distinctly unusual in her actions and interests. However, as we saw earlier, Hazel did begin to establish some close friendships and that developed with Harriet was to be a special one and to last throughout their primary school years. For interested readers, therefore, something of the continuation and outcomes of Hazel's primary school career may be tracked through the telling of Harriet's story in *The Social World of Pupil Careers* (Pollard and Filer, in press). In their own ways both girls had a creative, independent and mischievous streak. Hazel's deviance provided a source of amusement to many children and was certainly so to Harriet. For other pupils who were perhaps more conforming in the classroom it confirmed Hazel as being 'a bit odd'. Nevertheless, Hazel began to broaden her friendships and certainly to be seen by all the children as interestingly unique.

For Hazel's mother, despite her strategy of negotiation with Miss Scott, the year was still seen as having been very problematic. She summarized her feelings:

> Over the past few days I have been trying to analyse how I could sum up the changes and developments that have occurred to Hazel during the year. Overall I feel frustrated and concerned. Hazel's relationship with Miss Scott seems to have gradually deteriorated from bad to worse. Hazel seems to have accepted the unhappy situation and has withdrawn in many ways, especially in areas where she seems to have learning difficulties such as maths.
>
> She has difficulties in understanding the task in hand and having asked to have it explained again, and still not understanding, is too frightened to ask a third time.
>
> Hazel told me that she felt she had not learned anything more in maths than she already knew last year. I think this is probably an exaggeration but aptly expresses how Hazel feels about her own progress.
>
> (Mrs Farthing, parent diary, July 1989, Year 1)

The irony then, seems to have been that Miss Scott, Mrs Farthing and Hazel herself felt frustrated about Hazel's learning, but each perceived the situation in a slightly different way and, although Mrs Farthing did her best to negotiate between Hazel and Miss Scott and there was some reaching out at the end of the year, the necessary quality of communication was never established. Setting Miss Scott's circumstances aside, Mrs Farthing saw this as having quite a lot to do with Hazel's temperament and was mindful of continuities in her early behaviour:

> Right from when she was a baby, and I can remember it ... . Just simple things like when she used to still have just a bottle in the mornings ..., she must have been about 10 or 11 months, and she knew that she wanted her bottle first thing in the morning. If you didn't catch her at the right moment between sleeping and waking, she'd go all peculiar and have a little tantrum and would throw the bottle across the room and refuse it. And so you'd say, 'Right, right, OK, you don't want it now' and then she'd scream for it, but she wouldn't take it. In the end, once you'd managed to get her to have this damned bottle, she was fine. And I think she's a bit like that when someone says something to her now. If you use the wrong tone of voice with her, 'Hazel, do this', it's almost a case of, 'No!'
> (Mrs Farthing, parent interview, July 1989, Year 1)

Mrs Farthing was well aware that this sort of experience could occur again unless Hazel could either learn to adapt to new circumstances or could find a track through school and life in which she felt fulfilled.

> I hope for her own sake that she finds something she really enjoys doing and can make a career of it or something, but as long as she's happy in whatever she does, then that's the main thing. Because I think she is going to make life difficult for herself in lots of ways, I think she's probably her own worst enemy.
> (Mrs Farthing, parent interview, July 1989, Year 1)

Mrs Farthing awaited the next school year with some trepidation.

Matrix 5.2 provides an overall summary of Hazels Year 1.

Matrix 5.2 *Hazels Year 1, a summary matrix*

Family relationships	Peer-group relationships	Teacher relationships	Identity	Learning
Continued strong parental endorsement and development of Hazel's interests, such as dinosaurs and animals, and of her drawing.	Hazel loses previous close friends to other schools and class but continues to create and enjoy imaginative games into which others are invited.	Miss Scott frustrated by Hazel who does not talk to or relate with her. Feels she is 'extraordinary', 'withdrawn' and 'stubborn'.	Hazel is young within the class and amongst the lower attaining children.	Slow initial progress in reading, but movement following parent/teacher discussions. Hazel delighted by 'moving up a box' but her overall achievement disappoints Miss Scott.
Mrs Farthing provides much home support to Hazel in her reading, writing and maths, but also in terms of her relationship with Miss Scott.	Hazel still regarded as a bit odd by some children and is sometimes teased by boys.	Hazel frightened by Miss Scott and bored by much school work.	However, Hazel sees herself, and others see her, as artistic and knowledgeable about dinosaurs and dragons.	Makes slow progress at writing skills.
Hazel proud of the thought of having her sister, Katie, at school.	During year, Hazel develops wider friendships with a small group of girls – joining the clan' (Mrs Farthing). These girls largely accept the rules of her play, have similar experiences of boys in the playground and of Miss Scott in the classroom. The group are described by Mrs Farthing as 'Hazel's saving grace'	Hazel increasingly deploys evasion strategies such as withdrawal and daydreaming.	Enjoys her own imaginative worlds and games.	Hazel is 'strong-willed', very slow and resistant to some tasks, particularly with maths. Miss Scott tries to coax her.
Hazel loves Katie to play with her games, but also sometimes sees Katie as a 'little goody, goody'.		The relationship between Hazel and Miss Scott improves a little over the year following parental intervention, but rapport is very limited for most of the year.	Seen by Miss Scott as very unusual and a challenging child to teach.	Hazel needs to be 'drawn into' class projects and 'is often lost in a dream world'.
			Seen by other children as 'a bit odd' but her humour is appreciated.	Very artistic throughout the year and Hazel made a significant contribution to the rainforest project.
		The end-of-year whole-school rainforest project brings Hazel and Miss Scott together in exciting, creative achievements.	Hazel wants to achieve at reading, writing and other school work, but often prefers to withdraw when things get difficult.	
			Mrs Farthing very aware of continuities between Hazel's classroom withdrawal and her assertive early childhood strategies.	

5.5   HAZEL IN HER YEAR 2

Hazel, Year 2, relationships with parents at home

Hazel continued to receive a great deal of support from her parents and they would often engage in games and activities as a whole family. Drawing was a particular favourite and Hazel parents continued to be impressed by Hazel's skills and visual memory.

> Later that evening Rob was looking up some Inca/Aztec architectural designs and motifs for me and was doing some rough sketches, Hazel had glanced briefly at what he was doing. A little later she produced a drawing of a dragon with the same serpent's tooth design that Rob had put in his sketch. We were both amazed that she had noticed this after just a glance, and had remembered it well enough to draw from memory.
> (Mrs Farthing, parent diary, November 1989, Year 2)

Hazel's drawing of a family barbecue in the garden (Document 5.10), conveys both her artistic ability, her close identification with her imaginative world of dragons and, perhaps, her sense of an idiosyncratic self as she rises up and observes the scene with Katie to one side. Gran, incidentally, is simply resting on a lounger.

An important breakthrough in Hazel's perception of her reading also occurred at home. Mrs Farthing explained:

> Rob was bathing them and putting them to bed one night. Hazel said, 'Dad, you're really good at teaching me'. Because he'd said that, 'when you can't find a word sometim⁓ there's clues in the picture', and she'd got stuck on a word and he'd said, 'Well, what's the ⸳cture about?' and she'd said the word. She must have been aware of it before but perhaps not put like that. And Rob had said to her, 'Well, you're good at teaching yourself. You're the best person, you're the one that's learning and picking these things up'. And just then she picked up one of her other books, 'Scarry's Treasure' or something, that *we'd* always read to her in the past, and she picked it up and realised that she could read books that we had previously read to her. And she'd never really twigged that before, except for some very simple ones. ... She thought it was fantastic. Took a book to bed with her ... until eventually I had to take it off her because it was getting so late ... . She was so proud of herself that she could actually pick up this other book, I mean, I know she's not the best reader in the world, but she's not bad now and I think if she comes on the way she has been it will be fantastic.
> (Mrs Farthing, parent interview, December 1989, Year 2)

Hazel, Year 2, relationships with siblings at home

Hazel's relationship with her younger sister, Katie, continued to be characterized by both affection and rivalry, and this was particularly accentuated as Katie began school in this year. Hazel was very aware of Katie engaging with the same curriculum that she had herself faced in the past and, since Katie's approach to new challenges was usually to make a constructive attempt, Hazel often found Katie very tiresome. If the contrast in approaches became apparent, Hazel would often withdraw:

> We talk about maths and Katie will be interested and have a go and Hazel will just shout a few things like, 'Ten and ten is twenty', and if she goes wrong anywhere, she just doesn't want to know.
> (Mrs Farthing, parent interview, July 1990, Year 2)

Mrs Farthing expressed Hazel's dilemma:

Document 5.10   *Hazel, drawing of family barbecue, September 1989, Year 2*

Although Hazel loves Katie, I think she thinks of her still as being a threat, which is a pity. ...
They will even sort of cuddle each other and get on well. I don't think she'd really be without
her.
(Mrs Farthing, parent interview, December 1989, Year 2)

Hazel, Year 2, relationships among friends and in the playground

During this year, Hazel's relationship with Harriet continued to deepen and they began to
develop an independent identity in relation to other children, and particularly, as distinct
from the more dominant group of girls associated with Sally and Mary that we met in
Chapter 3 (pp. 53–4). Hazel and Harriet, set themselves a little apart, indulging in their
particular type of imaginative games and a somewhat sceptical sense of humour in relation
to their peers.

Really Harriet has been her mainstay and character wise ... they've got the same sort of almost
little naughty streak in them I think, ... well, *mischievous* streak rather than naughty. I think
they share the same sort of basic humour. Hazel has got a wonderful sense of humour. She
really has. On Harriet's birthday, they went riding together and she was just delighted.
(Mrs Farthing, parent interview, July 1990, Year 2)

Hazel continued to play imaginative games in the playground, as she told me:

I like dragons or dinosaurs, and I pretend I'm a family of dogs and sometimes a family of cats

with loads of kittens and puppies. And I can run as fast as anyone in the whole school on my hands and feet.
(Hazel, pupil interview, April 1990, Year 2)

This capacity to run faster than anyone else on hands and feet earned Hazel particular admiration from many other children.

In the classroom, Hazel would often sit with Harriet to do her work. They would talk together, and sometimes Harriet would guide Hazel. However, Hazel was not beyond rejecting her friend's assistance if she felt that her dignity was threatened, and Harriet would accept this with some amusement. Fieldnotes recorded one such incident:

Hazel is 'writing a book'. She sits with Harriet and is doing a picture of a dragon on every other page to go with her story. Harriet laughs and tells me, 'Hazel always writes about dragons'.

They discuss finishing their books, 'we'll do some every day and then we'll be going past the blank pages' (which they see as a landmark in the middle).

Hazel writes, 'then Tom had an idea ah (sic) buns and sausages'. Harriet looks at Hazel's writing and suggests that she must mean '*of* buns and sausages'. Harriet leans across, rubs 'ah' out and replaces it with 'of'. Hazel starts to get upset. She rubs 'of' out and replaces it with 'ah'. Harriet watches with a hint of amusement but she doesn't press the point. Hazel carries on writing and they chat about Gareth – 'he's the naughtiest boy in the school'.
(Fieldnotes, October 1989, Year 2)

Hazel did, however, have a period of friendship with a boy, Greg, who was seen as being one of the 'naughty children' in that Year 2 class. In the Autumn Term, the play within this friendship began to encompass the children's developing sexual curiosity and this was particularly stimulated by getting changed for PE lessons. On such occasions, some of the girls would go into the Home Corner to change and the boys made much of 'peeping'. Hazel was happy to join in the laughter when Greg declared that he had been, 'pushed in my willie when we was changing' and soon after she sat with Greg in the writing area engaging in a lot of unusually animated laughter (Fieldnotes, October 1989, Year 2).

Mrs Farthing reported that Greg had 'declared undying love' for Hazel and that he had begun to play regularly with Nimra, Harriet and Hazel (Mrs Farthing, parent diary, November 1989, Year 2). Hazel and her mother had talked about him:

Apparently they were standing out in the field one day and he came up and told her that he wanted to be her boyfriend and he loved her. I said, 'How do you feel about him?' And she said, 'Well, he's my boyfriend' and I said, 'Yes?' and she said, 'Well, I think I love him' or something like that. And I said, 'Why?' And she said, 'Because he loves me'.
(Mrs Farthing, parent interview, December 1989, Year 2)

This liaison occurred at about the same time as Sally and James were also supposed to be 'in love' and, in one sense, it reflected a playground fashion. However, it was also a process of learning about relationships. By the Spring Term Hazel's relationship with Greg had broken down as he reasserted his friendship with other boys. Hazel was no longer cast as a friend, as she saw it, more as a victim as she explained:

I don't like to play with Ned or Greg or Gary 'cos they're naughty. Sometimes they start chasing us and keep pulling up our skirts, and we tell the teacher and the boys have to stand by the wall.
(Hazel, group interview, March 1990, Year 2)

Throughout such episodes, Harriet continued to provide a strong source of friendship and solidarity for Hazel. They were able to develop together in ways which were relatively independent of both boys and other girls.

Hazel, Year 2, relationships with Miss George in the classroom

When she began in Miss George's classroom, Hazel was initially cautious and withdrawn. Miss George attempted to draw her out, and she soon found that, when Hazel became confident, her expression could be almost too wholehearted. Miss George reflected on the challenge which this posed for her:

> When she first came into the class, she was so totally withdrawn, she didn't speak to anyone or me. Even now there are times when she doesn't like answering the register ... . Now it's a bit like Pandora's box – if you pay her any attention, you have to think at the beginning of the day, 'Can I cope with the consequences?' ... because she's ... it's all bottled up inside, probably been bottled up for a long time and she gets so over exuberant ... one part of you thinks, 'Well I've got to make more fuss of her', and the other part thinks, 'I'm not sure I've got the energy – I've got to cope with the other children.'
> (Miss George, teacher Interview, November 1989, Year 2)

Hazel soon found that the classroom atmosphere was not threatening and that her teacher was outgoing and warm towards her. Over the summer, she had been continuing to work on her reading and in the new classroom situation she made rapid and enthusiastic progress. Mrs Farthing described this new turn of events and how it had led to Hazel's eager production of stories:

> Within about two weeks of going back with Miss George, she moved up to another reading box, so it happened all very, very quickly. In fact, she's still not brilliant, but she's OK, I was getting to be a little bit worried before, whereas now she's about probably what she ought to be. When I went in to see Miss George she seemed a little bit not quite sure about how to handle her. ... At the moment, I think she's wisely using Hazel's interest and channelling everything she needs to do via dinosaurs and things ... and these books she's been bringing home, the writing and spelling is atrocious, but at least she is doing it now.
>
> She doesn't stop at home though, she was writing something at home about a Christmas song she'd been learning. And she drew a beautiful picture on the front and then she wrote down all the words and everything about it and on Miss George's advice, I started doing a little bit of editing, but not to dishearten her – although when I read 'Max and the Frog' I fell about laughing with the 'frop shop'. I said, 'What's a frop shop?' and she loves it when I read it how she's written it as well, we are in hysterics reading it. ... I think 'Max and the Frog' is probably the best and it's the expressions that the characters have. There's a picture of Max, this dinosaur, in the bath and he's taken his dinosaur skin off and hung it up and it's the right colour hung up and he's in the bath and you can just see the top half of him and the soap is slipping out of his hand and there's all the right sort of lines for soap slipping out and it looks like a cartoon the way she's done it, it's brilliant.
> (Mrs Farthing, parent interview, December 1989, Year 2)

Hazel was delighted with this release of her imagination in a form which also pleased both her teacher and parents. She would become extremely excited when asked to read one of her stories to the class, revelling in the length and complexity of the account:

> Hazel has been writing. She seems to be full of tension as she reads her book to me and a group of children, but it is excited tension. She reads story after story about dragons, all beautifully illustrated. She is self-critical of her pictures and draws attention to one announcing loudly that it is, 'my bestest picture in the world!'. She reads in animated ways, without twiddling her hair or sucking her thumb.
>
> Later, with Miss George, she is selected to read a story to the whole class. She has everyone's attention and announces that, 'This is an absolutely long story'. The story is about some dragons going to a birthday party.
>
> She explains excitedly, with ideas tumbling out as she turns the pages, '... it's a Chinese

dragon ... in this one he's met his girl-friend ... here he's thinking of buns and sausages ... he's crying because no one will come to his party ... balloons for the dragons dancing ... he's lighting his birthday cake.'

Eventually, Miss George has to ask Hazel to calm down.

(Fieldnotes, October 1989, Year 2)

Hazel maintained this enthusiasm right through the year, supported by the interest of Miss George, Mrs Farthing, sister Katie and any other listeners who might be enlisted. Not least though, she derived satisfaction from the combination of her artistic skills with a new medium for expressing her imagination. As she said, 'I really love writing stories' (Fieldnotes, May 1990, Year 2).

This positive teacher–pupil relationship and associated progress and enthusiasm is not the whole story however, for Miss George was very aware that Hazel also had to acquire other basic skills, knowledge and understanding. Hazel was far less enthusiastic about many of these and progress was far harder to achieve. As Miss George explained:

Last week we almost fell out because we were doing some handwriting, so here she was away from what she wanted to do, and she was just refusing to do it, and I really had to be cross with her. I said, 'I don't care what you want to do, I am the teacher and I'm telling you that you are going to do it'. And she sat down and did it. But I think there is a point where she thinks that because I have offered her an ear to talk to and have tried to be as gentle with her as possible, I think there is a point where she thinks 'I can get away with murder'.

(Miss Scott, teacher interview, November 1989, Year 2)

This struggle went on throughout the year, with Miss George walking a delicate line between wanting to draw on Hazel's motivation and wanting to broaden her interests and curricular experiences. My fieldnotes recorded a case of this:

Miss George told me at playtime about her 'battle with Hazel'. Hazel doesn't want to do anything she hasn't chosen herself. She won't plan her work properly. She won't do maths. She rejects small group work, evades and sometimes even seems to sleep. Miss George commented that, 'Hazel has to learn that sometimes she has to do things. She's very bright and creative. I like that and I don't want to restrict her, but she's got to do some things she doesn't want. Her maths isn't good – but then she hardly ever does any! When she does things, she usually does them very well.'

(Fieldnotes, February 1990, Year 2)

By the end of the year, when Miss George was contemplating the loss of this class of children, she was quite sentimental about Hazel, having seen her as an enormous challenge, but also as a source of great fulfilment.

Of all the children in the class, Hazel is the one I think I shall miss most. I think it will be a wrench. Am I a masochist? Am I mad? What am I? ... You don't know what's going on inside, because if I tell her off she doesn't answer me. She just looks at me with those eyes. She doesn't say a thing. How can you tell somebody off when you can't even get them to agree that they've been naughty. I say, 'now that wasn't a very sensible thing to do was it?' and she just stares. Anyway, this is what I've written on her report. Her reading has improved immensely, she clearly loves writing but really as a vehicle for her main love which is drawing. Her written work is imaginative and interesting but I am surprised that despite the rapid development in her reading she's made little progress with her spellings. However, she can put me to shame and spell the name of every known dinosaur. Can't spell 'because' but 'diplodocus' – no problem. She argues that, 'if she can read it and so can I, why change it?' She's written some of her stories for Katie and I have observed her reading these enthusiastically to a group of reception children, which I thought was quite sweet. They were all sitting there, and she was showing them the pictures and they were absolutely fascinated. Perhaps she'll be a teacher or something. They have to be a bit odd!

This is what I've written for her mum, because I think I can talk to her mother. ... I've put that it's been a pleasure having her in my class and despite our little ups and downs I feel that we got on well together. Because I do think we have established a relationship. I feel very protective of her and worry about her because I know that she was unhappy last year and I worry that she might go somewhere else and be unhappy. ... I feel extremely protective because I think she's vulnerable. ... And I've put that she's as stubborn as a mule!
(Miss George, teacher interview, May 1990, Year 2)

Hazel was secure in her relationship with Miss George, though she recognized the tension which was inherent in her role:

Miss George does like me a lot I think. Sometimes she does get cross with me though ... mmmmm when I've not done enough.
(Hazel, pupil interview, July 1990, Year 2)

Hazel, Year 2, progress in classroom learning

As we have already seen, Hazel made considerable strides in reading through the year and both she and her parents were very pleased with her progression from books with substantial proportions of pictures to books with more reading challenge and, indeed, more status. One such book was given to Hazel on her birthday:

One of her presents included 'The Magic Finger' by Roald Dahl. She started reading it as soon as she unwrapped it and continued with it after her party. After the children had been put to bed I went upstairs to check on them about 10.00 pm expecting them to be sound asleep, Hazel was sitting up still reading. I said that she should be asleep by now and could finish her book tomorrow, to which she replied 'I'm ever so tired Mummy, but I've only got two more pages to read and this is the best book I have ever read, it's just like watching a video in your head'.
(Mrs Farthing, parent diary, July 1990, Year 2)

Hazel continued to enjoy 'watching a video in her head' and, as Miss George put it, 'Hazel's reading has improved immensely' (Miss George, report to parents, summer 1990, Year 2).

The story of Hazel's writing has already been recounted and again, Mrs Farthing and Miss George saw eye to eye on its strengths and weaknesses, with both commending its imaginative quality but being concerned about her spelling.

Document 5.11 below, shows a typical piece of Hazel's more confident and expressive writing. Here, she is conveying her excitement about observing and looking after some chicks which had just hatched in an incubator which Miss George had brought into the classroom. One chick had been named 'Silkie'.

Hazel's lack of enthusiasm for maths work was consistent across the whole year. In November, Miss George reported that Hazel 'just doesn't want to know'. In May her judgement was that Hazel has 'got no interest', whilst in her summer report to parents Miss George stated that, 'Hazel has no interest in maths and we have to negotiate one-to-one to get any done at all'. I asked Miss George to describe a typical negotiation with Hazel:

I'd say, 'Hazel, you're going to do a maths card today'. And then, 'the look' from her. 'Well, let's put it this way, Hazel, if you do one today I promise I won't nag you to do one tomorrow.' So she does it and sometimes she'll say, 'I want to do another one so I don't have to do another one this week.' Sometimes she will actually do it ... but I really have to be close ... and I have to sort of watch out for if she disappears somewhere – 'Hazel! Are you doing that work?'.
(Miss George, teacher interview, May 1990, Year 2)

I LOVE Silkie. becuse she
is sowe fluffey and it is
cyote and it peks the gifs sowe
etsnits food and it tris and it
srok it we nevur sobooley tris to
and evrey time ifm gowin hom I say
big to it.
I Love Silkie becose she is sowe
fluffey.

Document 5.11 *Hazel, writing about chicks hatching, April 1990, Year 2*

Miss George believed that Hazel genuinely found maths difficult, compared it with her new found confidence in reading and writing and related it to Hazel's tendency to withdraw into her imaginative world rather than attend to group or whole-class teaching opportunities:

> She'll quite happily tell everyone that 'I'm the best dragon drawer and I'm the best writer in the class'. Which imaginatively, she is. But I do feel that she loses out, because I try to do little games, number games and things, we add up the dinner register and things like that which I would say everybody else gets involved in and Hazel misses it. Because I say something simple like 'There are seventeen packed lunches and one going home, how many all together?' 'Hazel?' ... and she'll just look at you with those eyes and she'll say 'I don't know what you're talking about', as if she's just been in another world the whole time.
> (Miss George, teacher interview, May 1990, Year 2)

Drawing, however, was an activity in which she developed self-critically, as her mother explained:

> ... at last, is beginning to draw other things besides dinosaurs and dragons. She is very independent and does not want help or direction from me, although she does appreciate my interest and constructive criticism. She criticises my work too!
> (Mrs Farthing, parent diary, July 1990, Year 2)

Hazel, identity and learning in Year 2

This was a year in which Hazel flourished. The positive atmosphere of her Year 2 class-room and the joint interest of Miss George and Mrs Farthing provided conditions in which she could express herself and develop her confidence. Nevertheless, Hazel was still very self-directed and independent. Her sense of self and of her own priorities was expressed quite well in an interview with her during the Spring Term:

AP: What do you think about work in school?

Hazel: I like doing writing and playing with the home corner, or the post office and stories about cats, dogs, and definitely dragons and dinosaurs. I'm the best drawer of dinosaurs and dragons in the class. I pretend I am the dog or sometimes pretend I'm the lady in the post office. Best of all I like playing with Mobilo 'cos I can make a dragon out of it.

     Miss George says that I must get my maths book out but I don't like doing that as you have to think of the numbers, but I don't like doing that – I like playing best.

     I like imagining things. I love my favourite dreams, about the Rainbow Passage Way and the Blue Bell Passage Way and the Violet Passage Way – I go through the Passage Way and the Violet Valley and I end up at the Unicorn's castle, and Queen Unicorn takes me to Care Bear and My Little Pony land and I love them. My Little Pony and the Smurfs is great.

AP: Do you like learning new things?

Hazel: When I don't understand, I just say I don't understand and Miss George tells me what it means and I learn more. Or if I don't understand, I just say I don't understand and I just go away and do something else. Sometimes I feel grumpy and I just sit there then I do it all in a rush to get it done.

AP: Do you like doing other things – different from dragons and that sort of thing?

Hazel: Well, I'd like to play 'cows' but no-one wants to really. ... I think I'd like to go off on my hands and knees now. (Hazel zooms off, as if released!)

(Hazel, pupil interview, April 1990, Year 2)

Mrs Farthing wondered if she 'subconsciously encouraged' Hazel because, 'perhaps we're a bit zany and she gets it off us' (Mrs Farthing, parent interview, December 1989, Year 2), and she certainly admired and enjoyed Hazel's creativity and sense of humour. At the same time though, she was aware that some of Hazel's behaviour could be disruptive and was beginning to intervene with Hazel to help her adapt:

This running round on her hands and feet all the time apparently has been a problem. Miss George said she's had discipline problems with her too, where she's turned everything into a game, even signed her planning sheet, 'Dragon Man', and things like that. It's funny when you hear about it at home but it's not really when you are trying to cope with 30 odd children and you've got one who's making all the others run around on their hands and knees. We've had a word about that and she's not allowed to pretend to be a dragon at school anymore. She can be one at home but not at school. Which I felt really mean about, but I felt that was a little step in the right direction. We've also spoken about her trying to listen more and not to go off into a dream world. ... Everyone has a slight imaginary world actually, so that's OK, but it's controlling it.

(Mrs Farthing, parent interview, July 1990, Year 2)

Mrs Farthing was particularly concerned by the fact that, 'Hazel finds her imaginative world far superior to everyday life and, when things overwhelm her, she is likely to slip away and is just not aware of what is going on around her'. She felt that this dependency on her 'other world' would decrease if Hazel found more confidence and success in the 'ordinary world' and she was delighted that Hazel had found success in learning to swim.

As Mrs Farthing put it, 'to watch Hazel in the water is like watching a dolphin at play' (Mrs Farthing, parent diary, July 1990, Year 2).

For Miss George, Hazel had grown enormously in confidence and achievement:

> I feel Hazel has made progress this year. She answers both registers now. She has found her niche in the learning process and hopefully we can build on this and widen her outlook. It is unfortunate that she misses out on a lot of class lessons because she is so wrapped up in her own world.
>
> (Miss George, report to parents, summer 1990, Year 2)

Hazel herself, was very aware of her progress and had developed a positive opinion of herself at school which tended to discount the concerns which Miss George and her mother still had. She reflected across the whole of her time in the Infants and now faced the future in the Juniors with reasonable confidence:

> Hazel: I liked it in my first class but I didn't like it last year and I do like it in this class. Because last year, I always used to get told off. She thought I was very good at doing pictures but when I was doing my maths cards I just sat there, I didn't do anything.
>
> AP: What do you think it will be like in the juniors compared with being in the infants?
>
> Hazel: I like it in the infants best, but when I'm in my next class I'll be eight. The maths cards will be harder, but I'll be able to do better writing.
>
> (Hazel, pupil interview, July 1990, Year 2)

Matrix 5.3 *Hazel's Year 2, a summary matrix*

Family relationships	Peer-group relationships	Teacher relationships	Identity	Learning
Hazel continues to develop her drawing skills and imaginative expression.	Hazel begins to develop a particular friendship with Harriet.	Miss George sees Hazel at start of the year as 'totally withdrawn' but is 'like Pandora's Box' and becomes exuberant if given attention.	Hazel is amongst the oldest children in the class, though her relative attainment is low, particularly in maths.	Rapid progress with reading through the year. Hazel discovers that reading can be 'like watching a video in your head'.
A breakthrough with reading when Mrs Farthing helps Hazel realize she can 'work out' words and meanings and 'teach herself'.	Hazel can run on hands and feet as fast 'as anyone in the whole school'.	Hazel very happy during the year.	Sometimes mischievous in whole class sessions such as registration, PE or story time.	Hazel takes great pleasure from her written stories and reads them to others with great animation. Expressive, but less attention to spelling, handwriting and grammar.
Close affection and rivalry with Katie continues.	Often plays dragons and dinosaurs, or animal families in the playground.	Hazel's drawings are regularly praised. Hazel gets very excited and involved in converting her imaginative world into written stories.	Hazel sees herself as 'the best drawer of dinosaurs and dragons in the class'.	Hates maths and has to be enticed into doing tasks. Routinely evasive. Very limited progress.
Katie is alert, 'has a go' and tries to be good in the family. If Katie threatens to show Hazel up, Hazel rapidly withdraws.	Hazel and Harriet develop their humour in class. Harriet supports Hazel in class work, when Hazel will accept it. Hazel goes riding with Harriet.	By the Spring Term Miss George sees a 'battle with Hazel' emerging over things she doesn't want to do such as maths.	Hazel feels positive about herself in relation to reading and writing stories, felt she would be able to do the writing in the Juniors but less confident about maths.	Hazel's drawing continues to develop – 'the love of her life' – and the range of skills becomes increasingly refined.
	Hazel is mischievous in PE and plays with Greg – known as 'a naughty boy'.	Miss George tries to broaden Hazel's curriculum and becomes firm over handwriting and maths.	Mrs Farthing sees Hazel as 'a bit zany', as having 'a wonderful sense of humour' and as wanting to 'experiment with everything in sight'.	Hazel is conscious that if she doesn't understand she can get help from Miss George, not 'just go away' or 'feel grumpy and just sit there or do it all in a rush'.
	Grey is named as a boyfriend, but he gets into trouble playing 'kiss chase' and 'pulling up our skirts'.	Miss George thinks she's a masochist, but will miss Hazel the most when she leaves. 'A pleasure to have in the class, but she's very vulnerable ... and stubborn as a mule.'		By the end of the year, is seen by Miss George as having 'found her niche in the learning process', though Miss George still working to widen Hazel's interests.

5.6 HAZEL'S LEARNING AND DEVELOPMENT

The case study of Hazel can now be briefly summarized. In Figure 5.3, we can see Hazel's experience over the three years of her infant schooling in terms of a pattern of relationships.

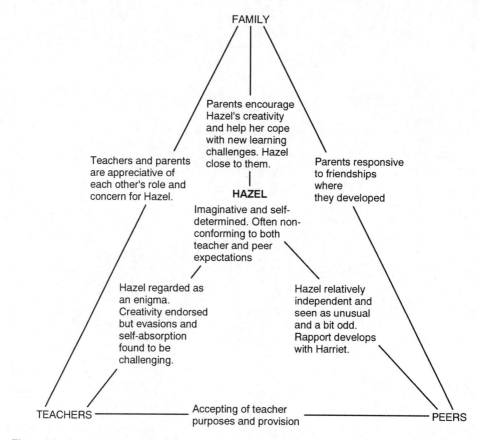

Figure 5.3 *Hazel's case-study overview*

As described more fully in the introduction to the case studies in Part Two (p. 37), this triadic representation depicts in the outer triangle, the social context within which Hazel learned and interacted and to which she could contribute, and, in the inner star, the dynamic relationship between Hazel and her family, peers and teachers. In the simplest of terms, within this context and web of relationships, Hazel's self-absorption and determination developed.

We can also think about Hazel's case with regard to the model of learning, identity and social relationships which was presented in Chapter 1 and elaborated in Chapter 4.

In respect of the question *Who is learning?*, we might consider Hazel's identity in terms of the particular influences of the intellectual and cultural resources within her family. For example, she drew on her parents' talents for artistic and imaginative expression and the family pleasure in sharing interests in natural history. We might also consider the simultaneous resource and threat to Hazel's status which her younger sister provided. She was both a valued companion for imaginative play and an observer of Hazel's learning struggles.

With regard to *What is to be learned?* we might think of the variations in Hazel's confidence, motivation and strategies when facing different learning challenges. For instance, whilst watching and learning from her father drawing, when playing with Harriet, when faced with maths tasks in the classroom or when in communication with Miss Scott before and after the commencement of the rainforest project.

The questions of *How supportive is the learning context?* and *What are the learning outcomes?* are very closely connected when considering Hazel's learning experiences. Classroom learning took place when Hazel enjoyed a measure of control and freedom to express her imaginative identity and, sometimes, following careful negotiation and coaxing by others. Her self-esteem increased in proportion to the opportunities accorded her for expression of her imaginative identity. Where control was denied her, or Hazel felt threatened by boredom or incomprehension, then withdrawal and immersion into a dream world took place. In such circumstances, communications ultimately broke down and relatively little school learning took place. Within the home, her parents' flexible response and efforts to understand and adapt to Hazel's learning stance were of constant value against the variable relationships which existed between Hazel and her teachers. A similar process can be detected in the development of supportive peer relations. Friendships were only gradually formed because Hazel needed children who could operate largely on her terms and who could share in an imaginative world of her devising. Thus the mainstream interests and activities of the majority of the girls, with its competitive struggle for classroom and playground status, remained an almost alien culture for Hazel, as her world did for them.

For Hazel, the issue of control was of primary importance. Indeed, her mother's major conclusion regarding Hazel's learning, arrived at through hard experience, was that force, domination and threats were almost always counter-productive. Where Hazel's identity and personal interests were built on and allowed to flourish, so Hazel's relationships blossomed and learning took place.

Hazel's case is an interesting example of the struggle for power in classrooms. Within the working consensus which had been established in their classrooms, Hazel's teachers certainly had the power to grant or restrict Hazel's capacity to exercise personal control and to express her imaginative identity. However, Hazel's strategies of withdrawal and evasion were consistently used to constrain or even reject teacher authority. For long periods, Hazel was thus able to avoid confronting her lack of knowledge and fear of maths.

As we have seen, the somewhat puzzled but affectionate consensus from her teachers was that Hazel was both fascinating and frustrating to teach. Her parents were very sensitive to her feelings and took care to mediate her responses as constructively as they could as she encountered new learning challenges. Gradually then, in a complex process which was often finely poised, Hazel moved forward and developed to accommodate herself to the external world of others.

Chapter 6

Daniel's Story

6.1   DANIEL, AN INTRODUCTION

Daniel's story again illustrates the influence of family life on the sense of identity and repertoire of strategic adaptions which a child brings to school. As the youngest of five children within an active, bustling family, Daniel was often concerned to seek approval by trying to please – to 'be gooder' as he once put it. However, in his quest to establish himself, he was vulnerable to teasing or criticism. He hated failure and avoided stress whenever he could.

How though, could he avoid stress at school? How could he develop friendships? How should he present himself to his teachers? What if he could not do the school work which was set for him? These were some of the main questions with which Daniel was initially concerned.

In Daniel's Reception year the theme of gender was particularly interesting when, although making reasonable progress at learning 'the basics', he experienced difficulties with other boys because of his special friendship with a girl, Harriet (the child who later became Hazel's closest friend). How could he cope with this? In his Year 1, Daniel experienced the somewhat stressed climate in Miss Scott's classroom which was a particular problem for him. One important way through this was to establish a close friendship with a boy, Andrew, and this special relationship provided solidarity and entertainment. Would this develop constructively and sustain his self-confidence, or might it produce 'silliness' which would get him into trouble? For his Year 2, as Figure 6.1 shows, Daniel was the youngest child in Miss George's class, but he got on well and made better academic progress. What though were the effects of his parents' views that he needed a more formal type of teaching than that provided at Greenside Primary School?

As Figure 6.1 shows, Daniel's relative attainment at literacy and maths was perfectly sound for his age. However, at no point was he among the leading children within the classes in which he was placed, and he often worried about his progress. At the end of Daniel's Year 3, his parents decided that he should leave Greenside Primary School.

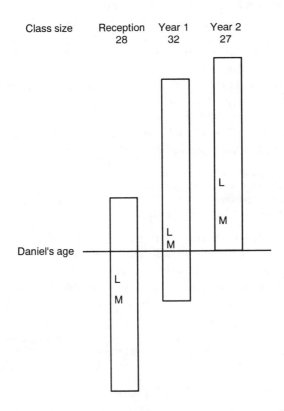

| Class size | Reception 28 | Year 1 32 | Year 2 27 |

Figure 6.1 *Daniel's structural position: age and relative attainment at literacy and maths in Reception, Year 1 and Year 2 classes (for an explanation of this figure, see p. 35)*

6.2 DANIEL'S FAMILY

As the family tree below shows, Daniel was the youngest of a family of five with some of his siblings being considerably older than himself.

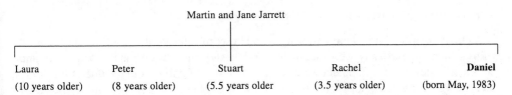

Martin and Jane Jarrett

| Laura | Peter | Stuart | Rachel | **Daniel** |
| (10 years older) | (8 years older) | (5.5 years older | (3.5 years older) | (born May, 1983) |

Figure 6.2 *Daniel's immediate family*

The Jarrett family lived in a conventional four-bedroomed, detached, 1930s house with a pleasant garden in the heart of the suburb of Greenside.

Daniel's father, Martin, was a senior manager in an advertising agency. Throughout the period of this study, he regularly worked very long hours, often into the evening. This work was a vital source of income for the family, but nevertheless its intensity meant that he was not able to be at home as much as both he and Mrs Jarrett would have liked. Child care for the young but growing family, and other domestic responsibilities, fell to Daniel's mother, Jane. This division of responsibilities was well established and remained throughout the period of Daniel's primary education.

Mrs Jarrett had been brought up herself in the suburb of Greenside, and, as a child, had attended Greenside Primary School. As she put it, 'it was not that different actually' (Mrs Jarrett, parent interview, March 1988, Reception). She was aware of the comfortable social and economic circumstances of most families in this part of Easthampton and was particularly conscious of their educational aspirations:

> I do understand why people are so keen for their children to do well. ... I don't think it is necessarily because they are social climbers, they just do not realise that this is a very narrow community. They assume that *everybody* has two cars, two televisions and the rest of it.
> (Mrs Jarrett, parent interview, March 1988, Reception)

Mr and Mrs Jarrett wanted the 'best possible' education for their children. However, they regarded the comprehensive school which was suggested by the Local Education Authority in the late 1980s as being out of the question for most parents in the suburb because of its social-class composition and relatively low levels of examination success. Indeed, Mr and Mrs Jarrett felt they had no option but to send their children to private secondary schools.

> I find it a very worrying thing really in this day and age. I wish we had the children more spaced out, because it is becoming a tremendous burden. Martin is from a very conventional background round here, and he wants them educated conventionally. ... But if you are in the bracket we are, you haven't actually got enough to pay full fees but you don't qualify for an assisted place.
> (Mrs Jarrett, parent interview, March 1988, Reception)

Mrs Jarrett accepted what she saw as some academic limitations of her children but valued other qualities such as having a rounded personality and self-confidence. However, at the point when Daniel was starting primary school, she was not certain that she had achieved this.

> Scholarships are out of the question with ours because we haven't got that sort of material. I wouldn't necessarily want them. The ones I know who do get them are not necessarily how I would consider 'well rounded' children. I would prefer them to have other things. I think confidence is an extremely important thing in life really, confidence in yourself. We haven't done awfully well so far... but hopefully you can rectify mistakes by the time you get to number five.
> (Mrs Jarrett, parent interview, March 1988, Reception)

As the youngest child, Daniel grew up within a set of family roles, routines and relationships which were already well established. When the study began, many of the common stages of children's development were represented in the family, from the difficulties of the teenage years, rivalry amongst the boys and the struggle of the younger children to establish themselves. Whilst there were inevitably some tensions, the children often played together and supported each other, including older children helping the younger ones. The following diary entry by Daniel's mother indicates something of the flavour of these dynamics, as they were when Daniel was four years old and in his first year at school.

> Daniel sleeps in the same room as his sister Rachel who is 7½. This morning they were up as usual at what feels like dawn but was probably about 7.00 am. They played together as is usual until 7.30 am when they were joined by next brother Stuart, who is 9½, when the playing got

more adventurous, consisting of hitting a balloon to each other without letting it hit the ground. This only lasted a few minutes as somebody always cheats and they fall out. Told to get dressed, which Daniel did without protest today. Rachel helped him with collar and cuffs but the rest he did himself. Says he has washed but I know he has not. Down for breakfast about 7.55 am. Shreddies put in bowl by Daddy with milk. Daniel sprinkled sugar in one place which was wrong so had to have more. Daddy leaves at 8.00 am with Peter who is 12. This morning Stuart puts toast on but Rachel butters Daniel's and her's. Daniel extremely pleased with himself as he has finished his breakfast before I came down-stairs having been stripping beds and sorting out washing. Back upstairs to wash and clean teeth. Daniel comes back down with wet hair combed the wrong way. Very pleased as he sees Stuart doing this to stop it sticking up. Daniel gets out Spiderman lunch box and Rachel's but hides them behind the door. The other two put coats on and get their packed lunch but cannot find boxes which causes some annoyance. Set off for school approx 8.40 am and is pleased to be early and one of the first there. Takes off own coat and hangs up carefully. Lunch box in wire basket under peg and takes book and word tin into classroom without a backward glance.
(Mrs Jarrett, parent diary, February 1988, Reception)

In this diary excerpt, we can see the bustle of family life, relationships among the children and the support given to Daniel by his father, mother and siblings to ease him through one of the busiest times of the day. We might also note Daniel's concern to please his mother, his awareness of and wish to emulate his brother and yet his capacity for making mischief as he asserts himself. Daniel is then pleased to be at school early and to feel that everything is well under control.

With a family of this complexity of interests and activities, there were inevitably some compromises. For instance, whilst Mrs Jarrett would normally work with Daniel on his reading, this role was sometimes passed to others. In the example below, Stuart traded the task so that he could avoid a different chore, but then did not attend properly to it.

Stuart given option of unloading dishwasher or doing Daniel's word tin and book, so chooses words but proceeds to play recorder at same time so Daniel interprets his own book. Does eventually do words. Known ones go back in tin, unknown in lid to do again. Slight altercation occurs when Daniel does not get 'looked' right first time, but insists he knew it really.
(Mrs Jarrett, parent diary, February 1988, Reception)

As we shall continue to explore throughout this case study, the family context was particularly important for Daniel. Rather than enjoying the exclusive attention which, say, an only child might enjoy, Daniel started as 'the baby of the family' and had to struggle to establish his place. As he gained in confidence and began to assert his identity, his family was already evolving under the complex momentum of many other inter-relationships, concerns and aspirations. Daniel was thus caught up in the circumstances and story of his family as a whole. Notwithstanding its own evolving development, it provided Daniel's base, as he began his encounters at school with teachers and a wider circle of peers.

6.3 DANIEL IN HIS RECEPTION YEAR

Daniel, Reception, relationships with parents at home

Daniel, as the youngest of the five children, had a unique relationship with his mother and, indeed, within the family. As Mrs Jarrett put it,

'He is the baby. I regret the passing of his babyhood, yes I do.'
(Mrs Jarrett, parent interview, March 1988, Reception)

However, family life was complex, busy and inevitably jostling, as each of the children developed their identities in relation to their siblings. In such a context, no one child could be indulged.

> Daniel has his moments. He moans and groans and he whinges if things aren't quite right. But we don't all have to make it so he doesn't have one of his turns, because the children are not allowed to behave like that. It is not tolerated in this house. ... I can't afford to let it happen. I am a very strong personality myself, so I tend to, sort of, 'give an instruction' which will be obeyed. There will be a lot of hassle over it but I won't give in over it.
> (Mrs Jarrett, parent interview, March 1988, Reception)

As the youngest child, Daniel did not always find his position easy. In particular, although he had to act within the family setting as a whole, his identification as the baby of the family meant that his perspective was not always taken seriously. His frustration could also contribute to family badinage.

> Occasionally when Daniel gets really angry he shouts at you, and this makes the others laugh. They always laugh at him if he gets like this and, of course, that makes him even worse – but in fact it makes me laugh as well. I quite like it. He is a very amiable, outgoing boy.
> (Mrs Jarrett, parent interview, March 1988, Reception)

As time allowed, Mr and Mrs Jarrett would get involved with Daniel, often with Mr Jarrett being sought out for some special activity whilst Mrs Jarrett managed more routine events and juggled with the children as a whole. The diary excerpt below is an example of this and it leads into a description of Daniel's relationship with his Grandpa.

> As soon as Martin returned from church he was roped in to help with the computer. Daniel wanted him to show him how to operate the lego motor with batteries and put the tracks on. Then he made four colour co-ordinated space rockets with his duplo lego. After lunch Daniel went to play with a friend. We walked, or at least I walked, Rachel cycled and Daniel rode on an old tricycle as the stabilisers have broken on his bike and he is almost ready to ride without them. Stuart stayed behind kicking a football in the road. Daniel was asked to stay for tea which he accepted as long as he could have marmite sandwiches.
>   When Rachel and I returned Grandpa and Grandma had arrived for tea. I think Grandpa was rather disappointed that Daniel would not be home until six. He gets on extremely well with small children and they love him. I think Daniel regards him as totally his property because as soon as he arrives he takes him over and insists on doing puzzles, reading books and drawing etc. As soon as he returned today, out came the coloured shapes to fit into pictures. Then out came his drawing pad and Grandpa helped him draw Father Christmas. Daniel put the belt and boots on and coloured it in. The thing about Grandpa (my father) is that he lets the children totally dictate the pace and the rules and what Daniel suggests he goes along with. No discipline seems to be needed.
> (Mrs Jarrett, parent diary, February 1988, Reception)

Daniel's relationship with his Grandpa seems to have been rather special for them both. Grandpa's interest in his youngest grandchild was perhaps matched by Daniel's appreciation of the luxury of sustained and relatively individual attention on his own terms.

Indeed, with four older siblings, Daniel was naturally concerned about his place in his mother's affections and was, perhaps, a little insecure. Mrs Jarrett's diary records an indicative conversation at bedtime.

> At 6.30 pm Daniel's thumb was in so decided it would be a good idea to get him into bed. Whilst washing him he said, 'I was his best Mummy, and Daddy was the best Daddy. Was he my favourite in all the family?' I never quite know how to answer this one so then he asked, 'Was he my favourite boy?' so we agreed that Mum mys love all their children but sometimes, when they are 'gooder' (his word), they are the favourite for a little while.
> (Mrs Jarrett, parent diary, February 1988, Reception)

Daniel's idea that a 'gooder' child can earn affection is an important one in understanding his strategic adaption to home life. It articulates directly with circumstances
within the family and with his appreciation of the needs of his parents. Again the parent
diary entry illustrates this context.

> We have a twelve year old who has his first end of year exams this week but does not know
> where to start with his revision so just does not do anything and walks around looking glum
> muttering 'I was never allowed to do that at this age'. A fourteen year old who never appears
> at all as she is convinced that life will end if she does not get at least 90% in her exams. When
> she does appear she bites everyone's head off if they dare to speak to her. This then makes the
> twelve-year-old mutter, 'Why is she allowed to speak like that?' A nine year old who is
> convinced that he won't be in the cricket team next week because he has been out for a duck
> two weeks running, but of course 'It wasn't my fault and anyway Mr Bland does not like me.'
> A seven year old who returned from Brownies fighting back the tears because somebody who
> had joined recently had gone straight into 'Road' whilst she, who joined in January, is only on
> 'Footpath'. Having tried to ascertain the significance of this, interspersed with many 'it's not
> fair's', we discovered that Rachel needs to do rather more work at these badges so now have a
> plan of campaign – but during all this many tears were shed over maths at school, rough games,
> a minute scratch and anything else she could dredge up. I felt a good nights sleep was required
> but that set her off again when she thought she was going to bed ten minutes earlier than usual.
> All this goes on in front of Daniel and must affect him in ways I would not like to imagine.
> (Mrs Jarrett, parent diary, June 1988, Reception)

Daniel, Reception, relationships with siblings at home

Daniel's older brothers and sisters were very important to him, not just because of his
affection for them but also because of their influence in his life at home. Because of their
age, relative maturity and the diverse activities in which they were involved, they provided
a range of role models for Daniel. Additionally though, they structured his life through
their interaction with him and with each other. The interpersonal dynamics of the siblings
were thus a vital element of the context within which Daniel sought to establish his own
identity. In March 1988 Mrs Jarrett provided a brief sketch of each of the children and their
relationship with Daniel, as it was then.

> Laura (aged 14) has got teenage problems. She probably feels she gets no attention at all. Her
> attitude is to withdraw into her room and shut herself away, interspersed with being quite nice
> from time to time but not consistently, so none of the other children know where they stand
> with her because one minute she is quite nice and the next minute the abuse. .... Certainly
> Daniel used to be quite fond of her and go into her room but he wouldn't dream of going in
> there now without tentatively sort of poking his head round the door. She is very difficult at the
> moment ... and she doesn't find it easy to relate to people. She resents being the eldest of the
> family.

> Peter (aged 12) is totally different from Laura. He is a much more openly affectionate child. He
> shows his feelings much more. He is very amiable and is liked by a lot of people. He always
> wants someone to play with – very gregarious. He is physically quite small. ... Peter is very
> articulate, very good sense of humour and relating to people. But he knows their weak spots
> and he finds Stuart's weak spots and continually puts him down.
>
> Peter used to like imaginary games just as Daniel does now. But he doesn't have much time
> to be nice to Daniel any more. He is working a six day week at school, so he is not around as
> much and he has a lot of homework to do but he used to play with him – those silly games
> careering round being different people. He would find a level to get on with Daniel quite well.
> I think he was actually quite fond of him.

Stuart (aged 9½) is a much bigger child and competes with Peter in size but not in maturity. Very aggressive in his behaviour in games and wants to win and can't bear to lose, but not aggressive at all in his attitude to people. I do an awful lot of correcting of him and I am aware that I do. I think he is a bit unsure of himself. He talks much more – he will explain things more. He tends to talk to you. ... I don't think he knows where he stands. I think Peter gives him a hard time. Upstairs, when I am not within ear-shot, an awful lot of verbal putting down goes on.

Stuart tends to go over the top when playing with Daniel. He gets that little bit too rough or, then, when Daniel gets silly, Stuart won't tolerate it. He just sort of wipes his hands of him then.

Rachel (aged 7½) is a law unto herself really. She fills every silence. She talks. She is not squashed by situations and tensions. ... Any frictions in the family just go over the top of her head. You can tell her off and you think you have really got through to her, and then she just moves on to something else and continues talking as if it is something that you have never said. I suppose it is a way of shutting out difficulties. She is very bossy. She mothers Daniel in a sort of way, which he likes. ... He likes and she likes. It is completely voluntary. She is never told to do it at all. Never told to button his cuffs ... but she does it without saying really. She is fairly outgoing and has become much more demonstrative since a hospital operation she had.

She wants Daniel out of the way if any of her friends come round. She said, ' I don't want my friends to come here because Daniel always wants to play.' She will play with him all the time at home ... and is very tolerant of him. But she will push him out if she has anything better. Daniel can't accept that. He cries and moans, 'she won't let me' and all the rest of it.

(Mrs Jarrett, parent interview, March 1988, Reception)

At a mid-point of his Reception year Daniel thus experienced Laura as withdrawing a little from her previous relationship with him as she encountered her 'teenage problems', Peter being preoccupied by his school work and routines and Stuart tending to go 'over the top' and become 'too rough'. At the same time he was aware of the rivalry between his older brothers and of the risks he might run in becoming involved in it. Not surprisingly, Daniel preferred the low risk strategy of keeping his head down which, in a way, was comparable to his strategy with his parents of 'being gooder'. Rachel, his sister closest in age to him, filled some of the space in caring for Daniel that had once been occupied by the now teenage Laura. In so doing she accomplished something of her own identity within the family. With her peers, however, she preferred to be less encumbered – much to Daniel's dismay. Daniel, in other words, had to accommodate to a set of relationships in which each sibling, quite properly, had their own concerns, priorities and strategies within the family. Daniel was well aware of this and, where he could, managed his action to ensure that he was not rejected. One example of this relates to his play with Rachel.

Today (Sunday) Daniel played 'Thundercats' with Rachel before breakfast, complete with all the voices and accents. But after breakfast until bedtime he had played out in the garden with Rachel and her friend Hannah. They have played Mummies, babies and dogs with Daniel the baby of course. He seemed to spend a great deal of the time pretending to be asleep in a large cardboard box.

(Mrs Jarrett, parent diary, June 1988, Reception)

Daniel's older brothers and sisters had, of course, passed through Greenside Primary School before and knew the teachers well. This was something of a mixed blessing in that, whilst they were supportive of his Reception teacher Mrs Powell, they tended to build up worries about the Year 1 teacher, Miss Scott.

The idea of going into a class with a preconceived idea of a teacher is not a good thing at all, really. Neither Stuart or Rachel have ever said anything detrimental about Mrs Powell and still

see her as the nicest, kindest teacher and think Daniel is lucky and tell him so, which helps. But they tell him that Miss Scott is horrible and I think that he is very likely to go to her next. In the school, she is renowned for being ... unsmiling, shall we say?
(Mrs Jarrett, parent interview, March 1988, Reception)

Daniel, Reception, relationships among friends and in the playground

Daniel entered school in the September of 1987 a little uneasily but with the great security of being with his great friend from playgroup – Harriet. Indeed, for much of the Reception year they were almost inseparable. Mrs Powell described this relationship at that time.

> He's got this best friend Harriet and I think when Harriet moves, he moves, rather than the other way round. Harriet doesn't need him quite as much as he needs Harriet. They were both in the home corner and I asked Harriet to come out because I couldn't stand the noise anymore and so Daniel said, I've played in it for long enough, can I come out as well? He follows her around.
> (Mrs Powell, teacher interview, September 1987, Reception)

Harriet and Daniel get on very well together, with Harriet being prepared, to some extent, to indulge Daniel.

> Daniel and Harriet are playing the maths game with cards (0-3) in which two have to be turned and added. Daniel has to think to recognise them and to 'add' them by counting. Even then he is very erratic with counting on the board. (Spacemen and rockets going from 'Earth' to the 'Moon'). Harriet is a little better. They negotiate answers and procedures. Daniel is ahead and announces 'I'm winning the game.' Harriet accepts this and says that she will catch up.
> (Fieldnotes, April 1988, Reception)

Daniel certainly became rather reliant on this friendship and it is easy to see it as, to some extent, mirroring his relationship within the family with Rachel. Indeed, in some ways, since the reciprocity was more consistent, it was more supportive and necessary for Daniel's adaption to the school context. Sometimes, when Daniel could not be with Harriet for some reason, then his insecurity would show:

> I told Daniel that Harriet could come and play after school as Rachel goes to Crusaders. But unfortunately when we got to school Harriet had a cold and was not going today. The tears rolled down his cheeks but I could not make out whether he was saying that he would have nobody to play with at school or he was upset that she could not come after school. As soon as we got into the cloakroom he approached the only other person there, Hazel I think her name is, and asked her if she would play.
> (Mrs Jarrett, parent diary, February 1988, Reception)

However, Mrs Jarrett felt that Daniel was simply too dependent on Harriet. She was concerned that Daniel needed to learn how to cope at school on his own and also that his close friendship with a girl might cause him difficulties in later years.

> Harriet has a very strong personality and Daniel definitely relies on her. I consider him to be very immature really. ... I do see it as a bit problematic. I am worried really how he would cope if he didn't have her. Children have very sexist attitudes as they grow older. ... Boys who play with girls have a very rough time when they get slightly older. ... It is not the same for girls. Girls who play with boys are not branded the same as boys who play with girls – you know what I am trying to say. ... I just want him to spend a part of his day uninfluenced by her really. They are in the same group at school. When I went to Parents' Evening the first thing Mrs

Powell said to me was, 'You are not really worried about Daniel and Harriet are you? I said, 'Yes, it is a very narrow situation and he is not getting what he could out of school really'.
(Mrs Jarrett, parent interview, March 1988, Reception)

During the year it was certainly the case that activities in the playground did become increasingly patterned by gender. Many boys, particularly those from a group of slightly older Reception children from the next class, took to a variety of fairly noisy chasing games which tended to dominate the playground space. Some of these boys were a little 'difficult' in class and had become known as 'Mrs Miles Naughty Boys' because of their behaviour. Daniel was very concerned to avoid any form of trouble with them. At the same time the girls, often led confidently by Sally, developed imaginative playground games such as 'Mummies and Daddies', 'My Little Pony' and 'cows' in which Daniel comfortably joined for much of the year.

From the latter part of the Spring Term onwards children became more aware of and accentuated the gendered nature of their play as 'kiss chase' became popular as a playground game. The period saw an assertion by both boys and girls of their respective group identities.

In this context, Daniel began to play more with some boys and *against* some girls.

Robert and Daniel get rather noisy trying on and joking about female wigs in the home corner. Daniel puts one onto Amy and she throws it off.
(Fieldnotes, June 1988, Reception)

Similarly, Harriet began to play more with girls and noted the change in their relationship.

Harriet, in interview, declares how she 'likes playing mummies and daddies and babies with Alice and Amanda'. She says that she 'used to play with Daniel a lot, but now she plays with Amy and Hazel. Daniel plays with Matthew and Barry now. Before he used to play mummies and daddies and babies but Daniel kept running away when I got an ice-cream for him'.
(Fieldnotes, July 1988, Reception)

Thus, towards the end of this Reception year, Daniel responded to both his mother's feelings and the changing nature of peer and playground culture by moving beyond the security of his previous relationship with Harriet. However, he was not immediately welcomed into the company of the boys, having been perceived, given his relative insecurity at starting school, as a 'bit of a baby'. In this transitional period he was a little bewildered as the following interview transcript indicates.

AP:	You were playing the cow game weren't you, just now? Did you like that?
Daniel:	*(Nods)*
AP:	Do you often play with Amy and Sarah?
Daniel:	*(Nods)*
AP:	You do. What about some of the boys? Do you play with them at all?
Daniel:	*(Looks rather blank)*
AP:	Not so much?
Daniel:	Only Edmund.
AP:	You like playing with him a bit, do you?
Daniel:	Yes.
AP:	Why do you like playing with him?
Daniel:	He chases girls.
AP:	Does he?
Daniel:	I chase them too.
AP:	You do, do you?

Daniel: Mmmmm
AP: Why don't you play with the others so much, do you think?
Daniel: *(No reply)*
AP: Not sure?
Daniel: *(Nods)*
(Daniel, video interview, July 1988, Reception)

In new situations Daniel was particularly uneasy. Thus he developed a real concern for going to play, or eat, at other children's homes or to birthday parties. Mrs Jarrett described one such incident in which the separation of boys' and girls' culture was becoming particularly clear.

> I had to persuade him to go. I mean, he had been to her house so many times I thought he would cope with it. I think it was Jonathan and Damien sitting on a rug and there was Amy and Mary, and Daniel's face was a picture. His mouth was quivering, and he was sinking into me as far as he could go and holding my hand. He didn't want to go. Jonathan and Damien said, 'Hello Danny, come and sit with us', just like that, but what did these two girls say? 'Look at Daniel, look at his silly face', he is 'crying again' sort of attitude. ... I don't know if it is the difference between girls and boys, I think girls are more prone to the cutting remarks.
>
> I did feel for him, I felt like saying, 'How dare you speak to him like this'. Because your protective instinct comes in and I felt so sorry for him, I thought no wonder the poor chap doesn't want to go, to be subjected to ridicule every time.
> (Mrs Jarrett, parent interview, July 1988, Reception)

Daniel, however, was caught somewhere between the cultures of the boys and the girls. At home, he found particular satisfaction and support from his sister, Rachel and at school Harriet had fulfilled a similar role. Now his play with the two girls was indeed beginning to pose an identity crisis, and yet Daniel did not feel anything like confident enough to take up the assertive style of the dominant boys' culture. Towards the end of the year, Mrs Jarrett noted Daniel's problem and his gradually evolving solution of identifying one, 'special' male friend.

> I think he doesn't feel secure any more. He hasn't got this person (Harriet) to rely on her. Also, he hasn't got a good friend amongst the boys. ... Also, he tends to like the more gentle one's. He had this phase of liking Robert but this seems to have tailed off ... and it's Andrew at the moment, but I think that is circumstances as opposed to them being great friends.
> (Mrs Jarrett, parent interview, July 1988, Reception)

Daniel was to retain and develop this strategy over the years and indeed his friendship with Andrew grew to become the cornerstone of his adaptation to school.

Daniel, Reception, Relationships with Mrs Powell in the classroom

At the start of the year, Daniel was sometimes a little disturbed when left by his mother at the start of the school day but he invariably soon settled. Mrs Powell discussed this with Mrs Jarrett and felt that he would gradually become more confident. Although Daniel would occasionally sit with Mrs Powell for comfort at the start of the day, he was seen as presenting 'no real problems'. Indeed, Mrs Powell was extremely experienced in the induction of young children to school and her calm and kindly approach was well suited to increasing children's confidence.

Mrs Jarrett had been a little concerned by Daniel's response to some simple work on 'basics' which had been begun at playgroup, and she was relieved by the more relaxed approach which Daniel showed in Mrs Powell's class.

> The funny thing is, at playgroup they had a small class where she taught them the basics of number work, exactly the same as Mrs Powell does with the word tin. He hated it and absolutely used to quiver when he went into the class, and couldn't bear it and worried about it dreadfully. And yet, he has never complained at school about the same situation, so it is obviously taught in a very different way.
> (Mrs Jarrett, parent interview, March 1988, Reception)

In fact, Mrs Powell's steady routines and her warmth towards the children seemed to suit Daniel well. Daniel began to trust and relax with her. This is illustrated by the ways in which, on many occasions at 'Review Time', he shared insights into some of his play with her. He often talked about models which he had made with Mobilo construction outfit:

> It's a bat machine – it catches people who are chasing after bats. It throws a bomb out and the person goes in there and gets covered in chocolate.

> I made an aeroplane. That's the front and that's the back. The engine is in there. It transforms into a caravan.

> It is a boat and it has another boat on it. It unclips and it is a paddle boat. It goes on the sea. The little boat keeps the big boat going. It transforms into a man and into a dinosaur.
> (Separate occasions recorded by fieldnotes, early Spring Term, Reception)

Mrs Powell had no doubts in telling Mrs Jarrett that she thought Daniel was 'lovely' (Mrs Jarrett, parent diary, February 1988, Reception).

However, as the year progressed, Mrs Powell began to increase the proportion of work on basic skills which the children were expected to undertake each day. Daniel found this restrictive and developed feelings which perhaps began to echo those he had at playgroup:

AP:	Did you like doing that maths?
Daniel:	No, I don't like it in the maths corner.
AP:	You don't like maths? Why's that, then?
Daniel:	Because I get a tummy ache then.
AP:	You get a tummy ache, do you? You get a tummy ache when it's maths time, do you?
Daniel:	Because I don't like it.
AP:	Ah. I wonder why you don't you like it? Is it because Mrs Powell tells you you must do it?
Daniel:	Yes.
AP:	Is that really the reason?
Daniel:	Yeah, it is. I get fed up with her, because she tells me other things what's very nasty.
AP:	Does she? Very nasty? What are the nasty things she tells you?
Daniel:	'Get on with it!'
AP:	You'd rather do something else, would you?
Daniel:	Yeah. I make loads of Mobilo best because it's good, because I like 'showing them'.
AP:	There's Mrs Powell *(showing a photograph)* and she's working with the children doing the writing, isn't she?
Daniel:	Yes. She's nice when she helps.
AP:	What does she do with you?
Daniel:	She helps me to write and read.
AP	And does she help you get it done better?

Daniel: Yes. ... I like doing the things where you can do it all on your own.
AP: Do you like it in things like the home corner then?
Daniel: Yes. Because the teacher isn't there.
(Daniel, photo interview, February 1988, Reception)

Towards the end of the year, Daniel again became disturbed about going to school. There were probably two main reasons for this. The most important may well have been the gradual tightening of the curriculum, with Daniel becoming particularly concerned to complete his tasks correctly and worrying considerably about 'being told off' – however mild the manner in which this might occur. Daniel seemed to interpret many teacher actions as 'being cross' and found them worrying. Perhaps he was influenced by the warnings from his siblings about what being in Miss Scott's class might be like, warnings which seem to have been confirmed by his occasional observation of her. However, it is also likely that his unease reflected his insecure relationships with his peers – having given up Harriet's friendship but not yet replaced it. For whatever reason, the result was serious:

> Daniel has been ill since last Friday with a high temperature. He has had nightmares and one night he woke in quite a state saying he did not want to go to school, nobody likes him and they are always cross. He did not like Miss Scott – 'She's got a cross face'. I think he was very hot and uncomfortable but he was very distressed. Today I mentioned that he would be going back to school tomorrow. Look of horror on his face – he does not want to go.
> (Mrs Jarrett, parent diary, June 1988, Reception)

Mrs Powell offered her normal calm, but firm, support, but neither she nor Mrs Jarrett were really able to connect with Daniel's concerns:

> When I drop him off at school, he is white as a sheet. ... He tends to be very withdrawn about it really, because he is very quiet. I mean, he feels it inside.
> (Mrs Jarrett, parent interview, July 1988, Reception)

There was then, never any fully understood reason for Daniel's fears. However, what is clear is that, notwithstanding his early trust in Mrs Powell, Daniel felt increasingly threatened by the demands of the curriculum at a time when the lack of the peer support he needed left him vulnerable and frequently isolated in the classroom.

Daniel, Reception, progress in classroom learning

Daniel's progress at the basics of literacy and maths were, notwithstanding his anxieties, a perfectly respectable average for that of the class. The report which Mrs Powell wrote for his parents in the spring of 1988 described him in the following terms:

> Daniel is keen to talk and read and has neat handwriting. He enjoys maths and has no trouble with the concepts. He is interested in all class activities and usually listens well. He is good at PE and creative activities and he enjoys imaginative play. He is happy and sociable and able to cooperate with others.
> (Mrs Powell, teacher report to parents, spring 1988, Reception)

Nevertheless, this apparently routine progress, which was undoubtedly the impression which Daniel wanted to present, hid some more personal struggles for Daniel.

Daniel began his programme of learning to read at school with Mrs Powell's system whereby his 'word tin' and reading book went between home and school. He was very pleased to have the status of 'learning to read' and valued both his progress and the special attention which he received from his mother:

> AP: What are these things here in these tins and piles?
> Daniel: That's for your word tin and that's for your book place. You have to read when you get home with them.
> AP: Who do you read them with at home?
> Daniel: Mummy. I sit on her lap.
> AP: You sit on her lap. Is that nice?
> Daniel: Yes.
> AP: Have you got lots of words in your word tin?
> Daniel: Yeah. I've got loads and loads of new ones. I like getting new words.
>
> (Daniel, child interview, February 1988, Reception)

However, with this progress went a certain degree of worry, for which sucking his thumb provided some comfort:

> He always sucks his thumb at night, all night as far as I can see. I go in and heave it out, and then there is all this suction and it goes back in again. He will put it in at night while you read a story – always when I am reading to him. And he puts it in between words when he is reading.
> I think sometimes, that I ought to leave the words if it gets late, and say 'to hell with it,' but he worries about it.
>
> (Mrs Jarrett, parent interview, March 1988, Reception)

Certainly Daniel made steady progress during the year. At school, when he was unsure of how to read something, he would insert meaningful words as he read and, in discussion, he could embellish stories intelligently. By the end of the summer Mrs Powell was confident that he had 'made good progress' (Mrs Powell, teacher report to parents, summer 1988, Reception).

However, Daniel's mother was less confident of his skill at decoding text, though she noted his enjoyment and understanding of stories.

> I found some old Ladybird reading scheme books and thought Daniel might be able to read Book 1 easily. He skipped through it and felt very pleased with his achievement, but the second one was more difficult and he soon got fed up with it. I had forgotten how boring they were. Managed to struggle through the book he brought home from school.
> He does enjoy being read to, particularly by grandfather who reads slowly and discusses things about the story with him. The ultimate punishment for not co-operating at bed time is no story – this is very rare. ... Daniel knows the stories and the sequence of events and is able to give reasons for why things happen.
>
> (Mrs Jarrett, parent diary, June 1988, Reception)

Overall though, reading was a source of pleasure and achievement for Daniel over the year.

Daniel's progress at writing was also sound and was achieved via Mrs Powell's daily, tried and tested Reception class programme of doing 'picture and writing'. With this daily exercise, Daniel made steady progress and filled at least four writing books over the year. His progress, in both representational drawing, handwriting and in expressing himself and his experiences, is well illustrated by the examples of his work in Documents 6.1, 6.2 and 6.3.

Unfortunately, for Daniel, the reality of such writing tasks was that they were 'the horriblest' activity which he experienced at school. This horror seemed to have two main components – boredom and a sense of the consequence of non-completion:

> AP: What do you think about when you're doing your writing?
> Daniel: I get a lot fed up.

This is me in the garden and the sun is shining.

Document 6.1 *Daniel, picture and writing about 'me in the garden', September 1987, Reception*

Monday   11th   January

I   am   playing   with

my   Thundercat   sword.

Document 6.2   *Daniel, picture and writing about 'playing with a Thundercat sword', January 1988, Reception*

I am helping mummy
I am helping mummy

make chocolate cakes
milk chocolate cakes

with chocolate on the
with chocolate on the

top.
top.

Document 6.3 *Daniel, picture and writing about 'helping mummy make chocolate cakes', March 1988, Reception*

AP: You get fed up. Why do you get fed up with the writing?
Daniel: Because it takes a too long time. .... I do it all, though.
AP: You do it all?
Daniel: Yeah. I don't like the teachers to tell you off.
AP: So you think it's best just to do it ... .
(Daniel, child interview, February 1988, Reception)

Despite his aversion to such tasks, Daniel's application and his developing reading skills began to produce the capacity for more independent writing. At the end of the school year Mrs Powell reported:

Daniel is willing to try to do his writing by himself and he is able to spell a few words. His handwriting is quite well formed when he takes time over it.
(Mrs Powell, teacher report to parents, summer 1988, Reception)

In maths Daniel again made steady progress within the fairly conventional curriculum provided by Mrs Powell. He learned to write numerals, practised one-to-one correspondence, engaged in some simple addition and subtraction and a variety of forms of measuring, weighing and other practical maths. Many of these activities were structured by the worksheets which Mrs Powell produced, as in the examples in Documents 6.4, 6.5 and 6.6 .

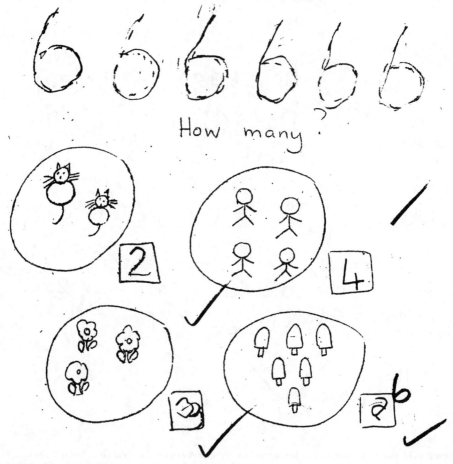

Document 6.4   *Daniel, sample number task, October 1987, Reception*

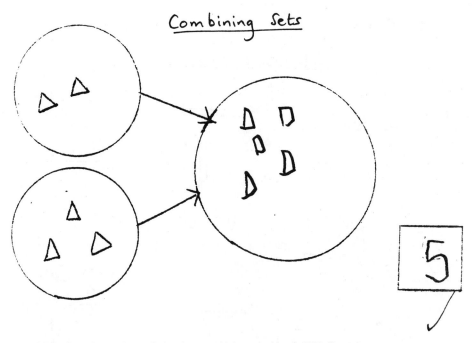

Document 6.5 *Daniel, sample number task on combining sets, March 1988, Reception*

Daniel was usually among the slower children to both start and finish such tasks, which, unlike 'picture and writing' often varied in the detail of what was expected. Daniel's concern to act correctly meant that he was regularly observed waiting and watching other children, so that he could be sure that he was approaching the task in the way in which Mrs Powell required.

As Mrs Powell noted in her report, Daniel did indeed like imaginative play, particularly in the home corner with Harriet and sometimes some of the other girls, or through the media of the sand or Mobilo construction equipment. When placing photographs of classroom activities in order, Daniel's ranking (from 'liked' to 'disliked') went: home corner, Mobilo, painting then maths and writing. The latter were, 'the horriblest, because you have to do them' (Daniel, photo interview, February 1988, Reception).

In Mrs Powell's perception then, Daniel made considerable progress during his first year at school. He settled in after an uneasy start and he achieved good levels of attainment in reading, writing and maths. However, the fact that he became so unsettled again towards the end of the year did upset his mother and she felt that, at that point, he 'had gone backwards' in his learning (Mrs Jarrett, parent interview, July 1988, Reception).

Daniel, identity and learning in Reception

Within his home and family, as we have seen, Daniel strove to establish his identity in a busy and complex interplay of relationships. As the youngest child, he watched and learned from his older siblings, tried to fill some of the niches they left, to take advantages of the opportunities they created and, gradually, to assert himself despite the inherent risks of so doing. As Mrs Jarrett put it:

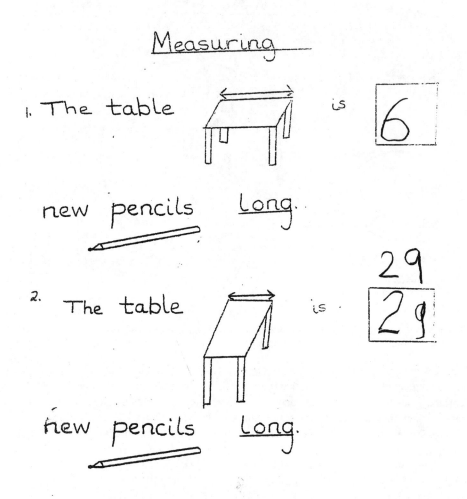

Document 6.6 *Daniel, sample measuring task, February 1988, Reception*

> I think that a lot of the aggro that goes on at home, although he is not involved in it, he is definitely aware of it. They are not a family that always get on particularly well. I don't feel they are great friends. There is a great deal of, 'He is not having more than me'. There is nothing concrete that has happened, but I am sure his identity is affected by all this.
> (Mrs Jarrett, parent interview, July 1988, Reception)

In this context, Daniel particularly valued the chances of special, non-risk attention from his mother, grandfather or others who offered it.

More actively, from his position of relative inexperience and weakness within the family, he adopted the essentially defensive strategies of watching, waiting and trying to 'be gooder'. This seemed to lead to a considerable reluctance to take any sort of risks, sometimes over the most mundane of issues:

> He gets very agitated if he doesn't do it as he thinks he should. He sets himself quite high standards. It has to be perfect. ... Yesterday, he got downstairs early for breakfast. Martin was still

down there. Daniel put this Weetabix in the bowl. He wanted to pour the milk on himself and he said to Martin, 'you will have to tell me when to stop.' He has to check everything. He wouldn't just judge it. He has to know. He doesn't like making mistakes.
(Mrs Jarrett, parent interview, March 1988, Reception)

Daniel also adopted some of the same methodical characteristics of his father and, when applied to eating, these were a source of both frustration and amusement among the family:

Mrs Jarrett:	It's awful, it's painful, it nearly drives everybody insane. He has to eat in certain order, never mixtures on a fork – it is a carrot into the mouth, a pea into the mouth, this is how it goes on.
AP:	He will go through the carrots and then goes through all the peas and then on to the next?
Mrs Jarrett:	Yes, I think he eats the meat first, that's the best. ... Martin is methodical. That's an understatement for him. He is absolutely meticulous. I am sure half the reason he is late at night, is because he is far too methodical at work.

(Mrs Jarrett, parent interview, March 1988, Reception)

For Daniel at school, his security came initially from his friendship with Harriet and his relationship with Mrs Powell. However, as the year wore on, he came to reappraise both sources of support. His friendship with Harriet was not endorsed by his mother and was further undermined by both girls and boys at school. Not only was such a friendship with a girl deemed 'cissy', but Daniel's tearful reaction and renewed unwillingness to come to school, to visit the homes of other children and attend birthday parties was seen as transferring to school the 'baby' identity with which he had grown up at home. Mrs Powell's pursuit of her curriculum objectives, combined with Daniel's fear of 'getting things wrong' or 'being told off' unwittingly compounded his unease. Mrs Jarrett noted the change in Daniel during the year and the depth of his and her concern:

He has definitely changed since Easter. He has become more and more insecure really. I can't really analyse his feelings. He is terrified of making a mistake all the time. ... I think he thinks too much. He reasons with himself, whereas the others tend to accept things a bit more than he does.
(Mrs Jarrett, parent interview, July 1988, Reception)

He seems to have lost confidence to cope with situations of which he is not completely sure. Birthday parties present problems now. He does not want to go anywhere that he has not been before. How will he know how to play the games? He might get them wrong. What will he have to eat? What if he does not like the food? I have persuaded him to go and he does seem to cope when there, but the look on his face of being abandoned is heart-rending. This feeling of insecurity was extended to school. He does not like the maths today. He does not know how to make the patterns with the buttons. What if he gets them wrong? Mrs Powell says he is OK, but he says he cries but she does not see him. His ability to learn is being affected by all this. At home he is reluctant to read or do anything connected with what he considers to be 'work'. ... Daniel does not appear to be making much progress at the moment in any direction.
(Mrs Jarrett, parent diary, June 1988, Reception)

Daniel was clearly sensitive to the perceptions of his mother and teacher regarding his school work. His mother recorded the following incident which she undoubtedly regretted:

I have upset Daniel and lost my temper whilst doing the word tin tonight.
We had read the book reasonably well. We then progressed to the word tin which I have sorted out into words which sound similar, i.e. 'ball', 'tall', 'wall', 'all', which he loves to get right all in a row. Then we do 'come', 'came', 'get', 'got', 'go' and, of course, 'saw' and 'was', which he always has to think about, and several other variations instead of reading them all parrot fashion. However, whilst doing 'ball', 'tall' etc. I asked him what they looked like and which letters were the same. Although he knew the similarity, he could not name the letters.

This for some reason annoyed me, particularly as he called 'l', 'r' – both of which he has in his name and, although he obviously knows the order in which they are written, he could not name them. Anyway I said something like, 'This is ridiculous. I don't know how Mrs Powell puts up with you if you don't even know what letters look like.' Whereupon he burst into tears and shouted, 'She likes me and says I do beautiful drawings', and fled upstairs and put himself to bed.

He reappeared a few minutes later, wrote his name and told me all the letters without any hesitation. I regret bitterly getting annoyed and would rather not lower his self esteem.
(Mrs Jarrett, parent diary, June 1988, Reception)

Daniel thus ended his Reception year feeling somewhat unhappy and vulnerable despite his very sound learning achievements. His mother, in particular, was concerned about him and, in her anxiety, she offered two main explanations:

I feel his progress is limited at the moment and I feel it is because he is not very happy and there is no way he is going to work well if he is not happy, is there?
I don't think he is very academic. He certainly shows no signs of being a genius to me. ... I think, perhaps, he is just thick actually.
(Mrs Jarrett, parent interview, July 1988, Reception)

The question of innate ability is, of course, one which is asked by many parents in one form or another as they bring their children up and perhaps it underpins the public fascination with so-called 'objective' assessments and examinations. However, in this context, Mrs Jarrett's comment was not meant seriously. The social explanation which she offered, relating to Daniel's happiness, was much more tangible because of the recently announced decision that Daniel's next class would indeed be that of Miss Scott. Indeed, Mrs Jarrett knew very well that Miss Scott's reputation, which Daniel's siblings had liberally catalogued, was partly accurate. She knew that the situation could be difficult for Daniel:

I worry about next year, because I don't think he is going to be happy, especially not to start with.
(Mrs Jarrett, parent interview, July 1988, Reception)

From Daniel's perspective, his predicament was indeed difficult. He was under peer pressure to make friends with boys, yet his previous security at both home and school had come from relationships with individual girls. Furthermore, Miss Scott, his next teacher, was renowned for strictness and for her treatment of 'naughty boys'.

An overall summary of Daniel's Reception year is provided by Matrix 6.1, overleaf.

Matrix 6.1 *Daniel's Reception Year, a summary matrix*

Family relationships	Peer-group relationships	Teacher relationships	Identity	Learning
Daniel is youngest of a busy family with five children. Mrs Jarrett takes 'no nonsense' line with all the children in order to maintain family routines and relationships as a whole. Mrs Jarrett has special relationship with Daniel, her youngest child. Generally seen as 'the baby' of the family, he feels a little vulnerable. Mr Jarrett is under pressure from his work and works very long hours. Struggles to define his place. Wants to do things 'correctly'. Sometimes laughed at when getting angry. Mother concerned, as she considers reading progress to be slow. Daniel is both supported and rejected by siblings as they pursue their own concerns and strategies. He is watchful of his older brothers and is closest to his younger sister, Rachel. They often play together unless her friends call.	At start of year Daniel has very close attachment to Harriet, which is continued from playgroup. This is seen as 'over dependence' and is discouraged by Mrs Jarrett. Daniel has an uneasy relationship with other boys and is very aware of the 'naughty boys' in the next class. More distinctive cultures of boys and girls emerge during the year and Daniel is criticized by some boys and some girls. Daniel is very insecure, for instance, crying when coming into school and being reluctant to visit other children's homes. By the end of the year, Daniel rejects his friendship with Harriet. He begins to develop close friendships with individual boys, thus replacing his previous relationships with Rachel at home and with Harriet at school.	Daniel somewhat uneasy at starting school but eased in by Mrs Powell's calm, warm consistency. Enjoys play at school and is confident to 'share' it with Mrs Powell and other children. Gradual drawing back as curriculum requirements for writing and maths are enforced by Mrs Powell. Daniel very worried about 'being told off', as he sees it, and sometimes fears he is 'not liked'. Daniel begins to be aware of Miss Scott and of teachers who are 'cross', particularly with 'naughty boys'.	Relatively low status – the 'baby of the family'. Sometimes seen as rather immature, unnecessarily meticulous and dependent. Sees himself as trying to 'be gooder' to earn parental affection. At school, Mrs Powell sees Daniel as a little immature but sociable and cooperative. He is among the older children in the class. Daniel is not confident with his male peers but distances himself from Harriet. Tries to adopt a close male friend, continues to feel vulnerable without one. A 'follower' in peer group culture and activities.	Hates failure or making 'mistakes' in any setting. If facing new learning challenges, likes the security of routines and procedures or confirmation of his approach. Progress and enjoyment of reading, supported by mother and other family members. Progress seen as good by teacher, poor by mother. Daniel feels supported by his teacher's confidence in his academic progress, despite his mother's concerns. Sound progress in maths and writing despite feeling 'bored' by the tasks which 'must be done'. Enjoys the open, non-threatening play of home corner and construction equipment.

6.4   DANIEL IN HIS YEAR 1

Daniel, Year 1, relationships with parents at home

Throughout Daniel's Year 1, his relationship with his parents continued in a similar pattern to that of his Reception year. His mother continued to be concerned about both his maturity and overall ability. She felt that Daniel was like his father in being very particular that things should be done correctly. However, Mrs Jarrett was supportive of Daniel and recognized the key necessity of helping him to believe in himself:

> With shoe laces ... he wanted these trainers and they had laces. I think I must have done them up twenty times on the first day because they kept coming undone, and I said, 'if you want to wear these trainers, you have to tie them up.' ... So we got out this rag dolly practice thing and we sat down and amidst great frustration and tears he couldn't get it right. So he wouldn't do it. That is his attitude – if you can't do it, you don't do it. Then, all of a sudden he got up one morning and put the trainer on and he tied a bow and it was absolutely perfect. And he's done it every time since. ... Once he knew he could do it, he will do it again and again because he knows he can do it. Before, he thought he couldn't do it.
> (Mrs Jarrett, parent interview, November 1988, Year 1)

Unfortunately, Daniel was particularly unsettled at the start of his year with Miss Scott and his mother was very aware of this. As she explained:

> He was very tense to start with. He didn't like the classroom situation at all ... the tension and the shouting that went on. ... I think that he found it difficult to cope with the tension that there was between the older boys in the class and Miss Scott. ... He used to come home and says things that had happened and I would say, 'I'm sure it didn't', that she didn't do that. He'd say, 'She did, she did and I hate her'. Now he just says he hates her but he accepts it. He doesn't really like her but he seems able to cope with it.
> (Mrs Jarrett, parent interview, November 1988, Year 1)

Mrs Jarrett was well aware that Daniel's paramount concern to do things correctly and to avoid any possible criticism meant that life in Miss Scott's classroom was often stressful for him. She attempted to negotiate with Miss Scott but Miss Scott perceived her as being 'overwrought'. However, Mrs Jarrett also had to negotiate with Daniel when one of his strategies became that of 'being ill' so that he could avoid school. He worked hard to convince on this point, but was a little naive, as his mother reported in relation to his remarks one evening:

> He said, 'If I say I'm feeling ill now, then you'll know that I'm ill if I say I'm ill tomorrow, won't you?'
> (Mrs Jarrett. fieldnote of conversation, March 1989, Year 1)

Daniel continued to relate well with his father at weekends when they would often work on odd jobs in the house and garden. On one such occasion, after Daniel had inadvertently swallowed a loose tooth, they discussed what should be done to convince the 'Tooth Fairies' that he deserved money under his pillow. Motivated by the need to communicate, Daniel wrote a letter to the fairies that was of considerably higher standard than that of his school work at the time, see Document 6.7, overleaf.

be ar fairies
my tooth came
out and I ate it
in my doughnut.
can you look in
my mouth· and you
will see it has
gone
Love   from
daniel.

Document 6.7   *Daniel, letter to 'Tooth Fairies', November 1988, Year 1*

Daniel, Year 1, relationships with siblings at home

Daniel continued his struggle to establish himself among his four older siblings. As his mother explained at the start of the year, 'He doesn't have his own individual slot yet'. However, by the end of the year he had begun to assert himself more:

He stands up for himself at home now. He's not trodden upon so easily. The others all get a bit fed up with the fact that he won't do certain things and he won't wear certain things – 'I was never allowed to be like that when I was his age' sort of attitude. But yes, he is more confident than he was.
(Mrs Jarrett, parent interview, July 1989, Year 1)

Nevertheless, Daniel still found it hard to make his case with complete confidence because of the bustle and competition for attention within the family.

Mrs Jarrett:	He can't express himself as well as the others, but it is coming. He was telling us walking across the field the other day about some incident and it was taking an awful long time, and even Rachel said, 'Oh, for goodness sake!'. You see he gets a lot of stick from brothers and sisters as well. Not just me. They say, 'What are you trying to say?' They're not prepared to sit there for five minutes waiting for it to come out. But he got there. They all say things and then ... the next one up puts them down.
AP:	But he's at the bottom.
Mrs Jarrett:	Yes, he's only got the cat!

(Mrs Jarrett, parent interview, July 1989, Year 1)

Daniel, Year 1, relationships among friends and in the playground

Daniel began the year seeking to continue to establish himself with other boys. Miss Scott noticed him as watching and taking cues from other boys. She characterized him as 'a follower' and 'certainly not a leader' who would either work on his own or with Andrew, 'a nice, pleasant little boy'. Over the year this friendship with Andrew was to flourish and deepen.

Daniel now expressed his rejection of involvement with girls and declared that 'All my friends are boys' and 'I like boys better than girls'. In the playground, he now played games such as chasing, 'off-ground-touch' and 'Superman' with boys such as Luke, William, Stephen and Andrew. The strength of the peer pressure and growing polarization of the boys and girls can be seen in the teasing of a boy who had deviated from gender expectations in the colour of his clothes and also in Daniel's perception of the girls' attempts to assert themselves.

Daniel:	We fight 'Girlie Gloves'.
AP:	What do you mean?
Daniel:	Girlie Gloves, but it's a boy really, and he's got girl gloves, so we call him 'Girlie Gloves'.
AP:	And, what do you do with the girls? Do you play with the girls at all?
Daniel:	No, I hate them.
AP:	Why do you hate them?
Daniel:	Well, they boss us around and things.

(Daniel, photo interview, November 1988, Year 1)

Despite Daniel's rejection of girls, he remained a little insecure among other boys. However, he derived increasing security and entertainment from his friendship with Andrew.

Daniel, Year 1, relationships with Miss Scott in the classroom

Daniel felt insecure and worried for much of his time in Miss Scott's classroom. He always kept a low profile and watched carefully to avoid getting into any sort of 'trouble' or being 'told off'. He was very aware of the risk that he might be her focus when she was 'in a bad mood'. He worked cautiously, checking at each stage. Miss Scott noted this. She was not sure how to interpret it but she suspected both pressure and 'over-protectiveness' from home:

> Daniel is a very slow worker, probably works his backside off at home. Typical Greenside syndrome in that they work so hard at home, they feel they haven't got the energy to work at school. ... But I haven't really got through to him at all really. ... He is a boy I haven't really sorted out and the problems come from the home I think.
> (Miss Scott, teacher interview, November 1988, Year 1)

Daniel was particularly aware of Miss Scott's tendency to shout at the children when teaching sessions became disorganized. This was highlighted for him by the comparative calm of his previous teacher and, even in the autumn of Year 1, he had begun to develop a form of resistance with his friend, Andrew:

> Daniel: Miss Scott's nastier ... because she shouts at everyone.
> AP: So what do you do when she starts shouting?
> Daniel: I start talking about her and going, 'I think she's a twit', and things like that.
> AP: You say that with your friends?
> Daniel: In my mind, so no one knows. Sometimes I tell Andrew. We're thinking about chucking her down the loo.
> AP: Chucking her down the loo?
> Daniel: And flushing her.
> (Daniel, photo interview, November 1988, Year 1)

The discussions which took place at this time between Mrs Jarrett and Miss Scott were somewhat inconclusive, with a considerable difference in their perceptions of the situation. As Miss Scott noted:

> Mum has said Daniel seems to have lost his confidence in himself as a worker. I feel it is more due to her hard attitude towards him one minute, and being over-protective the next.
> (Miss Scott, teacher record, November 1988, Year 1)

This situation continued somewhat uneasily for much of the year, with Daniel maintaining very cautious strategies within the classroom or even seeking to avoid coming to school altogether. Throughout, he wanted the security of the established daily routine in which his mother brought him to school and collected him.

However, Daniel did became more relaxed towards the end of the year. Mrs Jarrett felt that Daniel had simply 'come to terms' with Miss Scott, whilst Miss Scott saw this growing confidence as a product of his friendship with Andrew and their liking for 'being a bit silly at times':

> Daniel appears happier in himself and has struck up a friendship with Andrew. This has been good for him, boosting his confidence. In fact they both get boisterous and exuberant together. However, at the moment they display good co-operation, encouraging one another in their work. Daniel, as a result, is calmer and assured on arrival at school, and appears less reliant on Mum's presence.
> (Miss Scott, teacher record, May 1989, Year 1)

Daniel, Year 1, progress in classroom learning

Daniel's progress in school was sound over the year as a whole, though it is impossible to assess the effect of his sense of insecurity. The most graphic example of this was his faith in a 'magic conker' which he felt could help him with his writing. As Mrs Jarrett recorded in her diary:

> Daniel has a shrivelled up magic conker at the moment and this morning he thought he had lost it but it re-appeared in the other pocket. This caused a few minutes diversion at breakfast but was soon forgotten. ... At bath time the conker appeared again. It was put in the bath and washed, did several plunges and flights and was then carefully dried and placed inside the cardboard tube sword. I listened at the door whilst he was in the bath – he could not see me but I had overheard a few snatches of conversation with this conker so listened carefully. He told it he was going to take it with him to school and it could help him write his story and tell him how to write 'pop' and 'out'.
> (Mrs Jarrett, parent diary, October 1988, Year 1)

Indeed, writing was an activity which Daniel told his mum he hated:

> Writing is his big bug-bear. He is slow and finds it very laborious and dreads days when he has to write about anything. I don't think he finds writing down his thoughts very easy as he is much too concerned about getting the actual writing done to an acceptable standard.
> (Mrs Jarrett, parent diary, July 1989, Year 1)

Certainly, Daniel's written work did not show as much improvement over the year as might have been expected. For example, the story below, written at school in the summer, can be compared with his much earlier letter to the tooth fairies.

Overall, Miss Scott reported Daniel to be, 'still rather hesitant and shy' with regard to language development. She went on:

I had a prty an sunday
and I had a mgison
to my prty
then we had to go home

Document 6.8 *Daniel, writing news about his birthday party, June 1989, Year 1*

Daniel listens well and is becoming more responsive in class oral situations. He is reading with growing awareness although I am not sure if he really enjoys it. He needs to feel more relaxed and receive a lot of praise in order to boost his self-confidence.
(Miss Scott, report to parents, spring 1989, Year 1)

By the end of the year, Daniel had made good progress with his reading. Miss Scott gave this a high priority and praised him as he moved forward. Mrs Jarrett also read with him each evening in what was, by her account, 'a fairly teeth gritting exercise' during which she tried to 'encourage him and disregard any failures'. Daniel himself was determined to make progress and to show himself and his brothers and sisters that he could indeed 'read'.

Daniel, identity and learning in Year 1

Daniel's Year 1 was not easy for him. Whilst not quite secure in his position within his family, he also began the year on the margins of the boys' peer culture and faced a class-room situation which he experienced as threatening. In each setting he wished to avoid any risk of failure or humiliation – about which he was very sensitive. At home, he gradually began to assert himself. Among his peers, through rejecting girls, establishing his friend-ship with Andrew and developing some suitably boisterous activities with him, he began to feel more secure and relaxed. Throughout though, he faced the challenge of a 'high-risk' classroom and his fundamental insecurity affected him deeply. Mrs Jarrett's diary entry for the Summer Term conveyed something of this:

We have been counting the days until the end of this term. Each week is a milestone in the countdown to July 25th. Daniel has been at school two years now but still cannot go in on his own. Each day the same pattern has to be followed – into the classroom, packed lunch under the table, book in the reading box then a goodbye kiss. No deviations and always checking over his shoulder to make sure that I am still there. At least he goes, but it is not a pleasure and he is still constantly worried in case he does or says something wrong that will incur the 'shouting'.

In fact, today I overheard him telling Stuart and Rachel that he did not know what to do because sometimes Miss Scott says things have to be done one way, then she says, 'That's wrong' and you must do something else. He said he was told to put something away with Maurice and Peter, so they put it away, then Miss Scott started shouting that they must get it out again, they had done it wrong. So they got it out but she still shouted.

He went all red and the tears started to come out. I am sure he takes things to heart more than most in his class and I so wish that he got greater pleasure from his achievements, but all the time he is worried about mistakes. ... This has been the longest school year I can ever remember.
(Mrs Jarrett, parent diary, July 1989, Year 1)

Nevertheless, Daniel did move forward during the year. At the end, he saw himself as someone who could now 'read' and he took great pleasure from his rapport with Andrew and other peer activities. These were important developments, though overall a particular sense of insecurity remained when he was confronted with learning challenges which might expose him to adverse comment by others.

Matrix 6.2 *Daniel's Year 1, a summary matrix*

Family relationships	Peer-group relationships	Teacher relationships	Identity	Learning
Mrs Jarrett is concerned that Daniel's progress at reading is slow. Mr Jarrett gets frustrated that Daniel does not understand phonics.	An uncertain start to the year, but Daniel begins to associate more with other boys.	Daniel is frightened of Miss Scott, but Mrs Jarrett says he accepts that 'she is like that'.	Miss Scott sees Daniel as being insecure and nervous for most of the year – 'a follower'. He is one of the younger children in the class.	Daniel won't try with new learning at home unless he believes he can succeed – e.g.: tying shoelaces.
Mrs Jarrett supports Daniel as he becomes tense and unhappy at school.	Later, Daniel is very clear that 'all my friends are boys now'.	In the autumn, Miss Scott recognizes Daniel is unhappy but doesn't know why. She feels that Mrs Jarrett worries too much about him and is 'overwrought about all her children'.	Daniel sees himself as being vulnerable at school, and needing to minimize risks of being picked out by peers, or by Miss Scott in class.	In the autumn, Daniel has a 'magic conker' which he talks to and which he thinks will help him write his stories and do his spellings.
Daniel starts to negotiate that he 'feels ill' when pressure at school gets too much.	In the playground, he plays 'Superman' and chasing games.	Miss Scott is concerned that Daniel is 'so slow' and wonders if he 'works so hard at home, he has no energy to work at school' or if he is 'babied' at home.	He is cautious and alert for trouble. Even in the Summer Term, Daniel follows an established routine for going into school with Mrs Jarrett.	About his writing at school, Daniel tells his mother, 'I hate it and I'm not going to do it.' However, at home he writes a two-page adventure story and letters to the Tooth Fairy and Father Christmas.
Mrs Jarrett visits Miss Scott to explore Daniel's unhappiness.	Playtime is 'highlight of his day'.	Daniel thinks Miss Scott is 'nasty because she shouts at everyone'. He says 'I say in my mind she's a twit' and discusses with Andrew 'chucking her down the loo'.	He begins to hold his own at home, and feels more confident at school as his friendship with Andrew deepens.	In the middle of the year, Miss Scott feels Daniel is 'rather hesitant and shy' and 'needs to feel more relaxed' so that his learning can progress.
Daniel identifies with his father and helps him 'doing jobs' at weekends.	Daniel says he 'hates girls' and that they are 'silly'. He joins with other boys to 'frighten Girly Gloves' – a boy who has pink gloves.	Daniel develops a strategy of keeping his head down, trying very hard to avoid mistakes and trouble with Miss Scott.	Mrs Jarrett feels that Daniel has been unhappy and may have lost confidence in his ability to do school work. She is herself unsure of his capabilities.	Daniel enjoys some maths tasks and makes sound progress, but where he is uncertain he usually seeks reassurance before beginning.
Through the year, Daniel learns to stand up for himself more in family discussions, but is still vulnerable to being swept along or laughed at.	Daniel becomes increasingly dependent in classroom and playground on his close friend, Andrew.		Later in the year, Miss Scott sees Daniel as becoming more 'responsive, alert and confident' following his friendship with Andrew.	Over the whole year, Daniel and Mrs Jarrett are pleased with his steady progress at reading.
Siblings sometimes get impatient with him and his 'silly (babyish) voice'. Mrs Jarrett says 'he's only got the cat' below him.	Miss Scott is very clear that 'Daniel is a follower, not a leader', and sees Andrew as supporting Daniel.			
	Daniel becomes happier at the end of the year as his friendship with Andrew deepens.			

6.5   DANIEL IN HIS YEAR 2

Daniel, Year 2, relationships with parents at home

As we shall see, Daniel had a considerably more settled Year 2 at school. However, Mrs Jarrett wanted him to 'feel quite happy about going in' and therefore continued to both take and fetch him. Throughout the year she still feared that he might 'panic and turn around'.

They continued to work together on Daniel's school work when opportunities arose, with Mrs Jarrett supporting him in understanding new concepts and attempting to bolster his self-esteem:

> After an early tea Rachel went to Brownies. This always seems to give us more time and Daniel usually reads to me or at his suggestion does some maths. Today he asked for some sums – 'Subbuteo ones'. I deduced that this meant subtraction. I asked him what the sums at school look like and he said, they say 'minus'. We wrote this down in words, which he recognised. Then we wrote them with a minus sign. He seems to enjoy this more than anything that he considers 'work' – 'I am very good at maths', he said.
>
> When I suggest that he is very good at reading now he always agrees as if I am daft to think that he would not be good. Much greater self-esteem now. Much more confident as well.
>
> I try to do and say as much as possible to make Daniel confident but this is all contradicted by his brothers and sisters who say the most hurtful things to him (and each other) all the time. They will not put up with any favouritism and definitely no babyish behaviour. He is told in no uncertain terms that he has to stop.
> (Mrs Jarrett, parent diary, November 1989, Year 2)

Daniel, Year 2, relationships with siblings at home

As the youngest, Daniel continued to have to struggle to protect and assert his position amongst his four other siblings. At this time, Mrs Jarrett felt that, 'they do not get on well together' and that Daniel was particularly vulnerable:

> They are a family who have very strong differences, which they have to air all the time. There's this constant putting down of each other, which is not good, and it can't be good for Daniel, can it? So, his self-esteem is not very good. No matter how much 'building' you do, if there's constantly people ... And you can sort of see his bottom lip quivers quite often at things that are said to him, and he can't cope with it very well.
> (Mrs Jarrett, parent interview, December 1989, Year 2)

On the other hand, there were also more occasions when Daniel was able to join in jokes and activities with his brothers and sisters. For instance, Mrs Jarrett's diary records times when Daniel was invited to come to the local park with Peter and his friends who liked to 'talk and joke with him'. There was also one episode when Peter entertained the family, including Daniel, by reading from a library book on the 'facts of life'.

Daniel, Year 2, relationships among friends and in the playground

Daniel was the youngest pupil in his new Year 2 class but, fortunately, his friend Andrew also moved with him. Their relationship became very close indeed and they would often sit together to work, play together in the playground and visit each other's homes. They were many older children in the class and Daniel and Andrew were careful to keep out of the way of any 'naughty boys'. However, on the margins of the dominant group of boys, they developed a strongly shared sense of humour and, when with Andrew, Daniel was significantly more self-confident and relaxed than when alone. This was particularly noticeable at Daniel's house when, according to Mrs Jarrett, 'Daniel gets besides himself':

> I always think of Daniel as rather a gentle boy ..., but when he and Andrew are together they act like a couple of idiots and giggle all the time and fool around. This drives me to distraction and certainly irritates all the others. They never actually play any games that I would recognise but everything comes out, then they jump off the stairs and I am convinced that one day I will have to take Andrew home with some injury. The noise is horrendous and Laura can't concentrate on 'Neighbours' and gets very aggressive.
> (Mrs Jarrett, parent diary, November 1989, Year 2)

In other settings, Daniel's old insecurities sometimes returned, such as when invited to tea by children whom he knew less well. He feared being teased, worried about the food he might have to eat and worried too that he might be teased for being worried.

Daniel and Andrew played together whenever they could, but Mrs Jarrett began to be concerned that Daniel was becoming 'over dependent'. She was fairly certain that Andrew would soon be sent to a private school and she feared that Daniel's confidence would be very shaken unless he could establish other friendships. On the other hand, she recognized that, 'he's not going to progress at all unless he's got security.'. Other friendships were thus encouraged with Robert and Luke, but they never really compared with the rapport which was available to Daniel through Andrew.

Daniel, Year 2, relationships with Miss Sage in the classroom

Daniel was the only one of the children discussed in this book who was placed in Miss Sage's classroom during his Year 2, and discussion of her approach to teaching is thus dealt with briefly here, rather than within Chapter 2.

Miss Sage was a young teacher who had graduated in 1987 and had spent 1987/8 travelling in India and on a variety of supply teaching jobs in Easthampton primary schools. When discussing her educational philosophy, Miss Sage indicated her commitment to 'active learning' and explained that she wanted, 'children to control their learning as much as possible' (teacher interview, September, 1989). However, Miss Sage was realistic, rather than romantic, about this commitment and she felt that high levels of pupil control and forms of active learning could only succeed within a tightly organized structure for classroom rules and behaviour. Following the overall school policy, she thus used a strong topic as a source of cross-curriculum integration and as a focus for negotiation with the children. Miss Sage began the year using a simple organizational system in which the children recorded the activities in which they had engaged. From this base, Miss Sage gradually developed a classroom planning system with which children planned a programme of work for a fortnight. They used a matrix which set out curriculum activities in columns and the ten working days in rows, and they then ticked off each planned activity when it was completed. Planning took place among groups of children, with a child 'chairing' each group, and the activity requirements were weighted to ensure coverage of writing, reading and maths. Miss Sage monitored all plans and activities to ensure that there was appropriate curriculum balance. Whilst the children were able to self-direct their work for quite a lot of the time, Miss Sage also extracted groups for particular teaching purposes. Such group work might concern maths, science or a particular aspect of topic work.

Miss Sage's classroom organization was thus relatively complex and allowed the children a good deal of autonomy. It so happened that the class also contained many of the older Year 2 children in the school, including those who had once been known as 'Mrs Miles's Naughty Boys'. Miss Sage was aware, as she put it, that she had 'some lively children who could be quite a handful to handle' and her strategy was thus to maintain a tight framework of classroom rules within which the children were given scope for self-directed learning. The rules were discussed with the children on introduction and, if difficulties arose, Miss Sage would seek the children's views on a solution. Having led them so far into consultation, she would then interpret and enforce the rules very firmly. However, the children seemed to accept the legitimacy of this. As Miss Sage explained:

> They get on fairly well. Well, they know that I'll be on to them if they don't.
> (Miss Sage, teacher interview, November 1989, Year 2)

Daniel began the year by maintaining his low key, risk-avoidance strategies and, with Andrew, would watch for cues at all times. Miss Sage commented:

> Daniel is very quiet, but he started out seeking a lot of attention, especially when Andrew was away. He is inseparable from Andrew and seems lost without him. Very quiet.
> (Miss Sage, teacher interview, September 1989, Year 2)

However, he quickly appreciated his new teacher. Mrs Jarrett explained:

> As far as settling in goes ... I think he realised that life was so much easier. There wasn't the shouting. It's the tension that seems to have got to him. Once he realised that it wasn't there, he has not complained at all. Miss Sage wants them to be happy. I think a lot of people would say that's all she ever cares about ... but that is the most important thing.
> (Mrs Jarrett, parent interview, December 1989, Year 2)

Daniel gradually started to relax and, with Andrew and some others, even felt confident enough to be 'silly' – though he avoided being 'naughty'. His mother recorded his views:

> He said, 'She never shouts even when you're silly, just sometimes when people are naughty. She never shouts at me but she asked me whether I thought I was being silly on the carpet. So I said, "yes" because I was'.
> (Mrs Jarrett, parent diary, November 1989, Year 2)

His general view of school became much more positive, with Miss Sage being seen as 'very kind'. Daniel and Andrew began to 'have fun' more openly in the classroom whilst maintaining their clear desire to 'be good' and to avoid getting into trouble:

> Daniel: We like to be good, because we don't like being told off.
> Andrew: We try to be good 'cos we don't like being told off, 'cos you feel bad and get sent to the headteacher – but we haven't had that.
> Daniel: If we get giggly, we get told off a tiny bit sometimes – kind of just saying, 'just sit down and shhhh'.
> (Daniel and Andrew, pupil interview, April 1990, Year 2)

By the Summer Term, when Miss Sage was off work for a while with illness, Daniel had become so confident that his activities with Andrew, and now Liam, were seen by a supply teacher as a nuisance:

> Daniel is a very lively personality. He needs pushing, because he can be very silly. He can be very irritating. Daniel is very easily distracted because he's in a gang of three. He belongs to Andrew and Liam. They have a very strong bond, those three, but their behaviour is extremely

off to planet ~~Shape~~

onecs upon a time there
was a man called Bob. He
was an Astronaut. He had a
friend. His friend was called
fred. He was a Astronaut
too. One day they
went to Space in
a Space rarcit. They
travelled
.travald fro^through lots
galaxies
of Glaixsec . They
saw
sar lots of planets.
saw
they sor a strange
planet. So they went ~~to~~
They _landed_
ito. ~~and~~ landy on it.
when they got out
there _were_ Lots of
everywhere.
Shapes afree ~~wher~~
There was _were_ ~~a~~ _triangle_ tryangal

Document 6.9   *Daniel, story writing on 'off to planet shape', May 1990, Year 2*

houses   rectangle
huoSces   rectangal

trees.   ~~aree~~ ~~Wher~~
                  were
There   was   shapes
                        were
and   ~~there~~!!!was
      circle
suCal   thees.
                                 square.
a bush ~~went~~ Was squae
               saw
Then they sor a shaped
man. They said Hello
         asked   everything
and acked   why isereeking
shapes. ~~cus~~ ereeking
    Because   everything
was like this when I
      born.
~~was~~ bron.   ~~oh~~   ~~so~~

They got in to the
           rocket
space Rorcit and went

home.   A very good story, Daniel!

        — Well done. You have worked well.

the end

Document 6.9   *Daniel, story writing on 'off to planet shape', May 1990, Year 2 (contd)*

silly. It's just sort of giggling and twittering amongst themselves and not getting on with their work. They won't apply themselves. They'd much rather have a chatter and a gossip and a giggle among the three of them. It's got to the point where I won't let the three of them sit together because I know they're going to distract each other.
(Mrs Smith, teacher interview, June 1990, Year 2)

Daniel, Year 2, progress in classroom learning

Daniel made considerable progress in all areas of the curriculum during the year, and was increasingly prepared to take risks in trying things out. For instance, regarding his reading, his mother recorded:

Today he decided to read. I feel he is beginning to read well now, not just words he already knows but new ones as well. He is now attempting to build words with letter sounds. But he also makes some good guesses which usually pay off. He now thinks he can read well which boosts his confidence.
(Mrs Jarrett, parent diary, November 1989, Year 2)

Daniel's rapid growth in self-confidence at reading, and new understanding of phonics, began to be applied in his writing – with the opportune support of a student teacher who happened to be placed in his class. His mother explained what had happened in the Spring Term:

Miss Robinson – a student – was working with them and obviously provided more time and also a lot of gushing praise. But most of all he learnt to write with greater ease and also to construct words by sounds. This really seems to have boosted his confidence tremendously – he writes stories for pleasure at home. He even says he loves writing! Also the reading has improved dramatically, not gradually but suddenly. Miss Robinson gave him a part to read in their class service which did wonders for him. Now he remembers songs and rhymes far more easily and even enjoyed going to a singing festival this term even though he was doubtful at first what it would entail.
(Mrs Jarrett, parent diary, June 1990, Year 2)

This progress at story writing was also associated with Daniel's friendship with Andrew, for they had begun to set themselves joint targets. Daniel conveyed something of his pleasure and relief at their new achievements:

We like writing because we like stories and we like long stories. I didn't like it in Miss Scott's 'cos I had no ideas, but now we do seven page stories or ten pages. Writing is very good.
(Daniel and Andrew, pupil interview, April 1990, Year 2)

One example of such a story is provided by Document 6.9 overleaf.

However, Daniel still seemed rather lost when working alone without Andrew. This continued to be noted by Miss Sage and his forlorn looks across the room when they had been separated for some reason was recorded several times in fieldnotes. Daniel's sense of dependence on others was revealed by a conversation even very late in his Year 2:

AP:	How would you feel if your teacher asked you to do some new work?
Daniel:	Very sorry for myself, 'cos I might not know how to do it.
AP:	What might you do to try to do it?
Daniel:	I wouldn't know at first, so I would say, 'I didn't know how to do it'. And the teacher would tell me to get a book about it.
AP:	Might you get help?
Daniel:	Yes, my mum would help me go to the library and get some books and help me look at home.

(Daniel, pupil interview, July 1990, Year 2)

Despite such reservations, Daniel did make good progress during the year. Miss Sage reported to Mr and Mrs Jarrett:

> Daniel is progressing steadily in all areas of the curriculum. His writing style is beginning to mature and he is expressing his ideas with increasing independence. He still lacks confidence in his own ability and often needs encouragement to check and improve his own work. When he concentrates, he obviously enjoys reading and appears to gain a good understanding.
>
> Daniel works well in the maths area, especially at practical activities. His confidence has grown in his ability to tackle new problems and he needs less encouragement.
>
> (Miss Sage, report to parents, spring 1990, Year 2)

Daniel, identity and learning in Year 2

During his Year 2, Daniel became more relaxed at school, developed in maturity and made some significant breakthroughs in his learning. He was aware of the expectations on him and of the need to relinquish any residual 'babyish' strategies which had been used within his family. For instance, in November of his Year 2, when he had fallen over in the playground, he proudly told me, 'I didn't cry at all, even though I hurt my face'. When asked how he managed not to cry, he replied, 'Cos I'm getting bigger' (Fieldnotes). His friendship with Andrew and, progressively, other boys, also underpinned his confidence and provided him with a great deal of enjoyment. However, it also imposed expectations on him – one of which was a build up in pressure to relinquish being taken to school and collected by his mother every day.

Mrs Jarrett continued to be concerned about the way he settled in school and tackled school work:

> I do feel that he is more neurotic than some. He is a worrier and it's not going to change radically, I don't think he is ever really going to change, he's just going to come to terms with it, isn't he, hopefully. There are some kids that never do. Not all children love the school environment or can be expected to really.
>
> (Mrs Jarrett, parent interview, December 1989, Year 2)

In some areas however, such as doing maths cards, Daniel became much more confident when faced with new challenges:

> Daniel: I didn't like it before but I can do it now 'cos I just work out what I have to do and set it out and I go, 'de, de, de' (he points emphatically), and then it gets done. I feel better at it now.
>
> AP: Why is that, do you think?
>
> Daniel: I'm more confident because I learned it better, doing more cards, getting more practice and I'm not with Miss Scott any more. There's teachers that are much nicer.
>
> (Daniel, pupil interview, April 1990, Year 2)

At home, he showed resolve in learning how to knit and a new confidence that such an activity would be accepted by this male friends:

> Rachel was doing some knitting (she's hopeless) and after many handstands in the hall and 'I can't think of anything to do's', Daniel thought he would like to learn to knit. Now he's hooked, he did not want to go to bed and when he was still awake at 9.30 he said it was because he felt itchy because he wanted to knit!
>
> Earlier, whilst struggling with the knitting he said it would be quite alright to tell Andrew that he was learning to knit because Andrew knows not to laugh. And Robert would understand, he wouldn't laugh. Hope this proves to be true.
>
> (Mrs Jarrett, parent diary, June 1990, Year 2)

In the more public setting of Sports Day, some of the old fears started to resurface. Would he fall over? Would he come last? Mrs Jarrett reported on her conversation with him:

> Daniel said that before his race he had a tummy ache and did not feel well. I was expecting the worst, but he then carried on to say that as soon as he had run and come second, he felt perfectly alright. He then said it must have been because he felt worried and nervous.
> (Mrs Jarrett, parent diary, July 1990, Year 2)

Whilst his mother still felt that Daniel's 'main preoccupation was not to excel, but to do well enough not to attract any attention' (Mrs Jarrett, parent diary, June 1990, Year 2), Daniel remained very pleased with his achievements during his infant school years 'especially in writing and maths'. He was confident about his future but worried that his close friends were going to leave the Greenside School:

> The juniors will be good fun, 'cos I can meet new friends at playtimes. I don't know about the work. It won't be really hard. It might be quite hard but not too hard. .... I've got better recently – but the problem is that my best friend and my second best friend are going to a different school so I'll have to play with my third best friend, Robert. I won't have anyone to play with except Robert.
> (Daniel, pupil interview, July 1990, Year 2)

Mrs Jarrett recognized that Daniel had made significant progress during his year with Miss Sage. However, she also formed a clear view of the approach to teaching which would suit Daniel best. As she explained:

> My theory is that he likes to know what he is doing. If somebody says to him, 'Sit down and do that', he feels quite confident. That is what he must do and he can do it. But if he's given a choice to do things and a lot more freedom, he panics. I've seen it at home even now, panic sets in, 'What should I do?' I think he needs goals. He likes to know where he is. He likes order, he doesn't like wandering around. ... I think, from his point of view, he needed to feel confident in the basics, before he should have been forced into the situation where he had to plan and to decide what to do. So, from his point of view, I think it (the negotiated curriculum introduced at Greenside) is the wrong system.
> (Mrs Jarrett, parent interview, July 1990, Year 2)

Daniel was to be proved wrong in his predictions for his friendships in Year 3 as William's story in *The Social World of Pupil Careers* (Pollard and Filer, in press) demonstrates. However, It was both the departure of Daniel's close friends and the development of these perceptions of his mother regarding his educational needs that led to her decision that he should leave Greenside at the end of that year.

Matrix 6.3 *Daniel's Year 2, a summary matrix*

Family relationships	Peer-group relationships	Teacher relationships	Identity	Learning
Hurly burly amongst siblings continues and Daniel, though becoming more aware and competent, is still vulnerable.	Very close friendship continues with Andrew – almost inseparable. Additional friendships with Liam, Robert and others.	Initially, Daniel is still nervous of coming to school, but 'the tension soon went out of him' (Mrs Jarrett).	Daniel is the youngest child in the class, but he performs better than several other children in his school work.	Miss Sage feels 'Daniel is progressing steadily in all areas of the curriculum'.
Mrs Jarrett thinks a large family is often 'abrasive'. She 'battles it out' to maintain order within the family. However, she is aware of the 'constant putting down of each other' and notes how Daniel is upset by things that are said to him – 'he can't cope with it very well'.	Daniel and Andrew regard themselves as 'old friends'. They reject playing with 'naughty boys' and with 'Robert if he's being bossy'.	Miss Sage initially thinks Daniel is 'a nice, quiet boy'. She is concerned that he should be happy at school.	Miss Sage believes Daniel 'is lost without Andrew' at start of year. In the middle of the year, she notes that, 'he still lacks confidence in his own ability, and often needs encouragement to check and improve his own work'.	Miss Sage uses a classroom organization system in which children plan when to do much of their own work. Daniel is often rather bemused by this choice and skews it, for instance, towards construction activities.
Following last year's unhappiness at school, Mrs Jarrett takes and fetches Daniel every day 'in case he panics'.	Andrew and Daniel are very confident together out of the classroom. At Daniel's house they get very high spirited and 'career around' causing Mrs Jarrett to intervene.	Daniel thinks 'Miss Sage is very kind' and Mrs Jarrett notes that Daniel is 'much more relaxed and positive' and that Miss Sage is 'much more laid back'.	Mrs Jarrett sees Daniel as 'a worrier' who 'isn't ever really going to change'.	Mrs Smith, the supply teacher in the summer, introduces a strict system in which tasks are presented on the black-board for defined groups of children.
Mrs Jarrett is increasingly doubtful of the suitability of the Greenside approach to teaching, for Daniel and for other 'fairly privileged' children. She is aware of children being taken away from Greenside and feels that 'Daniel needs the basics before being asked to plan and decide what to do'.	Daniel is unwilling to go to play at the homes of other children, particularly if there are older boys there. He fears being teased, but his reluctance provokes it.	In the Spring Term a student teacher lavishes praise on all the children, including Daniel for his writing.	If faced alone with a new type of learning task, Daniel says 'I'd feel very sorry for myself 'cos I might not know how to do it'.	Daniel makes good progress in reading over the year. He begins to enjoy it and his confidence grows.
	Mrs Jarrett expects Andrew to leave Greenside at the end of Year 2, and sees Daniel as being 'overdependent'. She wants him to 'spread his wings a bit', but at the same time is aware that he is 'not going to progress at all if he doesn't have security'.	In summer, Miss Sage is ill and off school for a while. The supply teacher, Mrs Smith, sees Daniel as 'very lively' and 'often very silly in his gang of three with Andrew and Liam – they just won't apply themselves and prefer to have 'a gossip and a giggle'.	However, there was some growth of confidence in learning and in self during the year on familiar tasks or lower-risk activities, such as doing maths cards and learning to knit at home.	Daniel progressively enjoys writing over the year, which he almost always does with Andrew. He says, 'we didn't have any ideas in Miss Scott's, but now we do seven page stories'.
		Daniel and Andrew do not like being told off because 'Mrs Smith kind of shouts and we feel bad'. They decide to 'try to be good'.	By the end of Year 2, Daniel feels that he has done 'quite well' in the infants and that work in the juniors will be 'hard but not too hard' for him.	Daniel initially thinks, 'maths is my worst because the sums get harder' but by the end of the year says 'I've got better recently and now I'm very good'. This development is confirmed by Miss Sage.

6.6 DANIEL'S LEARNING AND DEVELOPMENT

A brief overview of Daniel's experience across three years of schooling can now be generated and may be compared with those of other children. This overview is first presented, in Figure 6.3, through a triadic representation of social contexts and the dynamic relationships between Daniel, his family, peers and teachers.

Here we see the context in which Daniel sought to cope with the experiences and challenges which presented themselves, and which led him to seek to avoid risks as he struggled to establish himself and build his self-confidence.

We can also reflect on Daniel's learning in terms of the questions within the model of learning, identity and social setting which was presented in Chapter 1 (p. 14) and elaborated in Chapter 4 (p. 98). If we first think about *Who is learning?* we might consider the identity which Daniel brought to school having been the 'baby' of his family and the significance of the strategy he developed of being 'goodest' of his siblings. We might further reflect on Daniel's learning stance in the light of his acute concern to 'get things right' academically and socially, his need to find a niche and to conform, all of which he exhibited in the peer group and in the classroom as well as at home.

For Daniel, it seems, the significance of *What is to be learned?* was almost inseparable from that of *How supportive is the learning context?* In relation to these questions we can note the greater confidence he showed in relation to those tasks which were facilitated by non-threatening family relationships. This might be compared with the vulnerability and fear of failure which often accompanied more tense situations, including many school tasks. For example, discussion with father over the Tooth Fairy dilemma and Daniel's need to explain matters in a letter can be contrasted with Daniel getting 'fed up' with writing that takes 'a too long time' and that gets finished because, 'I don't like the teachers to tell you off'. Similarly, we might compare the pleasures of learning games and reading with Grandpa, where Daniel was allowed to take the lead and dictate the pace, with the high-stakes learning of the reading scheme and word tin where learning could be measured and was exposed for the evaluation of family, teacher and peers.

With respect to *What are the learning outcomes?* in Daniel's case we might begin with formal academic outcomes. Daniel was, above all, concerned to be 'good' and so as the data showed, despite the stresses of his earlier years, his concern to get work done and avoid getting into trouble meant that his academic attainment was reasonable. However, though he hid much of his stress in school, as his mother clearly recognized, it badly affected his ability to learn and his progress on all fronts. His acute need to avoid getting things wrong also had adverse effects in terms of the informal learning outcomes relating to his self-esteem and social status. We might consider, for example, his approach to formal learning tasks in the classroom, his attempts to learn the culture of the playground or of party games, his need to avoid mistakes at home, even, at one point down to the pouring of his milk on his breakfast cereal. In each context of classroom, peer group and family, in situations in which Daniel's competence was open to evaluation, his preference was for relinquishing control in favour of the perceptions and structures supplied by others. Whilst such strategies may have enabled him to learn at least adequately in school, they tended to weaken his identity with respect to his competence as a member of a peer group and within the family. They reinforced his 'baby' image and thereby compounded his difficulty in establishing a satisfactory niche and identity among his siblings and peers.

Overall then, perhaps the issue of prime importance to Daniel was that of the social

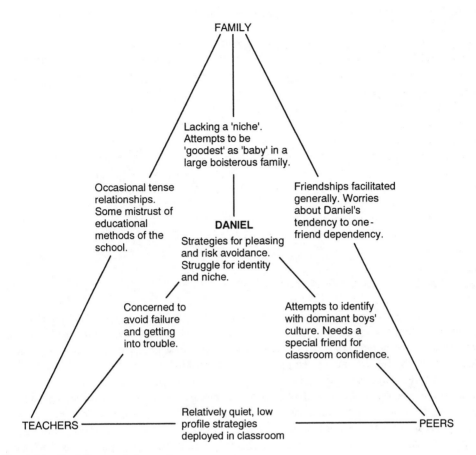

FAMILY

Lacking a 'niche'.
Attempts to be
'goodest' as 'baby' in a
large boisterous family.

Occasional tense
relationships.
Some mistrust of
educational
methods of the
school.

DANIEL

Strategies for pleasing
and risk avoidance.
Struggle for identity
and niche.

Friendships facilitated
generally. Worries
about Daniel's
tendency to one-
friend dependency.

Concerned to
avoid failure
and getting
into trouble.

Attempts to identify
with dominant boys'
culture. Needs a
special friend for
classroom confidence.

TEACHERS ——————— Relatively quiet, low
profile strategies
deployed in classroom ——————— PEERS

Figure 6.3 *Daniel's case-study overview*

relations and strategic resources available him as the youngest in a large, boisterous and sometimes abrasive family. In particular, they influenced the repertoire of strategic actions for fitting in and avoiding mistakes which he then brought to classroom learning and peer-group interaction. Such strategies linked to Daniel's sense of presentation of self. The identities of the 'baby' and 'the goodest' of the siblings were both readily available to him and, if anathema to his brothers and sisters, were a source of security in relation to his mother. The sense of identity which Daniel then brought to school had implications for his relationships there, as the threat to his sense of self-esteem and his social status became acute within peer-group culture. Gradually, however, Daniel's relationship with his 'special friend' seemed to provide the source of stability and a way forward for which, perhaps, he had been seeking.

Chapter 7

Sally's Story

7.1   SALLY, AN INTRODUCTION

This is the story of Sally, who came from a family, good humouredly described by her father as 'the poor relations' of Greenside school. However, this is the same child who was described by one of her teachers as a pupil who 'walks on water'. We met Sally initially in Chapter 3, as the best friend and competitive rival of Mary.

Sally was the daughter of the school caretaker and might be considered to have been at a considerable socio-economic and cultural disadvantage compared with other children at Greenside Primary School. Nevertheless she managed to out-perform most of her peers in the years reported here, not only in relation to academic achievements at school, but also in relation to non-school activities in the community and in popularity and in status among her peers. How did she do this? Was it due to Sally's unique sense of belonging and identification with Greenside Primary School? What contribution did her parents make? To what extent could Sally's success simply be attributed to her own energetic enthusiasm and her determined learning stance? But if so, then how did this arise and how was it maintained? How did Sally's circumstances and relationships at home, classroom and playground influence the fulfilment of her academic and athletic potential?

Figure 7.1 shows Sally's age and attainment in maths and literacy in relation to other children in the Reception, Year 1 and Year 2 classes in which she was placed.

From Figure 7.1 it can be seen that Sally's structural position in terms of the 'official' world of her classroom teachers was always a relatively high one. She was amongst the older children in her Reception class and was the oldest child in her Year 2. Her relative attainment in literacy was particularly high throughout and she was also a good performer at maths even when, as in her Year 1, she was among the younger children within the class.

7.2   SALLY'S FAMILY

Mr and Mrs Gordon lived opposite the school, in a modest, semi-detached house reserved by Easthampton Council for the caretaker of Greenside Primary School – a post which Mr

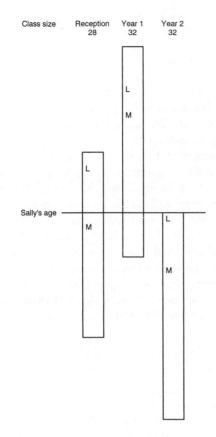

Figure 7.1 *Sally's structural position: age and relative attainment at literacy and maths in Reception, Year 1 and Year 2 classes (for an explanation of this figure, see p. 35.)*

Gordon held throughout the period of this study. Indeed, the family connections with the school and the local community were very close indeed.

Mrs Gordon worked at the local playgroup and made many contacts with other local families in that way. At the start of the study she also worked in Greenside Primary School as a cleaner and school meals assistant. In 1989, she acted for a period as a temporary class-room assistant.

Mr Gordon worked tirelessly for the school and in very diverse ways which often went well beyond the normal expectations of a caretaker's role. For instance, he assisted in coaching the football and cricket teams, worked with the children in making scenery for school performances and was often to be seen around the classrooms providing for teachers' practical needs. Mr Gordon was a keen sportsman and played cricket and football for local Greenside teams.

Mr and Mrs Gordon had a very positive outlook on life and they projected this in their relationships with others. Within the school, they were seen as a reliable source of sensible

Adrian and Gail Gordon

Sam (3 years older) **Sally** (born May 1983)

Figure 7.2 *Sally's immediate family*

and high-quality support. There were close-working relationships between Mr and Mrs Gordon and the teaching staff and they also mixed socially with some teachers. However, Mr and Mrs Gordon were aware of their status and roles in the school and were careful not to overstep their authority or to speak indiscretely.

Because of their close involvement with the school, Mr and Mrs Gordon had a great deal of knowledge about it and many shared experiences on a day-to-day basis. Thus, on most issues, they were uniquely placed to guide their two children as they began school and moved through it. Indeed, this had happened before, for when Sally began to attend play-group officially at the age of three, she had already been going 'in the background' with her mother. Regarding primary school, Sally was a regular visitor from the age of three when she would help her mother and father in their work and in maintaining what Sally regarded as 'my Dad's school' (Mrs Gordon, parent interview, March 1988, Reception).

Mr and Mrs Gordon took a very great interest in their children's development and progress at school, though they did not put them under pressure. Sally, for instance, in her Reception year, liked to share everything that had happened at school, and her parents would dutifully listen and respond:

> She must tell you what's gone on throughout the day from all aspects of school. ... Anybody who has time to listen, she will tell us all. She will go right through it with me and then with Adrian.
> (Mrs Gordon, parent interview, March 1988, Reception)

Roles within the family were well established and reflected many gender conventions. Of the two children, Sam followed his father in being very keen at sports whilst Sally modelled herself on her mother. The following brief extract from a diary entry gives a flavour of this:

> The afternoon was spent baking. Sally really enjoys this although the mess is greater when she helps. Sally's dad plays football on Saturday afternoons so after waving goodbye to him we usually do some baking.
> After we have washed up, we sometimes do some ironing. Sally puts up her own board and clothes horse. And then off we go. She likes to chatter about the things that have happened during the week.
> She often goes down to play with Amy who lives three doors down. Amy is ten but Sally gets on really well with her.
> When Sally's dad gets back from football she likes to know how the game went and whether or not he scored.
> (Mrs Gordon, parent diary, February 1988, Reception)

Sam was successful in the school teams, particularly in football and cricket. He worked hard at his skills and played his first games for the school at a relatively young age.

The Gordon's were a contented family who all seemed to derive a great deal of personal fulfilment from their involvement in Greenside Primary School. However, amongst the parents of children attending the school, and within Greenside more generally, they were clearly distinctive in terms of social class. This was reflected in the income and material resources available to Mr and Mrs Gordon and also in their previous educational and cultural experiences. Mr and Mrs Gordon were well aware of such differences. For instance, discussing Sally's great liking for 'disco dancing', Mr Gordon said:

> We live in an area where your girl goes to ballet or tap and your son goes to tennis lessons. And it is a bit different for us, we are like the poor relations. But, I mean, disco dancing is something that Sally loves, she enjoys it.
> (Mr Gordon, parent interview, July 1988, Reception)

Overt social-class issues were not prominent in the way Sally's friendships developed during her infant school years, for, as we shall see, her self-confidence and success at school were by far the more significant factors. However, Mr and Mrs Gordon were well aware of the way in which the educational ambitions of more wealthy parents were likely to impact on their own children:

> It is a worry really, when so many of the children from here go on to fee paying schools.
> Obviously the standard of education in the school is very good, but, as far as our children are concerned, unless something drastic happens with my wages, there is no way we can pay for them to go to fee paying schools. I mean, I am happy that the standard is high because it tends to bring our children with that. They go along with the mass, don't they?
> But there is a worry that we have to send Sam to Damibrook Comprehensive, which seems to have such a bad reputation. That is our biggest worry for the future – where he, and also where Sally is going to have her secondary education.
> (Mr Gordon, parent interview, March 1988, Reception)

7.3   SALLY IN HER RECEPTION YEAR

Sally, Reception, relationships with parents at home

Sally was in a rather unusual position as a pupil in having home and school so intimately connected by her parents' work. Indeed, unless she had been invited out to tea, Sally remained at the school each afternoon during term time, when most of the children went home. During the Reception year it was, as her mother put it, 'a set pattern'.

> Between 3.30 – 5.00 pm she stays within the school, usually in Mrs Powell's room (Sally's Reception class teacher), although she does enjoy going into other classrooms and experimenting with their puzzles and equipment. She has a very good relationship with adults and enjoys talking to all the members of staff at school. She likes to help the teachers whenever she can, particularly her own teachers.
> She never seems to worry about the extra hours she spends at school, in fact I think she rather enjoys them. When she has someone to tea after school she revels in giving them a guided tour of all the classrooms and telling them who teaches in which room.
> After tea she usually watches some of the TV programmes I video for her. She likes to help in the kitchen although at times she 'helps' just a little too much. She enjoys helping with the dishes. Sally had her friend Mary for tea tonight. They play happily in the school until it's time to come home. Sally enjoys 'entertaining' and I usually let her choose what they have to eat.
> (Mrs Gordon, parent diary, February 1988, Reception)

Sally understood the efforts of her parents to keep the school in good order and perhaps modelled herself on them in the ways in which she offered to help teachers. She learned a great deal about the school and, in identifying with her parent's responsibilities, was very aware of what it was, or was not, appropriate to do within the building. As she would say to other children, 'My Dad wouldn't like you doing that. ... You're not supposed to do that'.

Sally identified particularly closely with her mother and enjoyed chatting to her and helping her in jobs around the house. This extended to thinking that she could 'look after' her father and brother when her mother went out, or even going out with her:

> When school finished she was busy asking me about the evening I had planned. A friend was moving and I was going on a 'farewell meal'. All day Sally had been fine about this. ... We came home and she helped to prepare the meal, saying she would look after Daddy and Sam and not to worry.
>
> After tea she helped clear the table and then followed me upstairs to watch me get ready. She stands in front of the mirror copying as I put my make-up on. She loves being let loose on the real thing but tends to get everything rather messy.
>
> All this time she's asking me what I'm going to wear. What colour shoes and bag etc. Everything's fine until about ten minutes to go. Then she decides she doesn't want me to go. ... I tend to think she just hates to be left behind.
> (Mrs Gordon, parent diary, February 1988, Reception)

Sally very much enjoyed going to school through most of her Reception year and she wanted to share her experiences, particularly with her mother:

> She loves school and she talks about school what she has done throughout the day. ... She has a habit of when she is getting tired she likes to talk. She will tell you everything that has gone on throughout the day which is fine.
> (Mr Gordon, parent interview, March 1988, Reception)

Mr and Mrs Gordon helped Sally with her reading very regularly and directed their support as necessary:

> We took out from the word tin all the words that she had problems with ... and she had to think about them. We found at first she looked at pictures (in books) and guessed, like if she knew the letter 'b' and she saw a ball in the picture. Whereas with the word tin, she can't guess, she has got to look at what is there. And she worked things out from there which was wonderful.
>
> I mean, it is a ritual with us with her reading and her word tin every evening.
> (Mrs Gordon, parent interview, March 1988, Reception)

For Sally, the continuity and overlapping of experience between home and school gave her an unusual advantage as she embarked upon her Reception year at Greenside. As her mother put it:

> She knew the school, she knew the teachers, she knew most of the children and she was already there, 'at home' sort of thing.
> (Mrs Gordon, parent interview, March 1988, Reception)

Sally, Reception, relationships with siblings at home

Sally, aged four, and Sam, aged seven, were fairly typical of young siblings in their 'love-hate' relationship. As Mrs Gordon expressed it in her diary:

> Sally often finds the three year age gap between them very frustrating. She hates to lose at anything and as her brother feels the same way it often ends in confrontation.
> (Mrs Gordon, parent diary, February 1988, Reception)

She elaborated in interview:

At the moment they are at the stage where there aren't too many games they can play together because of the age difference. I mean, if they play something like noughts and crosses, she hates to lose. ... She is very competitive with him. Obviously in games where you need to use your brain, he has the advantage because of the age. I think that she finds that upsetting. She really would like to be the winner and if she can't win it is, 'I am not going to play'. It often ends up like that and then they will end up arguing. She has ruined it really because she won't play.

On the whole really they get on well – it is just, there are times. I suppose, like all children, they fight over various different things. ... They are very protective towards one another. If Sam was upset about something she would be very concerned and vice versa.
(Mrs Gordon, parent interview, March 1988, Reception)

Sam would certainly play with Sally both as a pair and in the context of family games. As the older and more experienced child, he would also talk with her about school and, in particular, help her with her reading:

Sam helped her with her book today. He enjoys listening to her read and helping her with the words she doesn't know. It's nice to see them sat together enjoying something that isn't going to end in tears.
(Mrs Gordon, parent diary, February 1988, Reception)

However, in the older child's failure to adapt to Sally's needs, there is a suggestion that Sam may well have been concerned with maintaining his learning status over his younger sister:

The trouble is he very often tells her words that he thinks she doesn't know, if she hesitates at all. This infuriates Sally. She sometimes needs a few seconds to sound the word out in her mind before she says them and Sam takes this as indication that she doesn't know the word. When he tells her she gets really annoyed.
(Mrs Gordon, parent diary, June 1988, Reception)

The desire to succeed and be well thought of that Sally exhibited in school seems to have had its origins in the family. In her relations with Sam as well as with her parents Mr and Mrs Gordon were well aware of Sally's strategic presentation of herself:

Sally is very aware of things around her especially what adults are saying. She nearly always takes sides in an argument. If her brother is being reprimanded for something she usually agrees with me and then will sympathise with her brother as soon as I leave the room.
(Mrs Gordon, parent diary, February 1988, Reception)

Mr and Mrs Gordon, elaborating on Sally's strategies, wondered if she was 'thinking a bit too much for her age' or being 'too clever for her own good'. They noted that, in this respect, Sally 'sometimes seems a lot older' and was 'quite cunning' (parent interview, March 1988, Reception).

Sally, Reception, relationships among friends and in the playground

Sally was one of the most popular children in the Reception class. She was very confident with other children and would often make the first move towards making friends with someone new. She particularly enjoyed 'looking after' new children and giving them guided tours of the school. Sometimes she might leave a slightly incorrect impression, explaining that, 'It's my Dad's school'. Mrs Gordon thought that she might suggest that 'Mrs Davison just thinks she runs the school. Daddy does it really'. Mr Gordon had had children come up and say, 'Did you actually build the school?' (Mrs Gordon, parent interview, March 1988, Reception).

Sally developed particularly strong and close friendships with a group of girls of which she and Amy and Mary formed the core, with Alice, Nimra, Amita, Sarah and Amanda also being associated with it. Sally was a strong influence within the group not least in deciding on play activities. Sally's mother described such games as, 'many and varied' and in the playground context those observed included skipping, hopping, catching, chasing and imaginary games such as 'My Little Pony' and 'Mummies and Daddies'.

Amy, Mary and Sally were very much 'best friends' at school and, as we saw in Mary's story, for Mary and Sally, this friendship was enhanced by going to ballet lessons together on Saturday mornings. Mrs Gordon felt that Sally was at her happiest when she was able to 'put on a show' which enabled her to demonstrate her dancing skills:

> She will make the most of any captive audiences she might come across. Dancing plays a big part in these shows together with singing. As well as ballet, Sally is really interested in disco dancing and has recently entered her first competition. She came fourth in the under 6's and won a trophy. This was proudly shown to her class (as well as anyone else she could find). I think she was rather pleased that none of her close friends had achieved such a feat.
> (Mrs Gordon, parent diary, June 1988, Reception)

This last diary entry hints at another aspect of Sally's relationships with her peers, for in many matters she was highly competitive. As her mother put it, 'although Sally will go along with somebody else's ideas, she does tend to want to be the "boss"' (Mrs Gordon, parent diary, June 1988, Reception). For much of the year, Sally's influence was largely accepted by her friends. After all, she did seem to know everything there was to know about the school and was completely confident within it.

Reading provided the most overt indicator of progress because of the school system for grading reading books. As we also saw in Mary's story, Sally took considerable pleasure in her achievement in relation to her friend:

> She has gone on to the 'grey books' and is terribly pleased because she has gone on and Mary hasn't yet. Anna (Mrs Inman) was saying that Mary is really working hard because Sally has gone on to the grey books. She wants to catch her up. So obviously there is a lot of competition between them. They really are quite competitive even at that age and aware of that. You wouldn't think that they would be that aware of the others.
> (Mrs Gordon, parent interview, March 1988, Reception)

Whilst for much of the year, Sally and her two friends had been inseparable, Sally's liking for being 'the boss' and the element of rivalry which crept into their friendships meant that the girls played with a wider range of children towards the end of the year.

Also towards the end of the Reception year, the girls found that their playground games were increasingly disturbed by boys. Sometimes this was inadvertent, as boisterous chasing or ball games spilt over into a girls' activity. On other occasions, the boys acted more deliberately, finding amusement in such intrusions. Another development was the game of 'kiss-chase' in which both boys and girls participated, but which the boys sometimes pursued 'too far' causing some girls to become upset. Sally, however, was often an active participant and could hold her own with the boys and turn the tables by threatening to kiss *them*. Mrs Gordon described Sally as being 'pretty happy' playing with boys and Mary and Sally being 'perfectly at ease' as the only girls at a boy's birthday party. However, Sally was sufficiently aware of boy/girl relationships to both tease her older brother about them and feel embarrassed herself:

She does get embarrassed with boys. Sam ribs her. Sally ribs Sam and says things like 'Laura thinks you're lovely Sam', and then Sam will retaliate and say, 'Well, you like Jonathan, or so and so', and she really gets embarrassed. So she knows, she is aware of the fact that girls have boy friends and boys have girl friends.
(Mr Gordon, parent interview, July 1988, Reception)

Whilst she was certainly confident and extrovert in her behaviour, as we shall see in the course of her story, Sally was highly conscious of her status in the eyes of other children and adults alike. As her mother put it:

She enjoys making people laugh but can get quite distressed if people laugh at her rather than with her.
(Mrs Gordon, parent diary, June 1988, Reception)

Sally, Reception, relationships with Mrs Powell in the classroom

As we have seen, Sally's relationship with Mrs Powell was established before she joined her Reception class. She looked forward to school with eager anticipation and, once there, she thrived on it. As Mrs Powell put it:

Sally is pretty well balanced. ... She is all things actually, she is good at academic things and she is very good at PE. ... Very sociable, very helpful, very kind. Odd flashes of spitefulness and what not ... but then they all show some of that. She is very keen on the rules, wanting to do things properly and she organises everyone. I can't fault her really. I know her so well because she stays on after school and gives me a hand. She used to come in and play in my room before she even started school you see. ... Her mum cleans some of the infant classrooms and her dad is a marvellous, cheerful fellow.
(Mrs Powell, teacher interview, March 1988, Reception)

Sally was attentive to every detail of school life and spent a great deal of time asking questions of Mrs Powell. Her mother reported that this even extended to Sally asking questions of Mrs Powell in her sleep, which slightly concerned her:

When she first started school she would talk in her sleep when she came home – and it was, 'Mrs Powell, Mrs Powell', and I could imagine her all day nagging, 'What's this? What's that?' She wants to know everything. She is very inquisitive. She is like a sponge really she soaks up all the information.
(Mrs Gordon, parent interview, March 1988, Reception)

As we saw earlier, Sally would also often play at 'schools' and this provided some insight into both her understanding of classroom rules and also her devoted study of Mrs Powell. Mr and Mrs Gordon reported one such episode:

Mr Gordon: Last night she was telling the class a story. She was Mrs Powell and it was 'Amy, you're misbehaving, if you don't want to listen to the story, you will have to ...' This was while we were watching the television and this was going on, on her own. You could hear her saying, 'Amy, don't do that to Amita,' etc. I thought that was wonderful last night.

Mrs Gordon: I think the funny thing about it is, you can actually *hear* Betty (Mrs Powell). You can hear the things she says in class and Sally is copying exactly the phrases that she uses. I think, 'Gosh, if Betty was sat here listening, she would roar'. Because it is actually the things she says, she will repeat them word for word and often in the tone that she uses as well.

(Parent interview, March 1988, Reception)

In the classroom Sally was an asset to Mrs Powell and could be trusted to do a variety of 'jobs'. Together with her friends, she was often entrusted with carrying the attendance and dinner registers to the school office, and sometimes, if she was fortunate, she would be awarded the supreme honour of carrying Mrs Powell's empty coffee mug to the staff room after her playground duty. Mrs Powell once asked Sally to fetch John to read to her. Without hesitation, Sally replied that John was 'away' and, having memorized the list of readers, asked if she should fetch Thomas, the next child on the list. She was thus immensely attentive, and she particularly enjoyed being able to participate in lessons and activities which Mrs Powell planned:

> Sally was looking forward to school this morning. She was taking a tambourine to play during the singing lesson. Any opportunity to take anything is always welcomed by Sally.
> (Mrs Gordon, parent diary, February 1988, Reception)

The relationship between Sally and Mrs Powell was warm and friendly, as the following episode, recorded in classroom fieldnotes, illustrates. It also shows the way in which Sally accepted the routine classroom tasks which she was expected to do and would both monitor Mrs Powell's teaching and also interrupt when she wanted attention. Mrs Powell's calm disposition usually enabled her to maintain something of a firm line with Sally's interruptions, however, on this occasion, when they were at the expense of Robert and Mary, she did not altogether succeed.

> After playtime Sally is sent to do her writing. She seems very cheerful as ever. She comes to show me her work on the letter 'k' which involves drawing and writing things which start with that sound. Her writing is big and bold and accurate.
>
> Mary comes to see what is happening and also shows me her colouring. Sally wants to sit next to Mary.
>
> When Mrs Powell comes over, Sally gets her book open at the right place and begins crayoning.
>
> Mrs Powell is showing Robert how to form the letters 'c', 'a', and 'g' and Sally watches intently. She listens to the explanation and joins in, telling Mrs Powell what she can do herself.
>
> Mrs Powell would rather not be interrupted and tells Sally to sit on her chair properly rather than 'side saddle'!
>
> Mrs Powell explains to Robert and tests him on initial sounds. She finds he has not written 'on his first clean page' and offers a friendly reminder.
>
> Mary comes to show Mrs Powell her pictures having done very little. Her task is also to draw things which start with the 'k' sound. Mary has made a start by drawing some 'keys'.
>
> Sally watches intently when Mrs Powell talks.
> Mrs Powell: What have you drawn, Mary?
> Sally interrupting: 'Keys', I recognise those.
> Mrs Powell continues looking at Mary's work ...
> Mrs Powell: ... 'Kaleidoscope' ...
> Sally: ... and I've done a football ... .
> Mrs Powell, turning to Sally: Oh well, you need someone 'kicking', don't you?
> Sally: ... and 'kissing'...!
> Mrs Powell: Well you need two people for that don't you?
> Sally: Yes.
> Mrs Powell: You need to make it a bit clearer than that!
> (Fieldnotes, January 1988, Reception)

Sally's relationship with Mrs Powell was thus a very close one. In the classroom episode above, although Mrs Powell's suggestion that Sally might 'need someone kicking' may have been a little pointed, the context was one of indulgence and they went on to share the joke about 'kissing'.

In summary, Mrs Powell maintained her calm classroom atmosphere through her firmness, routines and consistent programme of curriculum tasks and activities. The stability of the classroom enabled Sally to learn a great deal about it and she identified herself with Mrs Powell in a stance which could well be termed 'devotional'. For her part, Mrs Powell was fascinated by Sally's knowledge and attention to detail. She remarked, 'If I didn't turn up, Sally would sort the class out. That's the kind of girl she is really' (Mrs Powell, teacher interview, July 1988, Reception).

Sally, Reception, progress in classroom learning

Sally made very good progress in her learning of basic skills over the year. In literacy, she was one of the highest attaining children. In her records at the start of the year, Mrs Powell described Sally as, 'very willing to talk about her experiences and good at story telling', and this confidence in speaking seemed to roll over into her approach to learning to read.

As we have seen, Sally engaged with the process of learning to read very positively indeed, paying great attention to Mrs Powell's teaching and working hard at the word tin 'ritual' every evening with her parents. Mrs Powell recorded her impression at the start of the year:

> Cat box. Reading well at home and at school. She is reading with understanding and expression and obvious enjoyment. She knows most of the initial letter sounds.
> (Mrs Powell, teacher records, November 1987, Reception)

In the school system for progression in the reading curriculum, children moved from the simple books of Mouse, Pig, Teddy, Duck to Cat Box, and then through Alligator, Kangaroo, Rhino, Elephant, Cloud, Sun and Butterfly Boxes, until finally they arrived at 'Library'. 'Cat box' thus denoted the level of reading book which Sally had reached after three months of schooling, and was an achievement of which she was proud. Sally was also very aware of her attainment relative to that of most other children in her class.

> She is very concerned about what other children are doing and informs us who's on what box. She's very pleased that she's in the last box (in the Reception class) before going into Mrs Miles' class to check her books.
> (Mrs Gordon, parent diary, June 1988, Reception)

At the end of the Spring Term of 1988, Sally was also very pleased to be one of the first Reception class children to be told that she need no longer use a word tin.

Sally also began to experiment during the time she had in school at the end of the day:

> Sally often goes into other classes. She often sits after school in the book corner in the older infant classes, and just recently has been sitting reading the books. She is extremely pleased if she can read them and believes it to be a great achievement.
> (Mrs Gordon, parent diary, June 1988, Reception)

Sally developed her writing using the established procedure of doing a picture and some writing about it each day. As we saw in previous case studies, in this routine, the children would complete a drawing with coloured wax crayons and Mrs Powell would circulate to write some text at each child's dictation. The children then either 'copied over' Mrs Powell's writing or, as they became more advanced, 'copied under'. At a further stage, the

I was skipping out
in my garden. The
sun is shining. Later
it became dark

Document 7.1 *Sally, picture and writing about 'skipping out', October 1987, Reception*

children attempted to write some words alone. A new idea, which Mrs Powell tried with Sally despite being a little sceptical, was the use of a 'magic line'. Stemming from the National Writing Project, the magic line was to be used by children who wanted to maintain the meaningful flow of their stories when they did not know the spelling of a particular word. In such circumstances, they could insert a 'magic' line, or an initial sound and a line. Later, the teacher would support them in completing the words.

Sally was keen to use writing as a medium of expression and she moved quite quickly from 'writing over' to 'writing under'. Document 7.1 is from October 1987, shortly after Sally started school.

Sally also gradually began writing some words on her own. In the late autumn, Mrs Powell recorded:

> Sally usually has good ideas for her writing. Has recently been writing in her own book in spare time. Handwriting good, if she doesn't hurry.
>
> Can write on her own using initial sounds and magic line, spelling some words herself. Sometimes reluctant.
>
> (Mrs Powell, teacher records, November 1987, Reception)

However, Sally was not a keen user of the 'magic line' because she preferred to know how to spell the word correctly from the start. She would therefore 'ask for spellings' from whoever she could. At home, as Mrs Gordon explained, 'She drives me absolutely crackers "How do you spell this? How do you spell that?"' (Mrs Gordon, parent interview, March 1988, Reception). However, this difficulty did not diminish Sally's enthusiasm for communicating through writing, particularly as, towards the end of the year, she became more confident in spelling many of the more common words which she needed:

> Sally loves to write. She often writes notes to her friends, draws maps and cards – particularly get well cards if someone's not feeling well. She's pleased that now she can actually write some words without asking for the spellings.
>
> Sally is what I would call a compulsive writer. Any piece of paper which happens to be lying around usually gets written on. (The envelope for this Diary is a prime example. She even attempted joined up writing on the back which was a complete surprise as to my knowledge she's never done any writing of this sort). Very annoying when the piece of paper is important. She also makes up stories using words that she knows. They often don't make any sense but she spends long periods just messing around with different words.
>
> (Mrs Gordon, parent diary, June 1988, Reception)

In March of the Reception year, Mrs Powell officially reported to Mr and Mrs Gordon that Sally was 'forming most of her letters correctly', so that, from the Summer Term, as in the example of Document 7.2, Sally was able to use her writing to clearly communicate one of her other achievements.

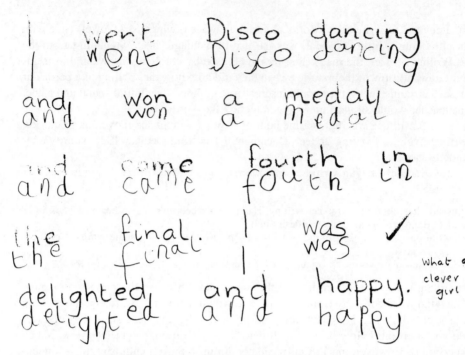

I went Disco dancing
and won a medal
and came fourth in
the final. I was ✓
delighted and happy. *What a clever girl!*

Document 7.2 *Sally, writing about disco dancing, June 1988, Reception*

5 5 5 5

Draw 5 🐱 cats

Document 7.3 *Sally, sample of number task on numerals, October 1987, Reception*

Sally did not seem quite as enthusiastic about maths as she was at literacy, but she certainly made good progress during the year. In the autumn, Mrs Powell noted her counting skills and worked on her knowledge of numerals.

She completed practical tasks, as set by Mrs Powell, such as this one, using a polythene bag containing three buttons:

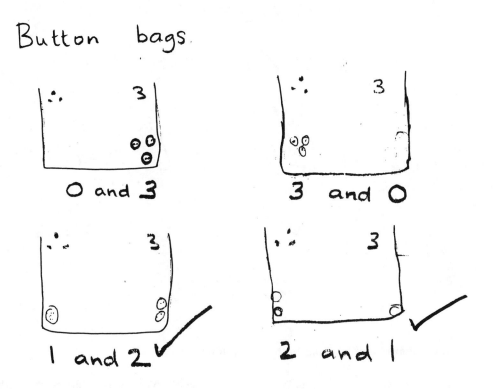

Document 7.4   *Sally, number task on addition, February 1988, Reception*

She quickly moved her on through activities related to the Peak Maths scheme, Stages 1–3, which she completed with, in Mrs Powell's words, 'no trouble'. Nevertheless, her skill's were not always reliable and she did have to work at her maths:

Mrs Powell's records documented Sally's achievements:

> Sally has had practice in addition to 10. Ready to continue with Stage 4. Did the Take away problem sheet easily. Measures length: non standard units. Choosing own units and some estimation. Balancing activities: non standard units. Money: Equivalence to 5.
> (Mrs Powell, teacher records, July 1988, Reception)

However, unlike the situation with Sally's reading and writing, there were quite a lot of children who performed at least as well as she did at maths

With respect to a range of other classroom activities, Mrs Powell reported:

> Sally takes an intelligent interest in all class activities. She is very good at PE and movement and enjoys games. She is attentive at listening times and often contributes to class discussion.
> (Mrs Powell, report to parents, July 1988, Reception)

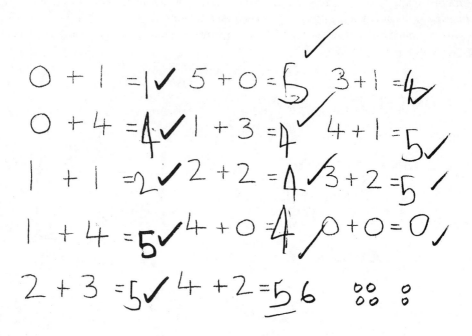

Document 7.5 *Sally, sample of number task on addition, March 1988, Reception*

Sally, identity and learning in the Reception year

During the Reception year, Sally continued to identify with, share achievements with and draw support from her mother and to be very proud of her father and of his role in the school. Sally was confident with almost all the adults whom she met. This extended to, for example, workmen repairing her house and Sally persuading them to get her bike in and out of the garden shed for her, and to her elderly nextdoor neighbour:

> We stopped to talk to the lady who lives next door to us who is a widow and only partially sighted. Sally often goes round to her house on weekends particularly Saturday afternoons. She has a small dog and Sally loves to stroke her. She sits and talks to Mrs Watson. You wouldn't think there was about fifty years difference in their ages. They sit and chat like two old ladies. (Mrs Gordon, parent diary, February 1988, Reception)

This self-confidence rolled over into Sally's approach to school work. This was not only important for her approach to new learning tasks, but it also constituted a point of difference between herself and her brother, Sam.

> She is *so* confident. ... Sam makes friends very easily, but he is not so confident in his approach to work as Sally is. As far as Sally's approach to work is concerned it is, 'Oh well I will get it. It doesn't matter if I get it wrong the first time because I know I will get it right next time'. Sam would sit back and worry more about getting it right the first time, where she would jump in with both feet regardless of the consequences. You know if it doesn't work out the first time,

not to worry we will have another go sort of thing. In that respect they are different really.
(Mrs Gordon, parent interview, March 1988, Reception)

Sally's confidence grew throughout the year and its culmination was her role in the disco dancing competition at the City Hall. Her parents were justifiably proud of her:

Mr Gordon   That was enormous to a little girl, standing up at the City Hall to a packed house. Out of the whole of the younger ones, Sally was the only one that did all the steps.

Mrs Gordon   She carries on regardless, even when those around her were just standing still. She carried on regardless, didn't she, trying as much to stick to the routine that they had worked out as possible? They did really well.

(Parent interview, July 1988, Reception)

The disco dancing was subsequently shown to all the children in Mrs Powell's class, earning great admiration from the other children.

Sally used her self-confidence and knowledge of the school with generosity. Mrs Powell, for instance, described her as 'always kind to children who are upset for some reason and always ready to help others' (Mrs Powell, teacher records, March 1988, Reception). Indeed, Sally was very often to be observed actively looking for 'ways to help' in the classroom. She was positive and thoughtful in trying to help, perhaps modelling herself on her parents.

Sally was thus very successful in all sorts of ways in her first year at school. She understood the school better than any, was known to many teachers, had unusually close parental support and worked hard for her achievements. However, one consequence of her high levels of relative attainment and acceptance was that Sally came to expect them of herself and was certainly concerned to maintain them. She was thus quite nervous of the opinions of others, such as Mrs Powell:

This evening was open evening. Several times, while I was talking to Mrs Powell, I could see Sally peering through the glass in the door. The thought of not knowing what was being said about her was almost unbearable.
(Mrs Gordon, parent diary, February 1988, Reception)

Sally was very interested in what Mrs Powell had to say about her the previous evening at open night. She was very concerned that everything was OK and that Mrs Powell thought she was a good girl.
(Mrs Gordon, parent diary, February 1988, Reception)

We see then that beneath Sally's confident approach to school work, and her willingness to 'have another go' when things went wrong, was a deep concern to be a 'good girl' and an aversion to 'getting it wrong'.

I think it boils down to the fact that she doesn't like to get it wrong. She likes to get it right. That is the way she reacts.
(Mrs Gordon, parent interview, July 1988, Reception)

If a mistake was made at home, Sally would acknowledge it and then look for reaffirmation of affection and, implicitly, of her identity:

If you take, for instance, if she drops something, if she breaks a plate. She wouldn't make any excuses ... she would cry and she would say 'I am really sorry' and that would upset her. When she cries, she really gets wound up about it – 'I am really sorry Dad', and all that. ... I don't know, I think she likes the cuddle after ... I think that is what it boils down to. She is a very sensitive girl, Sally. She is a very loving girl.
(Mr Gordon, parent interview, July 1988, Reception)

Thus Sally in her Reception year was certainly happy, confident, sociable, keen to help and successful, particularly in her reading, writing and dance. She valued and took pleasure in her achievements, as did her parents. Whilst Mr and Mrs Gordon did not highlight the attainment of Sally relative to her peers, it was nevertheless something of which Sally was very conscious. Although she was popular and had her close friends in Amy and Mary, she liked to do well, and if possible, do 'better' than her friends. During the Reception year, she managed this fairly comprehensively, with only her attainment in maths lagging a little behind.

Matrix 7.1 *Sally's Reception year, a summary matrix*

Family relationships	Peer-group relationships	Teacher relationships	Identity	Learning
Parents work in school and are very supportive of it.	Popular amongst peers.	Sally's familiarity with Mrs Powell before entry is built on a warm and friendly relationship form.	Sally had adopted an identity as a 'pupil' before starting school, and immediately sought to be helpful to her teacher.	High relative attainment, particularly with reading.
Sally spends time in classrooms after school, often helping Mrs Powell.	Enjoys supporting new children in class and guiding them around school.	Sally actively learns about the classroom rules, routines and procedures which Mrs Powell maintains. She rehearses teacher and pupil roles in her play.	High classroom and playground status.	Competitive in all settings. Is first to discard 'word tin' and delighted to move 'up boxes' in the reading system.
No clear division between home and school – parents in school, school staff in the home.	Likes girls' games best, but will play with some boys and holds her own in 'kiss chase'.	Sally likes to bring things in from home to support class topics.	Very strong identification with school.	Pleased with early 'writing under' but as her own writing develops is nervous about 'wrong spellings'. Nevertheless, becomes 'a compulsive writer' and likes to experiment. Correct letter formation and neat writing by end of the year.
Sally particularly identifies with her mother.	Will go along with ideas of others but likes to be 'boss'.	Likes to 'do jobs' for Mrs Powell, organize and help other children.	Seen by Mrs Powell as sociable, competent, kind and high attaining.	
Sally loves to talk at home about her experiences at school and to play at 'schools'. Mr and Mrs Gordon provide constant help to Sally with her reading and praise her achievements. Sally is usually a confident, relaxed learner at home.	Socially at ease with older children at home and school.	Takes great pleasure in helping Mrs Powell in the classroom after school.	Watches and models herself on her mother and teacher.	In maths, sound progression through Mrs Powell's programme of work.
	Competitive with friends in class, such as Mary and in gymnastic ability.		Transcends usual pupil identity by 'instructing', 'socializing' teachers (new and supply) and having social relations with teachers outside school.	Sally is highly attuned and responsive to school expectations.
Mr and Mrs Gordon prepare Sally for the possibility of going into Miss Scott's class.	Rivalry with friends also for teacher attention and approval.		Enthusiasm for cousin's disco dancing leads to competition success for Sally and fulfilment from dance.	When approaching new classroom tasks, Sally is highly cue-conscious and is concerned with the product should be 'right'.
Sally is competitive with her older brother but finds it difficult to win at games.			Ballet skills develop – puts on impromptu performances at school.	Regarded by Mrs Powell as 'attentive and intelligent'.
Sam helps Sally with her reading, though this sometimes leads to her annoyance.				
Sally sometimes 'is a bit too clever' in presenting herself to please parents, particularly if Sam is being told off.				

7.4 SALLY IN HER YEAR 1

Sally, Year 1, relationships with parents at home

During the second half of Sally's Reception year, her parents began to think that some preparation might be needed before the start of her Year 1 with Miss Scott. Mrs Gordon explained that Sally had been upset by her some years earlier:

> What happened was, when we first came here Miss Scott was going along the corridor and Sally couldn't have been much more than about three. As I was coming along with a tray it was, 'Oh get out of the way', and it upset Sally. She never forgot that, and she would sit at home and say, 'I am going into Mrs Powell's class, then I am going into Mrs Rock's, then I am going to skip Miss Scott's, then I am going into Mrs Miles'. Even up until about six months ago.
> (Mrs Gordon, parent interview, July 1988, Reception)

Mr and Mrs Gordon thus began 'to prepare' Sally for her new experience:

> Mrs Gordon: We had an idea that she would go in. Any other year she probably wouldn't have done but with the amount of late birthdays we had a fairly strong feeling that this is where she would end up. So we started to do what you would call a bit of a brain washing act from then. You know, 'Oh gosh, Miss Scott, great, you will enjoy it in there'.
>
> Mr Gordon: That's right, yes. And we made a point of saying, if Miss Scott did anything, we would say, 'That is really nice, isn't it Sally? Miss Scott is a really nice lady, isn't she?' and Sally probably started thinking, 'Well, perhaps she isn't as bad'
> (Parent interview, July 1988, Reception)

Mr and Mrs Gordon were greatly helped in this by a social event which Miss Scott had attended. Mr Gordon explained:

> It all stemmed from that Fun Day we had over at the village hall. The only people from the school were me and Miss Scott wasn't it, to start with. Miss Scott was ... Miss Scott, socially, is a super lady. She was great, bouncy, and things like that. And Sally saw her in a different light, dancing on the grass to this live band thing. She thought it was wonderful, and since then she has been fine.
> (Parent interview, July 1988, Reception)

The result of this preparation was that Sally became confident of going into Miss Scott's class, despite the fact that she knew from her own experience and from other children that Miss Scott could be a 'difficult' teacher to be with. Mr and Mrs Gordon were able to use their knowledge of the school to mediate one of the bigger challenges which Sally faced, her Year 1 placement with Miss Scott.

During Sally's Year 1, the Gordons continued to provide strong support to their children and to enjoy their progress. They were also conscious that they wished to avoid 'being pushy':

> Mr Gordon: It's just that Sally's so confident that we just leave her to her own devices. She doesn't need encouragement because she's so enthusiastic and we wouldn't stem any of it. The thing is she wants to start to ... she goes to ballet, she now does tap and she now does modern dancing. Now she wants to join the gym club. It's costing us a bomb, but we manage because it's something we feel she's quite good at and she enjoys it. If it means me buying one less packet of cigarettes a week, fine, because as Gail says, they come first really. I think nowadays, with parents, the kids seem to come first.

I can't remember when I was at school my parents encouraging me like this. ... They're expecting now to do so well, aren't they? I don't know whether it's just because we live in this area, but it seems to be they've got to really do well, which is pressure for them all the time. We don't encourage Sally. She just does her own thing. And we don't encourage Sam. We just praise when he does well, and he has done well in a lot of things.

Mrs Gordon: We don't push them at all.
Mr Gordon: No, we're not pushy parents.
Mrs Gordon: If they want to do it, fine. If they don't ... .
Mr Gordon: We're proud. We're very proud parents. We're very proud of Sally and Sam. Because they are super really. They are terrors when they are at home, but you get them in the school environment and they just don't step out of line, which is really nice. I'd rather have it that way.

(Parent interview, July 1989, Year 1)

Sally, Year 1, relationships with siblings at home

During her Year 1 there continued to be some rivalry between Sally and Sam, particularly at the start of the year:

Sally was very noisy tonight. Sam was practising his violin and she just wouldn't leave him alone. She jogged the music book, tapped the case and generally made a nuisance of herself. She ended by getting the recorder and joining in, much to Sam's annoyance. I don't know whether she resented the fact that he's learning an instrument and that she's not or whether it was my involvement in his practise. The fact that for 20 minutes he gets my undivided attention and she has to sit on the sideline. This is a bit of a reversal for Sally. She is a very forceful person and tends to overshadow Sam a bit. Not that Sam is a shy, retiring child, far from it, but just that she likes to be the centre of attention and is prepared to go to great lengths to get it.
(Mrs Gordon, parent diary, October 1988, Year 1)

Towards the end of the year, however, relationships had begun to settle and Mrs Gordon felt that Sally had 'matured in her attitude' so that there was 'not quite so much bickering as there used to be'. Indeed, Sam was 'actually quite proud of her, at times' and began to take pleasure himself in her achievements at school.

Sally, Year 1, relationships among friends and in the playground

As Figure 7.1 shows, Sally was now one of the younger children in her class. However, she was quickly able to strike up friendships with older girls as well as retaining those from the previous year. She was particularly pleased when she was close with one older girl, Hannah. In the playground, Sally continued to be seen at the centre of play, directing operations through the allocation of roles or assertion of a storyline. Among the favourites at the start of the year were 'mums and dads' and 'brothers and sisters', and 'Mr Wolf', 'Farmer's in his Den', 'kiss-chase' and skipping were still popular.

Of the younger children, Sally retained her close friendship with Mary and Sarah. Discussion of one of the most popular games elicited some of Sally's attitudes to boys, her experiences of them and her concern to avoid them:

Sally: I like playing lots of 'mums and dads' games and Amita chases us 'cos we're naughty babies.

AP:	Oh, you're the babies and she's the mummy. And who do you have for the daddy?
Sally:	Oh, we have a boy.
AP:	Which one, any one?
Sally:	Yeah, anyone who wants to play.
AP:	What do you think about the boys then?
Sally:	Well, they punch people and fight people. Hazel had a bleeding nose because William and Robert was pushing her over. You know that they're a nuisance because they hit people and stuff; they catch people. They like catching people.
AP:	They seem to. I noticed that they were sitting at the back this morning, weren't they?
Sally:	They're always sitting at the back.
AP:	Are they? Always at the back?
Sally:	I think they like it there because there's a lot of people there, a lot of boys. They don't like sitting next to the girls.
AP:	I notice that you mostly sit up the front, don't you? Why do you sit near the front near the teacher?
Sally:	Because I don't like the boys sitting next to me.
AP:	What happens if you are sitting next to a boy, what do they do?
Sally:	They try ... they punch you sometimes.
AP:	Do they do anything else?
Sally:	Yeah. Fidget.

(Sally, child interview, November 1988, Year 1)

In May 1989 a supply teacher identified Sally in the following terms, 'She's the dominant force in the class. She's bright. Everyone wants to be with her'.

Sally, Year 1, relationships with Miss Scott in the classroom

It may be recalled from Section 2.4 (p. 24) that, at the time of the study, Miss Scott was somewhat stressed and frustrated in her teaching. She had a reputation amongst parents for becoming irritable and sarcastic with children, even though her attention to the basics of the curriculum was appreciated. Sally, however, benefited from the careful preparation which her parents had made so that she thought positively about Miss Scott. Miss Scott also felt positive about Sally because of her appreciation of the work of Mr and Mrs Gordon. As she put it:

> Sally comes from a family which are a totally well adjusted, life isn't easy for them I know, it is not a bowl of cherries and hasn't ever been ... .
> (Miss Scott, teacher interview, September 1988, Year 1)

Miss Scott was also aware of Sally's exemplary behaviour and, in July 1988, had said to her:

> I am very pleased to have you in my class next year because I have got some naughty ones from the other class and it will be nice to have you.
> (Reported by Mr Gordon, parent interview, July 1988, Reception)

Despite this, once the year started, Miss Scott did report that she had been 'a bit of a shock' to Sally and that 'she looked a bit anxious at times when I was getting cross with others'.

Nevertheless, a special relationship did flourish. For instance, on one occasion at the start of the day Miss Scott was upset following earlier discussions with a parent about a child's reading progress. My fieldnotes recorded:

Some children are told off and moved for fidgeting. They are made to stand at the front.

Robert has been told off but he doesn't seem to think this is fair. He rubs his eyes, as if he might cry, and looks out of the window.

The children now sit very quietly and the atmosphere is rather tense. Sally, Sarah and Mary are in the middle of the carpet. Sarah sucks her thumb, Mary looks as if she might.

Robert is told to turn round. He scowls and his eyebrows furrow, darkly.

Robert gets eye contact with William who is playing with Richard on the floor with a sheet of paper.

Miss Scott: Right, now what are we going to do today?

Sally: (*Immediately*) I've no idea.

Miss Scott laughs – and the tone lightens.

Miss Scott: Well ... really we ought to make a display for the entrance hall. There's really some lovely work there, *and* I thought we could also make another light-house picture for the entrance hall.

(Fieldnotes, February 1989, Year 1)

Sally's interjection, picking up on Miss Scott's rhetorical question, caused Miss Scott to laugh at the naive presumption that she might really have been asking for Sally's opinion. In this way the tension went out of the situation.

Miss Scott admired and appreciated Sally so that in her end of year records she wrote:

A well adjusted child, her popularity does not affect her and it's not gone to her head. Works with alert interest and enthusiasm. Always with a keen response. Always keen to take on responsibility and be helpful and go on errands. For her, school is an extension of her home and this undoubtedly helps, but her outward going confident approach would be the same if her parents weren't so closely connected. She is reliable and conscientious, if a bit slap dash in approach but working with increasing skill.

(Miss Scott, teacher records, July 1989, Year 1)

We will explore this reference to Sally being a 'bit slap dash in approach' in the section below.

Sally, Year 1, progress in classroom learning

Sally did extremely well during her Year 1 and, associating with some children consider-ably older than herself, achieved a high relative level of attainment in maths and literacy (see Figure 7.1). She particularly delighted in 'making progress' and, if Miss Scott had a reservation about Sally's achievement it was that she sometimes worked 'to simply finish a task quickly, rather than to do it as well as she could'.

Sally was well aware of this problem and explained in interview that 'you've got to take your time, in case you get scribbly'. However, my fieldnotes also recorded some interesting examples of the difficulties of working amongst a group of peers, of the emphasis given by Sally's teachers on the appearance of her writing rather than its content and of the matching tendency of Sally to work to a formula through which she could both satisfy her teachers and be seen to 'be good'. The account below, drawn from fieldnotes, is one such example:

After lunchtime, at 1.30, Sally chooses to write and selects a 'story starting card'. It reads, 'Once upon a time there lived a king and a queen'.

Sally starts to draw a picture. She does a crown and then the rest of a king.

She is sitting at a table with Mary and Maurice. Maurice asks her for some spellings. He moves closer to her and she comments on, 'knockud', saying it is spelled correctly.

Sally completes her picture of a King and Queen within a few minutes and begins her writing. She rules a line across the top of her page and starts to write quickly.

She draws a second line with her ruler, Mary watches. Maurice interrupts Sally to take her ruler and jogs her as she draws a second line. She says, 'Oh Maurice'.

She gives Maurice her ruler and goes off with Mary to get a rubber. Sally and Mary agree no boys should use the rubber.

Sally starts to rule a line again.

Maurice has put numbers by each line so he knows how many lines he's done.

Mary says, 'Anyway, Sally can use my rubber and my pencil and my ruler!'

Sally changes places to the other side of the table so that she is nearer to Mary.

Sally talks to Mary but she keeps on writing. She draws a third line and continues to write quickly.

Mary sits beside her and says, 'I don't have to do anything'. Sally asks her if she has 'to do one of these cards', but Mary shakes head.

At 1.46 Sally finishes her fourth line and takes her story to the supply teacher to get it checked. She reads it out.

> Once upon a time there lived a king and a queen they are rech [rich]
> a door was open and a cat got in
> the king and queen they said to the cat you can stay here
> thank you said the cat The end.

The supply teacher says, 'Right, that's a nice little story. It's nice and neat isn't it, 'cos when you did it last week it was a bit untidy wasn't it?

(Fieldnotes, May 1989, Year 1)

In discussion afterwards, Sally explained to me that she had 'chosen writing 'cos I like drawing queens and kings' and that Maurice had been a nuisance because 'he kept on moving his arm' but then 'he sometimes does'. She had ruled lines because, as she put it:

> Last time my writing went up and down, up down, up down and I didn't have lines. So the teacher wanted me to do it again. So this time I did lines.
> I like learning new words, it doesn't take long and I don't usually use 'queen' so I liked that. That's why I chose that card, and I know how to do crowns.
> I like to be good, never naughty.
> (Fieldnotes, May 1989, Year 1)

Despite her considerable application and concentration on the writing task, Sally acknowledged that she had only written an amount that she thought would be sufficient to get the supply teacher to let her go and play:

> Four lines is OK cos she's a kind teacher. ... I like to get my three things done, so I do writing first to get it out of the way. But if you don't know a word you have to look it up. In a dictionary if you want to say 'Spain' you have to find 'S', so you say ABCDEF. ... and you have to go on to find it.
> I can do lots, but I'd rather do other things.
> (Fieldnotes, May 1989, Year 1)

Sally, identity and learning in Year 1

Mr Gordon was delighted at the progress that Sally made during the year and recounted Miss Scott's comments to him:

> Miss Scott has come to me a few times and said, 'I am amazed – I have given her a work card and maths card and I have explained nothing and she just sat down, worked it out.' Really good. Miss Scott says, 'She is so quick', which is lovely isn't it? And her reading – she is reading all the time ... suddenly this term it has gone in leaps and bounds. When she was in Mrs Powell's class she would talk about what she was doing but not so much maths – but now she

will come home and say I have done so many cards today. We are in a position where we can go in and have a look – 'I did all this today and I did all this today' – and she is so proud of it all, she is really bursting.
(Mr Gordon, parent interview, July 1989, Year 1)

Overall, Mr and Mrs Gordon felt that Sally was 'much more mature than last year' and had 'grown up a lot'. Mrs Gordon explained in her diary:

Sally's confidence and enjoyment of all aspects of life are a constant source of amazement to us. At school she seems to thrive on responsibility and at Christmas she was so pleased to be picked for the school play. She had the part of Babushka and we were very proud of her. She didn't appear to have any nerves and actually loved getting up there on stage in front of the whole school.
(Mrs Gordon, parent diary, June 1989, Year 1)

Matrix 7.2 *Sally's Year 1, a summary matrix*

Family relationships	Peer-group relationships	Teacher relationships	Identity	Learning
Parents had previously 'brainwashed' Sally out of worries about Miss Scott, and they continued to be positive about her throughout her Year 1.	High popularity. In threesome with Sarah and Mary. Aspires to friendship with older girl, Hannah, and greatly upset by any rejection by her.	Miss Scott appreciates Sally's family circumstances and finds her confidence and personality 'really amazing'.	High structural position and attainment in the class, considering her age.	Reading improves in 'leaps and bounds'. Sally is highly self-motivated and reads a great deal at home.
Sally can be demanding at home but is considerate and polite outside it.	Sally's group has positive 'good girls' identity with Miss Scott. They learn to anticipate or avoid teacher wrath.	Sally seen by Miss Scott as being, 'well adjusted', 'keen', 'responsible' and 'enjoys the attention she receives for it'.	Very great self-confidence. This flourishes through friendships with older girls, parental support and good progress in classroom learning.	The quantity of maths cards completed is source of pride to Sally. Sally adopts a 'slap-dash' or routine approach sometimes makes very good progress.
Parents resist pressurizing Sam and Sally. Just encourage, through praise when they do well.	Quick to adapt to the social and cultural differences in the middle-class homes of many of her friends.	Sally is wary of Miss Scott, but is more confident than most of the children and is prepared to take initiatives. Strives at all times to be helpful and 'good'. However, Sally prefers to help another infant teacher, rather than Miss Scott, after school.	Her major role in the Christmas play is a particular boost.	Some drift towards minimalist writing to satisfy teacher requirements.
At start of year, Sally still likes to be the centre of attention and will try to displace parents' attention from Sam – forceful in this.	'A leader', 'in charge' in playground. She is critical of boys but also plays chase with some.		Joins infant gym club. Watches junior drama club after school and unofficially joins in.	
Sally 'more mature' by end of year and Sam is sometimes proud of her.			Sees herself as successful in school and able to help teachers as well as being popular with her peers.	

7.5   SALLY IN HER YEAR 2

Sally, Year 2, relationships with parents at home

Sally continued to have close support from her parents throughout her Year 2 at school as well as their considerable pride at her achievements. Nevertheless, negotiations were sometimes necessary when Sally became determined about something. In such circumstances, she was prone to generate a tantrum, but her parents were generally very firm and insisted on negotiating compromises. Two examples from the diary illustrate two very common sources of difficulty with young children – food and dress.

> When we got home this evening Sally was extremely difficult about what she was going to have for tea. She couldn't have what everyone else was having. I left her to it. We all ate and she sulked. She came round in the end, and we made a compromise. Half of what she wanted and half of what I said she should have.
> (Mrs Gordon, parent diary, November 1989, Year 2)

> A theme that has been on-going in the last few weeks has been socks. Sally has one favourite pair that she wants to wear every day. I started by washing them every evening and drying them – a situation that soon became very trying. A firm stand was needed on my part. This morning I put out some socks for her to wear. Result tantrum with a capital T. Every time I do this she gets really annoyed, but I think she realises now that she can't have her own way all the time. I try to make sure they are clean as often as possible but make sure she knows that she's got to compromise as well.
> (Mrs Gordon, parent diary, November 1989, Year 2)

During Sally's Year 2 Mr and Mrs Gordon began to play an even greater part in the life of the school. In addition to her role as cleaner and 'dinner lady', Sally's mother took up a temporary post as a general assistant working with the teachers and children in the classrooms. They both continued to enjoy participating very fully in school activities, committing themselves well beyond the normal expectations of their jobs. These contributions were greatly valued by the teachers, as Mr Gordon explained:

> They've been very appreciative, from Mrs Davison downwards. I think they realise just how valuable we are, not just me, but Gail as well. Gail has done so much, and this last week or so I've done all the scenery for the play, I've painted the fireplace and built the chimney and done the cakes. It's really nice and we're enjoying it at the moment. It's nice to be involved in all aspects of school work, rather than just being regarded as the people who clean it, which we're not, are we?
> (Mr Gordon, parent interview, December 1989, Year 2)

From Sally's point of view, the consequence continued to be that she had a particular sort of 'ownership' and knowledge of the school. She continued to spend a considerable amount of time at the school – from 9 a.m. to 6 p.m. except when going out to tea with a friend. In addition, if she ever was ill or distressed for any reason, the support of her parents was never far away. For instance, fieldnotes record one occasion in the autumn of Year 2 when Sally showed me a new pen and pencil case and explained, 'I got it 'cos I was sick on Daddy's floor. He gave it to me for a treat'.

There were times, however, when Sally did not disclose things which were troubling her, even though she was able to obtain sympathetic support immediately. As Mr and Mrs Gordon described one occasion in interview (see below) and we will return to it in the discussion on Sally's relationships with her peers.

Mrs Gordon:	She went through a little patch, didn't she? I don't know whether it was a case of she was just a bit under the weather, or whether somebody upset her, we don't know. She wouldn't say. ... But she never mentioned a word, did she, Adrian?
Mr Gordon:	No. In the end, like Miss George came and said, 'Sally's crying again. She said she's not feeling very well.' So I took her out into the corridor and I said, 'Can you tell me what's up, Sally, because either somebody or something has upset you?' and in the end because I kept on to her so much, rather than tell me what was going on, she just made something up. She said, 'I'm finding the maths too hard, Dad, at the moment' – which to me is nonsense because Miss George says she just sails through maths, no problem. So I said, 'Do you want me to come into the classroom with you one day and sit down while you're doing your maths?' 'Yes'. So I did that and the maths card that she said she had a problem with was simple and she found it simple and I thought, Well, that's obviously not what was going on. She's not having difficulty with her maths but by telling me that she's having difficulty with her maths, it might shut me up and stop me asking her questions. Obviously, something upset her, I don't know what. She got very tetchy.

(Parent interview, December 1989, Year 2)

Sally, Year 2, relationships with siblings at home

A degree of rivalry continued between Sally and her older brother, Sam. Sometimes, this drew other members of the family in, and, on occasion, enabled Sally to claim some high moral ground. For instance, Mrs Gordon's autumn diary records:

> Sally is really argumentative at the moment, and the fact that Sam tends to wind her up doesn't help in the slightest. What started out as a quiet morning (at breakfast) ended with everybody shouting at each other, me shouting the loudest! Then Sally turned to me and told me not to shout because I'd disturb the neighbours! I'm not sure exactly what they were arguing about but it ended up with Sally getting really upset about it.
> (Mrs Gordon, diary, November 1989, Year 2)

The rivalry spurred Sally to start playing the recorder in the Autumn Term. This was something to which she had eagerly looked forward, but it was given particular impetus by Sam's violin lessons at school and the progress he was making. As Mrs Gordon put it, 'a touch of the, "anything he can do"'.

On the other hand, the two children also enjoyed each other's company and sometimes played at home together. Like her parents, Sally took a close and proud interest in Sam's achievements in the school's football and cricket teams.

> She came out to watch Sam play football for the school team. She's very supportive of Sam and enjoys cheering him on. Unfortunately it didn't help much they lost 9–0!
> (Mrs Gordon, parent diary, November 1989, Year 2)

Sally, Year 2, relationships among friends and in the playground

Sally continued to play with many of her schoolfriends from the previous year, though, if anything, she broadened her contacts, particularly among girls such as Harriet and Alice. In the playground, Sally and Mary described playing tig, making daisy chains in summertime, and 'looking after' younger children. As described in Mary's story, they avoided 'not normal' games like football and cricket.

Relationships with boys were somewhat mixed during the year. At times chasing games, including 'kiss chase', would be entered into wholeheartedly but on other occasions and as in previous years the boys were simply seen as a dominating nuisance. In interview, Sally was adamant that she and her friends did not play with, 'Gary, Greg, Barney and Philip, the naughty boys'. As she explained:

> We don't play with them because they spoil our game. They always play football. They always say, 'We're doing that'. They kick a football in our games. We have to kick it back otherwise they shout.
> (Sally, pupil interview, March 1990, Year 2)

Towards the end of the Autumn Term, it appears that the games of 'kiss chase' had gone rather too far and that some of the girls were finding the attentions of the boys oppressive. Mr and Mrs Gordon gave the following account of Sally's feelings at a time just after some children had been in trouble with the headteacher after being found to be showing too much sexually explicit interest in each other:

> Mr Gordon: Greg, who was a little lad in the class, who's quite lively apparently, he just walked up to me in the corridor and he said, 'You know, Mr Gordon, Sally's my girlfriend'. He was really chuffed to tell me that. I said, 'Really, Greg?' And I said to Sally, 'Did you hear what Greg said?' and she just broke down and cried, which was very unusual. I couldn't work that out at all.
> Mrs Gordon: She was really quite upset about that ... the only thing that I could think was that Greg ... .
> Mr Gordon: ... there was a problem.
> Mrs Gordon: ... there were a few problems over there about it ... and I wondered if Greg had said he liked Sally she thought, 'I'm going to get into trouble now', whether that ... I don't know ... but I know that there has been a lot of trouble with Greg and another girl, and whether she thought I might get caught up in all of that, I don't know.
> (Parent interview, December 1989, Year 2)

It seems likely then that, even at this young age, issues arising in the playground and connected with the emerging sexuality of the children were the cause of Sally's unhappiness in the Autumn Term. Throughout the year, Sally remained popular with boys as well as girls, and she continued to have other 'suitors' such as James. However, despite James's attentions, she would not accept him, or anyone else, as a 'boyfriend'.

The mixture of reciprocity and rivalry in Sally's friendship with Mary continued:

> I think she feels she needs to be competitive with most of her friends. ... There's always been something between Sally and Mary. We pooh-poohed it basically, but there's always been an edge. And they've fallen out a few times this term, Mary has been mean to Sally, Sally has been mean to Mary, so whether that has anything to do with it.
> I'm not sure whether it's this area. This area is very competitive. Parents make their children very competitive, which we don't personally like.
> (Mr Gordon, parent interview, July 1990, Year 2)

Certainly the circumstances of the two families were very different, with Mary and her family now living in a brand-new, split-level, 'lovely big house', enjoying a high standard of living and contemplating the possibility of private education for their three children.

Sally, Year 2, relationships with Miss George in the classroom

From the very beginning of the Autumn Term, Sally had acted as a 'helper' for Miss George, the young, newly qualified teacher in her probationary year (see Chapter 2). By this time Sally had had two years experience of 'looking after' children who were new to the school or who joined at unusual times of the year and, in a sense, she adopted this script for her support to Miss George. With her detailed knowledge of the teachers, the school and its routines and with her after-school availability for doing 'little jobs' in the classroom, Sally was a genuine asset to Miss George. As Miss George commented when asked about her:

> Oh yes. Sally is ... well, she walks on water. From the very first when I didn't know where anything was, Sally was there to show me, help me. I can't find any fault with her ... . She's so mature. I could honestly trust her to do anything.
> (Miss George, teacher interview, November 1989, Year 2)

This opinion was very similar to that offered by supply teachers during the year and, whenever opportunities to help teachers in the school arose, Sally was in her element. As has been suggested above, this could be seen as Sally emulating the supportive roles of her parents and she certainly earned similar appreciation.

As in other years, Sally was also very much to the fore in the class presentation of the Autumn Term. Her parents explained just how intensely and thoroughly she prepared for it:

> Mr Gordon: She introduced their class thing, which to her was fine. And she was a reserve for everybody else, 'cos she knew everybody's part – because we had a performance in the hall before their play, where she used the whole of the stage and she said, 'Good Morning, welcome to our service da da da da da da'. Then she went to the next spot, said their bit, and went on, right through the whole play, and then ran back from that end right back over there and said, 'and now we'll say The Lord's Prayer'. She did everything in that play, because I watched the day after and she knew everybody's line. Because Miss George had told her that there were two that were a bit iffy, they had coughs, 'could she step in if that was the case?' And she said, 'yeah', and she could have stepped in anywhere.
>
> Mrs Gordon: She wrote the words out and Miss George said, 'You're alright, Sally, you don't have to learn them, you can read them'. 'That's alright', she said, 'I don't need to read them, I know them.' She already knew them anyway.
> (Parent interview, December 1989, Year 2)

For a new teacher, such a strong safety net underpinning her first major class presentation to the school was very highly valued, though following this there was some criticism of Sally's prominence with the result that she was assigned a less central role in the Christmas performance – much, to her dismay, as we shall see.

Nevertheless, Sally's relationship with Miss George was close and based on reciprocity. Sally and Mary were both besotted with Miss George and would regularly say how much they liked her. They would sit attentively at the front of the class at story times, shoot up their hands to offer if a 'job' arose such as taking the dinner register to the school office and offer to tidy up at play time if tables were left in a mess at the end of sessions.

Sally's actions in class had much in common with Mary's main strategy of 'being a good girl' which has been described in Chapter 3. Thus, when asked if it mattered if she didn't do things the way her teacher wanted them, Sally had the simple reply that, ' I always does it right, and Miss George *doesn't* shout if I do it wrong.' I asked her:

> AP: Do you like learning new things?

Sally: I like to do them quickly and to get them down. ... If I can't do it, I ask the teacher.

(Group interview, April 1990, Year 2)

Indeed, Sally's answer here is a fair summary of her approach. She regularly gave indications of her goals in her 'planning sheets', which were used in the negotiation of tasks to be done within the class. Thus, in maths she wanted to 'use a card' in order to 'go onto Stage 3, Blue card' and in English she planned 'to write about my wedding' and wanted 'to work quietly'. Her emphasis was on neatness and on completion of tasks effectively and 'correctly', so that she could move onto the next. When she planned to play in the home corner it was to 'make a house' or 'play mums and dads', thus accommodating to the fairly conventional provision which had been made. She would take rather more initiative with regard to tasks than Mary, but like her, would ask Miss George if she was really unsure of what to do.

Miss George's appraisal of Sally at a mid-point of the year was:

She's involved in class topics. She's observant. She spots relevant sections or pictures in books she reads. She shares them with the class. She enjoys art and craft but she's not particularly artistic, though she does like anything musical or with movement. If they do little plays or anything she takes it so seriously. She stands perfectly. She's a delightful child. It's been a pleasure to have her in the class. Where would I have been without her at the beginning. 'Sally, where's so-and-so?'

(Miss George, teacher interview, April 1990, Year 2)

At the end of the year, Miss George remained committed to Sally – as Sally was, perhaps even more-so, to her:

Sally is a delightful child and it has been a pleasure to have her in my class for the last year. I shall miss her.

(Report to parents, July 1990, Year 2)

Sally, Year 2, progress in classroom learning

Sally's progress at reading was fairly straightforward – she continued the momentum she had established in her work with Miss Scott. Her parents explained:

Mr Gordon: She's not having any problems. Her reading is just going up and on and on.
Mrs Gordon: I think she's only got two more boxes and she's a free reader, she can choose then.

(Parent interview, December 1989, Year 2)

Well before the summer, Sally did indeed qualify to become a 'free reader' – a position, of considerable status amongst her peers, which her friend Mary was not to reach until the last weeks of the year.

Sally is now a 'free reader' and chooses her books from the library. She takes great pride in this and is really enjoying her reading. I think this is reflected in her writing, both in content and spelling. I am often very surprised at how good her spelling has got. She spells words that I wouldn't have thought possible, and is never frightened to 'have a go'.

(Mrs Gordon, parent diary, June 1990, Year 2)

At the start of the year, despite Sally's proficiency in spelling, Miss George was not entirely convinced by the quality of the content of her writing, perceiving her as 'playing the system' and producing stories which lacked imagination. As she put it:

> I'm a bit worried about her writing at the moment, actually. Because she's got no problems –
> it's very hard to find a fault spelling-wise or anything like that – but I have actually started
> saying, insisting on capitals and full stops, just by way of extending it. But I don't think there's
> much imagination there any more. ... I've more or less said, for the benefit of the others, that I
> would like them to do two Peak Book maths cards each week and two pieces of writing. Well,
> now I feel that that's just what she's doing. Two pieces of writing – and there's nothing in
> them. ... I really have got to find some way of stretching her.
> (Miss George, teacher interview, November 1989, Year 2)

Interestingly, when it came to writing stories, rather different approaches were apparent
in the classroom. Sally, James and Mary tended to take a relatively minimalist approach,
aiming it seemed to reduce risk and the time spent whilst still turning out a neatly presented
story. Hazel and Harriet, on the other hand, were more oblivious of the conventions and
expectations of class norms, and often sought both intrinsic satisfaction from their stories
and some glory from length.

Sally was aware of some of Miss George's reservations about her writing, as emerged in
an interview:

> AP: What do you think about work in school?
> Sally: I think it's nice 'cos you do hard work and it's brilliant, 'cos we've got new
>   things in the home corner. But I'm not sure about writing, 'cos I don't have
>   such good ideas.
> (Pupil group interview, April 1990, Year 2)

Sally did, however, work at her weakness and by the Summer Term, with Miss George's
encouragement and advice, she had made significant progress. Miss George explained
that:

> Her stories have become more imaginative – because they went through a phase where they
> were a bit routine. ... And she started structuring them and using chapters and now she's
> writing a chapter every day and they are becoming more interesting because she's following
> on. Her spelling is excellent and anything she does get wrong is a slip of the pencil. I've put (in
> a draft report to parents) that I think she's observant. She notices spelling patterns.
> (Miss George, teacher interview, May 1990, Year 2)

Sally's progress in maths was very sound, though not exceptional and, importantly, not
as rapid as that of her friend Mary. Sally did sometimes get upset about her progress in
maths and it was a subject on which she would strive to improve when at home. Her father
explained:

> She does a lot of maths work at home, not through us, it's her own choice. You're in the
> kitchen and she'll shout out, 'Dad, give me a sum' and you'll say, '13 and 19', and she works
> that out, which is really good at six years old. She knows how to borrow 10 and carry it across
> and all that. 'Ask me another', she loves that.
> (Mr Gordon, parent interview, December 1989, Year 2)

Miss George wondered if the period when Sally was upset at school was related to her
maths progress:

> She's experienced one or two problems with her number work. She went through a phase
> where Adrian and Gail were quite concerned because she was crying ... and she said it was
> because of her maths. Afterwards I wondered if that was because Mary was way ahead of her,

outside insects

Some of class 4 were looking for insects we found a beetle and then we found a nother one and a Spider and an ant a bloodsucker and a centipede. I didn't Lik any of them. I was running when someone calls that they have seen something and it is always a bloodsucker, and one crawled up me

Document 7.6 *Sally, writing about minibeasts, May 1990, Year 2*

I don't know. Am I reading too much into it? But she didn't complain to me that there was something she couldn't do. She didn't seem unable to do it.
(Miss George, teacher interview, May 1990, Year 2)

By the end of the year equilibrium seemed to have been established. Although Sally was a little behind Mary's level on the Peak Maths scheme, she had, as Miss George put it, 'come to terms with the growing complexity of her maths number work' (report to parents, summer 1990, Year 2). Mr and Mrs Gordon seemed content, but they noted the influence of new approaches to teaching maths which slowed down Sally's overt progress through the scheme.

Sally seems to be progressing well through the maths scheme. ... [although] we were expecting her to be further on than she actually is. I must say less emphasis seems to be placed on the scheme. Maths problems, quizzes etc., seem to be used alongside Peak which means that at the end of the day less time is spent on Peak and therefore progression through the book is slower.
(Mrs Gordon, parent diary, June 1990, Year 2)

Together with her friend Mary, Sally continued to attend Saturday morning ballet and dance lessons. She took exams for different types of dance and appeared in public performances held at the prestigious King George's Hall. Her mother recorded her justifiable pride in these achievements:

Last time I wrote the weekly diary Sally was looking forward to her Ballet Show at the King George's Hall. Prior to that she had a modern exam at Christmas. She gained a 'first degree honours pass' in this, the highest pass. I don't know who was most pleased, us, her or her dance teacher. Sally excels at modern, more so than the ballet. Ballet is quite formal and restricted and you can always see Sally's personality bubbling away under the surface. Modern allows that to come to the front. Although a highly commended pass in her recent ballet exam shows that she's also successful in this too.

The show at the King George's Hall was a great success. Sally enjoyed the whole thing and showed no sign of nerves at all. I, on the other hand, was a bag of nerves from start to finish and had a headache for four days!
(Mrs Gordon, parent diary, June 1990, Year 2)

Looking back at Sally's year, Mrs Gordon recorded in the diary:

... I think she has had a very good year. Her reading has improved ... her vocabulary and spelling. ... Her maths has progressed steadily. ... She's thoroughly enjoyed the science, her art work, I think, has improved although dance and movement are always going to be her first love. ... Music has also played a big part this year. She's joined the Glockenspiel Club and has played in three concerts this year. She also plays the recorder and this is coming along quite well too. ... On the whole I think her confidence is growing, tempered with the odd hiccup which keeps the ego in line!
(Mrs Gordon, parent diary, June 1990, Year 2)

Sally, identity and learning in Year 2

Sally's identity in many respects continued to flow from her detailed knowledge of the school. In the clubs and after-school activities which she attended whilst her parents worked, she had plenty of opportunity to renew this knowledge, to see other teachers at work, to meet other children and to develop some of her own interests and skills.

She's quite taken up now with all the clubs because the ones that she doesn't actually go to as such, she goes along to watch all the others. She goes in and watches the junior gym club. Tuesday nights she does drama, unofficially – it's supposed to be for the juniors but she goes along and, you know Sally, she doesn't sit on the side lines for long. She's there, she's in there, sort of business. On Wednesday, there's nothing on a Wednesday, just Stamp Meeting. She doesn't join in that. Thursdays she goes to Cru Club up at the church. On Fridays she usually goes out and watches the football, goes out with the younger boys, so there's something to occupy her and lately she's been in on the Glockenspiel practice. I know she's been in the hall with Mrs Smart. They've been doing gymnastics on the beam. They've worked out a little routine. I think they watched some of the juniors doing it. I think that's what it was and they've been copying it on the beam, pretending the bench was a beam and doing things on that, so they've got plenty to occupy them at the school. She doesn't seem to get bored at all.
(Mrs Gordon, parent interview, December 1989, Year 2)

As we have seen, the rivalry with her friend Mary often surfaced, both in school work and in their out of school dance activities and perhaps such rivalries fuelled Sally's feeling that, despite her existing real achievements at school, she always needed to strive for more. For instance, she was very disappointed when, having become a 'glockenspiel player', she was not given a central speaking part in the infant's Christmas Play for parents. Her mother explained the position:

This has upset her terribly. She was in tears. We tried to explain that with so many children in the infants, it stands to reason that she can't always have a major part in school productions.

We told her that playing an instrument is a very important responsibility – but Sally didn't quite see it that way. Hopefully she'll get over this and enjoy the part she has to play.
(Mrs Gordon, parent diary, November 1989, Year 2)

Mrs Gordon continued the story in interview:

> Mrs Gordon: Having got over the disappointment of not actually having a part, then Sally decided that she was going to be best on the glockenspiel. I think she's decided that, 'Alright then, I'll be best at the glockenspiel instead'. She's quite happy about it now. I think she'd be even happier if she could sit on top of the piano and play it.
> Mr Gordon: With a spotlight on her!
> (Parent interview, December 1989, Year 2)

When the position between the friends was reversed and it was Mary's turn to be disappointed, Mrs Gordon attempted to help Sally think about her friend's feelings:

> She's extremely excited about the forthcoming ballet show at the King George Hall. This year's production is Alice in Wonderland. Sally's been chosen to play the little Alice when she shrinks. I believe she'll be going on and off stage during the production. She also has to sing a song.
> It's very difficult to try and stop her from getting too carried away, especially as Mary goes to the same class. I've noticed that if Sally's chosen to do something and Mary isn't then Mary takes it to heart. It's difficult to try and explain to a six year old that they have to consider other people's feelings especially when I'm as excited as Sally! But I think on the whole Sally is very receptive to this and I'm sure wouldn't deliberately show off, she just gets a bit carried away in her excitement.
> (Mrs Gordon, parent diary, November 1989, Year 2)

Here then, we have examples, in her disappointments and in her successes, of Sally being guided by her parents, as she was by her teachers, to become aware of and reconciled to the feelings of other children. She was, in other words, being helped to come to terms with her own success, helped to manage her identity and enthusiasm for learning in socially acceptable ways.

Sally did, however, face a particular challenge of her own during her Year 2, that of learning to swim, which she initially found difficult. It provides a good illustration of her determination to overcome setbacks in learning:

> AP: Could you tell me about this swimming business? It sounds very interesting ... hitting a problem.
> Mrs Gordon: Our first failure really of anything significant. Up to now most things she's had a go at have come easily, it hasn't been a problem and the swimming is just not coming as easily as she thought ... well, as we thought really. I put her in for this course of 10 weeks and I thought, because she's very, very confident with armbands, she's not frightened of the water ...
> Mr Gordon: But it frightened her because the lady put them in the deep end which is 8 or 9 foot. They've got single armbands you see and depending on how good a swimmer you are, they'll add or take away, and they put her in with one on straight away and she wasn't ready for one and she went straight down and the lady had to fish her out with the net, which really threw her. I was there then, that was the only time I went.
> Mrs Gordon: It hasn't frightened her, has it?
> Mr Gordon: Well, it did then, she didn't want to get back in. It frightened me, I was almost in there and the lady said, 'Don't worry'. She was fine after she'd cried a bit and she came and sat with me ... and they put another two armbands on her then and she was fine. But that worried her.

AP: So she had a shock then ... .

Mr Gordon: And I'm not sure whether ... because, Sophie's taken to it quite well, Sophie who's gone with her, and I'm not sure whether Sally can handle the fact that one's doing it and she's not. She may try too hard.

AP: Do you think she's going to grit her teeth and stick with it, or do you think she's going to fade out of it?

Mrs Gordon: She wants to carry on. She wants to go on, so it hasn't put her off, she's not frightened of getting back in.

Mr Gordon: We took them to the Oasis last Sunday and she made a conscious effort to take her armbands off as much as she could, and she was saying, 'Look Dad', and she'd swim, and I haven't seen her swim before so I was quite impressed with that.

Mrs Gordon: It was that initial shock of finding that she couldn't do it as easily as she thought she was going to, and that somebody else found it much easier than her.

(Parent interview, July 1990, Year 2)

Sally was clearly supported by her parents in her struggle to learn to swim, but the account above also reveals her own determination, particularly given Sophie's success. Indeed, Sally felt that there was very little school learning that she could not at least make a good attempt at. When shown a photograph of herself facing a new challenge, she talked about her feelings and about the strategies which she might adopt:

AP: Here's a picture of you Sally, when a teacher has asked you to do some new school work. How do you feel when you get new work?

Sally: I'd want to do it 'cos it's fun, but I didn't want to do it in the picture 'cos I was frightened and scared that I might get it wrong. Learning things is good 'cos it's useful.

AP: What might you do to try to do the work?

Sally: Go through it with a calculator for maths or with a dictionary for writing. Watch and listen to the teachers.

AP: Might you get help?

Sally: Not get help. I like to get on with it on my own, 'cos you want to try to do it, 'cos 'if you try you'll learn it', my Mum says, and, 'if you don't try you won't learn it'. I have a go at my maths and when I'm on books, My mum and Dad say the same. My brother had a go at cricket and football, and did very well and he's in the team.

(Pupil photo interview, July 1990, Year 2)

Sally then, was as keen to 'have a go' and 'do it right' at the end of her infant school education as she had been at the start. She had achieved much – with a positive self-image, and being well regarded by her peers, her teachers and her family. At the same time, Sally was gradually learning how best to take account of others around her.

As Mr and Mrs Gordon summarized it:

Mr Gordon: We feel, ourselves, that she's had a really good infants, she's gone through the infants so well. And she's grown up, she's now quite grown up. Even her sense of humour.

Mrs Gordon: I think she was born that way! No, she does have her periods where she jumps up and down and waves her arms about when she doesn't get her own way. Like most kids her age I suppose really. On the whole, though, her outlook is quite mature for her age.

(Parent interview, July 1990, Year 2)

Matrix 7.3, overleaf, reviews the Year 2 as a whole.

Matrix 7.3 *Sally's Year 2, a summary matrix*

Family relationships	Peer-groups relationships	Teacher relationships	Identity	Learning
Mr and Mrs Gordon continue to actively support Sally and take pride in her achievements.	Sally is popular with peers and broadens her friendships.	Constant helper to Miss George and seen as being totally trustworthy – 'walks on water'.	Sally is the oldest in the class and enjoys high relative academic attainment.	Agreement that, overall, Sally has 'a very good year'.
Their support is particularly necessary when she encounters a difficulty, such as in learning to swim. Sometimes when Sally is determined about something, negotiations are necessary – but a tantrum from Sally is also possible.	However, her close friendship and rivalry with Mary continues.	Sally entrusted with the key coordinating role in the autumn class production. Learns all lines and underpins presentation.	Sally's considerable successes in public ballet performances and in dance examinations are very important. Mrs Gordon thinks that, 'dance is always going to be her first love'.	Steady progress in reading to achieve 'free reader' status by middle of year. Excellent spelling.
Sally continues to enjoy being so involved with the school. This encompasses her helping time after school and doing some school work at home. Mrs Gordon becomes a general assistant which increases involvement in school and availability to Sally.	Sally declares that she and her friends 'do not play with the naughty boys' because 'they spoil our games'.	Sally and Mary 'besotted' with Miss George.	In school, has 'an answer for everything', and 'knows everything' concerning the classroom and much about the school. Sally is a determined learner, even when rebuffed.	However, increased tendency to play the system in terms of working 'just enough'. Seems to watch, listen, work swiftly, get it right, enjoy completion.
	Nevertheless, she plays 'kiss chase' with boys, but has some upsets with Greg and fears of 'getting into trouble'. She rejects 'boyfriends'.	Sally on constant look out for opportunities to 'do jobs'.	Gets involved in school clubs, including junior gymnastics and drama club.	Slightly minimalist approach to writing early in year – neat and correct, but not much imagination. Sally feels she 'doesn't have such good ideas'. However, she recognizes the problem and, in the summer, she produces stories of higher quality.
On some issues in relation to her peers, Sally no longer shares her feelings with Mr and Mrs Gordon.	Sally plays in the junior playground after school.	Sally aims to 'be good' but this is sometimes interpreted as 'neatness' and completion of tasks at the expense of quality.	Sally has a very strong self-confidence, tempered, as Mrs Gordon put it, 'by the odd hiccup which keeps her ego in line'. For instance, Sally suffers from any failure to 'star'. Soon picks herself up, though, determined to succeed as ever.	Sound progress in maths though a difficult mid-year patch when Sally is upset and seems not to understand non-scheme tasks. Sally often seems satisfied by completion of a set number of work cards. She is also very aware of Mary moving ahead of her in maths work by end of the year.
Sally and Sam continue to sometimes argue.	Continues to have older friends out of school.	Miss George sees Sally as 'a delightful child'.	Sally is devastated by not having a speaking role in the Christmas play. She is determined to be 'the best glockenspiel player'. Begins to adopt a 'junior identity' before entering juniors and is seen by parents as 'quite grown up and mature for her age'.	Sally is upset by her difficulties in learning to swim, in particular in not moving up a class with her friends. However, she is determined to continue, and does.
Sally too young to join violins like Sam but learns recorder instead.	Sally is 'competitive with most of her friends' (Mr Gordon). Is 'just ahead' of Mary in most areas of school work and dance.			
Sally takes pride in Sam's sporting achievements.	Sally pleased to win prize at Cru Club – the first to memorize a verse.			
	Chosen to co-star in ballet production. Achieves a high award in an examination for modern dance.			

7.6 SALLY'S LEARNING AND DEVELOPMENT

The case study of Sally can now be briefly summarized. First, in Figure 7.3 (p. 223), we can see Sally's experience over the first three years of her schooling in terms of a pattern of relationships. As with the overviews of the other children, the triadic representation depicts, in the outer triangle, the social context in which Sally learned and interacted and, in the inner star, the dynamic relations between Sally, her family, peers and teachers. The central feature of the overview is Sally's self confidence through which she managed to transcend the normal pupil identity.

The second way in which we can summarize the case study is with regard to the model of learning, identity and social setting as presented in Chapter 1 and elaborated in Chapter 4.

So, with the question of *Who is learning?* in mind we could consider Sally's sense of identity in the context of her unique position in the school. On the one hand, Sally's parents described themselves as 'the poor relations' of middle-class Greenside. On the other hand, this seems to have been more than compensated for in Sally's case by her sense of family 'ownership' of the school and her close identification with it. The resource of the school building, social relations with the staff and access to knowledge about the workings of the school to which her parents' roles and relationships in the school gave Sally access, were crucial to the confident and powerful edge which she had over her more middle-class peers.

The resource which her special access to the school gave Sally, as well as her undoubted enthusiasm, were also significant in a consideration of *What is to be learned?* For example, she was learning the games and puzzles of the infant classrooms before she became a pupil. She was reading the books of the older infant classes before she was in those classes or officially on those reading stages. She unofficially joined in with junior drama and gym clubs after school. A recurring feature of Sally's learning is thus that she transcended the usual pupil identity in terms of age-related stages and had sampled the content, as well as the social and physical contexts of much of her learning, ahead of her peers.

With regard to *How supportive is the learning context?* we know that such support was almost complete. She had to face few of the stresses associated with independence and separation from parents in the adaptation to school life, and the 'maturity' ascribed to her by her teachers, whilst being justified, should be considered in that light. Where she did face difficulties, for example in coming to terms with her entry to Miss Scott's class, her parents were in an ideal position to anticipate and to intelligently divert her fears. We might consider as especially important the network of supportive social relations stemming from her parents' care and commitment to the school and support for the changes under way, the reciprocal value and appreciation which they were accorded by the staff and their popularity among Sally's peers.

In answer to the question *What were the learning outcomes?* we might highlight the social status and self-esteem which Sally earned. Her desire to please, to be best and to 'star' were the driving force behind much of her classroom learning. If Sally was minimalistic and formulaic in her approach to some classroom tasks, concerned with balancing speed with neatness to keep ahead of peers and please her teachers rather than prioritizing intrinsic satisfaction or concern for content, then it has to be said that it was a highly effective strategy. An important learning outcome for Sally was her consistently high attainment.

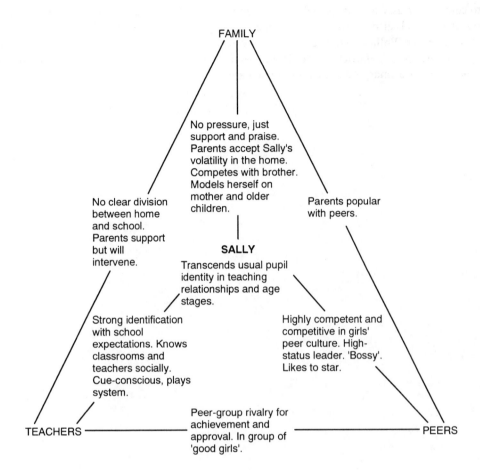

FAMILY

No pressure, just support and praise. Parents accept Sally's volatility in the home. Competes with brother. Models herself on mother and older children.

No clear division between home and school. Parents support but will intervene.

SALLY

Transcends usual pupil identity in teaching relationships and age stages.

Parents popular with peers.

Strong identification with school expectations. Knows classrooms and teachers socially. Cue-conscious, plays system.

Highly competent and competitive in girls' peer culture. High-status leader. 'Bossy'. Likes to star.

Peer-group rivalry for achievement and approval. In group of 'good girls'.

TEACHERS

PEERS

Figure 7.3 *Sally's case-study overview*

Having distilled Sally's story with respect to some of the major themes concerned with the social context, her classroom learning and identity, we now may consider some key issues that emerge.

The issue of relationships, in particular home–school relationships is of particular interest in Sally's story, because of the lack of any clear division between the social worlds, the concerns and the commitments of Sally's parents and of the school. Sally's case is unique in the descriptions of the roles, relationships and resources which instigated and supported her close identification with the school; an identification which seems to have had major consequences for the confidence, status and self-esteem of a working-class child in a traditionally middle-class neighbourhood and school.

Learning outcomes were also a significant aspect of Sally's story, not least because the sort of outcomes for which she strived were beginning to present her with problems. At the point where her story closes she was beginning to have to come to terms with her own success, to cope with sharing the limelight with others and with occasional failure and learning to be aware of the feelings of others who were less successful. Sally was still fairly young at the close of the story but, as she moved through her junior school career, she had to come to terms with her special position within the school and the potential threat to her popularity, and, at one crisis point, to her learning, that it posed. In *The Social World of Pupil Careers* (Pollard and Filer, in press) we shall meet Sally again through the eyes of some of her peers, Harriet, Sarah, Robert and William, and will be able to track further aspects of her primary school learning and career.

Chapter 8

James' Story

8.1   JAMES, AN INTRODUCTION

The case study of James at Greenside Primary School is a rather sad one. James became rather unsettled at school initially and was never fully accepted by his peers. There were also some misunderstandings and weak relationships between his teachers and parents.

Over the period of the study, James' mother, Mrs Tait, suffered from the debilitating condition of Myalgic Encephalomyelitis which is more commonly known as 'ME' (Macintyre, 1989). This is a post-viral syndrome which the ME Association, founded in 1976, describe as having the primary symptom of abnormal muscle fatigue combined with impaired brain function and other effects which are similar to influenza. The disease was recognized by the National Health Service in 1987 and there has been a struggle for its public acceptance in the face of scepticism. Something of this is conveyed by the title of the ME Association's 1994 leaflet, 'Prisoners in a World of Disbelief'. As we shall see, Mrs Tait's illness was not fully understood by either the teachers at Greenside or by the mothers of other children. How then, would this affect James and his development?

On the face of it, James might have been expected to have flourished in his primary school. The socio-economic status of his family was high and both parents put great value on academic attainment. James' mother was a former primary school teacher with an awareness of the value of a wide range of stimulating learning experiences within supportive and sympathetic family relationships. The Taits also held firm views on some aspects of popular culture, such as television viewing, and made efforts to ensure that their children learned to be well-mannered in company. Although the most conservative and traditional of the families in the study, the Taits regarded their approach to education as being conventional for families of their background.

But how would these family circumstances and values influence James' coping strategies at Greenside Primary School? Why, after his Year 2, did James become so unhappy that his parents decided to send him to Easthampton College, an independent school? What were the factors that shaped his school experience into a downward spiral of misunderstandings and anxiety?

Figure 8.1 shows James' relative age and attainment in maths and literacy for his Reception, Year 1 and Year 2 classes at Greenside Primary School.

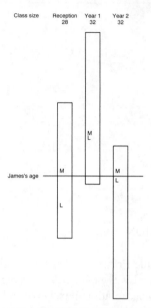

Figure 8.1 *James' structural position: age and relative attainment at literacy and maths in Reception, Year 1 and Year 2 classes (for an explanation of this figure, see p. 35)*

It can be seen that, as for several of the children in this study, James moved from being of average age in his Reception class, to being one of the youngest in Year 1 and then one of the oldest in Year 2. This reflected the age-based allocation of pupils in the 1.5 form of entry school but it also meant that some friendships were disrupted when particular individuals were split up. James' relative school performance in maths was always a little higher than his relative attainment at literacy, though this primarily reflected his weak writing rather than his relatively good reading. At no point was James a 'high flier' within these classroom contexts, though his annual attainments were perfectly creditable.

8.2   JAMES' FAMILY

Graham and Helen Tait

Laurence
(3.5 years older)

James
(born January 1983)

Figure 8.2 *James' immediate family*

At the start of this study, Mr and Mrs Tait lived in a pleasant, detached 1930s house in an established part of Greenside. However, they did not feel entirely relaxed there, finding some of the neighbours a little diffident towards them. When James was in Year 2, they moved to a newly built, luxury house on the other side of the suburb.

Mr Tait was an active businessman, owning and managing a successful wholesale distribution company. Mrs Tait had trained and worked as a primary school teacher. However, as indicated above, at the time of the study she suffered from ME. As she put it:

> The muscles don't work. I start the day very bright and go down hill during the day until I am right out by the evening.
> (Mrs Tait, parent diary, January 1988, Reception)

Mrs Tait was thus unable to be as active as she wished and, in fact, needed help in maintaining the home and family. The two boys, Laurence and James, played their part in this:

> We eat high tea together. Boys lay table. Mum cooks, Dad puts dishes in dishwasher. It is the boys' chore to empty the dishwasher and put everything away. As I have not a great deal of stamina, they help by doing certain set chores. They fought at first not to do them, but now accept them as a matter of course. James has always seemed to feel grown-up and important when helping. Only when he is really tired at the end of term or when unwell is he difficult.
> (Mrs Tait, parent diary, January 1988, Reception)

As the above reference to 'high tea' perhaps indicates, the Taits consciously upheld many middle-class conventions and saw these as a contribution to their children's upbringing and education. Thus routine outings and family treats were also learning experiences whereby the children could receive training in suitable manners and a broad, cultured and Christian education.

AP:	You talked about taking them out to dinner, Sunday lunch time, providing them with a situation to get their manners right and that kind of thing, does that happen incidentally or have you got a sort of programme of social learning or ... .
Mrs Tait:	I have a programme, yes. In the holidays I try to pack in as many different experiences as Easthampton has to offer. I get a young lady to take them on boats, up towers, round all the churches. Whether they will or no, I get them taken. So if they have to say, write an essay, they will have some material to draw on. I feel ..., I taught in Damibrook [a local council estate] for a year and I noticed what barren lives they lead and the children came out that way. So I try to give them a rich diet you know.
Mr Tait:	I think we try not to have very much of them doing childish things if you like, so if we go out, we tend to go out more lunch time than evening time and they come with us, so we involve them in the meal and the fact that they don't throw the bread rolls around etc.

(Parent interview, March 1988, Reception)

The whole family often attended the Morning Service at the local church, for which the children put on their best clothes and were expected to behave appropriately. During the week, they attended 'Cru Club', an evening activities club for children run by the church.

The Taits saw the values, expectations and conventions which they upheld as being normal and unexceptional among families such as theirs. However, as the above discussion shows, they also recognized that their children's experiences were not generalizable to a wider community.

Mr and Mrs Tait thought of James very affectionately. For Mr Tait, he was, 'a pretty normal little chap if you like, perfectly happy going to school', whilst Mrs Tait drew attention to his, 'nice, funny, easy-going nature'. As she elaborated:

> We think he is a dear little chap and he has not given us a minute's problem. He is very lovable.
> (Parent interview, March 1988, Reception)

James was 3.5 years younger than his only sibling, Laurence, and this position in the family was significant. James' strategy seemed to be to aim to conform, almost at all costs:

Mrs Tait: He wants to be seen as 'good'. It doesn't trouble Laurence if he is bad, but James wants to be good and if he gets told off he is instantly on the verge of tears, whereas with Laurence it doesn't affect him at all. I would say James seems softer, he is a softer person that one can affect him at all ... He is a softer person that one can affect more with discipline.

AP: But more vulnerable in a sense?

Mrs Tait: Yes, which surprised us because he looks tough. He is built as a large, muscular chap and he is always beating up Laurence! So we thought, 'We have got a toughie here', but inwardly he seems to have sensitivity. ...

AP: If he is told off when he has done something wrong, how does he take to that?

Mrs Tait: He will cry as if you have broken his heart to a point where you wish you hadn't told him off. He is so upsetting to watch he gets cut to the core and it will take him maybe a whole day to come round because he has been so upset.

(Parent interview, July 1988, Reception)

During James' infant school years, whereas Laurence tended to take particular notice of his mother, James looked up to his father:

Mrs Tait: He is 'Daddy's boy' and the other one is 'Mummy's boy'. He identifies with him in every way, he wants to work with him, be with him. Daddy tends to do more telling off because he is not geared up for children. I am used to the hurly burly but Dad comes home after a long time and he wants them to ... .

AP: ... be quiet?

Mrs Tait: Yes, and that will affect him of course, because he wants to be the apple of Daddy's eye, to be in favour, ... so that affects him.

(Parent interview, July 1988, Reception)

At the time, Mrs Tait felt a little marginal among the social networks of mothers which developed within Greenside. Prior to starting primary school, James was one of only a few children who had attended a private nursery school outside the area and the friendships which often stemmed from a sustained period of participation in the Greenside playgroup were not established. Furthermore, throughout most of James' infant school years, Mrs Tait was unable to get out a great deal because of her medical condition as a sufferer of Myalgic Encephalomyelitis (ME). Unfortunately, ME was not well understood at the time and indeed it tended to be caricatured in the media as a psycho-somatic illness. In the context of this 'common-sense' view, it is not perhaps surprising that a number of mothers and teachers were sceptical about Mrs Tait's condition. Some simply felt that she was reclusive. Certainly, she was only rarely able to collect James from school and was thus not able to establish relationships among other mothers at the school gate which might have refuted such speculation. Additionally, because of her difficulties in managing at home, Mrs Tait felt that she had to put a limit on visits of James' friends 'coming to tea'. The unfortunate consequence was that the family was perceived by some other parents and teachers as setting themselves somewhat apart from the rest of the community.

Mr and Mrs Tait had high educational aspirations for their children and Mrs Tait had considered teaching the boys at home:

Well, I was a teacher and I felt convinced that I could tutor my children and I could get them into Easthampton College (an independent school) on a scholarship, I thought, 'the sky is the limit'! Then I actually had to tackle the children and found that what they wanted to do was not

what I wanted to do, so I have had to lower my sights considerably. We sat Laurence for the King Edward's College exam (an independent school) and he was a borderline case. He would have got in but he won't write a decent long story, so he failed. So I am gradually coming back from the heights to reality and am now thinking of Halberton Grammar School (a state school) whereas my husband is determined they shall go to Easthampton College, so we are in a conflict situation.
(Mrs Tait, parent interview, March 1988, Reception)

Mr Tait felt that, 'the age of 10 or 11 is about the crucial sort of time, when you have really got to start getting things completely right educationally' and he wanted the children to have 'the best possible start'. However, he was not convinced that state education could provide it:

> I am not happy with the way the state education has gone. I feel particularly with Laurence, he is likely to be lead astray and needs a more disciplined situation which is why I am hoping that we, resource wise, will have enough to wrap them that way. Obviously the same thing applies to James, although because it is too early yet to see how James is developing, it is difficult at this stage to see where we would want him to be going if you like. Really, we are looking to perhaps having to pay for them to get an elitist start, if you like, by not having to mingle with things which are going to have negative effects on them.
> (Mr Tait, parent interview, March 1988, Reception)

In summary, James' family was traditional and conservative in outlook and whilst James' father and mother held somewhat different educational views, they shared high aspirations for their children. They were fearful of the erosion of standards in modern society and supported clear Christian values and a strong code of good manners and behaviour. They also, as we shall see, wanted the boys to learn to 'stick up for themselves'. James particularly identified with, and wanted to please, his businessman father.

8.3   JAMES IN HIS RECEPTION YEAR

James, Reception, relationships with parents at home

Some important aspects of family roles and dynamics are illustrated by the following extract from Mrs Tait's diary, relating to the start of a school day.

> James wakes at 7.00 but rises at 7.15 when Daddy brings up early morning tea. He then plays with elder brother Laurence until 7.30. Father firmly tells both boys to get dressed as they would play until 8.30 if left to their own devices. 7.45, breakfast – boys help to lay table and carry mugs, now empty downstairs. There is much bossing of James by Laurence which James usually accepts but sometimes resents, when a scene ensues. Daddy supervises breakfast. He sits there in a silent daze whilst boys bicker and sometimes poke and hit each other. Father tolerates a certain amount of horse-play but shouts when it becomes too much to restore peace. Meal is always cereal, milk, toast and honey and tea. Sometimes orange juice as well. 8.15, boys help clear table then run upstairs to clean teeth, brush hair and get last minute things for school. James remembers the morning routine and cooperates easily. Whilst Laurence always has to be told to get on with teeth etc. Boys make their own beds before school. Today I ask Laurence to load up the washing machine for me and set it going. James wants to help too. Boys quarrel over who shall carry what. Laurence is always dominant James will retaliate by thumping him or appealing to adults for support. 8.35, husband drives boys to school. If the weather is dry like today he drops them at bottom of hill and they walk up to school at the top. James is quite happy to walk off to school as long as he is with Laurence.
> (Mrs Tait, parent diary, January 1988, Reception)

Mr and Mrs Tait were uneasy about the mixture of violent, sensationalist and pap television output which they felt was provided for children on national networks and on videos. They believed that it displayed inappropriate values and could be damaging.

> 4.30 pm: We ... sit down to watch a video of 'Ghost Busters' which to my amazement is an awful horror film. I was told it was a children's film! James and Laurence enjoy it – I am more horrified than they are, although in places they bury their heads and don't look. Finally I realise it is not suitable and turn it off. ... James goes along with this. Laurence cries and has a temper tantrum. At this point my husband arrives home and is angry that temperament is being shown. He is not keen on anyone demonstrating emotion. More trouble ensues. ... Boys sent to play upstairs. Father eats his evening meal in peace.
> (Mrs Tait, parent diary, January 1988, Reception)

With her teaching background, Mrs Tait was very aware of the value of direct experience in children's development and she accepted the consequent need for flexibility and responsiveness. This is illustrated by her account of a shopping trip in which she not only indulged James but also interceded on his behalf with his father:

> We all pile into the car and drive to Easthampton. I go into a jeweller because a ring has been made smaller for me and I must collect it today. Suddenly we realise James is missing. He is on the pavement trying to catch in his cupped hands a steady stream of water from the corner of the awning. His arms and hands are soaked but he is very happy and passers by smile indulgently at him. My husband shows anger which is a pity and tells him to stop. I think it must have been a lovely experience.
> I go back and sit in the car whilst father and boys go to a man's clothes' shop. The boys enjoy these outings. They both skip and dart about examining everything in sight. The rain seems to make it more enjoyable for them.
> (Mrs Tait, parent diary, January 1988, Reception)

This awareness of the value of experiences and activity also underpinned Mrs Tait's perception of children's TV programmes 'taking over' from more worthwhile pastimes. However, she acknowledged that the children took a different view:

> 5.30: Boys are delivered home. They have a drink and some food, then we watch TV. It sounds repetitive and boring that so much TV is watched but until the evenings become lighter they cannot go out on their bikes or into the garden after school. I have tried setting up activities such as a craft table or water play area, but they only stay for about 10–15 minutes at most and then get bored and restless.
> (Mrs Tait, parent diary, January 1988, Reception)

Mr and Mrs Tait thus took the all-round education of the children very seriously, including their social competence and manners.

James, Reception, relationships with siblings at home

James' relationship with his older brother, Laurence, was a rather uneasy one of affection, rivalry and occasional dependency – not at all uncommon for siblings. Mr and Mrs Tait explained the ways in which the boys saw themselves and interrelated:

> Mr Tait: I suppose really, Laurence sees himself as being the first child and being the elder brother and he is quite bossy and dominant in that respect, but at the same time Laurence is now also getting very helpful and therefore is thinking of himself as being a junior adult which is a role that he fills – he does things like the washing machine, he actually sets it going. ... So James in fact in

many ways looks up to him and copies him as much as possible. But then when Laurence gets too bossy James will basically hit him, or generally not put up with it any longer – so the role is very much of being dependent and looking after him. If I am having a tussle with Laurence, James will come rushing up and attack me – don't hurt my brother – that sort of situation. And on the days when Laurence is away and he is on his own here he is lost. Conversely when he has had enough of Laurence during the day here or the weekend, say a wet weekend, he will just disappear and he will go up to the bedroom and play with lego or something of that nature quietly all by himself for as much as an hour or more and not want or need Laurence. But I suppose the fact that he knows Laurence is about is ... .

Mrs Tait: Laurence very much resents it if I give James too much love or cuddles. Laurence sees it as his right to be more loved than James and for a long time he really ... I was sure he adored James. Once when James was ill he was really upset and then I went to school on open evening and read in the book that he said that James is a pain at times. I spoke to him last night. I was explaining something and he said well he gets on my nerves at times, or something like that so maybe there is a split coming. That he doesn't like this dependency on him all the time maybe, I don't know.

(Parent interview, March 1988, Reception)

The latter comments reflect the fact that James seemed to be either engrossed in an activity of his own choosing or, if not, tended to 'follow Laurence like a shadow'. Laurence resented this.

However, the two boys certainly enjoyed each other's company when they chose to play together:

As the sun is shining and the day is warm I take Granny and the boys for a drive. We go out to the Common and stop. Both boys get out and play for three quarters of an hour on the grass. They find a large pool in a hollow and play 'boats' on it with flowers and leaves. A large quantity of mud adheres to both boys.

(Mrs Tait, parent diary, January 1988, Reception)

At the same time, they were clearly beginning to differentiate themselves within the family as they began to establish their individual identities:

We have an early cooked tea together. We eat fish fingers, potato waffles and tinned tomatoes. James eats well and likes to try different foods whereas Laurence is fussy and only eats certain things. Lots of horse-play and rivalry at the table. I try to stop this so as to encourage 'good manners'. James likes to please and be well thought of so conforms to my requests quite easily. Laurence is tougher and more resistant to requests.

(Mrs Tait, parent diary, January 1988, Reception)

Of course, Laurence's age enabled him to assert himself in some respects, not least verbally, despite Mr Tait's preference for reserve. This may well have been a continuation of the pattern which had been established during the years in which Laurence had been an only child but, in any event, it tended to squeeze James out until, if given an entrée, his own account would spill out almost uncontrollably:

On the whole James is a quiet child who doesn't talk about himself very much. He seems to be watching and observing all the time. My husband likes silence and James finds this easier to comply with than Laurence. If asked to recount his school day he runs on in incoherent tirades for ages and can't be stopped, so I wonder if we should encourage him to speak more. He obviously has a lot to say. Normally all verbalising is done by Laurence who would talk 14 hours a day non-stop unless checked occasionally. The rest of us don't get much of a look in. We switch off into our own thoughts so probably James does this too.

(Mrs Tait, parent diary, June 1988, Reception)

James, Reception, relationships among friends and in the playground

James enjoyed a fairly conventional set of 'boys' games and activities.

> James enjoys playing cricket, football, chasing games and riding on his bike. He will also play
> with cars, boats and lego for long periods quietly by himself or with others. His ball skills are
> good. As good as, or better than, his eight-year-old brother. He loves water play and will stay
> engrossed for three times as long as his brother at the same age.
> (Mrs Tait, parent diary, June 1988, Reception)

However, until the end of his Reception year he had not really developed close friendships
either at home or at school.

At home Mrs Tait described their 'fairly strict neighbourhood' in which 'nobody let their
children out'. This changed in the summer when children of Laurence's age began to play
together and, although James would join in, he was not always secure:

> Local children to play with have also emerged at last, after living in this area for 8 years. Two
> families in our road with compatibly aged children have started to call for James and Laurence
> to go out and play.
>   From this small nucleus has grown a large group of children who now play together both in
> the street and our back gardens. James mixes well but is under-dog in large groups containing
> older children. He cannot cope at times in the large street group and crying and tantrums occur.
> He runs indoors to his parents for a hug and cuddle and then wishes to rejoin the group. I have
> noticed from observation at the window that he is put upon by others, not least his brother, but
> he usually is placid and takes it in good part.
> (Mrs Tait, parent diary, June 1988, Reception)

At school, James again found it difficult to establish close relationships, perhaps because
there too he was still learning acceptable ways of relating within a group of peers. At times
he presented himself as 'being very good' at school and, as Mrs Tait put it,

> being the policeman and telling those naughty boys they mustn't do that sort of thing. The
> bossy type.
> (Mrs Tait, parent interview, March 1988, Reception)

This alternated with a tendency to latch on to children or visitors and to want to kiss them
– or indeed, animals:

> It is really odd. We have some cats now who have moved in with some neighbours. So James
> starts kissing the cats, and the other boys are saying 'Oh James, for goodness sake, you silly
> child'. So I hope he is learning that you only kiss Mummies and Daddies. Little boys don't like
> to be kissed by others.
> (Mrs Tait, parent interview, July 1988, Reception)

The kissing continued late into the year, when James had begun to establish friendships:

> He loves other children generally and tends to kiss them a lot to show his affection which they
> often object to. This is because I have always kissed him a lot and he thinks it is how you relate
> to others!
> (Mrs Tait, parent diary, June 1988, Reception)

However, James was physically large for his age and his capacity to fight had been
developed over many years of sparring with his much older brother. Mrs Tait was aware of
this:

> I went to his sports day and I particularly watched to see how he interacted with the other chil-
> dren. He seems to be somewhat tougher. When the two boys are at home they are always
> fighting, pushing and squabbling and I don't take a lot of notice but I noticed him go behind a

friend or two and just give them a little poke to say – I am here look at me – and they would look round and say ugh-ugh or something and I didn't think that was very funny. I was wondering if he comes across in the classroom as slightly aggressive.
(Mrs Tait, parent interview, July 1988, Reception)

In fact, James' 'toughness' had been apparent much earlier in the year with regard to his behaviour in the playground:

Mrs Tait:	He came home early on and he said, 'I stand against the wall Mummy and stick my leg out and everyone who comes towards me, they leap up in the air and fly up really great'. I said, 'You mustn't do that James, you will cause a very bad accident', but it doesn't put him off. He will come back and say 'I really whopped so and so' and I say, 'Well, did he hit you back?' and it is, 'Oh yes'. He is not a bit put off by conflicts.
Mr Tait:	Yes, it is a very much a rough and tumble situation, there is no sort of thought there of playing cowboys and indians or whatever they do nowadays. But it is very much about, isn't it?
Mrs Tait:	... I would have looked at the bushes or looked at the birds or the grass – that doesn't seem to occur to him at all. It is all people and what he is doing to them sort of thing.
Mr Tait:	Son of his father, I suspect.
Mrs Tait:	Yes, my husband's family have got commandoes, boxers and all that sort of thing, I don't know if that is coming out in James.

(Parent interview, March 1988, Reception)

Mr and Mrs Tait would certainly not have endorsed aggressive playground behaviour from James. However, it is important to note Mr Tait's reference to the violent nature of society which 'is very much about'. Both Mr and Mrs Tait felt that it was necessary for their children to stand up for themselves and 'not allow themselves to be pushed around' (Mr and Mrs Tait, parent interview, July 1988, Reception).

We can see in the above that James had incorporated in to his behaviour some of the qualities of each of his parents. He exhibited some of the strength and unemotionality that he perceived in his father and his father's family together with some of the gentle demonstrativeness which was a feature of his relationship with his mother. These contrasting strategies were clearly highly adaptive to managing home relationships and could be combined successfully in that context. However, James' relative slowness to adapt his behaviour to meet the expectations of his peers meant that, for much of the year, he was rather isolated or peripheral to the main friendship groups of boys and girls. Certainly he would join in games and playground activities but he was rarely at their centre.

Mrs Tait was aware of this and sought to help in a variety of ways. For instance, the children attended 'Cru Club' at the local church and she reported:

At the club I hope James will find friends, possibly one to bring home. They will also learn about the Bible and good Christian values.
(Mrs Tait, parent diary, January 1988, Reception)

In interview, she elaborated her point about friendships:

I felt also they would meet children there. I hoped they would make a good friend that I could have home to tea. I keep hoping there is this ideal child who could come to the house and be fairly quiet, so that I can have that. So I am hoping they will bring somebody home.
(Mrs Tait, parent interview, March 1988, Reception)

As indicated above, Mrs Tait's health also restricted the number of times other children could 'come to tea' – an important indicator of friendship for children of this age and community. As Mr Tait put it:

> It is a difficult situation really. Most of his playing at home is with his peers or with friends of
> ours who are not connected with the school at all.
> (Mr Tait, parent Interview, March 1988, Reception)

However, by the end of the year James was beginning to make more genuine friends in
school:

> Lately James has gained several friends from school. This has taken a long time ... . At last we
> have requests from mothers for my child to go to their homes. James gets on so much better
> with a child who is keen to be with him than one which I have artificially introduced in order
> for him to have a 'friend' to play with. There is harmony and rapport between him and friends
> that have developed over time in class.
> (Mrs Tait, parent diary, June 1988, Reception)

James' friendships were indeed very special to him as they emerged. In the case of his
particular rapport with Dustin, which Mrs Tait noted in her diary, it may have seemed that
the relationship was reciprocated. However, James continued to interact in ways which
were a little surprising to his mother:

> With very close friends such as Dustin in his class, he tends to cuddle up. This I find odd, to
> see two little boys with their arms around each other. Maybe it is natural and I haven't noticed
> it elsewhere. They also gaze at each other! I wonder how long this friendship will last. It seems
> as if it might be an enduring one.
> (Mrs Tait, parent diary, June 1988, Reception)

James, Reception, relationships with Mrs Powell in the classroom

James had attended his nursery school since the age of three and Mrs Tait knew that he
had adapted well. She was thus confident that he could successfully make the transfer to
primary school as, indeed, he did:

> We felt he was used to school so we didn't make a big thing about it being full time coming up.
> I didn't want to get him worried about it. So I just took him in on the first morning and said, 'I
> will see you in the middle of the afternoon'. Once he saw a large group of children and a large
> classroom he didn't wish to stay and he clung like mad, but we were quite firm and left him. I
> think it must have taken about a week before he seemed happy and then he loved Mrs Powell,
> he loved everybody and everything. It took about a week.
> (Mrs Tait, parent interview, March 1988, Reception)

James' relationship with Mrs Powell, his teacher, was a positive one right from the start,
despite an element of misunderstanding and lack of knowledge of the circumstances of his
mother. Indeed, Mrs Powell believed Mrs Tait to be 'reclusive' rather than suffering from
any form of medical condition. She found James to be a little insecure at first, but she
warmed to the way in which he talked to her and she noted his step-by-step growth in
confidence:

> James is a super little chap really. His mum, I've heard on the grapevine, is a recluse. She
> pretends she's ill, she's in her bedroom all the time and doesn't get up and doesn't go
> anywhere and you wouldn't think so to talk to him because he's great. I think he's a little bit
> unsure of himself but he would come and ask you or talk to you if he felt unsure. He seems
> quite happy. He stayed to school dinners today. He's going to stay all day. ... He was going
> home in the afternoon and staying there, and I wondered how it was going to be because I
> wondered whether perhaps she liked to have them at home with her if she was like that.
> (Mrs Powell, teacher interview, November 1987, Reception)

James settled into the classroom routines very well. He was attentive and made satisfactory progress. Mrs Powell found him compliant and 'no trouble'. Indeed, this certainly appeared to be James' intention. He responded positively to her calm and sympathetic style and recognized both the extent of choice which he had in the classroom and the ways in which Mrs Powell supported the children in learning tasks. A discussion, when looking at some photographs of classroom events, illustrates these perceptions:

AP:	And what's happening here in this picture?
James:	There's Mrs Powell. She's doing Edmund's writing for him – just doing the writing which he's saying.
AP:	Does she do that for you as well?
James :	Yes, she does it all the time.
AP:	Does she tell you what to do as well?
James:	Well, sometimes she does, but sometimes she doesn't. Because sometimes we can do it ourselves and sometimes we can't do it ourselves.

(James, photo interview, February 1988, Reception)

However, whilst James wanted to please Mrs Powell by 'being good' and by completing his work as she requested it, there were signs that he did not always enjoy it. This seemed to apply to work in maths particularly. This was also approached in the photo interview:

AP:	I think Hazel looks a bit sad, doing her maths sheets, don't you?
James:	Yeah.
AP:	And what do you think she's thinking?
James:	I know what she's thinking about. Because all the others have almost finished. ... I did mine full speed. ...
AP:	Who's this?

(showing a picture of James himself, doing maths, and looking very bored indeed)

James:	Me! I've got my hands in front of my face.
AP:	Do you enjoy doing maths?
James:	I prefer playing with the Mobilo.
AP:	Do you? Why do you like that better, do you think?
James:	Because it's just so good.
AP:	Well, isn't maths so good?
James:	Not unless I do it quicker. Because if I lose all my energy, I can't do it very quick.

(James, photo interview, February 1988, Reception)

For James then, it was necessary to complete maths fast, so that he would not be left alone. It was not, in itself, very exciting and it was vulnerable to his 'loss of energy' if he was not able to complete the tasks on time.

James' approach to maths also provided a particular example of his disposition to check with Mrs Powell his understanding of any new task. Classroom observations showed the regularity with which he would seek confirmation from her, or, if she was not available, would be reluctant to commit himself. This was something which Mr and Mrs Tait also noticed at home:

Mrs Tait:	That is a great thing with him wanting to be right and not to upset anybody – to a point almost of over reaction it seems to me at times.
Mr Tait:	That's right, yes.

(Parent interview, March 1988, Reception)

When James was asked how he felt if some school tasks were 'very hard', he responded by saying, 'Not very easy. I don't like it when it's hard, thank you!' (James, photo interview, February 1988, Reception). Whilst Mrs Powell was, of course, the originator of such 'hard work', she was also the source of support and reassurance. She offered it freely and consistently and James was able to rely on her to bolster his confidence.

The overall impression of James which Mrs Powell formed was of 'a happy, sociable boy who co-operates well with the other children' (Mrs Powell, report to parents, spring 1988, Reception). There was thus a reciprocity in their relationship which was a source of some strength for James.

James, Reception, progress in classroom learning

Mrs Powell, Mr and Mrs Tait and James himself, all felt that he made sound progress in the basic infant school curriculum over the year. The steady provision of relatively routine tasks, which was the pattern provided by Mrs Powell, seemed to suit James' desire for a relatively high degree of clarity in the expectations which were made of him. Although Mrs Tait recognized James' achievements during the year, she also had high expectations of him. However, at the end of the year she judged that his performance was 'very average' for the class as a whole (Parent interview, July 1988, Reception).

James made sound progress with his reading over the year. Mrs Powell was content with this and, somewhat enigmatically reported to parents:

> He has made a start at learning to read.
> (Mrs Powell, report to parents, Spring 1988, Reception)

Mrs Tait, who regularly helped James with his 'word tin' and reading book at home, also commented on his progress during the year and on the particularly significant achievements which occurred at the end of it:

> This seems to have been fairly easy for him. He manages the 'look-say' method well, rather than building up with the sounds of the letters. He has blind spots with a few words such as 'here' and 'saw' and cannot, after a year at Greenside School, master them out of context. Whereas 'sunshine' and 'grandfather' come easily to him! He gets great satisfaction from making strides forward, knowing more and more words etc.
> Yesterday, 28 June, he read a whole 'proper' reading book to me with very little help and was deliriously happy with his achievement. He said he had moved from the 'red' to the 'brown' box and was very pleased. Unfortunately this doesn't mean much to me. I shall ask at open evening what the colours signify.
> (Mrs Tait, parent diary, June 1988, Reception)

With her background as an infant schoolteacher, Mrs Tait understood quite a lot about young children learning to read and recognized the value of warmth and encouragement from parents:

> James enjoys the challenge of reading. If he makes too many errors in a row, when going through his tin of words after school, he gets exasperated and won't continue. He needs to be encouraged by successes. Lavish praise of course, spurs him on to greater efforts. He enjoys the closeness of mother/father when reading and sees it as a time of 'togetherness'. He loves being read to by an adult, preferably whilst being tucked under your arm.
> At bedtime, when alone in his room he plays story tapes to himself for pleasure.
> (Mrs Tait, parent diary, June 1988, Reception)

However, Mrs Tait also noted that James, 'rarely picks up a book and looks through it out of choice. Only if I ask him to do so' (Mrs Tait, parent diary, June 1988, Reception) and later, in interview, linked this lack of enthusiasm to James' preference for watching television.

Mrs Tait: I am surprised that James doesn't volunteer to read some of his little books quietly himself, because he is coming on quite nicely there. He is a real TV addict which I find quite sad because that is very passive isn't it, just watching?

AP: What sort of things does he like to watch?

Mrs Tait: All the cartoons. Laurence and I like to watch films, but James can't sustain an interest in that so he wanders off. But all the cartoons – anything very lively, noisy and colourful and he is there.

(Parent interview, July 1988, Reception)

Mrs Powell felt quite positive about James' progress in writing. In September, he had been limited to 'copying over' her text, with very simple pictures, as is illustrated below:

By the Spring Term, James had graduated to 'copying under' and his pictures had become a little more detailed. Interestingly, in the example below James drew on some of his television viewing as a subject for his 'picture and writing'.

Throughout the year, as she did for all children, Mrs Powell provided a mixture of writing tasks designed to produce greater pencil control and correct letter formation. James conformed with this routine without demure, and made very satisfactory progress (see Documents 8.1 and 8.2).

James is happy to talk about his experiences and has ideas for his writing. His handwriting has improved, he is copying underneath and can make many letters correctly.
(Mrs Powell, report to parents, spring 1988, Reception)

However, it is necessary to record that James was not excited by his writing at school and seemed to find it quite difficult. As often happens in classrooms, the content of his writing was sometimes missed in a concern for its form. For instance, in May 1988 James completed a story which was, for him at the time, exceptionally long. It was 'copied under' from Mrs Powell's handwriting and it read:

We went swimming in a stream and we went swimming in a swimming pool and the second time we went in the river I went without armbands.

Whilst Mrs Powell may well have talked with James about what was undoubtedly a major swimming achievement, her written comment was an injunction to 'try to be neater!'.

Mrs Tait noted that James was not very eager to write, nor indeed, had he ever been:

He never offers to write at home. If I ask him to write in a birthday card for someone, he produces fairly good outlines and it appears to be easy for him to copy my writing on to paper. However, he has no interest in paper, pencils or crayons. As a baby he would not make shapes or scribbles on sugar paper with paints or crayons.
(Mrs Tait, parent diary, June 1988, Reception)

Exploring this a bit more in interview, it became apparent that James' reluctance to write may have been related both to his identification with his father and with his attempt to differentiate himself from his brother:

He is not keen to do anything at home. He doesn't volunteer to get a bit of paper and a pencil in front of him which Laurence likes to do and always has. But Dad is not that way. My husband is not academic or wouldn't write a letter. So I suppose if he is copying my husband as a role model and he doesn't see him doing it he doesn't bother.
(Mrs Tait, parent interview, July 1988, Reception)

We are going for

a walk to the park.

W

W ee

Document 8.1 *James, picture and writing about 'going for a walk', November 1987, Reception*

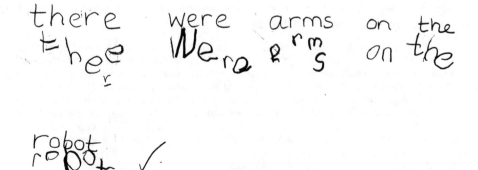

I was watching T.V. and

there were arms on the

robot

Document 8.2 *James, picture and writing about 'watching T.V.', February 1988, Reception*

James worked through the various stages of early number work. According to Mrs Powell's records, he could count up to ten when he started school and the tasks he initially engaged in started him on numeral recognition, one-to-one correspondence and ordinal numbers. James worked from the worksheets which Mrs Powell provided but he did not always understand the tasks. For instance, in the worksheet (Document 8.3) which he completed in the Autumn Term, he managed to 'colour the 3rd teddy' with help, but could not manage to 'colour the 4th car' on his own. Despite their simplicity, it is unlikely that James would have been able to read the task at the time and it seemed that he needed a great deal of support.

James expressed himself clearly on this topic:

> AP: Well, how do you feel about doing your maths?
> James: Not very happy.
> (James, photo interview, February 1988, Reception)

James' solution, as we saw in a previous section, was either to work fast so that he could complete tasks whilst other children were around, or to pause and check his understanding with Mrs Powell herself. Unfortunately, the former strategy could not always be fulfilled because of James' speed of working or because of his relative marginality amongst his peers. The latter strategy was dependent on Mrs Powell being available to explain and support James, which, with the demands of the class as a whole, could not be assumed. Maths thus became something of a trial for James and he would often be seen in the maths corner, sitting alone, chewing his pencil and looking about in a somewhat bewildered way. He stayed, because he wanted to be compliant, but he could not always complete the tasks because he did not understand them.

This is not to say that James did not make steady progress in his maths, for indeed he did. By the end of the year he was doing simple addition sums up to ten, as is illustrated in Document 8.4.

However, James did not enjoy maths and it was a source of tension and stress to him. It was a medium from which he could neither escape, nor demonstrate competence in the way that was so regularly expected of him.

James, identity and learning in the Reception year

In a great many ways, James' parents had a very positive, all-round image of James. This was so both at the beginning and end of the Reception year:

> We sit together on the sofa. James and I go through his tin of words and his reading book. ... James has an excellent memory and repeats the wording of his book back to me. He is not reading it however. We feel pleased with James' mental capacities. He has a good retentive memory and comes out with wise observations at times which astound us. He is very much aware of what goes on round him and doesn't miss a point. His senses are keen too. His hearing is such that he can hear my husband's car door and footstep before anyone else has heard anything. Similarly his sight is very keen and also his sense of smell. His reaction to temperature is extreme also. As a joke we often think of him as being related to 'Superman' and ask him if he will go out and lift up the car for us.
> (Mrs Tait, parent diary, January 1988, Reception)

> A willingness to help others and at times an uncanny knack of knowing how someone feels and expressing his sympathy, marks James out as a very warm and caring child. He is not very assertive and happily takes a back seat to his brother who likes to 'star' in things. He seems

Colour the <u>3rd</u> teddy

Colour the <u>4</u>th car

not understood

Document 8.3 *James, number task on ordinal number, November 1987, Reception*

passive *but* when he has had enough of anything, he goes 'pow' and whatever was annoying him gets floored. He knocks Laurence (twice his size) to the floor at times. He seems 'switched off' quite a lot but he is in fact learning and taking in all he sees. His intuitive and observant

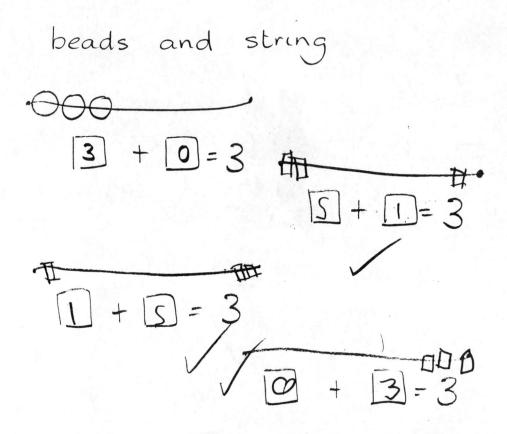

Document 8.4 *James, number task on addition, May 1988, Reception*

comments are sometimes amazing. Not only is he absorbing data, he is thinking it through and coming to conclusions of his own.
(Mrs Tait, parent diary, June 1988, Reception)

These two diary entries convey Mrs Tait's very high expectations of James, even as a four-to-five-year-old. However, whilst these attributes may have been apparent in the home setting, they were not always demonstrable in the more crowded and boisterous context of the school classroom and playground.

As we saw in Sections 8.2 and 8.3, Mr Tait also wanted the children to 'grow up' and away from 'childishness' as soon as possible and this too was a considerable influence on James. He sought opportunities to demonstrate his growth and achievement:

A great feature of James' life is being grown up and achieving success in a step of development such as doing up his own buttons. His comparisons are about age – 'I'm older than he is' and 'I can do that as well, look!'. He wants to be like Daddy. Grown up, going to work, making money etc. His ambition is always to help Daddy in his business whereas his brother wants to be a vet and an artist. James seems to be very down to earth.
(Mrs Tait, parent diary, June 1988, Reception)

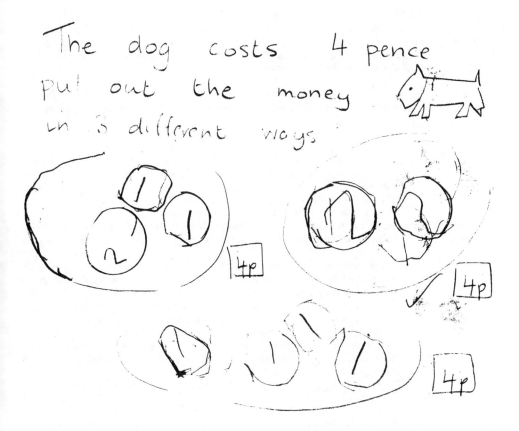

The dog costs 4 pence
put out the money
in 3 different ways

Document 8.5 *James, number task using money, June 1988, Reception*

Mr and Mrs Tait were aware that they were setting their sights high for James, and might be asking rather a lot of him. They noted that he often showed signs of insecurity:

Mr Tait: The trouble is a lot of people and probably ourselves at times as well, take him for being older than he actually is because of his size, but he is very young and insecure at times. He still very much ... when he gets tired, he grabs his teddy bear.

Mrs Tait: Yes, and in goes the thumb.

(Parent interview, March 1988, Reception)

It seems likely that Mr and Mrs Tait were right about the danger of 'taking James for being older than he actually is' and it could be argued that James' major problem in his Reception year was that the expectations on him were beyond his capacity to deliver. Expressed most simply, there appeared to be a tension between the expectations of James from home, and his capacity to achieve them in school. From his perspective, when expectations were satisfied he was deemed 'good' by his adult significant others. When expectations could not be realized, he feared being 'told off' or earning disapproval. Managing this dilemma was tiring and it could be upsetting if the situation went out of control or seemed impossible to resolve:

The thing that upsets James is being told off ... . He seems to try his best to get on with others,

to be 'nice', and well thought of. If he fails he gets upset. Being over-tired is a problem too. His school week exhausts him and if there are late nights too, he becomes unbearably crotchety. Nothing is right and you can't please him. Work such as reading, after school, has to be carefully timed otherwise he can't do any extra work and will react badly with a tantrum.
(Mrs Tait, parent diary, June 1988, Reception)

However, one of James' strategies was to bottle up his own feelings, and simply to present himself in ways which he felt would please the adult with whom he was interacting. Mrs Tait was well aware of this:

Mrs Tait:	He tries to say the right thing, at the right time, to please you.
AP:	Yes. I wonder what he really thinks about things, because he tends to be so good at presenting the image that he feels I want to see. I presume he does that with you?
Mrs Tait:	Yes, he does it all the time.
AP:	But I wonder what he really feels and thinks about it.
Mrs Tait:	Anything to avoid conflict or trouble. If he thinks you want him to say he loves something, then he will love it. How do you get to the truth? I don't know.
	I almost wish he would be a little more open so that one could perhaps help or understand him a bit more. He tends to want to avoid conflict even if you pursue something with him or chase him up about something. He will either physically disappear or just be inscrutable. You can't get through. Now that is me, that is what I do, so maybe he is following me in that.
AP:	Well, it will be very interesting to see how that develops.
Mrs Tait	Yes, it would be nice to see. If one saw him looking a bit down and at times he is sucking his thumb like mad so you know there is a problem, and you can say to him, 'what's up?' and he will say, 'nothing, nothing'. It would be nice to be able to find out how to help him if he has this problem.

(Parent interview, July 1988, Reception)

This account has drawn extensively on parental perspectives because, in James' case, his mother and father seem to have had a particularly important influence. However, it is worth noting that peer culture also began to penetrate during the Reception year as James became exposed at Greenside Primary School to language and ideas which, in 1988/9, were outside the chosen cultural world of his family. Mr Tait explained his perception:

One thing we have noticed now is that, before he went to school he was extremely innocent and he wasn't rude and he wasn't cheeky. That side of things is becoming greater. He is now being told off more at home than he ever was before because he is just getting a little bit rude if you like and I think it is just obviously what he is learning from others.
(Mr Tait, parent interview, March 1988, Reception)

For both parents too, the aspiration remained that James should one day move out of the state-maintained school sector and into a private independent school. This hope underpinned the high expectations which they had of him.

Matrix 8.1 *James' Reception year, a summary matrix*

Family relationships	Peer-group relationships	Teacher relationships	Identity	Learning
Mrs Tait aware of educational value of new experiences and tries to provide them.	James presents himself to adults as 'being good' with others, but is also quite prepared to be assertive and, at times, aggressive with other children.	Seen by teacher as 'a super little chap who is a bit unsure of himself'.	Seen by parents as generally confident but with a fear of being lonely. Seen as warm, caring, but not assertive.	Very sound progress made in reading, writing and maths.
Parents value manners and social etiquette, though boys also taught to stick up for themselves.	Some of James' behaviour, such as kissing people at school and initially limited TV knowledge, seen as strange by other children.	James finds it hard to engage in some school activities and is prone to wasting time.	Seen by many other children as being 'a bit odd'. Unusual with kissing, less aware of TV culture and occasionally aggressive.	However, James not keen on maths, which causes him to become lethargic.
'Good Christian values' taught through home, Cru Club and church.	Relatively few friendships derive from school initially, though later very close to Dustin.	Mrs Powell supportive and calm in setting and evaluating work tasks.	Seen by teacher as a happy, sociable and cooperative boy.	Dislikes reading books independently at home.
Parents uneasy at some television programmes for children and restrict viewing.	Friends at home initially limited, but develop during the year with older children. James is sometimes insecure in such groups.		Very aware of milestones in growing up – doing up buttons, etc.	Seen by mother as being 'very stable, constant and just plodding along'.
Mrs Tait supports reading and maths but James often tired after school.	Enjoys cricket, football, chasing and riding his bike. Likes water play.		Wanted to be like Daddy and be seen to be 'good'.	Progress seen by parents as inadequate for passing independent school entrance exams.
James 'looks up' to elder brother Laurence but there is rivalry too. Laurence is talkative whilst James quieter.			If told off, is unhappy and prone to cry alone.	
James often seeks the support and affection of his mother.				

8.4   JAMES IN HIS YEAR 1

James, Year 1, relationships with parents at home

At the beginning of the year, Mr and Mrs Tait were surprised when James did not settle well into his new class. He seemed to be anxious both about going to school and about his learning and, early in the Autumn Term, he often woke in the late evening. Mrs Tait did what she could to reassure him, and for most of the year, she put a high priority on trying to ensure that he was happier in the classroom and with other children.

> We awake to the sound of James crying somewhere in the house. This is now the usual thing since James started in Miss Scott's class. We find him and comfort him. ... The new class has affected James in that he is most insecure and has constantly to be loved, hugged and reassured. He also cries if he cannot read his book or words or encounters any difficult situation. Formerly he was happy, stable, seemingly carefree and able to take everything in his stride. Parent night is due soon so I shall make enquiries as to what is going on!
> (Mrs Tait, parent diary, October 1988, Year 1)

Mrs Tait continued her slow recovery from ME and was a little more active around the house, though still unable to go out much. She remained concerned about the suitability of many television programmes being broadcast for children:

> We all watch Fawlty Towers on video. I wonder whether it is suitable for James as it can be violent and has some bad language. ... It annoys me that the TV fills so much of James' spare time, but no matter how I try, he gravitates back to it whenever I leave him alone. I try to get him to draw or play with something else, but it lasts at most for 20 minutes and then it's back to the TV. At least a lot of children's programmes are informative such as Blue Peter, Hartbeat etc., I feel positively angry with the endless stream of mindless cartoons that are shown. It reminds me of hypnotism or drugs.
> (Mrs Tait, parent diary, October 1988, Year 1)

James and his older brother, Laurence, also continued to do some homework with their mother. She explained the routine and James' approach to working at home:

> Every Sunday morning we had a session regularly, the two boys, giving them a bit of homework. If it's the thing that's happening, James is quite happy. But if I say, out of the blue, out of routine, 'Sit down and do some writing', then there's a million excuses to go and play in the garden. But once you've got him sat down, he's very conscientious, quite eager and his attention span is quite long. He has this lovely diligence about him and workmanlike attitude, which is really nice to see. And of course if he's done something nice, he's very happy and he shows Daddy, gets quite proud of his achievements, which is nice. I don't know how to overcome this anxiousness with him, but maybe as he gets older he'll get more confidence.
> (Mrs Tait, parent interview, July 1989, Year 1)

James, Year 1, relationships with siblings at home

In the first part of the year, there was not much change in the relationship between Laurence and James. There continued to be, 'much argument and bad feeling between the boys over helping round the house' (Mrs Tait, parent diary, October 1988, Year 1). Mrs Tait was aware that her illness was an additional pressure on the boys but felt that they were not always as responsible as she would have wished:

All they want to do is play or watch TV, which I think is unfair, especially as I am a semi-invalid.
(Mrs Tait, parent diary, October 1988, Year 1)

Later in the year, James began to assert himself more and to challenge the previous dominance of his brother:

There's a lot of conflict .... because the older son wants to be boss – incredibly bossy. Up to now, James has taken every order. James is emerging now with thoughts and wills of his own and just fighting constantly the whole of the weekend, the whole of the evenings. The only way to get peace in the house is to put the television on and sit them down. Or to give them some work to do that they are absorbed in. But if you put them in the garden without much to do, you can guarantee within 10 minutes there's a fight. And it must be because James now just won't be trodden on, he won't be told. ... James is physically aggressive to the elder boy to get his own back when we're not looking. When you leave the room, he'll sort of trip Laurence up or stand on his foot and then Laurence comes dashing up, 'He hit me, he hit me', and you think, 'Of course he did, because you've been goading him for half an hour'. It's very difficult to get peace at the moment.
(Mrs Tait, parent interview, July 1989, Year 1)

James, Year 1, relationships among friends and in the playground

James had some difficulties in establishing friendships both among the children living close to his home and in the playground at school. In the case of the former, it seemed that he was simply rejected by children who were, for the most part, rather older than he was. Mrs Tait recounted a specific incident:

Friends call to ask the boys to play outdoors. After a short while James is crying his eyes out outside a neighbour's house. ... It seems the others rejected him and wouldn't play with him.
(Mrs Tait, parent diary, October 1988, Year 1)

In the case of the playground, Mrs Tait felt that there was a distinct possibility that James was teased or bullied, though this had not been observed by the school staff:

We found him coming home (from school) very badly physically knocked about and bumps on his head and cuts. I thought he was being bullied quite badly and I got quite worried. I have always said, 'Never fight, because you will get into trouble'. Then I got so fed up with it, so I said, 'If they come up and vandalise you give them a thump back'.
(Mrs Tait, parent interview, November 1988, Year 1)

Mrs Tait felt that James really wanted to 'be in' with other boys' play. However, as in his Reception year, this was not entirely easy for James because of the particular identity which he had developed within his family and because of his restricted access to important elements of child culture. For instance, one playground game at the time was 'Thundercats', deriving from the television programme, and, as Mrs Tait observed, 'I have tried to stop him watching Thundercats'.

Mrs Tait was, however, well aware of James' fierce desire to be accepted and did what she could to support him:

He wants desperately to *get in* with one of the lads ... he desperately doesn't want to be different. He's very fussy with his clothing for example. If you want him to wear something that he hasn't had before, we might have a scene because he'll look odd or look different.
(Mrs Tait, parent interview, July 1989, Year 1)

Happily, towards the end of the year, Mr and Mrs Tait were able to facilitate a way forward for James' friendships through the local church:

> I'll tell you what we have done recently which has helped him tremendously – my eldest son started in the choir at St John's and I've been confirmed from there and we are now regularly church goers. We meet two of his class mates there and this has cemented the friendship, so they are now his best friends at school and he's allowed into the cricket game and the football game. He's a lot happier because of this, so that was the entry for him.
> (Mrs Tait, parent interview, July 1989, Year 1)

James, Year 1, relationships with Miss Scott in the classroom

James was one of the youngest children in Miss Scott's class and was rather wary in his relationship with her, particularly at the start of the year. She consciously began by seeking to establish her authority over a group of older 'naughty boys' whom she knew had moved up to her class and she was aware that, at times, 'James watches with amazement'. James did indeed attempt to keep a very low profile and would tend to observe, monitoring Miss Scott, requiring confirmation of expected tasks and avoiding taking initiatives. Miss Scott felt that he was 'nervous, agitated and very affectionate – but in a silly way, like kissing your hand'. She explained her view of how James had settled in and of the visit of Mrs Tait at Parents' Evening where the question of his relationships with other children was raised.

> James is anxious to get everything done right, to please. I can remember hearing last year about this mum who has some sort of problem ... . She was very anxious and overwrought I think at parents' evening, in that she seemed to think he hadn't made friends, or he wasn't making friends, or Gareth was being nasty. ... Anyway, James didn't come up to me, he didn't complain, but there was this nervous, agitated behaviour which I took as being highly strung. ... He works well, always wants to do, to get it right, but he actually, the last few weeks, settled in much better I would have thought.
> (Miss Scott, teacher interview, November 1988, Year 1)

Mrs Tait's perspective of her meeting with Miss Scott suggested that Miss Scott had little understanding of James' needs at the time.

> So parents' night came, I went in and she was totally unaware of what type of child he really was. She kept saying, 'He is very highly strung', and I said, 'No he isn't'. Then she would say, 'He is fairly new to school' and I would say, 'No he isn't, he started at two and three quarters'. Then it was, 'He is very poorly coordinated and clumsy isn't he?' and I said, 'No, he never ever has been'. So she just looked at me and said 'Oh'. I was quite cross, trying to remain very calm, and sort of said well something is happening, he has been got at or vandalised in some way or another and she just hadn't an idea. She made a note by his name saying, 'Very unhappy'.
> (Mrs Tait, parent interview, November 1988, Year 1)

Despite this difficult start to the year, Miss Scott did work to help James feel more confident and, as the class as a whole settled, this gradually had some effect. However, she retained her basic feeling that much of James' unease derived from home:

> James' complex character and anxieties were formed obviously prior to school and no matter how much praise and encouragement and 'come on James' he is given, his nervy disposition remains deep within. Less rarely seen this term, but obviously still there.
> (Miss Scott, teacher record, March 1989, Year 1)

The difference in perspective between James' mother and his teacher was obviously not easy for him and was probably a major contributing factor behind his general unease.

However, James' confidence in Miss Scott did improve during the year as he began to be more comfortable with the routine classroom tasks and to make progress. He was particularly satisfied by his reading. He did well here, finding that decoding came quite easily to him and that stories held much interest. Miss Scott regularly heard him read, thus providing a period of one-to-one attention which was important to him. James' progress at reading pleased Mrs Tait who also visited the classroom on an open day to see the children at work. She was shocked by the class size of thirty-two children and felt very sympathetic towards Miss Scott:

> I went in on open day and I deliberately sat in his class, and I was just horrified because the children on the maths table with me were saying, 'What do I do Miss?', and I was teaching them and helping them and I knew they'd been sitting there for ten minutes and I thought they were day dreaming just because they didn't know what to do, and poor Miss Scott, someone has got to hear reading, and she's got this huge queue for words and I thought well, there's no way, is there, that potential is going to be realised with these children.
> (Mrs Tait, parent interview, July 1989, Year 1)

She also felt that James had now become 'used to Miss Scott' and that it had been 'a matter of him toughening up and meeting people with a different approach' (Mrs Tait, parent interview, July 1989, Year 1).

James, Year 1, progress in classroom learning

As we saw in the previous section, James made much more progress in the second part of his Year 1 than he did in the first. With his brother, he worked at home as well as at school and Mrs Tait certainly thought that he was 'not being stretched enough' at school (Mrs Tait, parent interview, November 1988, Year 1).

However, reports from Miss Scott convey the changes in James' approach during the year:

> *Language development:*
> Quiet and shy, but becoming more confident in his approach. Listens well, hesitant to join class discussion. Reading with growing confidence in his writing, and willing to write on his own.
> (Miss Scott, report to parents, Spring 1989, Year 1)

> *Social:*
> James has grown in confidence and is revealing a happier, more relaxed self. He is more aware of his peers, seeking their attention and friendship and is less reliant on the adult. Growing in self control and widening his horizons, and beginning to assert himself as he grows in maturity and awareness.
> (Miss Scott, report to parents, summer 1989, Year 1)

At successive Parents' Evenings there was something of a rapprochement between Mrs Tait and Miss Scott as they explored their interest in James' progress at basic skills.

Document 8.6 provides an example of a picture and some writing by James which dated from June of 1989, the end of his Year 1.

By the end of the year, now appreciating the challenges which Miss Scott faced, Mrs Tait obtained her support to maintain James' progress over the summer holiday. She too recognized his insecurity but she hoped to increase his attainment so that he could sit an examination for entrance to King Edward's College.

We got some hew rabit and
ml rabit ranaround The garden..
hpitey Ishis ha

Document 8.6 *James, picture and writing about pet rabbits, June 1989, Year 1*

His school work we've been very pleased with. His reading has come on very well; I do some every night. Miss Scott is going to let me have some school books, reading books, through the holiday and some maths books. His maths, I feel, isn't as far ahead in school as it could be, so I'm going to try and push him in the holiday. His writing is just coming. He's very anxious – I got him to write a letter to Granny and he asked me how to spell every word. And I kept saying, 'It doesn't matter, do your best', so he's a bit anxious and knotted up. But his outlines and his ideas are fine, really good. He's worried about spelling.
(Mrs Tait, parent interview, July 1989, Year 1)

James, identity and learning in Year 1

Overall, this was not an easy year for James. In the autumn, and still only aged 5½, he still liked to be 'babied' by his mother.

He likes to come to me and pretend to be a baby, sit on my lap.
(Mrs Tait, parent interview, November 1988, Year 1)

Indeed, James grew up in the calm of the family home in which his affectionate support for his mother was particularly valued because of her needs in relation to ME.

However, the identity which was appreciated at home was not the same as that which could give James credibility with his peers in his neighbourhood or at school, and he initially found himself somewhat isolated and occasionally teased.

At home, James' father provided him with a rather different role model and Mrs Tait saw signs of a new identity emerging:

> He is going to be like my husband I think. My husband is a man who doesn't need anybody – he left home at 18 and never looked back and shows all the signs of having that kind of a mentality. So whilst James is babyish now, I think he will be like my husband so I don't worry about him too much.
> (Mrs Tait, parent interview, November 1988, Year 1)

The more independent approach was, indeed, reflected in the acceptance by Mrs Tait that James would have to 'thump back' if bullied and 'toughen up' as he adapted to Miss Scott's teaching style. Sometimes, however, James would take this quite a long way in his relationship with other children and would almost lose control. Mrs Tait expressed these two elements of James' behaviour particularly clearly:

> He seems to everybody to be totally, totally placid and laid back, but if he does get angry, it's just phenomenal. He absolutely goes out of control, bananas. But it's very rare.
> (Mrs Tait, parent interview, July 1989, Year 1)

It seems that James was far from settled in terms of his own sense of identity. Facing quite different sets of expectations in the settings of home, playground and classroom, he often found it difficult to present himself with confidence.

> Everywhere you go, it's just apparent that he wishes to please and wants to conform, and if he can't get it right, if he gets baffled and can't see the way to do the right thing, he does get dreadfully upset. Any number of cuddles and reassurances don't work because he's got to go and face the situation again on his own.
> (Mrs Tait, parent interview, July 1989, Year 1)

Nevertheless, James did learn about new social situations and he did mature during the year. Miss Scott's final record about him was a positive one:

> James has been much happier recently and is indeed coming out of his shell at last. Noisy, excitable outbursts as he begins to make moves on his own to others and build up his self-confidence. Much more aware of his peers, seeking their attention and friendship, and less reliant on the adult as a result. Still nervy and sensitive, but becoming more in control of himself and his nerves, and though his noisy outbursts of energy show a change in his self control, he is at last widening his horizons and beginning to assert himself.
> (Miss Scott, teacher record, July 1989, Year 1)

Matrix 8.2 overleaf provides an overall summary of James' Year 1.

Matrix 8.2 *James' Year 1, a summary matrix*

Family relationships	Peer-group relationships	Teacher relationship	Identity	Learning
Parental support for James in a nervous start to the school year – reassurance in going to school and for school work needed.	Previous friends are mainly in other class. James is now the youngest child in his class.	James very anxious of Miss Scott at start of year and is initially unhappy at school.	James 'likes to be babied' at insecure start of year, but is 'coming out of his shell' with self-confidence growing by end.	Poor progress at reading and maths at the start of the year.
Mrs Tait's unease with some TV programmes continues.	James continues to find it difficult to be accepted by potential friends in neighbourhood and at school. Not allowed entry to playground football.	Miss Scott sees James as 'nervy' and 'highly strung'. She attributes these characteristics to his mother.	Wishes to please others – children or adults but not always sure how to do this.	Mrs Tait's 1-to-1 home teaching enhances performance but this is not always reproduced in school contexts.
Regular 'home work' sessions with mother, with higher levels of achievement by James than are produced at school.	Has series of scrapes and bumps in playground – suspected bullying or aggression?	Parents report James' disturbance at Miss Scott's classroom shouting and lack of calm. They believe James is 'not stretched' academically.	Normally placid, but can become very angry and lose control.	Developing progress during year after relations with Miss Scott settled and her rapprochement with mother on basic skills. By end of year, good reading progress, some anxiety on writing. Sound progress on maths at school though James not confident. Does more advanced work at home with support of mother.
Frequent conflict with older brother, Laurence, over household chores and in play.	James desires to watch children's TV and wear the 'right' clothes – he is 'desperate not to be different'.	James monitors Miss Scott in class. Often looks worried.	Mr Tait provides an 'independent' role model.	
Initially James accepts Laurence's dominance in play but becomes more assertive – with resort to aggression when feeling slighted.	Access to playground games following parental links at church with parents of other boys.	Very cautious in tackling learning tasks – particularly with maths.	Mrs Tait feels James looks 'tough and robust' but 'has a soft centre'.	
At end of year, Laurence continues to be very verbal and requires parental attention: James quieter and now 'more secure'.		Later, James settles and relationships with Miss Scott become more routinized – though James still cautious.		

8.5   JAMES IN HIS YEAR 2

James, Year 2, relationships with parents at home

Patterns of family life, and James' role in them, continued in his Year 2, as illustrated by the following excepts from Mrs Tait's diary:

> 7.0 am James woken by Daddy with a cup of tea. He pulls back the curtain. James slumbers on. ... I usher James into the bathroom and give him a shower. He does not like the shower pouring on his body so I take it off the hook. Then he enjoys the wash. Daddy is impressed with his clean, smart appearance. I have managed to get him to wear a tie! Down to breakfast. Empties dishwasher with Laurence. The routine is the same as a year ago. They still fight about who does what. Neither boy actually wants to do any chores. ... James whizzes upstairs to play in his room. We hope it is to clean his teeth! I supervise tooth cleaning and hair brushing. He is a very affectionate, loving child and always gives me a big hug when I brush his hair.
>
> 6.30 pm Laurence goes off to cubs. I go upstairs with James to get him ready for bed. With his throat problem I want him to get as much rest as possible. He is a good child and is easy to put to bed if you tell him why it must be so early. I read with him in my bed. He reads me 'Mouse Tales' from the library. He loves to read and is proud of this achievement. His maths too is good for his age. Although at school he is still doing adding up to ten, at home he can do taking away tens and units and simple multiplication, as well as adding tens and units.
> (Mrs Tait, parent diary, October 1989, Year 2)

Mrs Tait continued to gradually recover from the ME from which she suffered and she put some of her new energy into supporting James in his approaching examination for King Edward's College. She worked hard with him, discussing the requirements with him, but also being realistic about his strengths and weaknesses:

> I've just got to get him through the exam, that's all, but I don't think the writing side is sufficient. That's his weak spot. They have to do a lot of intelligence tests and I think James is fine on that because he sees the point in everything, he's quite bright, but the handwriting is going to be insufficient quantity. ... He says, 'If I want to get in Mummy, what do I have to do?' And I've told him about the exams and said look you will have to write about a page, etc, etc, whereas he's making a tremendous effort with the reading and the maths, nothing on the handwriting side. So it might just be a family failing, I don't know, it's just one of those things.
> (Mrs Tait, parent interview, December 1989, Year 2)

Looking back on this time from the summer, Mrs Tait explained what had happened:

> The usual problem with Mummy at home, they don't want to sit and settle to work. They seem to think that's for school. I did manage to push James forward on the maths quite considerably but I felt that even whilst I was doing that, the background wasn't there. It was a kind of rote learning because I was showing him this and he was memorising it, but he didn't totally understand. So I stopped doing that. He failed the King Edward's exam. He came out and said it was absolutely 'pimps', which we thought was a really bad sign.
> (Mrs Tait, parent interview, July 1990, Year 2)

Overall, she felt that James needed to be encouraged to be more independent and wished that 'he would start to move on'. It seems that James had not entirely shaken off his 'baby' image and sometimes, in fact, would still depend on it:

> You see, if we go out and have family gatherings, grannies and aunties will see him struggling with an orange and will dash over, do his orange for him, 'There you are'. He seems to know the ploy is to look a bit helpless and people will dash up.
> (Mrs Tait, parent interview, December 1989, Year 2)

James, Year 2, relationships with siblings at home

The rivalry, affection and conflict between James and his older brother continued at home, despite their mother's attempts to reduce their conflict:

> The relationship between the brothers stays the same. James loves Laurence and follows him around. Laurence doesn't want James around a lot of the time so conflict ensues. Laurence picks on James endlessly verbally which I hate. James wallops Laurence when he can't stand any more and I don't blame him. I asked them why they must continually be in conflict. It upsets me. They say they like fighting. Perhaps it is part of growing up! I would like a harmonious home but I don't think I'm ever going to have one.
> (Mrs Tait, parent diary, June 1990, Year 2)

James, Year 2, relationships among friends and in the playground

James moved to his new Year 2 class with most of the children with whom he had begun to relate in the previous year. However, he had few particularly close friendships at this time and seemed to play, somewhat pragmatically, with a variety of children in the playground. His mother noticed the same pattern:

> I pick James up from school. We drive to Easthampton College to fetch Laurence. James talks non-stop very rapidly all the way there. He has it seems given young Master Jones 15 piggy-backs around the school grounds. This I have doubts about. He received 2p for his trouble. His current friends are Ewan (who came to tea and said I looked like James' grandmother!!) Dustin and Francis. His close friends seem to vary. Not many come home to tea as I value a nice, quiet, peaceful life and hate the noise and chaos that ensues when we have people in to play. James doesn't get asked out much, possibly because I don't have boys here. Stephen is also a good friend and a boy I like very much.
> (Mrs Tait, parent diary, October 1989, Year 2)

In the latter part of the Autumn Term, James did develop a particularly close relationship with Sally (see Chapter 7). This followed a time when he had been off school because of tonsillitis and she enjoyed looking after him. James declared, 'I love Sally and I want to marry her'. However, this was one of several such liaisons in the playground at the time and it did not last far into the Spring Term.

James' friendship with Dustin gradually became stronger and, in a May interview they told me that they were 'best friends'. Talking about the playground they indicated that they were both concerned at being picked on and bullied by older boys and they were no longer playing with girls, 'apart from 'kiss-chase':

Dustin:	I try to avoid Gary, 'cos he knocks me about ... and Mark does.
James:	And Gareth because he's horrid and very rough. Whenever you, say handball when you are playing football, he'll say something like, 'If you do that once more I'll punch you in the face.'
AP:	I see. And do you play with girls at all?
James:	No! Apart from 'kiss-chase', but definitely not with Lena 'cos she always dives on you and kisses you.

(Friendship group interview, May 1990, Year 2)

Of course, as some of the girls found, 'kiss chase' can itself be a form of sexist bullying but it is interesting that James and Dustin were aware that they risked embarrassment from girls who could turn it to their advantage.

James suffered from tonsillitis and was off school for several periods. Around Easter

1990, he had an operation. The illness and periods of absence seemed to break up his attempts to form friends and, by his mothers' account, made him particularly vulnerable to bullying in the Summer Term. Miss George also felt that 'he was somehow not part of the class community' at this point, though overt bullying was not observed in the playground. However, Mrs Tait reported:

> There is one boy in particular and he and two friends gang up on James all the time. If I manage to have a heart to heart with James, he cries. He's in an awful state because these children are so beastly and I said, 'Well, stand by the teacher in the playground', so then they come up and say. 'Who's a baby then?', and they taunt him. One thing he doesn't want to be is a baby, so he goes away from the teacher and braves the place. ... For some reason these three boys just go for James. Whether sometimes just the sight of him incenses them, who knows? You can't tell. But they made his life hell. And he's not secure enough to hit them back or do whatever it is that was necessary, he hasn't stood up for himself. He's just come home all upset and bottled it up. (Mrs Tait, parent interview, July 1990, Year 2)

James begged his mother not to interfere (Mrs Tait, parent diary, June 1990, Year 2) so the problem remained unresolved and was an undoubted source of unhappiness for James.

On a more positive note the house move which the Taits made in the spring of 1990 was a great success for James' social life. The house was on a new estate and social relationships among the children living there were at a formative stage. James was able to join in and form relationships quickly, though some of the old problems remained. Mrs Tait explained these developments:

> Recently we moved house and he adapted to his changed environment well. Indeed we have all blossomed in the new house. In this road there are many children eager and keen to play with my boys and they are overwhelmed with offers of playmates. The house is now often full of little boys. This is wonderful for us and a complete change from the cold indifference of our last road.
> Cricket is the most popular game here and large games develop in our back garden. I notice James often gets upset and put out over small incidents so I expect he is the same at school. He complains people don't like him and won't play etc., but possibly he is over sensitive to others' remarks or behaviour.
> It becomes obvious that James likes his own company and if a local boy stays and plays too long James goes off on his own to his room and ignores his guest. Also, I cannot get him to play with anyone he doesn't care for. He will not have 'stage-managed' friendships.
> (Mrs Tait, parent diary, June 1990, Year 2)

Generally, however, the move was a very positive one and James was happier. However, his difficult experiences with peers at school were certainly one of the factors which contributed to Mr and Mrs Tait's decision to send him in the following year to Easthampton College, with his older brother.

James, Year 2, relationships with Miss George in the classroom

James started off the year feeling greatly relaxed by the new atmosphere of Miss George's classroom and by the relief from the tensions which he had experienced with Miss Scott. Mrs Tait was delighted with this and with Miss George's commitment to James' development:

> He is very happy. He thinks Miss George is wonderful. She doesn't shout. He just can't stand shouting for some reason. She's very kind and he moved into that class very smoothly. Straight away she discovered his reading ability was above the book he had, so immediately he had a

new book. She's very much on the ball and I went to see her on parents' night and said how pleased I was that she'd progressed the reading and she said she'd try and progress the maths in the same way, and I think she has. And he loves her personality and the class of children he's with of course he knows from Mrs Powell's as well, and it was just so easy this year. There were no problems at all. He's been very happy. ... She's a gentler soul, and he's a gentle soul so that goes down very well.

(Mrs Tait, parent interview, December 1989, Year 2)

However, Miss George herself found that James was difficult to understand and that he was very insecure. She reported:

He's prone to fits of tears for no real reason. ... One time, it was because he thought he'd lost his book and it was on the floor all the time. He's very anxious. Sometimes I think it's because he thinks he can't do something, and actually if he sat down or if he came and asked ... he probably could.

He just needs reassurance. He's becoming more agile. He was quite clumsy at one point but I think he's going to gym club and I think that is helping him. As far as *any* academic work is concerned, he really doesn't want to know. His mother spoke to me at parents' evening about him going to King Edward's College and she didn't think he was doing enough of anything. He will fulfil the minimum if watched, but he won't volunteer to do any more, but since parents' evening I have noticed that he's making more effort to do more writing, which is obviously because he's been told to at home and the content is very unimaginative – it's just writing for the sake of writing.

(Miss George, teacher interview, November 1989, Year 2)

Unfortunately, as the year went on, and as the episode illustrated in the next section shows, James continued to have a weak commitment to carrying out his set tasks in the classroom. This was a source of frustration to Miss George who knew of the high expectations being made of him. I talked to James and his friend Dustin:

AP:	Does it matter if you don't do things the way your teacher wants them?
James:	Yes, she gets in a flaming mood sometimes, and she shouts at you. Greg gets into trouble most. I get worried, 'cos if I don't feel too well, I get worried and the secretary says, 'I bet that's because you don't want to do any work.' They don't believe me. If I get upset, I just wait for playtime and then I think, 'Na, na, ... na, na, ... na, na,' and then I zoom off in a Porche.

(James and Dustin, friendship group interview, May 1990, Year 2)

James thus began to think more in terms of how to escape from the school work with which Miss George presented him, than he did in terms of how to engage with it. His mother noticed the same tendency and recorded it in her diary in the summer:

Unfortunately James' attitude towards school has deteriorated. He was very happy in Year 1 with Mrs Powell. He had an unfortunate year with Miss Scott which seems to have blighted his view of life at school. Miss George was a great success last September and we had hopes that he would regain his enthusiasm. He has now developed an aversion to Greenside Primary School and I could not find out why. His teacher seems sound and fair to me but then I have only seen her fleetingly. James says she shouts which is a thing he cannot stand at any price. I explained that shouting is sometimes necessary but he will not have this. He thinks all unpleasant scenes are to do with him and he seems to feel involved in all class disharmony.

(Mrs Tait, parent diary, June 1990, Year 2)

Miss George speculated that James' learning efforts were dissipated by the work he did at home, and that a lack of consistency in approach was causing problems. In any event, the very positive expectations with which James started the year, were not entirely sustained in the rapport between himself and Miss George at the end.

James, Year 2, progress in classroom learning

As we have seen, James did not engage as fully with school tasks as he might have done. Perhaps this was because he was not sufficiently motivated, could not understand or felt confused by differences in the teaching approach and expectations from home and school. A fieldnote of James tackling some writing at school provides an example of his use of strategies:

> I watch James as he does some writing one morning. It is now about 11.0 and, apart from play-time, he has been at work since 9.30. He clearly hasn't been relishing this work – spending quite a bit of time looking about and chewing the end of his pencil.
>
> At 11.05, James declares that his story is finished and I go across to see him. We talk. He explains that, the last time he wrote, Miss George had asked him to copy out some words for which he had used 'magic lines'. He explained, 'I didn't like that, so I did my easy story today'.
>
> I ask him how he decides what to write about. He explains, 'I just do a normal picture and then I think, – well, what can I write about that?'
>
> I probe further: 'How do you decide what to draw?'
>
> James replies, 'I just do whatever – something normal. You see, I do a lot of writing at home. I've got books and books, so I don't do as much at school really'.
>
> James explains how, when he is doing writing at home, he gets words from his mother on bits of scrap paper. As he puts it, 'she helps me'. By implication, though he doesn't say so, James doesn't think much of the 'magic line' procedure.
>
> At 11.15 James goes off to show his writing to Miss George and to negotiate moving on to a new task. However, he has spelt 'want' and 'mummy' incorrectly. Miss George writes them below his story and asks him to practise his spelling by writing out each word underneath her correct version.
>
> James returns to his seat, takes his rubber and corrects the words in his text and then begins to write 'want' and 'mummy' four times.
>
> He gets me to check that he has done this correctly and returns to show Miss George. Miss George looks at James' book and says, 'Well done. Now lets see if you can remember now.' Can you spell 'want'? James writes 'want' on a piece of paper, then attempts 'Mummy'. He begins 'Mam ...' and pauses as Miss George indicates some doubts. James corrects himself. 'Well done. Good, now you can put it away,' says Miss George. James is noticeably relieved and returns his writing book to his drawer.
>
> James gets out his 'planning sheet' on which he had planned to do maths next. However, he looks at me and says, 'You don't *have* to do it, you can rub it out'. He rubs out the reference to maths and inserts 'reading'. He explains, 'You don't have to do maths every day'. Then, with a light air, James disappears into the Reading Corner and takes up a comfortable position with a book. He is quickly immersed and remains until dinner time.
>
> (Fieldnotes, October 1989, Year 2)

Here we see a minimalist approach to a routine school task and an acknowledgement by James that he felt he had plenty of writing practice at home. The different procedure for obtaining spellings is noted, with the 'magic line' procedure (in which pupils maintain the expressive flow of their writing by simply indicating a word they are unsure about and then return to it) being found more tiresome than being 'given' words directly. This was not at all uncommon, for whilst being given a word involves no risk, the magic line procedure invites the child to make an attempt at the spelling, with a much higher chance of failure. Having passed through Miss George's evaluation of his story writing, James altered his planning sheet to avoid doing maths and to take him into the shelter and enjoyment of a good story book.

I once asked James if he liked learning new things. He replied with admirable frankness:

I don't mind usually, or I'd try to feel ill or get the worst cut ever in the playground so I could go home.
(James, friendship group interview, May 1990, Year 2)

Miss George noted the level of work which James produced at school in the early part of the year, but she was not sure what to do about it.

He's got the ability to write imaginatively but ... everything's repeated, 'I saw a tree', and, 'the tree was big', and, 'that's the tree' ... and tomorrow's story will be virtually the same with a few words rearranged.
  With his maths, again, he is reluctant. No problems when he does do it, but of course his mother has pointed out that he's doing long multiplication, or something, at home, so he shouldn't have problems. Again, perhaps he's bored. He can obviously do more challenging things.
(Miss George, teacher interview, November 1989, Year 2)

As an example of James' differing experiences of maths at home and school, we can contrast two examples of number work carried out by him. Document 8.7 shows work done at home in December 1989, in which Mrs Tait had written a variety of forms of sums for James to complete (see Document 8.7).

In contrast, Document 8.8 shows work from James' school maths book carried out some eight weeks later. The form of the work is less traditional and the level of challenge is much reduced but James was expected to set out and complete the task himself, using work cards.

Later in the year, Miss George was clear that 'James' reading has taken off', particularly since he was given the right to choose his reading books from the library. However, as she wrote in her report:

He's still rather a reluctant story writer, but continues to make progress with his handwriting and spelling, the latter as a result of his widening reading practices.
  James doesn't find maths number work difficult, but I have not observed him actively partaking in practical activities and he frequently has to be reminded of his planning obligation.
(Miss George, teacher interview, May 1990, Year 2)

For James though, a major part of the problem remained that he wanted more personal help and reassurance than was available to him at Greenside Primary School. In the Summer Term, when the interview below took place, he was also beginning to worry over what might await him at a new school and was very aware of his lack of close friends within his class:

AP:	How do you feel if you are asked to do some new school work?
James:	I feel a bit worried. I think that I might get it wrong and, if I go to Easthampton College I might have to do 100 lines or something.
AP:	What might you do to try to do the work?
James:	I don't really know. I would just have a think and then, when Miss George tells me the secret of how to do it, I'd dash and get all the things I need.
AP:	Might you get help from other people?
James:	Not from my friends 'cos they are not very helpful. What's worse, when I ask them to tell me, nearly everybody won't help me, even though Miss George says they should help. I don't know why it is. They help lots of other people when they ask, but they don't help me.

(Pupil interview, July 1990, Year 2)

James nevertheless was writing with more fluency by the end of the year, as Document 8.9 shows.

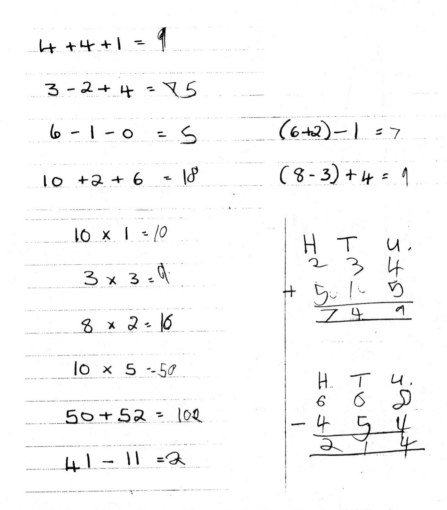

Document 8.7 *James, samples of number tasks completed at home, December 1989, Year 2*

James, identity and learning in Year 2

As we have seen, James felt rather insecure socially during the year. In fact, in the autumn, he had taken to asking other children if they 'liked him'. Mrs Tait told me that:

> He asks this question of all sorts of people and often at what seems inappropriate times. It seems to show a great need in him to be thought 'ok'. I can't see why he should think he isn't liked! (Mrs Tait, parent diary, November 1989, Year 2)

Unfortunately for James, this feeling of wanting acceptance and to 'belong' within his peer group was not satisfied at school during the year and he remained, somewhat isolated, on the margins of peer culture and playground activities and with a vulnerability to being 'picked on'.

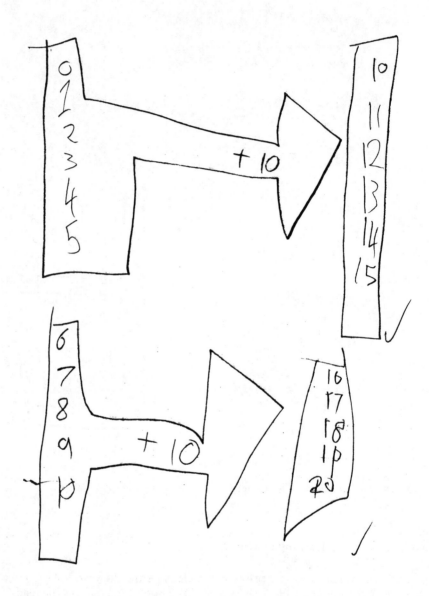

Document 8.8 *James, number task at school, January 1990, Year 2*

James' initial rapport with Miss George also broke down as she attempted to get him to 'knuckle down' to more work in school. She described what she had written in her personal records:

I've put in my own reflections that he's one of those children you have to keep an eagle eye on because he doesn't plan at all well. I think partly because he misses a lot of school and also

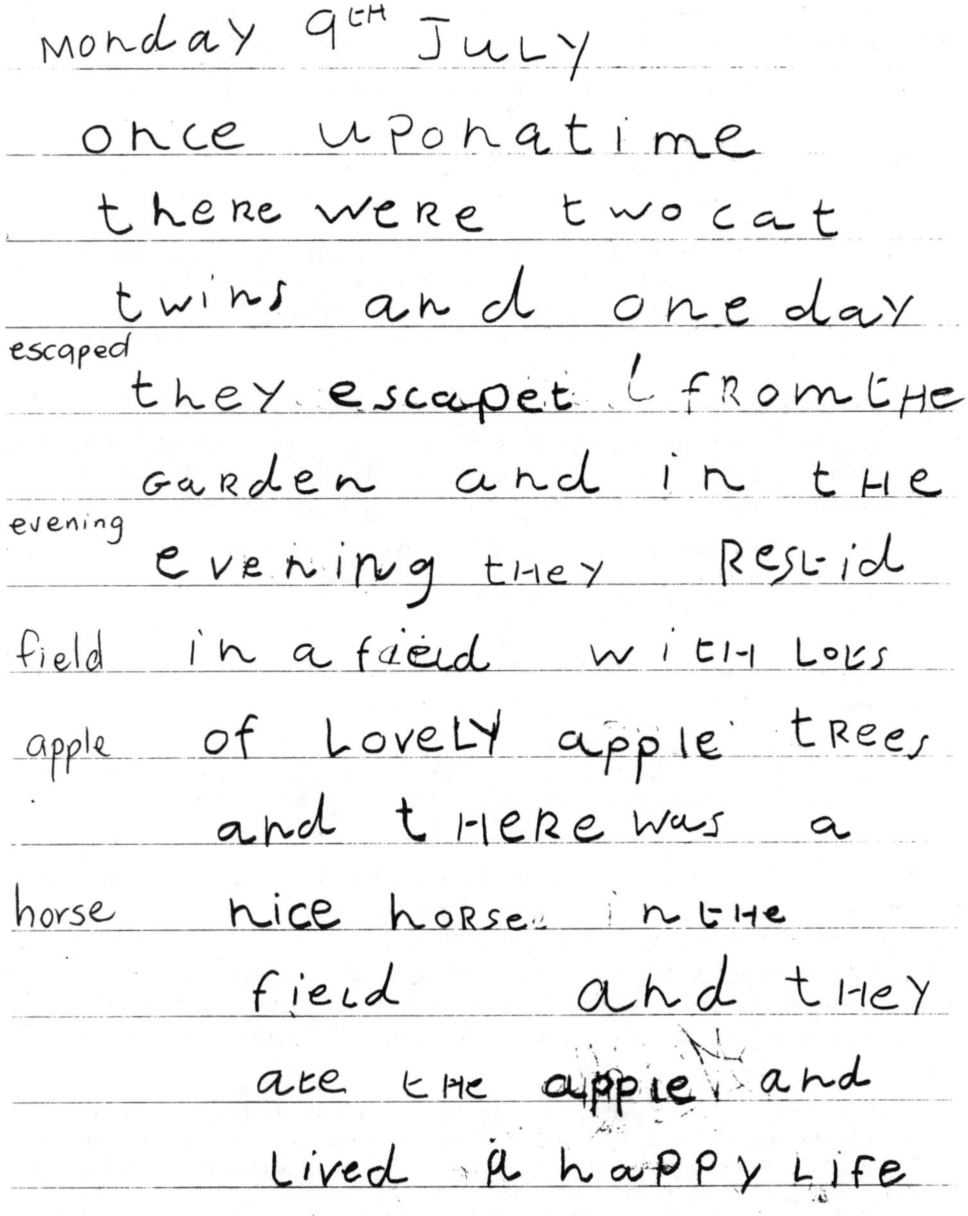

MonDay 9ᵗᴴ JuLY

once uPonatime

there weRe twocat

twins and one day

escaped

they escapet ⌐fRomtHe

GaRden and in tHe

evening

evening tHey Restid

field in a fáeld witH Lots

apple of LoveLY apple tRees

and tHeRe was a

horse nice hoRse in tHe

field and tHey

ate tHe apple and

Lived a haPPy Life

Document 8.9 *James story writing about cats, July 1990, Year 2*

because I think he probably does a lot of school work at home. He's jaded by the time he comes to school. He'd rather play. His mother doesn't approve of the system at Greenside I think – these are my impressions. And I think she puts pressure on him which he isn't emotionally or intellectually capable of taking.

(Miss George, teacher interview, July 1990, Year 2)

In the summer, reflecting back on the infant years as a whole, I talked to James about these influences on his learning and it was clear that, at this point, whilst he was confident of the support of his parents, he was very uncertain of the position of his peers and teacher:

AP: What do you think your friends think about how you have got on in the infants?
James: I don't know.
AP: And your teacher?
James: I don't know.
AP: What about your parents then?
James: They think I've done really well. Like I asked my dad this morning what he'd think if I had a bad report and he said, 'I don't think you'd ever have a bad report.' And my mum thinks I done well, and she's bought me a little green book with times tables and sums and I've done it all in about a month.
(Pupil interview, July 1990, Year 2)

Home and family life certainly provided James with his most important sense of security and personal affirmation at this time. Age seven, and despite having grown taller than many other children, he remained relatively dependent on his mother and still needing a lot of help with basic activities such as dressing and washing. As Mrs Tait put it:

'He does not seem to want to be independent', and 'We still cannot get him to put down his Teddies when he is at home or get him to stop sucking his thumb!'
(Mrs Tait, parent diary, June 1990, Year 2).

By this time, Mr and Mrs Tait had taken the decision to send James to Easthampton College and he had been accepted. Mrs Tait explained:

He will get the smaller classes and the more teacher attention. He seems to need this one to one guidance constantly. So we feel he'll get that at Easthampton and there's a broader curriculum. He also knows quite a few little boys that are going, so he's got support there.
(Mrs Tait, parent interview, July 1990, Year 2)

James himself had mixed feelings about the impending move. On the one hand, he was delighted because he felt it would give him the same status as his older brother and, in particular, he expected be able to visit the 'tuck shop' and 'buy sweets after school'. He also felt that he would be able to keep up academically and would be away from the children who teased him at Greenside. On the other hand, he feared that he would have to develop new friendships and might again be marginalized. I asked him what it would be like:

It will be totally and utterly horrid, because I don't know anybody there. I won't have any friends to play with so I'll just be left out of all the games and I won't be able to do anything. But I think I'll get on well with learning things, especially because most of the children here are all ruffians, especially in the infants. Greg and Gary are ruffians. I think I might be able to manage the learning alright. I don't really know actually. And there's one good thing about it – after school you are allowed to go up to the tuck shop.
(James, pupil interview, July 1990, Year 2)

In fact, as the Postscript (Section 8.7) shows, the move turned out to be a great success for James.

Matrix 8.3 *James' Year 2, a summary matrix*

Family relationships	Peer-group relationships	Teacher relationships	Identity	Learning
James is still supported in washing, dressing, etc. but moves towards requiring more independence.	James is somewhat isolated at start of year but, during the autumn, sustains particular affection for Sally – 'his girlfriend' – and this reflected in playground 'kiss-chase'.	James responded to Miss George's enthusiasm at start of year and is seen by his mother as 'very happy'.	Initially, Mrs Tait is concerned that James may be seen by peers as a 'Mummy's boy' and effeminate.	Excellent reading progress following reassessment of appropriate book levels, mother's support and James' enjoyment of stories.
The family enjoys events together, such as Sunday church and lunch out.	Some closer friendships develop with other boys at school – Dustin and Francis.	However, Miss George finds James prone to tears, anxious and making minimal effort with work.	Mr and Mrs Tait project great confidence in James, actively support him, and perceive him as able and sensitive.	Reluctant to write and stories bland, functional and unimaginative.
James still tends to follow and depend on Laurence. They often argue – Laurence will tease and James will fight. Chores are a continuing source of conflict.	Mrs Tait's need for 'quiet home life' limits visits home by James' friends.	Later, James is concerned at Miss George shouting – even when he is not involved.	Seen by mother as self-confident and growing into 'the young man'.	In maths James performs with mother's help at home at much higher level than he can achieve at school.
Mrs Tait sets her target 'to get James through entrance exam for King Edward's College' – and provides regular tuition in maths and English. Late in year, parents decide to send James to another independent school, Easthampton College.	James is off school during the late Spring Term with tonsillitis.	By the summer, relationships with Miss George weaken as James continues to avoid or minimize his work effort.	Seen by teacher as emotionally and intellectually insecure and as evasive in class.	In class, he expects to need help and believes in learning 'the secret of how to do it'. Reluctant to engage in practical work.
	Some teasing and bullying during the year continues with James as victim.	Miss George adopts 'firm, no nonsense' strategies. James sustains evasion strategies.	Seen by peers as 'a bit odd'.	
	In Summer Term, James' class peers withdraw help with school work.	Miss George wonders about the effect of home tuition on James' attitudes to work at school.	James very concerned about whether peers 'like him'.	
The family move to a new house opens up social opportunities for James.	James' friendships around the new home blossom.		James seems confused and unsure of his identity.	
			James delighted to be leaving the school and 'the ruffians'. Expects rapid progress in learning and anticipates privileges such as the 'tuck shop'.	

8.6   JAMES' LEARNING AND DEVELOPMENT

James' case study can now be summarized in the same ways as those of the other children in this section. First, in Figure 8.3, we can see an overview of James' experience over the first three years of his infant schooling in terms of patterns of relationships.

Here we see the influence of the social context provided by relationships between James' significant others and his interaction with them, resulting, in summary, in his 'anxious and insecure' presentation of self at school.

A second way to reflect on James' case is with regard to the model of learning, identity and social setting presented in Chapter 1 and elaborated in Chapter 4.

With regard to *Who is learning?* we might think of James as a child trying to shape an identity in school, wanting to please and 'fit in' but who was often confused about how to do so. For example, the contrasting strategies of demonstrativeness and toughness which

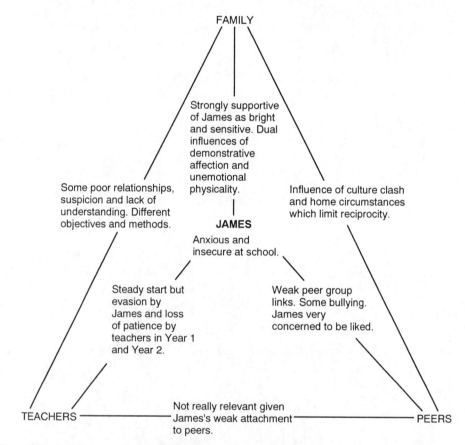

FAMILY

Strongly supportive of James as bright and sensitive. Dual influences of demonstrative affection and unemotional physicality.

Some poor relationships, suspicion and lack of understanding. Different objectives and methods.

Influence of culture clash and home circumstances which limit reciprocity.

JAMES
Anxious and insecure at school.

Steady start but evasion by James and loss of patience by teachers in Year 1 and Year 2.

Weak peer group links. Some bullying. James very concerned to be liked.

TEACHERS ——————————— Not really relevant given James's weak attachment to peers. ——————————— PEERS

Figure 8.3   *James' case-study overview*

were adaptive to James' home life but inappropriate in school, combined with his insecurity within the culture of his peers, meant that adaptation was slow. Acceptance from his peers and their necessary support in the classroom was often not forthcoming.

As learning at home and with the family was particularly significant in James' case study, we might consider questions of *What is to be learned?* and *How supportive is the learning context?* in relation to that context. In this, it is interesting to draw comparisons between James' and Sally's stories with respect to the relationship between parental support and the content of learning. We have seen that James' parents were highly supportive of his learning at home, as were Sally's (see Chapter 7), but the nature of that support, its aims and the processes involved were different in the two cases. For Sally, the emphasis of family support was on her freedom to follow her enthusiasms and to chose, with parental time and commitment following those choices. For James, parental support was more strategic and professional. Although James' parents also derived great pleasure from their children's learning, there was also the emphasis on providing appropriate educational experience, guiding away from the culturally inappropriate and on remedying the perceived shortcomings of Greenside Primary School.

When we consider *What are the learning outcomes?* for James, then we must identify his anxiety when help was not at hand, either from teacher or peers, his minimalistic approach to fulfilling teacher requirements and a range of strategies for the avoidance of class work. Although James, as we have seen, made reasonable progress in his curriculum work, it is likely that his learning stance and low self-esteem caused under-achievement at school, despite his teachers' efforts to increase his commitment. His higher-level achievements at home with the support of his mother, clearly had little effect upon his confidence at a lower level of challenge at school. Add to this his uncertain status in the eyes of his peers and it seems that James' social identity, learning stance and attainment at school were on a downward spiral.

At the core of James' unhappy experiences were home–school relationships and the story is of misunderstandings, poor communications and a clash of expectations between parents and teachers. The mismatch between home and school experience and expectations had consequences for James in terms of generating anxiety in both generally and with specific regard to learning.

In terms of identity, we see a child growing up in a situation of relative tension and difference between the culture of the home, and the cultures of school and of the peer group. The result was James' inability to forge a classroom and playground identity which was acceptable to him or generally acceptable to his peers. Rejection by peers, loss of self-esteem and loss of patience by his teachers followed. As the Postscript below suggests, greater coherence between the home and school was achieved by the move to independent education.

8.7   POSTSCRIPT

It is appropriate to provide a brief postscript on this particular case study. This is based on discussions held with Mrs Tait and her notes on a draft of this case study which date from the autumn of 1994, since, in the case of James, other forms of data-gathering ceased when he left Greenside Primary School in the summer of 1990.

Over the previous four years, there had been three particular developments. First, James had settled very quickly and happily into his new school, Easthampton College. He had been able to re-establish some previous friendships from his time at a private nursery school and this new rapport deepened as James moved, year by year, through the College. As Mrs Tait explained:

> We had no problems with 'friends' at Easthampton College. Their social life took off instantly.
> ... James blossomed and went on from strength to strength.
> (Mrs Tait's notes, September and November 1994)

Second, James had flourished at his school work, becoming much more confident and performing at what Mrs Tait felt was a high standard. She explained that 'the more formal situation and greater emphasis on the Three R's had suited him'. James was also active and successful in sports such as rugby and cricket.

Finally, Mrs Tait had gradually recovered from her illness, regained her strength and had then been able both to fully satisfy her commitment to her family and to take up her previous, pre-teaching career as a secretary/personal assistant which she combined with private tuition work. She had also became particularly active in the Easthampton Group of the Myalgic Encephalomyelitis Association, building up its membership, advising ME sufferers and lobbying for greater recognition of the disease.

Chapter 9

Learning, Identity and Social Relationships: Case-study Comparisons

9.1   INTRODUCTION

In this chapter I aim to compare across the case studies and thus elaborate the theoretical model which was first introduced as 'questions' in Chapter 1 and then developed as 'an initial analysis' in Chapter 4. This strategy is possible because we have now met *five* of the children whose learning and development have been studied. Comparisons between them will, in particular, be used to identify factors of similarity or variance which seem to have been particularly significant.

I would argue that the stories of the children are likely to resonate with the experiences of others because they provide examples of fundamental processes in human experience, through which individuals develop and act in society. However, at the same time, the families, school and community around which these case studies have been constructed are particular and are not representative of the diverse, differentiated patterns of experience, learning and becoming which certainly exist in all societies. We, therefore, need to be very cautious regarding generalizations about the specific forms through which social processes in learning might be manifested.

The structure of the chapter reflects its task in elaborating the theoretical model which has evolved through the book. It thus revisits each of the basic questions and reconsiders the model presented as Figure 4.3 (p. 98) in the light of comparative data from the case studies. Cross-referencing between the chapters may be helpful.

9.2   WHAT WAS THE INFLUENCE OF THE MACRO-SOCIAL CONTEXT?

Of course, the experiences of the families and children reported in this study derive from what, at one level, was a shared experience of time and place within the wider socio-historical context, as was described in Chapter 2. One could simply say that they all lived in a relatively affluent suburb of a southern English city during the late 1980s and early 1990s.

However, their relationships to that wider social context varied. For instance, in terms of economic security we can consider the income-generating jobs held by the parents. Neither James' or Mary's mothers worked outside the home but their fathers were self-employed and seeking to develop their businesses in the 'heady days' of late-Thatcherism. They directly faced the stress which follows from accepting business risks but they also exercised considerable control over their working context. Daniel's mother worked at home to support her family of five but the pressures of the time were just as intense for his father, with his role in marketing. He faced repeated productivity targets as the company he worked for sought to maintain its competitive advantage. Hazel's mother was at home and then in teacher training but her father worked for a nationalized company which was privatized, 'refocused' and 'downsized' over the period of the research thus causing a degree of uncertainty with which the family had to live. Sally's mother and father both worked for Greenside Primary School, were employed by the local council and, unlike the other house-owning families, lived in a house which was 'tied' to the caretaking role which Mr Gordon fulfilled. They faced the insecurities of those in the public services at the time with round after round of reorganization, budget cuts and uncertainty as 'contracting out' and the impact of local management of schools took hold. There were differences, in other words, in the security and permanence of the families within the community context which directly related to external developments in the wider macro context. The directions of economic growth and of public policy were not inconsiderable factors in shaping these lives.

We could also consider the stance which each family took in respect of values, culture and education. James' family could probably be deemed to represent relatively 'traditional' forms of both the English middle-class conventions which dominated and in respect of their attitudes to education. At the other end of the spectrum, Hazel's parents manifested middle-class values in much more liberal, imaginative and divergent ways and also had more flexible child-centred educational views. Ranged between them we might place Daniel's, Sally's and Mary's families. Sally's case is, of course, particularly interesting because of the more working-class roots and circumstances of her parents. Sally's parents recognized the type of service role which they occupied in Greenside but also felt that significant opportunities were available for their children. Relationships with the more middle-class families evolved through involvement with playgroup, school and sporting activities, the friendships of their children and their own self-assurance. These links, combined with Sally's own exceptional self-confidence and popularity at school, reduced the extent to which social-class background might have affected Sally's integration at Greenside Primary School. Indeed, as we have seen, her parents' work for the school made it possible for them to support her in ways which were not open to the parents of other children.

9.3 HOW WERE THE CHILD IDENTITIES FORMED?

The factors influencing the sense of identity of each child must, of course, first be sought in the home and in the years from birth. In the early parts of each case study there is reference or allusion to this stage of life with parents commenting on what may seem to be intrinsic characteristics of their children. However, as we saw in the parallel discussion in Chapter 4, section 4.3, no way has yet been found to identify the relative contributions of natural endowment and social nurturing in individual development and, although we will maintain awareness of innate characteristics, the main focus in this book is on social factors. We begin with the most important of these – each child's relationships in the family, among peers and with their teacher.

Relationships

Four of the five case-study children were the youngest and last child in their families, with Hazel breaking the pattern as an oldest child. Daniel (fifth child) was positioned very overtly as 'the baby of the family' and Mary, Sally and James (third, second and second children respectively) each also had to struggle to assert their identity in their respective family context. In every case, there was rivalry among the siblings as the younger children strove to achieve status and recognition and, in each case, the younger child both tried to identify with their older siblings and to differentiate themselves from them. Thus Sally would look up to and defend her brother Sam and support him in his football, but she would also 'get him into trouble' and was determined to challenge him at music and through dance and gymnastics. The younger children thus grew up and evolved their identities in the wake of the biographies of their older siblings. The children's development should thus be seen as being symbiotic rather than just sequential, for each provides a vital element of the social context for the other. In the case of Hazel, we find a situation in which she was very aware of her younger sister, Katie, developing beside her. Some of Hazel's actions, and some of her relief when she had a breakthrough such as with her reading, were very clearly developed with half an eye on her sister's progress.

Of course, the focus around which these sibling rivalries were played out concerns the attention and affection of parents and, in particular, of the mothers. In this regard there are also some significant points of comparison concerning gender and the availability and consistency of role models.

Three of the case studies are of girls, Mary, Sally and Hazel, and in each of their stories there is clear evidence of the ways in which they identified with their mothers at this age. For Mary and Sally this was very explicit with experiments with dressing up, make-up and role play, sharing of some domestic chores and discussion of how they might fulfil future female roles. These role expectations seem to have been very important in the girl's adoption of 'being good' as a strategy through school. Hazel's case was less stereo-typical in some ways, though the dragons, dinosaurs and cows of her imaginative worlds were usually set in nuclear families not unlike her own. Perhaps her creativity and divergence was itself partly a product of identification with her mother, for there were similar attributes in her biography. Hazel and Sally may have seen more of their fathers than Mary did, and certainly they were also both influential; Hazel's through encouraging her expression through drawing and interest in animals and Sally's through his presence in the school and strong encouragement and pleasure at her achievements.

For the two boys for whom case studies are presented here, Daniel and James, gender identification seems to have been more difficult at this age and both saw relatively little of their fathers except at weekends. Prior to going to school, as demonstrated in Chapter 6, Daniel's best friend at playgroup had been a girl called Harriet and he also enjoyed playing with his sister, Susan and her friends. Both Daniel and his mother enjoyed the warmth of their special relationship when it could be expressed in their busy family, but 'being the baby' was also used by Daniel's older brothers as a form of ridicule. As we saw, when Daniel's mother and peer-group pressure dissuaded him from being friends with Harriet, it was some time before he developed new friendships. When he did, particularly with Andrew, he remained rather dependent. James was also arguably somewhat confused during Key Stage 1, with rather different role models being provided by his mother and father. He was both expected to be affectionate, caring and conformist but also to be 'tough'. Outside the home, James sometimes found it hard to judge appropriate behaviour. At its most obvious, this was manifested through his phase of kissing children, teachers or visitors in the classroom and yet his willingness to fight other children very hard. The available evidence does not enable us to judge the extent to which this aggression resulted from him being teased by other children, or led to it.

In each of the cases which are discussed above we can see the transfer, from home to school, of very important aspects of each child's identity. Relationships with parents were formative and they continued to be developed symbiotically with siblings. When each child entered school the picture was complicated further by their relationships with a wider range of peers and with teachers.

Regarding peer relations at school, the most obvious initial factor is gender with the cultures and distinctive activities of boys and girls being immediately apparent in playground and classroom contexts throughout the study. The pressure to conform which was placed on Daniel in the Reception year until he gave up his friendship with Harriet (pp. 154–6) is a particular example of this but at a much more general level we have repeated evidence of the interactive process through which distinctive gender cultures developed and contributed to individual identities. The girls developed particular patterns of play activities – imaginative play involving family roles, play with small apparatus such as skipping, rhymes and small dance routines whilst the boys tended to run around more, dominating the playground space with more boisterous chasing games. When the boys chased the girls, were rough or intrusive in their play, or too insistent in 'kiss chase', the girls would respond by asserting their solidarity together – 'no boys, no boys' (pp. 43–4). Gender identities were thus asserted through exclusion as well as by inclusion.

Of course, there were also individual differences in the positioning of the children in terms of peer culture. Of the case-study children, Sally was particularly influential among other girls, linking up with older girls and promoting gendered activities through her relationship with friends such as Mary. The two girls embodied the strategy of 'being good' in school. Hazel, on the other hand, set herself apart from such conformity and developed her own self-determined strategies (on which, in due course, her later friendship with Harriet was to be founded, see Pollard and Filer, in press). Of the boys, neither Daniel nor James were particularly influential in the development of peer culture. Both were rather marginal to the boys' peer groups and, throughout these early years at school, they followed rather than led. However, whilst Daniel was eventually accepted by his peers, perhaps because of his sense of humour, James seems to have been progressively excluded. The five children's experience of peer culture was thus very varied. For Sally and Mary it provided a means of reinforcement of the identity developed at home whilst, for James, the playground was an uncertain, and at times threatening, context.

Of course, the children's interaction varied in respect of the successive teachers whom they encountered but broader tendencies can also be identified. Sally, for instance, was always prepared to negotiate with her teachers to redefine expectations and rules. She was sufficiently self-confident and socially aware to do this, even with Miss Scott. Mary, particularly in Reception and Year 1, was more conformist. She also wanted to 'be good' but sought to achieve this by watching and following rather than by taking initiatives. Daniel and James also tended to adopt low-risk strategies, with both children sometimes worrying about their teacher's responses to their work. Whilst Daniel derived support from his friendship with Andrew, James was more alone. Hazel, of course, was more inclined to withdraw from her teachers and, as in the playground, to prefer her own non-conformist activities. With Miss Scott a pattern of deviant, evasive strategies began, but she largely pulled back from these during her year with Miss George.

Reflecting back to the analysis of friendship groups which was made in *The Social World of the Primary School* (Pollard, 1985a), children in 'joker groups', 'good groups' and 'gang groups' expressed a range of children's classroom strategies in relations with their teachers. A similarly differentiated pattern is apparent in the children's relationships with teachers in this study and this is an analysis which we develop further in the sequel to this book (Pollard and Filer, in press). For instance, we might say that the *redefining* strategies of Sally are akin to those of the 'joker groups', whilst Mary, Daniel and James, tended to exhibit *conformist* strategies of 'good groups'. 'Gang group' *deviance* was not often evident in this school at Key Stage 1 but, in Hazel, we do have an example of a different type of response to school in *non-conformity*. The challenge for Hazel's parents and teachers was to persuade her to face and succeed at the curriculum of basic skills. The typology of career strategies which we offer in Pollard and Filer (in press) is elaborated from notions of pupil conformity and we use it to distil patterns of identity and career trajectories whilst taking account of the dynamic nature of social relationships over the full seven years of pupil's primary school education.

Having compared the relationships of the five case-study children with their parents, siblings, peers and teachers there should be a sense of the similarities and differences between them and of the ways in which these relationships informed the emergent sense of identity of each child. However, following Figure 4.3, we also need to consider two more factors which contribute to identity – 'potential' and 'resources'.

Potential

That each case-study child had a unique physical, intellectual and expressive potential is both undeniable and important to recognize, but that does not make it any easier to either judge or trace. Indeed, as has been indicated earlier, the work of psychologists and neuro-biologists in studying brain functioning, inherent capacities and the role of external stimulation in their development is still unfolding and attempts to apply their new insights were not made in this study. However, the most important influence on identity is the element of potential which has been realized at any particular time and this is something on which comment is certainly possible.

For instance, in terms of physical development during the period of study which is reported in this book, Sally seemed to be the most physically agile and expressive child, closely followed by Mary. The physical development of Hazel, Daniel and James was developed and expressed more informally though running (on all fours in Hazel's case), chasing and, for James, in occasional exhibitions of 'toughness' or fighting. These differences were reflected in the comments of parents and teachers and, in turn, in the ways in which the children saw themselves, acted and were seen by others. The dance and gymnastics of Sally and Mary were particularly important to them but other physical landmarks, such as the loss of 'baby-teeth' or learning how to swim, enhanced the self-image of each of the children as they were achieved.

Regarding intellectual and expressive development there were also clear and important differences in the children's development. For instance, Mary's emerging self-confidence with maths was based on the application of a more methodical logic which she seemed to develop as a five- and six-year-old, whilst Hazel's exceptional skills at drawing provided a vital element of individuality, self-esteem and status. Sally's success across the curriculum suggested that her intellectual potential was being drawn on more broadly, whilst for Daniel and James their relative lack of self-confidence in school may well have meant that part of their potential was unfulfilled over this period.

Resources

In terms of material resources, it is estimated, from occupational and housing indicators, that a rank order from the less to more wealthy families might have risen from Sally's to Hazel's, Daniel's, Mary's and to James' family. This range in material resources was reflected in some of the activities available to the children, such as holidays, in toys (with ownership of a fashionable bicycle being particularly important), and eventually, in the opportunity which the more affluent families had to send their children to private, fee-paying schools. However, having said that, material wealth did not seem to be a major factor in informing the children's sense of identity at Key Stage 1 in this school. Perhaps social differentiation was not sufficiently overt for children of this age to recognize the differences in life-chances which were likely to follow and certainly, the patterns of friendships among the children studied did not reflect this factor during Key Stage 1.

The cultural resources on which the children drew were arguably more important. The culture within each family reflected the values, priorities and practices of the parents, as mediated by other family members. The extent of this mediation varied considerably, with Daniel's family being particularly influenced by the social dynamics of the five siblings – but this influence was much less in the other families, where the children were both fewer and younger. The case-study accounts show how most of the parents relaxed with and enjoyed playing and working with their children, though there is some variation in the nature of these activities with, for instance, Hazel's parents seeming to involve themselves *with* her interests, rather than, say James' mother who often sought to *extend* his education beyond his immediate interests. Both families visited museums, went for walks together and enjoyed reading books, but they did so in quite different ways and with different forms of engagement reflecting, to a large extent, the child-rearing expectations and cultural assumptions of the parents.

The media, in the form of television, comics, toys and other merchandising, were also important influences on the children and sources of both entertainment and cultural resource. Again however, this influence was mediated by the family through, for instance, parental policies on television watching. In the case of James, his parents' reservations about some children's entertainment protected him from the possibility of being frightened, but also limited his access to some knowledge which might have helped him in establishing his credibility with his peers at Greenside Primary School.

One of the most significant areas of cultural resource in this study concerns gender. The case studies provide a lot of evidence, year-by-year, of the ways in which the girls monitored and modelled themselves on their mothers, female friends and female teachers whom they admired. Sally and Mary, in particular, developed ways of relating together, often cooperatively. Their strategies for protecting their interests against boys drew on well-established forms of female solidarity both at home and in school. Similarly, the boys were influenced by male images and by the male peer culture of the school. However, there were no male teachers over the period reported here, James and Daniel saw relatively little of their fathers and were on the margins of the main boys' peer groups. They had fewer first-hand experiences of and direct interaction with male culture, and their confidence within it was thus weaker than the comparable female identification of Sally and Mary.

Two significant aspects of parent's views concern their attitudes to peer culture and to the school's educational approach. The tendencies are represented on Matrix 9.1

Matrix 9.1   *Summary of parental endorsement of peer culture and the school's educational approach*

	Higher endorsement of school's educational approach	Lower endorsement of school's educational approach
Higher endorsement of peer culture	Sally's, Mary's and Hazel's parents	
Lower endorsement of peer culture		James' and Daniel's parents

Whilst all the parents were supportive of their children's social and educational development, Daniel's and James' were less sure about the peer-group relationships which developed and of the pedagogic approach of the school with its emphasis on the 'negotiated curriculum'. The greatest contrast here is between Sally's parents who encouraged her friendships and the work of the school as a means of giving Sally new opportunities and James' parents who eventually felt that school context was constraining his fulfilment of potential both socially and intellectually. James, of course, was not very happy at school and although, from some perspectives, the cultural resources available to him might be deemed to have had more social status than those available to Sally, the important point is that they were not as *appropriate* to the Greenside Primary School situation which James faced each day.

Consideration of a particular use of linguistic resources, to support children's school learning, shows a similar picture. Sally's parents talked with her a great deal, discussing her experiences openly and supporting her new enthusiasms even when they may have been unsure where they would lead or quite how best to support her. James' mother on the other hand, a qualified teacher, had strong views on what should be taught and offered explicit teaching sessions at home which were somewhat different in approach from those used in school. Thus again, whilst the linguistic and cultural resources might, in some senses, have seemed to offer more opportunities for James, the match with his other experiences and with his intrinsic motivation was less good. Mary's and Hazel's parents provided cultural and linguistic resources which were relatively well suited to supporting their children in Greenside Primary School. Though they may not always have had full confidence in teacher's perceptions and judgements, like Sally's parents, they took their cues from them and, when their children were particularly challenged with, say, their early reading, they were able to support them effectively.

Thus, in terms of the formation of *school* identities of these young children, the main conclusion which might be reached from this discussion is that material, cultural and linguistic resources seemed to reinforce and stabilize each child's emergent identity where they were consistent with the expectations which existed within the school and within each class. Where they were less consistent, they could also lead to more insecurity and less self-confidence.

9.4   WHAT DID THE CHILDREN HAVE TO LEARN?

Learning challenges

The case-study stories document a very wide range of *learning experiences* through which the children were challenged. Many of these were associated with maturing and growing older. For instance, from the Reception year we have a range of simple things such as Sally learning to bake and to help with the ironing, Mary to tie her shoelaces, Hazel to get herself ready for school, James to 'lay the table' and help with family chores and Daniel to get himself dressed and even to overcome his reluctance to sprinkle sugar on his breakfast cereal. Facing such new experiences and learning challenges are the day-to-day manifestation of the gradual transition from dependence to independence, from the world of the infant to that of the child, adolescent and adult. They reflect the gradual acquisition of competence and of successive layers of skill and understanding.

However, facing such new experiences and acquiring such competencies simultaneously challenges established images of oneself and patterns of existing relationships. Thus more difficult personal and social adjustments also become necessary. In the case-study stories we can see that each child faced the necessity of such personal and social adjustments as he or she encountered successive new experiences over the three years which were reported. Hazel's overarching challenge was to control her self-determination and absorption so that she could connect more with the concerns of others; Sally's successes meant that she had to learn to come to terms with other children being in the limelight; Daniel struggled to be more self-confident at home and school, such as holding his own in family discussions and going into school on his own; James faced the challenge of managing his identity at home and in school and in becoming accepted by his peers; whilst Mary strove to build up her self-confidence and to identify and pursue her strengths.

We can thus identify considerable similarities in the children's gradual engagement with new experiences through maturation, as mediated by cultural influences, but there was rather greater variation in those learning challenges which were more personal and social.

In terms of the *learning tasks* which made up the school curriculum, the children faced similar challenges as they were introduced to successive stages of the infant school programme of 'basic skills'. Of course, the main focus was on reading, writing and number. These areas of learning took up about two-thirds of the time available for instruction, were emphasized by teachers and parents and were subject to relatively overt evaluation, categoric assessment and reporting. Most of the time the children were concerned to do as well as they could, thus satisfying the expectations of significant others such as parents, teachers and, as awareness and status grew, peers.

For the most part, learning tasks associated with the basic curriculum were relatively routinized and systematizsed across the classes. Thus, in reading the children worked from their 'word tins', through 'reading boxes', towards 'Library' and were supported by the consistent and regular activities of reading to their teacher and reading at home. In writing, the 'picture and writing' task with the 'writing over' and 'writing under' routines of Mrs Powell's class gradually gave way to encouragement of 'magic lines', 'looking up spellings' and 'creative writing' in Miss Scott and Miss George's classrooms. In number, the sorting and matching activities and work sheets provided in Reception were replaced by the sequenced cards of *Peak Maths* which, by Year 2, provided the predominant form of task-setting in maths. In each of these curriculum areas, the pattern of progression was well understood by teachers, parents and many children. The nature of new learning challenges was thus predictable and, though it might be unexciting in itself, could be taken to signify personal achievement and used to denote status.

The major exception to the pattern of curriculum tasks described above concerned James, who faced an extended curriculum, particularly in number, from the coaching which was provided by his mother at home. Otherwise, the families accepted the leadership of the teachers in setting formal curriculum learning tasks.

Learning stance

Three aspects of learning stance have been previously identified; self-confidence, motivation and strategic resources. Matrix 9.2 summarizes the relative stance of the children.

Matrix 9.2 *The children's self-confidence, motivation and strategic resources.*

	Self-confidence	Motivation	Strategic resources
Mary	Gradually evolved more self-confidence as she established herself among her siblings, in respect of friends such as Sally and in 'safeclassroom environments such as Miss George's classroom	Strong, competeitve and determined to succeed despite initial challenge of learning to read. Connected to 'being good' strategy and sense of identity. Some intrinsic motivation also, particularly with dance.	Socially aware, influenced by mother and worked at developing her own strategies in order to achieve social and curricular successes.
Hazel	Highly confident in areas of her own selection – drawing, running on all-fours, imaginative worlds – but initially low in reading andwriting until break-through. Low confidence in maths throughout.	Highly motivated and intrinsic motivation in areas of own interest, but withdrawal from imposed and/or threatening areas of learning. Great enjoyment of drawing, later writing stories.	Sophisticated in expression through drawing, but otherwise strategic resources rather limited because of low social awareness and withdrawal.
Daniel	Low self-confidence at home and at school as she strove to establish his identity among his siblings and to develop secure friendships among his peers.	Wanted to learn and make progress, but arguably as a means of gaining security and acceptance rather than for its own sake.	Relatively limited range of strategies. Reluctance to move beyong passive conformity adn risk avoidance, ans his later lurch to 'silliness' did not support curricular learning.
Sally	Very confident of her own capabilities in all areas, linguistic, athletic, expressive, academic.	Very highly motivated to succeed in school which was connected to pleasing teachers and her concern to 'be good'. Great enjoyment of dance.	Relative competence and social awareness producing a wide range of strategic resources for her age.
James	Low self-confidence in school, primarily because of lack of peer-acceptance an dsome ambiguities in home-school expectations.	No evidence of intrinsic motivation except in respect of reading story books. Otherwise, seemed reluctant in school and motivated only by the need to satisfy the expectations of others.	Cautious approach and limited range of strategies used in school, but regular 1-to-1 teaching at home seemed to broaden approaches.

Perhaps the biggest contrast revealed by Matrix 9.2 is between Hazel and Sally. Hazel's absorption in her personally rich imaginative world was matched by her tendency to simply withdraw from activities which did not interest her. There were many of these at school, with the most consistent examples being provided by maths curriculum tasks. Even her Year 2 breakthrough into writing stories took the relatively immature form of a new, excited immersion. For Hazel then, she was either totally engaged in learning through expression – or determined to avoid learning challenges which did not attract her. In a sense, the situation was really rather clear-cut for her, with her mother and teachers working to build on her positive interests and to encourage her to develop more balanced, intermediate ways of approaching learning. Sally, on the other hand, was the most socially aware of the children and was very alert to adult cues and adult ways of doing things. With her very involved and encouraging parents, her extensive experience of the school even before she officially started and her detailed knowledge of progression within the reading, writing and maths curriculum systems, she was very self-confident and highly motivated. Thus, whilst she may not have been as original as Hazel, her determination to succeed and eagerness to 'help' and learn from adults meant that her repertoire of learning strategies developed relatively widely. She would listen, ask questions, make an attempt, seek advice, discuss, compare, try again and evaluate in her attempts to do her 'best'. However, as we have seen, because her view of her 'best' was so attuned to the views of significant others, her motivation was often more extrinsically geared to completion and success rather than to more intrinsic goals.

In considering Matrix 9.2 as a whole, there seems to be a relationship between the range of learning strategies developed and children's determination to engage with and succeed in the largely adult-controlled flow of learning challenges with which they were presented. Where children lacked the interest (Hazel) or the confidence (Daniel and James) to engage with these new challenges, they tended to deploy a relatively narrow range of tried, tested and defensive strategies. When children were more determined to succeed (Sally and Mary) they worked harder to develop, expand and refine a range of strategies, drawing on available cultural resources as modelled by parents, teachers, peers, siblings or others. Of course, the children's disposition to learn, their stance, did not stay constant, so that, for instance, both Hazel and Daniel's approach developed in their Year 2, and James began to open out in his Year 3 when he had moved to a new school.

9.5   HOW WAS SUPPORT PROVIDED IN LEARNING CONTEXTS?

This is a potentially complex section because it calls for consideration of a range of factors associated with support in learning contexts for each child in each year for each setting. I will reduce this complexity by using a summary, Matrix 9.3. This addresses home and playground settings for each child but it conflates both the three-year period being reported and the two identified factors – 'opportunity to learn' and 'quality of teaching and assistance in learning'.

Matrix 9.3 provides very brief summaries but they perhaps offer sufficient cues on which to base a consideration of the two basic propositions regarding factors which condition support for learners within social contexts.

Matrix 9.3 *The children's opportunities to learn and quality of assistance at home and in playground settings*

	The home setting: opportunity to learn and quality of teaching and assistance in learning	The playground setting: opportunity to learn and quality of teaching and assistance in learning
Mary	Open and supportive family context with positive relationships in which Mary developed her postition as youngest child and only daughter and gradually contested the dominance of her brothers. Many examples of mother scaffolding Mary's understanding through conversation.	Mary was part of an active, popular and successful group of girls – though occasional rivalry with individuals. She contributed to and learned much from her friends, particularly with regard to enjoyable games, activities and parrying the dominance of boys.
Hazel	Hazel's parents were very supportive of her enthusiasm for natural history, drawing and self-expression. Hazel was watchful of the successes of her confident younger sister. Her mother was increasingly active in mediating Hazel's attempts to adjust to school requirements, most successfully with reading.	Hazel was self-sufficient in imaginative play and set frameworks within which others learned how to play with her. At this age, she was relatively unreponsive to learning how to play within other chldren's games and was not pressurized to do so. Accepted as idiosyncratic.
Daniel	Busy and often boisterous family context in which Daniel, as the youngest child of five, struggled to establish himself. He felt very vulnerable to criticism. Daniel's learning was supported by older sisters and brothers as well as by his parents. His reading was supported by his mother whenever possible.	Daniel was accepted among his peers but found it hard to relax without the security of a 'special friend'. In Reception, he learned that 'boys should not to be-best-friends with girls' through being teased. He wanted acceptance but continued to be insecure in his peer group and particularly with older children. Latterly, he became inseparable from Andrew and, through him, learned to feel more comfortable with his peers.
Sally	Very close family with the unique experience over the reported period of all four family members attending or working at Greenside Primary School. Relaxed, positive climate with parental pride in children''s achievements and active engagement from both parents. Sally aware of and emulating, her older brother but modelling herself on her mother.	Sally was the most popular and self-confident child within the year group and she led the way in playground games adn many out-of-school activities. She learned from this active engagement and from the older children with whom she was friendly.
James	Considered provision and selected experiences consciously provided by James's mother with some protection from external child culture. Additional home instruction set goals different or beyond those of Greenside Primary School and with high stakes to fulfil parental expectations and match older brother's achievements.	Learning was largely defensive as James sought to cope with peer relationships and child culture within which he was not fully accepted. He found this hard at Greenside, latterly suffered from teasing and learned to fight back.

The first proposition is that the 'opportunity to learn' is dependent on social understandings and power relationships which affect children's willingness, or otherwise, to take risks in learning and to assert a degree of control. Sally, for instance, felt able to do this at home and in the playground in ways which James could never attempt. Similarly, Daniel's relative vulnerability in both settings could be contrasted with Mary's determination to work through her family and peer relationships to establish herself. In a sense, she recognized and assessed the two power contexts and worked to develop a range of strategies within them. Hazel, relatively self-absorbed and with her interests and imaginative expression supported at home, was less directly touched by the playground context at this stage of her development.

The second proposition is that the 'quality of teaching and assistance in learning' is dependent on affective and intellectual support as each child approaches his or her 'zone of proximal development' (ZPD) for particular forms of understanding, knowledge and skill. The level of generality in the summary makes this hard to specify without returning to the case studies themselves. However, there are examples in respect of the playground setting of both Daniel and James lacking affective support. Daniel later found this through his friendship with Andrew, but Sally and Mary had benefited from their mutual friendship over a much longer period and, despite their ups and downs, had greater confidence and understanding of peer relationships. Perhaps, when it comes to learning about relationships, falling in and out of friendships which have an underlying security actually provides a type of experiential scaffolding across the ZPD? Being marginalized and teased, as James eventually felt, is likely to be a less positive learning experience unless some form of emotional support and help in analysing what has happened is available.

Turning now to the classroom settings, we also have a multifaceted picture. In one sense, the classrooms were identical for each of the five children (setting Daniel's Year 2 aside) and we can compare them in terms of how supportive each class was as a learning context.

For instance, we might say that Mrs Powell's Reception class work was underpinned by an established working consensus with well understood and accepted conventions and routines. Although the very young children had much to learn about school life, they accepted Mrs Powell's authority and she used her power with sensitivity to their needs and interests (as she perceived them) as four-year-olds at the start of the year. She provided a supportive classroom climate in which it was possible for pupils to take risks and exercise some, albeit limited, control. The context for learning was relatively secure. Similarly there are many examples of Mrs Powell providing affective and intellectual support for children as they approached a ZPD which was associated with a learning challenge (for instance, with Mary and Sally's work on 'sounds' on p. 195). It is probably true though that many of these examples of Mrs Powell's work with these very young children are stronger on the affective side than in terms of intellectual challenge.

Thinking about Miss Scott's classroom we would have to acknowledge it as having been experienced as a rather difficult environment for many of the children. Whilst Sally coasted carefully through it, with some careful parental preparation, the other children found Miss Scott's unpredictability difficult to cope with. The working consensus was thus more fragile, with the teacher's power being more in evidence to assert class control and, at times, to criticize or cajole children for their work or behaviour. The classroom was perceived by pupils as a high-risk setting in which they thought very carefully before attempting to act independently or exercise control. In terms of the quality of teaching and assistance in learning, affective support for children was not consistent and this had the consequence that intellectual support, though sometimes offered in quite precise ways, often seemed to be perceived by the pupils as more of a threat than an opportunity.

In Miss George's classroom a very positive working consensus was established with many children flourishing as they related to this newly qualified, warm and outgoing teacher. The children found the classroom climate enabling and were certainly more relaxed and willing to take risks. The opportunity to learn was thus not constrained by the social setting. In terms of the quality of teaching and assistance in learning there was also plenty of affective support, with Miss George developing very close relationships with many of the children and working with them sensitively. However, given her relative inexperience in classroom management and lack of experience in teaching the early years' curriculum, Miss George was not always as able to provide the children with intellectual support at the ZPD as she would have wished. At this point in her career, she had neither the classroom time, the diagnostic skills nor the subject knowledge to provide very precise support.

We thus have a description for each of the classrooms at a general level. However, we need to look more closely, for the five children who have been studied did not have identical experiences within these classrooms. Indeed, although the learning contexts were mostly the same, the different structural positions and relationships of the children meant that the contexts were experienced in particular ways. The result was *differential access* to assistance in learning.

Sally provides an example of a child who, whilst listening and working very hard, would seek her teacher's attention if she had any doubts about what she should do or at completion of the task. She was sufficiently self-confident, mature and successful to make this statement as true in the relatively high-risk context of Miss Scott's class as it was during her time with Mrs Powell and Miss George.

Hazel provides a different example. In Mrs Powell's class this 'unusual little girl' was tolerated in a supportive and routinized way. Miss Scott found that Hazel would not conform to her expectations and began to think of her as frustrating, withdrawn and stubborn. Hazel certainly attempted to evade much of the work with which she was presented – until there was a short period of rapprochement during the 'Rainforest Project'. In Miss George's class Hazel found that her teacher was fascinated by her drawing and made a concerted attempt to develop her expressive writing. For the first time she was one of the older children and, with her book of 'Max and the Frog', she made a major breakthrough in her self-perception as a writer, from which, in that respect, she never looked back.

James, on the other hand, was, for Mrs Powell, 'a super little chap who is a bit unsure of himself' and whom she tried to draw out. With Miss Scott he remained rather worried by the situation and, although making sound academic progress, was still regarded as cautious and 'highly strung' in class. By Year 2, in Miss George's class James' unhappiness with his peer relationships and additional home tuition began to affect his approach to school generally. Miss George found it hard to be patient with his reluctance to engage in classroom tasks.

Mary, 'kindly and friendly' for Mrs Powell, fitted into and contributed to the working consensus of her Reception classroom. She was supportive and supported and, with that reciprocity, she adapted to school and flourished. With Miss Scott she felt a need for more defensive and cautious strategies to 'avoid being told off' and tried to reduce risk and ambiguity as much as possible before seeking teacher help or evaluation. This was interpreted as evidence of 'a lack of full motivation'. In Miss George's class, with relief, she formed a very close relationship with her teacher, almost of adoration, in which she vied with her friends to 'be most helpful' and began to explore her potential through particular progress at reading and maths.

For *Daniel*, his experiences in his Reception class were challenging and Mrs Powell found him to be rather immature and lacking in confidence. Whilst her classroom routines and calm manner gradually gave him more confidence, he was concerned by her progressive requirements that he carry out curriculum tasks because he might 'do it wrong'. This became an overarching concern in Miss Scott's class, where Daniel felt very vulnerable and, at times, frightened. Again, he sought reassurance to reduce risk and task ambiguity before committing himself, hence Miss Scott's perception of him as 'hesitant and shy'. He moved on to his Year 2 as the only one of the five case-study children reported in this book to be placed in the 'much more laid-back' Miss Sage's class. He became more settled and relaxed and, with a great deal of effort, gradually became more confident in tackling new learning tasks in the classroom.

For each pupil within a cohort, in other words, classroom contexts are both the same and yet are different. They are the same in that the pupils may well all be present at identical times, adjust to similar expectations and often engage in similar curricular activities. However, they are different because each child experiences the classroom in the light of their particular structural position, learning stance, interests, strategies, identity and cultural background. The ways in which each child interprets the classroom setting, acts and learns is bound to reflect this differential positioning and to lead, in consequence, to differential experiences and outcomes.

9.6   WHAT WERE THE PERSONAL OUTCOMES OF THE CHILDREN'S LEARNING?

We have seen that a whole range of factors associated with social relationships, identity, learning stance, social context and forms of support affect a child's learning. What then of the outcomes?

Following the arguments advanced in Chapters 2 and 4, it is helpful to focus on three types of outcome and these are summarized for each of the children, for Key Stage 1 as a whole, in Matrix 9.4.

Of course, Matrix 9.4 summarizes outcomes of the learning cycles across Key Stage 1 as a whole and thus obscures and conflates outcomes which could have been reviewed for each year or more regularly. In any event, it makes the point clear that whilst formal, curriculum attainments are an important contribution to long-term learning, they will have more impact when they also explicitly build up self-esteem and social status. If this occurs, a positive cycle starts to be completed because of the ways in which self-esteem and social status contribute, in formative ways, to identity, self-image and engagement in future learning challenges.

Thus for example, we see the ways in which Sally's achievements reinforced her self-confidence and how Mary gradually succeeded in her efforts to establish herself. Hazel's diverse and idiosyncratic achievements were precisely reflected in her self-perception and in the views of others whilst, in different ways, Daniel and James suffered from their lack of confidence and social acceptance. It is interesting, in fact, that neither of the boys was unsuccessful in terms of the school's judgements, though both mothers were uneasy at the level of their achievements and not entirely confident of their capabilities. From evidence of reports of their attainments in the schools to which they were later sent, they may have been performing below their potential. Thus, for both children at the time,

Matrix 9.4   *The children's curriculum attainment, self-esteem and social status*

	Basic curriculum attainment	Self-esteem	Self-esteem
Mary	Relatively good achievements each year, but maths particularly good.	Growth in self-esteem. Initially worried by her reading, but delighted by eventual maths achievements.	Part of popular group of girls and well thought of by peers.
Hazel	Relatively low achievement, particularly with maths, in each year.	High self-esteem with particular pride in drawing and, later written stories.	Viewed with some indulgence and many children unsure how to relate to her.
Daniel	Steady but moderate achievements each year.	Uncertain of self-esteem. Some insecurity in family relations which overlap at school and in cautious self-presetation.	Not confident among peer groups and seen as rather dependent with uncertain social status.
Sally	High achievements across all subjects in all years.	Very high levels of self-confidence in all settings and activities.	Influential peer-group leader and very high social status amongst peers.
James	In school terms, sound relative achievements each year, but parents had higher expectations and feared under-achivement.	Worried about himself, confused by differences in home–school messages.	On margins of peer groups, relatively low social status and, at times, exclusion from peer activities.

their lack of self-confidence and their compromised social status may have affected the quality of their learning attainment. The view that they would 'get on better' with more formal teaching methods was important in the decision by the parents of James and Daniel to send them to other schools to finish their primary school education and, in the case of James, his parents also hoped for, and found, peer and school cultures which were more consistent with the expectations which he experienced at home.

This discussion completes the comparative review of the five case-study children at each point of the learning cycle, We can therefore turn towards a more holistic conclusion.

9.7   WHY DOES CHILDREN'S APPROACH TO LEARNING DEVELOP AS IT DOES?

The previous comparison and discussion of the patterns of and influences on the learning of the five case-study children strongly warns against any simplistic responses to the question posed in this section heading. Indeed, perhaps we should be thankful that there can never be a complete answer, for, if certainty were possible, much of the fascination in education and the diversity in life would have been removed. Nor, of course, can this book do any more than make a contribution to discussion, analysis and understanding in this field. What though can we say?

The focus on the 'social world' of children's learning has enabled the construction of what it is hoped are 'credible stories' of five children's learning which will have some resonance with the experiences of readers as children, parents or teachers.

Additionally, each case study illustrates the application of the cyclical model which has been introduced Figure 1.2, p. 14 and Figure 4.3, p. 97 and can also be represented by it. There are thus some grounds for suggesting that the model is at least a useful way of identifying and analysing the social factors which are involved in learning. The model, at its level of abstraction and as a representation of some fundamental social processes, has some portability and could be applied and developed further in relation to children in other contexts and circumstances. It attempts to encapsulate important analytic elements of a model of social influences on learning.

However, whilst the comparison of the five case studies in this chapter does suggest some patterns which may exist in the impact of different types of social relationship, for instance in relation to continuities and discontinuities in family, peer and teacher cultures and relationships, it does not permit the production of substantive generalizations. If anything, our discussion reinforces a sense of the uniqueness of each child and the fact that, whilst all the factors identified in the model are likely to be 'in play', they can change and interact in very diverse ways.

Returning though to the aims for this book which were outlined in the Introduction, we can be more confident if we accept the role of the model in supporting the development of a reflective awareness of social factors and processes which influence the stance which young children take towards learning. Thus, accepting the level of abstraction, we can present a further analytical representation of the major argument of this book. This is provided in Figure 9.1.

The *spiral* of learning, identity and career represents successive cycles of the model which has been introduced throughout this book and which was represented in Figures 1.2 and 4.3. It can been imagined turning annually, through the school years of Reception, Year 1 and

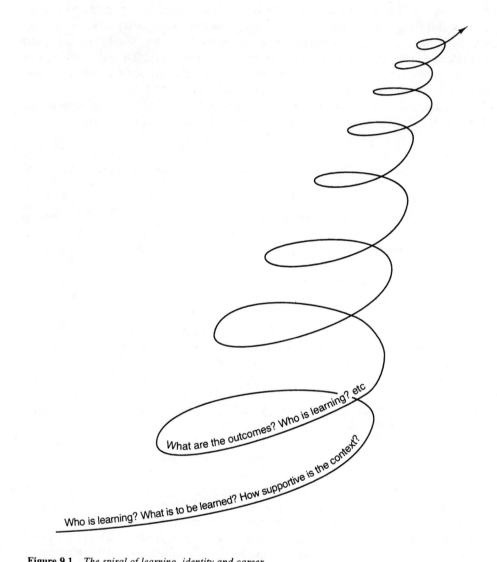

Figure 9.1 *The spiral of learning, identity and career*

Year 2. However, the spiral clearly starts at birth and, moving on through the formative years and schooling, continues throughout life. The spiral describes the recursive nature of experience and provides a starting point for the analysis of 'pupil career' which Ann Filer and I have developed in *The Social World of Pupil Careers* (Pollard and Filer, in press).

In the case-study stories of the five children who feature in this book, we have seen their lives spiralling and unfolding through three annual rounds of the cycle of learning and identity. Sally, over this period, seemed to have moved confidently, ever onward; Mary found her successes and also developed ways of coping and fulfilling herself; Hazel faced some challenges to her self-absorption and began a process of adaption; Daniel still felt vulnerable but began to develop more confidence whilst James was unable to overcome differences in home, school and playground cultures and a lack of peer acceptance.

As suggested above, it is inappropriate to attempt to draw conclusions about the long-term consequences of these spiralling patterns over the period of time from Reception to Year 2 which has been reported. However, the case-study stories were completed in late 1994, when the children had reached the age of 11 and had completed their primary education. Both continuities and changes were evident even over this relatively short intervening period and, as each child began his or her secondary education in the 1994/5 academic year, it was already apparent that each child's spiral was again turning and that the impact of new social settings and new experiences would be clearly detectable, overlaid on those of the past.

Part 4

Reflecting

Chapter 10

On the Research Process and Validity of the Study

10.1 INTRODUCTION

This chapter is intended to describe the research design, methods and the process of the research which is reported in this book, to offer my reflections on them and to help readers in forming judgements about the validity of the analysis which has been constructed.

Put very simply, the book is a study of social influences on the learning of a small cohort of white, middle class children attending one 4–11 primary school in southern England. The children's experiences, perspectives and behaviour were researched in family, class-room and playground contexts, together with the views of parents, teachers and peers. The main argument is that the 'social world' of young primary school children has a consider-able influence on their sense of personal identity and thus on the ways in which they engage with curriculum learning in school.

I see the study as being part of the mainstream of qualitative research in the sociology of education with its focus on natural settings, concern for the perspectives and understand-ings of people, emphasis on social processes and inductive attempt to generate analysis. The specific approach is ethnographic and, when I began, I was particularly influenced by the field-guides of Schatzman and Strauss (1973) and Burgess (1984), the argument for research 'reflexivity' presented by Hammersley and Atkinson (1983) and by my own previous experience as an ethnographer (reported in Pollard, 1985b,1987b). With this back-ground, I adopted a classic case-study approach, with its associated strategies of observing, participating and developing personal rapport as a means of trying to understand the perspectives and actions of people within the case. Of course, the results of such an approach are highly susceptible to specific factors such as the nature of the sample case itself, the quality of the relationships which the researcher builds up, the range and validity of the data which are collected and the analytical procedures which are employed to build an interpretation. These are some of the issues which I will address below.

However, it is also useful to have an overview of the phases, basic process and time-scale of the research and this is provided in Figure 10.1.

Figure 10.1 shows that evidence was gathered from children, teachers and parents over the seven years of their primary school education, but that material from only the first three years has been used in this book. It then represents the process through which the final text has been produced. This has been one of interaction between data gathering, interpretation, writing, validation, theorization, comparison with other research and response to academic, respondent and professional comment. Needless to say, this tidy diagram does not convey the practical and intellectual struggle to sustain the project, construct an interpretation and decide upon and execute a strategy for dissemination.

		Access, data gathering and descriptive analysis as used in this book.			Data gathering continuing (as used, with earlier data, in Pollard and Filer, in press)				Completion of of this book
Pupil year	Pre-school	Reception (age 4/5)	Year 1 (age 5/6)	Year 2 (age 6/7)	Year 3 (age 7/8)	Year 4 (age 8/9)	Year 5 (age 9/10)	Year 6 (age 10/11)	Year 7 (Secor school)
School year	1986/87	1987/88	1988/89	1989/90	1990/91	1991/92	1992/93	1993/94	1994/95

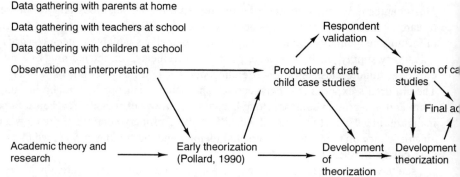

Figure 10.1 *A simplified representation of phases of the research process for this book*

The chapter also provides information to enable the question of the *validity* of the research to be addressed. Does the account accurately reflect the phenomenon studied? I aim to demonstrate that the study has internal validity because of the way in which it has drawn on a wide range of data sources over a sustained period of time, with the benefit of respondent validation, triangulation and comparison. However, I make no claims that the *specific empirical findings* are generalizable. Notwithstanding this, in Chapter 11 I argue that the *theoretical analysis* of processes which influence children's approach to classroom learning is relevant well beyond the parameters of the case. This claim rests on theoretical inference and on my invitation to readers to engage in reflective application of the analysis to their own lives as children, parents and/or teachers.

10.2 GETTING STARTED

Selecting the case-study school

The selection of Greenside Primary School for the case study was part of a comparative strategy. At the start of 1987, I envisaged starting two parallel ethnographies based around schools serving communities with contrasting socio-economic circumstances. Comparative methods (Glaser and Strauss, 1967) could then have been deployed in an integrated analysis. However, at the same time, I was aware that detailed, seven-year longitudinal studies involving parents, children and teachers would inevitably be intrusive and were likely to be impossible without particularly strong support from the headteachers, teachers and parents. A major factor in selection thus became that the schools should have supportive headteachers who would be likely to remain at the schools over the period and that teachers and parents would support the study. I was also aware that, whilst the conditions of my work made it possible for me to gather data at one school on a one day per week basis, I needed external funding and the appointment of a research assistant if a second school was to be studied. Whilst I was contemplating these problems, the opportunity arose to study at Greenside Primary School.

I first heard of Greenside Primary School through an academic friend who told me of interesting innovations in classroom organization which were being introduced by a new headteacher, Mrs Davison. On visiting the school, I found Mrs Davison to be very welcoming. She was interested in my research concerns and we struck up a rapport which was to last throughout the entire study. As we saw in Chapter 2, in which details about the school are provided, Greenside was Mrs Davison's second headship and she was confident in her values, educational aims and management style. Furthermore, she was at least as committed as I was to taking account of the perspectives of children in educational provision and she had some, generally positive, awareness of my previously published work. I decided that the opportunity for such support was too good to miss and I thus, despite the distances involved, began to negotiate access.

Meanwhile, I applied to a national research funding agency, the Economic and Social Research Council, to begin work at a second case-study school in inner-city Easthampton. Negotiations with the school were initiated and agreement reached in principle. The sample there would have had a wide mix of social class and ethnic backgrounds. However, despite the support of referees, my application was one of many for which sufficient funds were not available. The study thus developed at Greenside alone and in later years was supported by the Leverhulme Trust. It is also worth mentioning here that a second study with a similar research design and in a contrasting school was subsequently started by Ann Filer, as the site for her PhD, work which was focused on assessment and which I supervised. When she successfully completed her doctorate, we were able to get ESRC funding to complete the tracking of her cohort to the end of their primary schooling. We intend to publish those findings in Filer and Pollard (forthcoming).

Research identity, the negotiation of access and identification of the pupil sample

My relationship with Mrs Davison was, without doubt, the most significant factor in both setting up and sustaining the study at Greenside Primary School. I believe that we both felt sufficiently confident of each other's value positions and trusting of the other's judgements to be open, frank and honest at every point. In particular, I was careful to keep Mrs Davison informed of each new phase of the research, to seek her advice and to minimize any disruption to the school. On her part, she was enormously supportive in legitimating the study with governors, parents and teachers and she respected my commitment to maintaining the confidentiality of the data which I collected from others. It was, in my judgement, a professional and respectful relationship, without which the study would not have been possible.

At the start of the study I had a research role within my higher education institution and was concerned at the view of me which Greenside teachers might hold. However, during the term before the study was to begin, I spent a day a week in one Reception class working with the teacher, Mrs Powell. This was important in establishing my identity for I was able to draw on my experience of teaching infants (for seven of my ten years in schools), which had ended just five years earlier, and also to demonstrate that I both cared for young children and understood the practical difficulties of teaching. In the September of 1987, Mrs Powell was very helpful in assuring parents and her colleagues of the non-threatening nature of the study. In successive years I moved, somewhat unpredictably, to work with the teacher or teachers to whom my cohort of children had been allocated. By then, a relationship with most of the teachers had been established and the study had been explained and discussed at staff meetings. I was able to anticipate the teachers who were likely to receive the case-study pupil cohort in the succeeding year and to spend some time in preliminary discussions. They, in turn, had many opportunities to talk to teachers in whose classrooms I had previously worked. Some of the teachers knew of some of my academic work, such as the teacher-education textbook *Reflective Teaching in the Primary School* (Pollard and Tann, 1993, first published in 1987), and of my work as director of the National Primary Centre (South West) which was active at the time. I believe that such knowledge was taken to indicate two things: first, that I had some expertise and, second, that I was basically sympathetic to teachers.

In the late summer of 1987, following the advice of Mrs Davison and knowing that the teaching staff were content, the governors agreed their support for the project, subject to the consent of parents. Thus, at the start of the Autumn Term 1987, the parents of twenty-six children in Mrs Powell's Reception class were invited to a meeting to hear about the project. The meeting was well attended by mothers, with a few fathers also coming. I described the issues in which I was interested, with particular emphasis on learning, pupil experiences and the influence of family, peers and teachers. I explained the data which I hoped to gather from parents, in which two sets of diary entries were to be particularly important, and the time scale of the study. I set out the ethical code which I proposed should frame the study. The first principle was that nothing would be done if it was likely to be harmful or distressing to the children. This underpinned the whole project. Second, the code stated that all data would be held confidentially and would not be released to anyone else, parent, teacher, child or peer. However, there was provision that this principle could be broken if I, as the researcher, came to know of something which I felt to be 'seriously damaging' to the child. It was agreed that, in such circumstances, I would return to the person from whom I had gathered such information and urge them to act. If they would or could not, then it was agreed that I could break the principle of confidentiality. The ethical agreement also recognized my need to keep records, make analytical judgements and, eventually, to publish research results.

The response of the parents rather surprised me, with the parents of twenty-two children being willing to become involved. Perhaps, coming at the start of their children's full-time education, they were pleased to find someone who seemed to be as interested in the development of their children as they were. Perhaps too, they were sympathetic to the overall aims of the study. It is certainly the case that the parents were reassured by knowledge that my wife and I had our own children, then aged nine and six, and had very recently experienced the feelings of parents as their children start school. This theme resonated throughout the period of data gathering, with occasional discussion of the educational progress of my children (at their local infant, junior and comprehensive schools) providing an element of reciprocity as fieldwork progressed. As self-evidently white and middle-class myself, and with generous sponsorship from the head and class teachers it is likely that any potential threat which I posed to these families was minimized, which may well not have been the case had I worked in an inner-city school. In any event, the outcome from the meeting was a long list of children whose parents were both willing to participate and who did not expect to move their children from the school during their primary education. Of these, I selected the five boys and five girls who were the oldest children in the class, since I was advised (incorrectly as it turned out) they were likely to stay together as a group through the school. I was then delighted to begin focused observations of the children.

There are both disadvantages and advantages in this sample. Whilst the gender balance provided some interesting contrasts, reflecting the school's overall intake at the time, only one child, Sally, was from a working-class family and all the children were from indigenous, white, English homes. Reflecting the school's class allocation policy, the children were also all rather young, with birthdays in the Spring and Summer Terms. On the other hand, as the study progressed the differences amongst the individual children became increasingly clear, despite the apparent relative similarities in their social circumstances. Indeed, I came to view the emergent uniqueness of each individual and the subtle variations in the social influences on them as being at least as interesting as the major differences which might have been highlighted by a more contrastive sample. However, had it initially been possible to develop my preference for a comparative ethnography in an inner-city context, the analysis would undoubtedly have developed in different ways and raised different issues. This conception may still come to fruition in Filer and Pollard (forthcoming). Perhaps the greatest apparent advantage of the Greenside sample was the resonance which it provided with my own biography and circumstances. As I suggested above, this probably eased access and fostered the trust which is an essential condition for any such long-term study which goes close to the personal intricacies of family and classroom life. In fact contact was maintained with nine of the ten families throughout the project. One child, Martin, moved away from the school after the first year and further data collection was not attempted.

My relationship with the parents remained positive throughout the study. We sometimes met informally at school, had biannual meetings at their homes to discuss their child and I organized occasional meetings of all parents together. The latter, in the evening with light refreshments, were used to thank parents for their participation, to report back on some aspects of progress, to maintain awareness of the general purposes of the study and to remind parents of the ethical framework within which it was being conducted and of the issues which might arise at the point of publication. A final group meeting, in July 1994, was used to launch the respondent validation process and it included a full exposition of the emergent theory and its relevance to education policy. At all times I tried to be frank and honest with the parents, to share with them my genuine fascination and enjoyment in seeing their children growing up and my uncertainties about how to make sense of what I observed. I believe though, that they tended to maintain some respect for me as a 'researcher' and felt I must, therefore, 'know' something. In conversation, I more commonly traded some of my experiences as a parent than my experience as an academic. For instance, sibling rivalry was no stranger to my family and, as time went on, like the parents in the study, my wife and I faced decisions about where to send our children for their secondary education. Our decision, to support our local comprehensive, was noted with interest by some of the parents but my strategy, and that of Ann Filer when she joined me, was to share the dilemmas of parenthood rather than make judgements. My aim was to be empathic without being intrusive. However, there is no doubt that my educational values differed significantly from those of some of the parents and this, reinforced by the relative infrequency of our meetings and by my non-participant observational role, was a guard against over-identification.

Regarding my identity and relationship with the children during the years reported in this book, I have no doubt that I was successful in developing a close rapport with them, and yet I was certainly viewed as being somewhat 'strange'. Here was an adult who was often at school, but who did not behave like a teacher, parent, dinner supervisor or classroom assistant. He wandered around the classroom and playground, watching activities, chatting with children and occasionally asking questions and recording their replies in his notebook. When asked what he was doing he would explain that he was, 'writing a story about what children think about school'. The children, with no other experience, accepted their pet researcher and joked about him. 'Was I a spy?' 'Was I Superman?' Those who know me personally will know that the latter suggestion was extremely far-fetched, but it reflected my ownership of some spectacles which reminded the children of Clark Kent. It was an excellent basis for speculation and entertainment – in which I happily indulged. I was able to draw on my experience as a teacher of young children, as a parent and as someone who has always enjoyed the freshness of young children's imagination and their humour and been fascinated by the complexity and intensity of their concerns. As in my previous research with pupils, I found that the children loved to be listened to and have their views taken seriously. This, of course, was simple for me because, unlike their teachers and parents, I had no responsibility for the children and no authority position to protect. Whilst I was never required to 'tell them off', I could indulge the children by simply being interested in them. Unconditional positive regard (Rogers, 1969) in these circumstances is relatively easy and, when the children were young, the main data-gathering problem was in sharing out the available time and preventing myself being monopolized by particular individuals. At no point was there pupil resistance to participation in the study.

10.3 COLLECTING DATA

The annual data-gathering schedule

When beginning this longitudinal ethnography, I was aware that it was not possible to be confident of the questions which I would want to address at the end. This problem was inherent in the combination of an extended time scale and the exploratory nature of the research. Thus, unlike the relatively pragmatic, inductive enquiry of more conventional, cross-sectional ethnographies prioritizing the generation of grounded theory, this longitudinal study required the use of a theoretically informed, annual, data-gathering schedule. Only such a structure could ensure that comparable data would be available for each of the seven years which the study was projected to last.

In summary, data were collected from parents, pupils and teachers in the settings of home, playground and classroom. Parents kept diaries, with two recording periods and associated follow-up interviews each year. Pupils were observed in the playground and classroom and some video-recordings and photography were also used. Pupils were interviewed in groups and individually, and examples of their work were collected regularly. Fieldwork using participant observation was regular in the school, with a target of one day per week over the period. In addition to naturally occurring conversation, the teachers were interviewed using a semi-structured schedule twice each year. Teacher records of children's attainment, reports to parents and other teacher-assessment data were collected. Table 10.2 summarizes the annual data-collection schedule and Section 10.3 gives a little more detail on each method of data-gathering.

	Parents	**Child**	**Class Teacher**
Autumn	Diary	Observation	Interview and discussions
	Diary interview	Video Photo interview	Video
Spring		Observation	Discussions
		Sociometry	Video
		Group interview	
		Video	
Summer	Diary	Observation	Interview and discussions
	Diary interview	Work interview	Records and reports

Figure 10.2   *The basic, annual, data-collection schedule*

Data-gathering methods

Parent diaries   were provided in the form of large, stiff-backed books and it was made clear that these would ultimately become the property of each family. The diaries were completed twice each year for a period of one week and in all but one case the diarist was the mother. For the Autumn Term diary entries, parents were asked to record a simple narrative of routine family events which took place. This was done day-by-day, with particular reference to the child within the family on whom the research was focused. The Summer Term entries were used to provide an overview of the year as a whole, with parents being asked to consider their child's learning progress, social, emotional and physical development and key social relationships and experiences. Diaries were normally issued and returned via the school using sealed envelopes to preserve confidentiality. The length of diary entries varied by diarist but each settled into a routine and provided between four and twenty pages of written text for each recording period. Although the completion of the diaries were sometimes hard to fit into busy family schedules and could be seen as a chore, there were no cases where they were not completed.

Parent interviews   were used to follow up each diary entry, thus occurring twice each year. They took place in the family home at a mutually agreed time and, in a third of the families, fathers regularly participated. The interviews were conducted informally, often over coffee and in the manner of discussions. Nevertheless, the conversations were structured by the diaries which had been written a week or so earlier or by other topics which I introduced for each interview. They were thus used to further explore interesting events or issues, to provide contextual information and to provide supplementary accounts. All of these interviews were tape recorded and later transcribed. No parent interviews were missed. The parents seemed to enjoy talking about their children and reflecting on their progress with someone who was, indeed, almost as interested as they were in their child's unfolding story.

Classroom fieldnotes took two forms. Some were general records of classroom events, routines and episodes which were intended to provide contextual information. However, most were more focused on the activities of particular children. With a data-gathering commitment of one day per week, I aimed to write detailed fieldnotes on the classroom activity of each one of the ten target children for two teaching sessions during each term. Thus, over the years, a considerable number of accounts accumulated. Recording took place in stiff-backed notebooks with a clear separation of the descriptive fieldnotes from analytic comments.

Classroom photographs were used to provide an easily accessible visual record of the classroom settings and activities. When the children were young, photographs were used as a basis for some pupil interviews but later they became more useful as spurs to my memory regarding classroom layout, equipment, routines, etc. They also provided a source of interest and amusement for the children and at meetings with parents.

Video recordings made in the classrooms focused on either general routines or on provision for mathematics and basic literacy skills. The children were initially interested in the camera and were occasionally shown recordings. However, after a while their behaviour when recording was taking place was not noticeably affected. Some video recordings were also made of school events, such as 'class assemblies' and the annual nativity play. The sound-track on the latter was often reasonable, whilst classroom audio-recordings were usually difficult to transcribe and were much less useful than the visual evidence which was provided.

Playground fieldnotes took the same form as those of the classroom but were focused on manifestations of pupil culture and on peer-group activities, with particular reference to the target children.

Video recordings were made in the playground each Spring Term to document play activities and were later used to stimulate group discussion on aspects of peer culture and relationships.

Pupil documents, such as samples of school work or pictures from home, were collected both routinely, at the end of each year, and pragmatically when opportunities arose or when particularly interesting examples occurred. For most of the period of the study it was school-policy to retain completed work rather than send it home at the end of the year, and I was able to collect these original documents. Each child also had a 'folder of work', later a 'portfolio', in which carefully selected samples of their school work were placed each term, often with annotations by the child or teacher following discussion between them. Other records about the child were kept in the portfolios which were shared with parents at parent–teacher meetings.

Pupil interviews occurred in many ways. Most often they took the form of *ad hoc* discussions which cropped up in the flow of classroom or playground events. I would wander around as an interested observer and conversation was initiated by pupils or by myself. In the playground this occurred very regularly, but in the classroom care was necessary to avoid disrupting teacher intentions for the session. More formal, individual interviews were held in the Autumn and Summer Term of every year. These usually took place in the pottery room of the school which was a small, closed room close to the classrooms and which was infrequently used. In it, it was possible to produce good-quality audio-recordings for later transcription. Such interviews were always semi-structured by issues or topics which I wanted to introduce but were approached very flexibly indeed. This was particularly necessary when the children were very young and photographs of classroom activities were used as a focus and stimulus for discussion on some occasions. The Autumn Term interview was used pragmatically to cover topics such as settling into the class, relationships with peers and teachers. However, the Summer Term interview was more structured and normally began with discussion of a specific example of the child's work and then sought pupil views on their year as a whole before looking forward to the next school year. Group interviews, based on friendship groups, were held each Spring Term and were focused on playground activities, friendships and aspects of child culture. On some occasions video material was used to stimulate such discussions. For all interview rounds, additional children beyond the target group were interviewed and sometimes this amounted to the whole class taking part. This was done to decrease the awareness of the target and other children which might have affected their behaviour, to gather data on others to provide comparative and contextualizing information and to satisfy a pressing pupil demand for 'their turn'.

Sociometry was used towards the start of each Spring Term to provide a check on friendship patterns and to contribute to the selection of pupil groups for interview.

Teacher interviews occurred very regularly indeed in conversational mode in the classroom or staffroom and they tended to focus on specific incidents in which the children had participated or on the intentions, process or outcomes of teaching sessions. However, such discussions were preceded at the start of each year by a semi-structured interview focusing on each teacher's basic biography, educational philosophy and preferences for classroom organization, pedagogy and curriculum provision. At an early point in each year, the teachers were also asked for their impressions of all the children in the class. The Summer Term teacher interview was also semi-structured and provided an opportunity to review the work and development of the class as a whole and of the individual children. The semi-structured teacher interviews took place wherever the teacher would feel most comfortable. Several took place at the teacher's homes in the evening, eased by a bottle of wine. One was held in a pub.

Teacher documents were studied and took three main forms. First, there were each teacher's records, made for their own administrative and teaching purposes, and to which I negotiated access from each teacher in turn. Second, there were the official school and LEA record systems which were completed regarding each child. Finally, there were the official reports which teachers made to parents. Greenside Primary School provided short written comments for literacy, maths, topic work and social development in each Spring and

Summer Term and I was given full access to copies of these reports. It was these documents, together with examples of pupil's work, which an experienced infant teacher, Kath Henry, and I used to map the 'structural position' of each child in each classroom as a rank order of maths and literacy attainment (see the Introduction to Part 2 and the start of each child case study).

School fieldnotes were made at selected school events using the same procedures described earlier. For instance, I observed at school assemblies and performances and at a limited number of evening meetings for parents and staff meetings.

School documents of various sorts were studied. These ranged from policy statements on curriculum subjects and on curriculum planning to timetables and annual schedules, minutes of staff meetings and letters and newsletters to parents.

Headteacher interviews were formally conducted once each year to provide contextual information about the development of the school. This semi-structured interview was taped for later transcription. Liaison with the headteacher was regular at other times and, in particular, regarding the negotiation and maintenance of access.

10.4 INTERPRETATION AND ANALYSIS

Given the longitudinal nature of the study and my desire to make year-by-year comparisons, straightforward use of the classic ethnographic method of analysis involving progressive focusing was not open to me. If I had narrowed the focus to issues which seemed interesting in the first year, I might have missed factors which emerged later. I therefore maintained the annual data-gathering structure which is described in Figure 10.2. However, this meant that there was a very considerable accumulation of data – which I filed by child and by year.

A brief attempt to develop a coding scheme to classify each small element of data very quickly proved itself to be both mechanistic and impractical and there was a period during which I feared that the volume of data could prove unmanageable. However, I felt that the basic research design was fundamentally sound and my previous experience gave me some confidence. I therefore continued to collect data, to read other research work, reflect in my research notebook and generally puzzle on how to interpret the material which I was collecting.The longitudinal design, though contributing to some analytical difficulties, also provided time to consider how to solve them.

Gradually, I began to adopt a more open interpretive approach to analysis which was very close to that advocated by Hammersley and Atkinson (1983). Drawing on Becker and Geer (1975), Weider (1974) and Lofland (1971) they promised that such an approach could 'enhance the fertility of the theoretical imagination' (1983: 178) and this was certainly one of my specific intentions. I began to develop my familiarity with the data I was collecting by making an increasingly close study of it. I wrote more specific analytic comments to myself, trying to relate the perceptions and behaviour of the participants to my impressions of relationships in the classroom, playground and home settings. Additionally I maintained my established interest in symbolic interactionist studies of classrooms and developed my reading of social constructivist work such as Bruner (1986) and Tharp and Gallimore

(1988). I continued to feel that there was potential in the synthesis of the two theoretical approaches and that something of the kind was implicit in the work of educationalists such as Rowland (1985). At a relatively early point, this led to my attempt to conceptualize factors affecting learning contexts and to posit a cyclical relationship between learning and identity (see Pollard, 1990). In a gradually evolving process, I thus built on concepts which were identified from the participants, on issues which I had sensed to be important within the classrooms, homes and playground and on my reading. I also discussed my emerging ideas extensively with my wife, Ros Pollard. We drew on our experiences as children, parents and teachers to reinforce or contest aspects of the models which I began to produce.

In conjunction with this unfolding approach to theorization, I introduced a way of managing the data more effectively. The most important decision was to define my basic 'units of analysis' in terms of each of the children (10 initially), each of the main settings (3) and each year (7). Over the full study, this projected no less than 210 child/setting/year units of analysis, but at least it provided a clear structure within which to attempt to integrate the diverse forms of data.

The data-management system underpinned the construction of what I began to call the first level, *descriptive analysis* in which summarizing matrices were drawn up by child/setting/year. These were descriptive overviews which could be referenced back to data sources and which, ultimately, developed to become the basis of the children's case studies which form the bulk of this book. These overviews made the data more manageable and eased the struggle to identify patterns in the children's learning stories as a whole. Ann Filer's role in this was important when she joined me in June 1991, for she brought a fresh eye to the material when she studied the early data sets as part of her familiarization process. Although I drafted each of the case-study accounts, Ann and I had innumerable discussions to produce the 'stories' for each child which were then offered to the parents for respondent validation.

The *theoretical modelling*, which constitutes a second level of analysis, also continued to develop over the whole project. As described above, this derived from interactive engagement with the participants directly, the raw data which had been collected, the descriptive analysis, academic theory, other research and discussion with close colleagues – a process which is indicated in Figure 10.1. At the same time, I wondered about the relationship of the emerging analysis to changes in education policy and school practices in England and Wales and I engaged in other research work, in particular that of the Primary Assessment, Curriculum and Experience project (PACE) (Pollard *et al.*, 1994). The culmination of this theoretical development, frozen in December 1994 and no longer constantly evolving, is Figure 1.2, Figure 4.3, Figure 9.1 and their associated chapters. Its wider relevance is discussed in Chapter 11.

10.5   THE STRATEGY AND ETHICS OF WRITING UP

For several years, in parallel with the struggle for descriptive and theoretical analysis, I worried about how to write up and communicate this study. Essentially the project itself imposed three important requirements: that longitudinal development was shown; that the holistic influence of the social contexts and relationships was demonstrated and that the voices and perspectives of the participants could be clearly conveyed. Further, I had identified *two* themes within the seven-year project as a whole; children's learning and pupil career – but how to present them? There were also two particularly important variables, the individual children and the social contexts which they experienced – could they both be represented? A more pragmatic factor was that changes of school meant that there were Greenside Primary School case studies of seven children over each of the seven years and of two children (James and Daniel) over each of their first three and four years at the school. Finally, there was the publisher's liking for books of between 70,000 to 100,000 words. The result was a large number of possible book structures and outlines and sample drafts of material in which the strengths and weaknesses of each approach were explored and discussed with Ros Pollard and Ann Filer. Whilst I wallowed in the complexities and dilemmas which I had identified, they argued for the simplicity and meaningfulness of basing the writing up around 'child stories'.

A fascinating account of ethnographers' strategies in constructing their texts is provided by Atkinson (1990) in *The Ethnographic Imagination*. He demonstrates how literary conventions are used to convey findings and arguments and to attempt to convince readers of the authenticity of accounts. This was compulsive reading and provided a particularly strong discussion of the use of narrative as a way of representing social action. As Atkinson puts it:

> Time, causality and agency may all be conveyed at an implicit level in narrative form. ... The sociological imagination is conveyed through the interplay of narrative and more formal, overt statements of sociological theory and proposition. The narration of people's doings not only arranges them in sequence, but also conveys consequence. The narrative has an internal coherence (beginning, middle and end, and so on) whereas the relations *between* narratives furnishes a broader framework of relevance and coherence.
> (1990: 105)

Furthermore, Atkinson illustrates how there can be 'a very potent narrative contract available between the text and the reader' (1990: 113).

The combination of human interest in the child case study stories, suitability of the approach for the forms of data processing which had been developed and opportunity for interpolation of narrative and analysis was very attractive. However, the clinching factor in deciding to construct the text using narrative case studies was the opportunity which the strategy provided to invite readers to engage with the text and to reflect on its meaning and connection with their own lives. The result, of course, is the book which you have been reading.

Having made the decision to present the findings using narrative case studies, the questions of length and focus had to be faced. Drafts suggested that the longitudinal, holistic and 'voice' requirements needed about 20,000 words for each child story and, with nine case studies available and the two major themes of learning and career to address, the solution was to produce two books. This is what Ann Filer and I have done. The present book focuses on learning and is based on five children over three years. The second (Pollard and Filer, in press) is focused on pupil career and is based on four *different* children over *seven* years though, of course, children from the first book do feature in it. In the second book, *The Social World of Pupil Careers*, the theoretical analysis is extended further.

However, even having made these difficult decisions, within the present book there has been a tension between length and holism which has led to the production of some shorter and some longer accounts of children's learning in particular years (see the Introduction to Part 2).

A number of ethical issues in the process of writing up, remained. The ethical code which had been agreed at the start of the study (see p. 292) was maintained without problems. However, part of this agreement was to treat data from children, parents and teachers confidentially and this meant that it was only at the writing-up stage that each party formally learned of the perspectives of the others. Anonymity from each other was clearly impossible to provide. I was extremely concerned about this, fearing for the possibility of people feeling uncomfortable by their portrayal in the accounts or by awareness of the perspectives of others, and I deliberately reminded people of the problem from time to time.

In the construction of the text, I determined that nothing would be included unless it was directly relevant to the story or argument, thus eliminating a great deal of fascinating data which would certainly have been included by a journalist. This was a challenge at times. For instance, there was a lot of data on school change which could have been written up, and there are many under-explored areas of the overall data set. With the help of Ann Filer and the adult respondents, I also considered, edited and negotiated any element of data which, though relevant and necessary, might be particularly sensitive to the children or others. At the same time though, I was anxious not to sanitize the accounts and, where conflict, misunderstanding, tension or anxiety had been important to the children's experience, I wanted the case studies to reflect it accurately. It was not, however, my purpose to be evaluative nor to dwell unnecessarily on data or incidents which might be disturbing to individuals. The construction and refinement of the case-study texts was thus the product of many judgements, as dilemmas within the relevant data for each case were faced.

In fact, when the moment for respondent validation of the draft child case studies and teacher vignettes came, significant amendments were requested by only one parent and by one of the teachers still in the school with whom the validation was conducted. For both teachers and parents, the validation took the form of pre-meetings in which Ann Filer and I explained the overall analysis, our view of its relevance and procedures for gathering their views. Anonymized draft texts for each teacher or family were then issued for confidential consideration. Sometime later, each had a personal follow-up meeting with Ann Filer and myself in which amendments and developments were made to the texts. Drafts of Chapter 2, on the school context and including the vignettes of teachers no longer in the school, were also validated by the headteacher. Overall, I was very pleased by the responses. The existence of the diaries and the continuing discussions and involvement in the school over so many years seemed to have resulted in perspectives which triangulated coherently, although that is not to say that some of the parents and teachers did not feel somewhat uncomfortable when reflecting in this way. The more analytical chapters (1, 4, 9 and 11) were written last and were not offered for respondent validation.

There remains the question of the children's responses to these case-study stories and of how they may feel about them in the longer term. The decision of whether to show the draft material to the children was raised with all the parents and explicitly left to them for decision. Ann Filer and I offered to discuss the drafts further with any child, but were not asked to do so. Several of the parents who gave their children access reported their child's amusement – 'it seems so long ago' was one response – and, in these cases, any necessary mediation was undertaken by the parents. In our validation discussions, no parent expressed concern about their children's perception of the stories and most seemed to feel that the text expressed much of what they knew already and, in many cases, had shared with their children through the diaries (which, towards the end of the study, were being used in several cases for reminiscing rather like family photograph albums). The case-study drafts were only made available as the children left Greenside Primary School for the last time as eleven-year-old 'leavers' in July 1994. In pupil eyes, the case-study stories were thus 'history' and, for the children, a new world of secondary education was absorbing all their attention. Nevertheless, one can never really tell how the children will respond as adolescents or as adults, and this remains a concern. I hope though that a wry smile or an occasional laugh will be raised by some memories from the past, that they will understand a little bit more both about themselves and about those who cared for them and, if they are saddened by anything that they read, that they will understand that their experiences have much in common with those of millions of other children. There are aspects of these stories that stand for the experiences of us all and from which we can all learn.

10.6   ASSESSING VALIDITY

A strength and defining characteristic of ethnographic research is the way in which the 'self' of the researcher is used as a research tool. There is a conscious and deliberate attempt to establish rapport with the subjects of the research in order to empathize and understand their perspectives, actions and interactions. This is an essential means of obtaining data about the subjective meanings of people's lives, without which no interpretive study can even begin. One must listen, observe, talk and ask, then describe and try to understand. Finally, one must search for patterns and attempt to generate a more abstracted, yet validly grounded, analysis. However, given the close involvement of the researcher at every point of the research process, there is an obvious question about the extent to which he or she influences the findings.

To assess the validity of this study, I would suggest that it is first necessary to accept the aims of the research in documenting and analysing social influences on children's approaches to classroom learning. Second, an attempt must be made to distil the main claims which have been made, probably with reference to Chapters 4, 9 and 11. Having done that, the reader must then form judgements about the appropriateness and quality of the data which has been presented and about whether the interpretations which have been offered are justified.

Hammersley *et al.* (1994) suggest that three main strategies are available to qualitative researchers in working to maintain validity: the use of unobtrusive methods of gathering data, as in 'non-participant observation'; the use of respondent validation; and the deployment of triangulation in terms of data-gathering methods, times, situations and researchers. Each of these can be assessed from the details of the research process which have already been provided, but I will also comment on them below.

Unobtrusive data gathering

Validity is strengthened to the extent that 'natural' social processes are undisturbed. I would argue that my low-key, non-participant role, extended over such a long period but with only limited presence at any one time meant that my influence on the social processes occurring in home, classroom and playground was very slight. In the pressing flow of everyday life, there were more important things for parents, teachers and children to do than to worry about the research project, and this largely overcame any special awareness of my presence or role. Maintenance of this unobtrusiveness was also one reason for deferring any major publications about the study until the children had left the school.

However, it would be naive to suggest that I had no influence on those whom I studied. My relationship with each teacher often began with some nervousness but then settled down over each year. I gathered data on all pupils from each teacher and did not emphasize the identities of the sample. In data gathering with the children, I disguised those in whom I was particularly interested – but the cohort were still very unusual in having a researcher taking such a close interest in them. On the other hand, they knew of nothing else. My judgement is that the greatest reactive effect may have been with the parents. This accumulated over the years. As the diaries were maintained and biannual discussions went on I was aware of how often they commented on the extent to which the study had caused them to reflect on their children's development. However, I have no examples of parents reporting taking particular actions because of the study.

Respondent validation

Confidence in validity may be enhanced when the subjects of the research recognize and affirm the findings as being an accurate representation of their experience. As I described in 10.5, respondent validation procedures were used with all parents, with teachers still in the school and with children when mediated by their parents. They were consulted about those parts of the text for which they were the focus. This process was carefully managed and spread over a period of several months, thus providing plenty of opportunity for discussion. One child case study and one teacher vignette were further developed in the light of the comments received, but, notwithstanding the very real challenges of reflecting on the past in this way, the overall perception was that the texts were accurate representations of the processes which had been experienced.

Triangulation

Validity is likely to be strong if a variety of types of data is collected, in different times and situations and if more than one researcher is involved. As has been shown in 10.3, a wide variety of data was certainly collected in this study, over an extended period and from three main social settings. This multiple triangulation should offer some confidence in the findings. Whilst only one researcher was involved in the collection of the data used in this book, a second researcher, Ann Filer, and an experienced headteacher, Ros Pollard, made a significant contribution to the interpretation and analysis of that data. The analysis also benefited from the comments of several other academics.

10.7   CONCLUSION

This methodological account could be developed much further, but it is hoped that sufficient information has been provided for readers to understand the technical aspects of the research design and data-gathering methods and to form a judgement on the validity of the findings.

I would argue that the study provides an *empirically valid* account of the issues on which it has been focused but I make no claim for the empirical generalization of specific substantive findings. The details of the case studies concern the children who have been studied and no others.

However, *theoretical inference* has been used to construct models which represent these empirically grounded findings in more abstracted ways. This has been done to facilitate comparison and reflection on the social influences on children's learning in a wider range of settings. Forms of theoretical generalization *are* therefore invited and I hope that one way in which this will occur is through the resonance which the accounts may generate with the direct experience of readers.

In Chapter 11 which concludes the book, I exploit these theoretical representations in exploring the *relevance* of the study.

Chapter 11

On the Relevance of the Study for Parents, Teachers and Policy-makers

11.1 INTRODUCTION

In this chapter we return to the questions which provided the starting points for this study (see p. x) and which are now listed above as the titles of the three sub-sections. Through explicitly addressing these questions, my aim is to review the analysis which has emerged and to consider its implications.

11.2 HOW DO SOCIAL FACTORS INFLUENCE THE FULFILMENT OF CHILDREN'S LEARNING POTENTIAL?

In answering this question, we can begin by recalling the model of socio-historical, intra-individual and inter-personal factors which was introduced in Chapter 1 to 'position' this study.

At the socio-historical level, the present study contributes to a growing body of inter-national research which demonstrates how social factors influence children's learning. Such work has recorded how children strive to fulfil their potential in circumstances which vary considerably both *across* and *within* societies. How, we might speculate, would the case study children have fared if they had been born elsewhere, into a different configuration of wealth, health, education, culture, language and security?

The countries and societies of the world exhibit vast differences in wealth, debt, health, education, environment, industrial and agricultural development, hunger, migration and forms of political control (Thomas, 1994). These differences relate to the social and economic histories of different parts of the world – the nature of ancient civilizations, religious beliefs and indigenous cultures, colonization, wars, struggles for independence and the emergence of national and international economies. Within particular societies social differences can be at least as great, with wide ranges in wealth, power and life chances. Such socio-historical factors produce huge differences in the economic and political circumstances in which children learn. Cultural variations are at least as important and these are becoming increasingly well understood by linguists, sociologists and anthropologists (see for instance, collections such as those of Rogoff and Lave (1984), Richards and Light (1986), Whiting and Edwards (1988) and Woodhead *et al.* (1991)). Building on Vygotsky's work, Bruner (1986, 1990) thus proposes a 'cultural psychology' and Wertsch (1991) argues for 'sociocultural' studies of human action and agency.

Of course, we cannot be sure how Mary, Hazel, Daniel, Sally and James would have fared and learned had they been born in families and societies facing different socio-historical circumstances. However, we can say that the socio-economic and cultural circumstances of the children's families produced values and expectations which were broadly consistent with those of the school and also provided a range of experiences and cultural, linguistic and material resources which supported the formal education offered by the school. The patterns of the children's learning and the development of their identities would not have emerged in the same ways as they did if it had not been for the socio-historical circumstances of relatively well-off and secure homes, the classrooms and play-ground culture of Greenside and their setting within a southern English city.

This book has not been primarily concerned with *intra-personal factors* though I have characterized children's 'learning potential' as being a product of such psychological and genetic influences. However, as I first suggested in Chapter 4, this is a considerable simpli-fication because it is becoming increasingly clearly demonstrated by psychologists and neuro-biologists that social and cultural factors make an important contribution to cogni-tion and brain functioning (Meadows, 1993). In essence, the assumption of fixed genetic potential within the brain has been challenged by research which highlights the importance of inter-connections between nerve cells. These develop or atrophy through *use* as well as through physical development and such use, of course, primarily occurs in social contexts through interaction with others. As Meadows puts it:

> Stimulation from outside the brain shapes these networks and is necessary for sorting out precise sensory and cognitive systems. Connections not only proliferate, a large proportion of them die, so that what is left is more specific and effective. ... Both maturation and experience are necessary for such developments. ... The nervous system develops in a social context.
> (1993: 274/5)

Children's learning potential is thus influenced by social factors from a very young age and on, throughout life. It is well beyond the scope of this study to demonstrate how that happens, but the case study stories offer accounts of differing social processes and patterns of interaction which, on the psycho-biological analysis above, are likely to be related to the successive intra-personal capacities of the children.

The book has been primarily concerned with *inter-personal processes* as children grow up and learn through their relationships with parents, siblings, peers and teachers and in this respect that we can again address the question, 'How do social factors influence the fulfilment of children's learning potential?'.

Figure 9.1, on page 284, represented the culmination of the inter-personal processes which were identified and discussed in Chapters 1, 4 and 9 following descriptive case studies of the children's stories. It shows a spiralling process through schooling and through life, in which individuals form identities, encounter learning challenges in partic-ular social contexts, are influenced by both formal and informal outcomes and thus develop their sense of identity and self. To that extent, the 'self', as Rowan Williams wrote, 'is what the past is doing now' (Maitland, 1991). It is the product of the individual learning in society.

A considerable number of important social influences have been identified in this book but perhaps the most important concerns *relationships within the family*. These have particular significance to any child because they provide the first, formative learning experiences. The results are deep emotional ties with parents and siblings and a particular nature and range of material, cultural and linguistic resources which affect capacities for certain types of action, self-confidence, motivation and learning strategies. Of course, for some children, perhaps where abuse or neglect occurs, these influences are likely to harm their school learning. Increasingly, there are also disjunctions caused by family breakdowns and divorce, the implications of which may be hard to predict. However, for most children, relationships within the family provide the formative influence on their sense of identity and a context of relative security as they progressively engage with the outside world.

Young children face two major sources of challenge as they begin to make their way outside the home. Relationships with other children is the first and each child has to learn how to accommodate themselves to the perceptions and interests of others. This takes some time and, as we have seen, some children are more successful at it than others. Friendships will grow as reciprocity is established and, through peer culture, these are likely to become a source of support in encounters with adults (Rubin, 1980). However, it is a long time before most children feel able to cast off the support of parents even as they build their alternative forms of solidarity with their peers. Parents, in this sense, are there to be used. They must offer support, advice and correction when their child needs it, but they must also learn to stand aside and allow space for experimentation as the child's independence grows.

The second major source of challenge to children comes from schooling and this could be seen as a more difficult form of 'assault'. After all, whilst the implicit rationale for playing with friends is 'to enjoy doing things together', the activity of teaching is based on the proposition that 'change should be affected in the child'. Thus we have the underpinnings of Waller's (1932) analysis of classroom life in which conflict, though rarely overt, is inherent. Jackson's (1969) analysis of the 'crowds, praise and power' which characterize classrooms sets out some of the conditions through which changes in children are to be brought about. To those, we might add reference to the curriculum which has to be learned and the fact of changes which, in most schools, pupils meet year-by-year as they encounter successive teachers. These are considerable challenges, particularly if, as in the case of Mary, Hazel, Daniel, Sally and James, you are starting out in primary school only a few months after your fourth birthday. The case studies provide many examples of the ways in which the children's parents provided emotional, intellectual and practical support for their children as they encountered the challenges of new situations, new teachers and new learning at school. The mothers, in particular, were constantly available in roles such as enthusiast, audience, confidante, interpreter, advisor, nurse, therapist and teacher. If we recall, from the Introduction of Chapter 1, Bruner's discussion of children as 'protagonists' – as agents, victims and accomplices in the praxis through which they engage with life (1990: 85) – then we begin to see parents in those families as *mediators* of the external world. They provided an emotional, physical and material infra-structure and a known, secure base from which their children struck out, and returned, in their engagement with new experiences and in their progressive struggle towards independence. Parents and carers of young children, in whatever family configuration or circumstance, thus have an absolutely vital role in education, for they are the most significant reference point with regard to children's identity, learning stance, the scaffolding of understanding and the valuation of learning outcomes.

The importance of the parental role has, of course, been identified many times before (e.g.: amongst the most interesting, Tizard and Hughes, 1984; Wells, 1987; Grant, 1989; Athey, 1990) and there are innumerable 'practical guides' (e.g.: Topping, 1986; Macbeth 1989). However, the educational potential of *parent-teacher partnerships* has not yet been fully realized. For instance, in England and Wales during the early 1990s, teachers struggled with curriculum and assessment workloads and with new forms of accountability and, though progress was made in some schools and LEAs, the deepening of partnerships with parents to support pupil learning was not a national priority. The tone of the *Parents' Charter* (DES, 1992), requirements to publish decontextualized assessment data and the promulgation of 'parent choice' as a means of creating a 'market' in education so that competition would increase standards, all missed the real educational point. Indeed, I would argue that the notion of 'parents as consumers' does not recognize the vital role that mothers and fathers play in supporting children's identities, self-confidence and learning. The danger is that it can create detachment and division.

This study thus reinforces the view that parent–teacher partnerships to support pupil learning should be developed with a clear sense of purpose and collaboration wherever possible. However, the issue is a complex one and should not be left at the level of rhetoric or superficiality. Is it possible, for instance, that policy-makers might understand how early learning is supported through experience, discussion and instruction and see the significance of the social contexts and webs of relationships within which children learn? Are there politicians who might then provide steady, long-term, practical policies to facilitate the provision of appropriate support in families and schools? Could courses on parenting be offered, perhaps following on in the UK from the Health Service support for new mothers and babies? Could more comprehensive forms of pre-school education, if developed as recommended (National Commission on Education 1993), provide complementary support to parents on educational aspects of their role? Setting the *Parents' Charter* aside, could there be a national *Parents' Guide to Early Education* spelling out the complementary roles of parents and teachers in a cooperative style? Could training on the essential role of parents be provided for teachers, and become a greater focus for student-teacher courses? Could there be special funds for schools to support parent–teacher partnership on the curriculum? Could the content of the National Curriculum and suggestions for other worthwhile learning activities be made available in an accessible form for parents? (For an unofficial attempt see Pollard, in press.) Could national assessment procedures be developed in *formative* ways bringing parents, teachers and children together, rather than risking division? Could national school inspection procedures reflect the full importance of home–school partnerships? Additionally, considering the range of socio-historical circumstances in the England of the early 1990s (Central Statistical Office 1994), could there be particular economic and social policies offering support for families with children who face significant poverty and could the particular needs of single-parent families be addressed? I would suggest that, over time, such policies might do a great deal more to realize the potential of the nation's children than, for instance, the production of crude league-tables of school assessment results.

The second question with which we started this chapter is more specific and relates to children learning in classroom contexts.

11.3   HOW DO YOUNG CHILDREN BECOME EFFECTIVE CLASSROOM LEARNERS?

Addressing this question sociologically requires us, once again, to consider the individual child within classroom settings. In particular, I will highlight the ways in which children *manage their identities* and *negotiate with others* in respect of the two major factors which were identified in Chapters 4 and 9. These were the 'opportunities to learn', which are reflected in classroom relationships and the working consensus, and the 'quality of teaching and assistance in learning' which mainly stems from teacher knowledge and skills.

These characteristics of the classroom social setting are intimately connected to the nature of what Walter Doyle has called 'academic tasks' (Doyle, 1986; Doyle and Carter, 1984). Doyle and Carter argue that:

> because academic tasks in classrooms are embedded in an evaluation system, they are accomplished under conditions of ambiguity and risk. *Ambiguity* refers to the extent to which a precise and predictable formula for generating a product can be defined. *Risk* refers to the stringency of the evaluation criteria and the likelihood that these criteria can be met on a given occasion. (1984: 130)

Managing identity and the negotiation of opportunities to learn

Doyle suggests that risk is 'closely tied to the accountability system in classrooms' and, in this respect, his argument about academic tasks is connected to the analysis of the working consensus and structure of power relations which I reported in *The Social World of the Primary School* (Pollard, 1985a) and have built on in Sections 4.5 and 9.5 of this book. Put simply, when teachers and pupils have negotiated a mutual understanding of the social rules and expectations which underpin classroom order, then the risk to pupils acting or engaging in academic tasks within the boundaries of those understandings is relatively contained. Where teacher power is less constrained by such negotiated understandings, then academic failure is more threatening to pupils because of the unpredictability of teacher response. Doyle's analysis of risk in undertaking academic tasks is thus closely connected to the sociological analysis of 'opportunities to learn' in classrooms.

In *The Social World of the Primary School* I argued that there are two major sources of support and claims on the allegiance of pupils when they act in school – their peers and their teachers. I suggested that 'enjoyment' of school was associated with obtaining a satisfactory balance between the expectations of these two sources and that a tendency to satisfy peers, teachers or juggle with both, could be associated with the 'gang groups', 'good groups' and 'joker groups' which existed within the peer culture of 11 and 12 year-old children whom I had studied. Galton and Williamson (1992) have drawn attention to the resonance of this analysis to the 'attention seekers', 'hard grinders' and 'easy riders/intermittent workers' of the ORACLE study (Galton *et al.*, 1980) and to other similarly compatible work (Bennett's 'sinners' and 'saints', 1976, and Measor and Woods' 'knife-edgers', 1984). In a sense this is not surprising, for the analysis reduces to the fact that pupil options are basically quite limited. They tend to either challenge teacher authority, conform with it or negotiate for a pattern of relationships which best satisfies their interests. In the sequel to this book (Pollard and Filer, in press) Ann Filer and I have developed an analysis of the variations of these patterns across contexts and over time. However, for the moment, we can simply note that such patterns of action are a product of the processes in which child identities are deployed in classroom settings to produce characteristic patterns of coping strategies.

Regarding social factors within classrooms, and leaving intra-individual factors aside, the most 'effective learners' are likely to be those children who can manage their classroom identities so that they derive support from both their teacher and other pupils. Such pupils – 'jokers', 'knife-edgers' or 're-definers' – will not reject or cut themselves off from teacher support, nor will they offer a relatively blind obedience. Rather, they will seek to manage a positive identity with both their peers and their teachers and thus to maximize their opportunities to learn whilst not losing their peer-group status. In the three school years which have been reported in this book, the case study children occupied a variety of structural positions regarding attainment and popularity. Indeed, in section 9.5, we saw how each child was perceived by his or her teachers and the implications which this had for the assistance in learning which was offered. Being able to negotiate and maintain a viable 'presentation of self' (Goffman, 1959) in the particular social context which a classroom represents to a child, is thus a necessary precondition of stable engagement with learning.

As we have seen, the 'opportunity to learn' is a product of the working consensus, social understandings and power relations which obtain in a classroom. It follows that young children become effective learners when their strategies and presentation of identities are, or become, well adapted to those social conditions. Indeed, we have seen the ways in which this worked in the cases of Mrs Powell's, Miss Scott's and Miss George's classrooms.

What though, beyond opportunities to learn, of negotiating high-quality teaching?

Managing identity and negotiating assistance and support in learning

We could answer the question of how young children become effective classroom learners by simply saying that such pupils are both open to teacher assistance and are fortunate in being provided with a constant flow of appropriate instruction, questioning and encouragement. In Figure 4.1, on page 92, I presented a social constructivist model of an adult acting as a 'reflective agent' to scaffold the learning of children across their zones of proximal development. This is a positive conception of the way in which high-quality support and assistance in learning can be provided. Unfortunately, however, this is an optimistic scenario in terms of both teacher and pupil behaviour. Indeed, HMI have repeatedly raised concerns about teacher expectations when their observations have shown routinized teaching in association with pupil drift (e.g.: DES, 1978, 1982, 1985). However, as I have argued elsewhere (Pollard, 1985a: 186/7), these strategies represent a particularly comfortable mesh of teacher/pupil interests.

The classroom challenge facing teachers is considerable and we know from a succession of studies (e.g. Galton *et al.*, 1980; Edwards and Mercer, 1987, Tizard *et al.*, 1988; Alexander, 1992) that the provision of sustained, individualized instruction with high levels of cognitive challenge in large classes is very difficult indeed. Despite this, the largest observational study of the early 1990s showed that individualized work still took up approximately 40 per cent of teaching time in English classrooms at Key Stage 1, with almost 20 per cent for group work and 40 per cent for whole-class instruction (Pollard *et al.*, 1994). Indeed, it was recognition of the difficulty of achieving high-quality individualized work which led Bennett and Dunne (1992) and Galton and Williamson (1992) to study various forms of group work, whilst Alexander *et al.* (1992) simply advocated that there should be an increase in whole-class teaching. However, the pressure towards routinization is just as great on the pupil side and, on this, Doyle and Carter's study (1984) is again useful. They studied a very experienced teacher teaching written composition in English to three classes of children of different abilities in a junior high school in the south-western USA. The challenge of the various writing tasks were characterized as being 'higher-level' or 'minor' and the children's responses were observed over a three-month period. The main empirical finding was that, if the pupils were confronted with higher-level tasks which required them to think independently, they immediately sought to reduce task ambiguity. They deployed strategies such as 'asking public and private questions about content and procedures', 'slowing down the pace of classroom events' so that the teacher had to clarify task requirements to maintain classroom order and gradually persuading teachers to compromise on their more open-ended and challenging intentions (1984: 148).

Here, then, we see the power of the conditions which produce a mesh of teacher–pupil coping strategies. Teachers need time, subject knowledge and high levels of skill if they are to be able to support young learners at the highest levels of effective learning. Pupils need to be sufficiently confident of their identities and abilities to be able to work with ambiguity within classrooms – but most are not. Unfortunately then, both parties cope by negotiating a reduction in cognitive challenge and task ambiguity, thus tending, over time, to recreate routinization, drift and lower expectations than are probably justified. This is not an easy process from which to escape.

However, to be more positive about how children become effective learners, I would suggest that the implications of this study are that young children become effective learners when their self-confidence is high, the classroom social context poses manageable risks and they receive sufficient appropriate instruction and support. The need for suitable social conditions in classrooms complements the necessity for appropriate levels of cognitive challenge – a theme to which I will return below in addressing our final question.

11.4 ARE POLICY-MAKERS JUSTIFIED IN FOCUSING ON CURRICULUM AND ASSESSMENT TO 'IMPROVE EDUCATIONAL STANDARDS'?

Following the Education Reform Act of 1988, the early 1990s saw the implementation of a national curriculum for England and Wales. The curricular framework was not dissimilar to those in many other countries (Meyer *et al.*, 1992) with provision for the 'core foundation' subjects of English, maths and science and for 'other foundation' subjects of history, geography, technology, art, music and physical education. Religious education was also to be taught. The initial specification for the National Curriculum caused considerable difficulties and stress for teachers and schools (Muschamp *et al.*, 1992, Campbell and Neill 1994, Pollard *et al.*, 1994; Pollard, 1994) and the government finally accepted that it was overloaded, fragmented and unmanageable after a report by Sir Ron Dearing (1994). The National Curriculum was then 'slimmed down' and a new framework, ostensibly giving teachers more scope for professional judgement, was introduced from September 1995.

The introduction and form of the National Curriculum can be seen as the product of competing interest groups and ideologies within the Conservative Party which was in power in the late 1980s, but its educational justification was provided by a long sequence of research reports (e.g.: Bennett, 1976; Alexander, 1984, 1992; Bennett *et al.*, 1984; Galton *et al.*, 1980; Barker-Lunn, 1982) and evidence from Her Majesty's Inspectors (e.g.: DES, 1978, 1982, 1985) which showed the variability and poor quality of much previous curriculum practice. The ideals of the post-Plowden (CACE, 1967) 'golden age' of progressive, child-centred primary education represented important aspects of the values and commitments of many teachers (Proctor, 1990; Nias, 1989), and they still did in the early 1990s (Pollard *et al.*, 1994), but they were not generally realized in classroom practice. As Campbell and Emery (1994) put it:

> The years before the Education Reform Act revealed, not a golden, so much as a rather leaden, age. HMI identified a narrow curriculum, emphasising literacy and numeracy through repetitive exercises; work in science was patchy and haphazard; standards in the social subjects were lower than might be expected; (there) was often an undifferentiated focus on the pupils in the middle levels of attainment within a class, and expectations of able children were undemanding. Continuity and progression in curriculum experience had remained elusive and assessment and record keeping, other than that in the basic skills of reading and number, were rarely systematic.
> (1994: 10)

Campbell and Emery argued that this situation had arisen because of the almost complete absence of public policy on primary education and they suggested that teachers should be seen, 'as much as anyone else, as victims of this policy vacuum and not its creators' (1994: 10). Certainly, the principle of having a national framework for curriculum was consistently supported by most teachers (Pollard, 1992a; Pollard *et al.*, 1994).

In summary then, the evidence suggests that, in English primary schools of the 1970s and 1980s, standards of pupil attainment and forms of classroom practice were not entirely satisfactory, though to some extent this was masked by the ideology of 'child-centredness'. In that context therefore, a national curriculum framework and related assessment procedures could certainly be seen as being justified as an attempt to improve educational standards.

There are many advantages in having a nationally specified curriculum. The framework provides a guarantee of pupil entitlements and sets clear educational aims around which teachers, parents, pupils and educational administrators can work together and which the public and industry can understand. These aims provide a focus for the assessment activity of teachers and underpin procedures by which teachers and schools become publicly accountable. The national curriculum may also be seen as a means of providing shared experiences, skills and knowledge, and thus contributing to national cohesion, as in the case of England (Tate, 1994). As an organizational device the existence of a national curriculum makes it possible for teachers and schools to plan for coherence and progression in pupil experience and for those concerned with teacher supply, training and professional development to make rational decisions on priorities.

However, national curricula may also be contentious, as the English experience certainly was (Galton, 1995; Kelly, 1994; Simon, 1992). The central imposition of a curriculum framework was seen as undemocratic and constraining of innovation whilst its strong *subject-based* emphasis was regarded as being particularly inappropriate for young children whose interpretation of experience is not differentiated in such ways (Blenkin and Kelly, 1992). The ordering and specification of subject content were also highly problematic issues. On the first, it was argued that the setting out of a linear syllabus for each subject may not fit the pattern of a child's actual interests and growth in understanding and, indeed, there are no subjects in which a rank ordering of subject matter cannot be challenged (see Ernest, 1991, for instance, on maths). Regarding subject content, debates on inclusion, exclusion and appropriateness raged throughout the early 1990s. There was particular reference to the subject of History, in which it was argued that too much emphasis was being given to a traditional type of English history, and to English where criticism focused on requirements for speaking and writing Standard English, reading of 'classic' texts and implausible standards for the attainment of seven-year-olds. Many commentators felt that the National Curriculum did not reflect the cultural diversity of modern society and the needs of bilingual children. Such debates are likely to continue.

On balance, this brief review of curriculum policy in England suggests that the provision of a national curriculum framework was a *necessary,* if poorly executed, contribution to the improvement of educational standards. However, in my view, it was not *sufficient.* I will present this argument through a consideration of the work of Neville Bennett, which has had a considerable influence on the thinking which has underpinned educational change in the past decade. This is graphically illustrated in the references to the 1992 'discussion paper' on Curriculum Organisation and Classroom Practice in Primary Schools (Alexander et al., 1992) which was the Secretary of State for Education Kenneth Clarke's attempt to 'get rid of 1960s theories' which, in his view, had produced 'a happy chaos in the primary classroom' (Clarke, 1991b). The discussion document, known as the 'Three Wise Men's Report' was unusual as a product of the Department of Education of the time because it explicitly set out to review 'available research evidence'. However, of sixty-one non-governmental or HMI citations, no less than sixteen came from Bennett or from his colleagues at the University of Exeter (Carré, Desforges and Wragg) who have focused on subject knowledge and teaching skills. Parts of the report are an almost specific endorsement of this work. For instance:

> Our own view is that subject knowledge is a critical factor at every point in the teaching process: in planning, assessing and diagnosing, task setting, questioning, explaining and giving feedback.
> (Alexander, Rose and Woodhead, 1992; paragraph 77)

Bennett's early work aimed to identify factors which enable teachers to be particularly 'effective' (Bennett, 1976) and he focused on 'formal' and 'informal' teaching styles. However, as he later argued (1987), whilst the initial work identified some interesting patterns and descriptions, it lacked explanatory power and made few connections with actual practice. It was superseded by a model in which the teacher was seen as the manager of the attention and time of the pupils. A key indicator became the amount of time which the pupil was 'on task'. In the early 1980's Bennett's interest turned to the analysis of what he and his collaborators termed the 'quality' of classroom tasks, with quality being defined in terms of the degree of appropriate match between the task and children's capacities (Bennett *et al.*, 1984). Following the work of Shulman (1986, 1987), Bennett began to focus on teachers' subject knowledge and found considerable weaknesses in both curriculum knowledge and self-confidence (Bennett and Carré, 1993; Wragg *et al.*, 1989; Bennett *et al.*, 1992). He also focused on the management of cooperative group work as a way of increasing the classroom effectiveness in the presentation and implementation of curriculum tasks (Bennett and Dunne, 1992).

Neville Bennett's work represents a sustained and consistent attempt to develop and test a model of teaching and learning. His successive studies have focused on different parts of

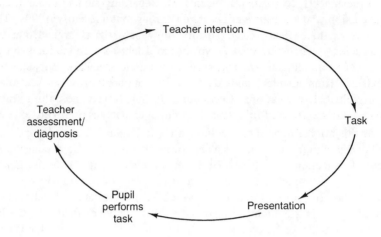

Figure 11.1 *A simple teaching cycle (Bennett, 1987)*

an emerging model (Figure 11.1) as used in Bennett (1987), Bennett and Kell (1989) and Bennett and Dunne (1992):

The very important point which Bennett and his colleagues have empirically documented is that breakdowns can, and do, occur regularly between each stage of this 'task process' within the teaching cycle.

Just as the National Curriculum sets out the knowledge, skills and understandings to be taught, Bennett's work provides a plausible and worthwhile analysis of how subject matter could be presented to maximize classroom 'effectiveness'. However, on the basis of the findings of this book it suffers from a lack of attention to learners and to social influences on the teaching and learning contexts which they experience. The model thus appears as a technical model of teaching – one which is dominated by the teacher, with pupils 'performing' to externally determined tasks. It is necessary, but it is not sufficient, as an analysis of teaching and learning in primary schools.

What happens though, when Bennett's analysis and that of this book are combined? Using the simplest form of each model and with some adjustments of presentation, this is attempted in Figure 11.2.

Figure 11.2 represents the two major actors in school education, teachers and pupils, and the two major processes, teaching and learning. The upper cycle uses the four questions on learning, which were first introduced in Chapter 1, to represent the analysis of this book in its simplest form with its focus on pupil learners as *children* with identities and learning dispositions which are developed, fostered or constrained by experiences within the social contexts of home, classroom and playground. Below it comes Bennett's five-part model of a 'teaching cycle' which has been expressed through questions. It represents teachers' work, which could well be within a national curriculum, in presenting appropriate tasks to pupils. The two cycles overlap at the point of the presentation of tasks within the socially-framed learning contexts of classrooms and both cycles should be seen as being located within the wider, socio-historical context.

My suggestion is that, at root, the two analyses are complementary. Whilst neither is sufficient, I would argue that both are necessary for an understanding of primary school education. Taken together they represent two of the most important strands of educational thinking concerning the interaction of the child and the curriculum, the socio-emotional and the cognitive. In a sense, the model legitimates the commitment by English teachers to maintain the quality of pupil experiences, as recorded in the PACE project (Pollard *et al.*, 1994), and English parents' consistent wish for their children to feel comfortable with relationships and the ethos of their primary school – which research evidence shows is a higher priority for them than concern for 'academic results' (Hughes *et al.*, 1994). This, of course, is a strength of the class-teacher system which remains a resilient form of organization in schools for young children.

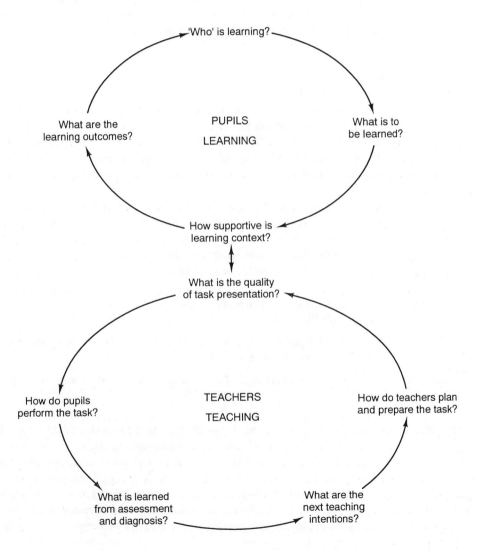

Figure 11.2 *A complementary model of teachers teaching and pupils learning*

Seen another way, the model suggests that whilst English policy-makers in the late 1980s and early 1990s were correct in principle to introduce a national curriculum framework (leaving aside the issues of implementation on which they failed so dismally), they were certainly wrong to ignore and condemn the views of those who attempted to assert the importance of the perspectives and needs of children as learners. The most obvious examples of this came from the Secretaries of State for Education in the early 1990s. Thus Kenneth Clarke claimed that primary education was dominated by 'an all-embracing and dogmatic orthodoxy about how children should be taught' (Clarke, 1991a) whilst John Patten suggested that it was 'trendy teacher educators' promoting '1960s theories' who were responsible (Patten, 1993). This 'discourse of derision' (Ball, 1990) was foolish and shortsighted. Drawing attention to the interests of children as learners need not indicate a sentimental hankering for some mythical past. Indeed, it simply draws attention to the educational necessity of engaging with each pupil as he or she develops as a person. We are fortunate that parents and teachers have never forgotten this reality.

11.5   CONCLUSION

This book as a whole has presented a cumulative analysis through engagement with the case-study stories of the social relationships and learning of five young children in an English primary school. I hope that it has provided a means through which readers will have reflected on their own childhood; on those of their children at home, if a parent; and on their pupils at school, if a teacher or student-teacher. Perhaps it has stimulated reflection of each sort?

I have also argued that, in the case of England, the National Curriculum and assessment innovations of the early 1990s failed to take appropriate account of pupils as developing, social individuals and as learners for whom the quality of learning experiences matters considerably. However, from what we now understand about education, I would not go as far as the assertion of the Hadow Committee of 1931 that:

> The curriculum of the primary school is to be thought of in terms of activity and experience, rather than knowledge to be acquired and facts to be stored.
> (Board of Education, 1931: 139)

for this does offer an unhelpful polarization. On the other hand, an assertion by the Prime Minister in the early 1990s, John Major, that:

> Children don't go to school for an 'experience'. They go to learn the basic skills they are going to need in later life – being able to read, write and do sums.
> (Major, 1994)

is also wide of the mark because, as this book has shown, children cannot avoid receiving experiences at school and elsewhere which will be of importance to them. In this context, it does seem to me to be the case that, whilst it is not always possible to ensure that children feel a sense of fulfilment and enjoyment in facing new learning challenges, these are appropriate intrinsic qualities to aim for in educational provision in schools and elsewhere. Additionally, as we have seen, such experiences are influential in the development of identity itself, and through identity, in the development of the citizens who create our societies over the long term.

Even if a directly instrumental view is taken, on the analysis of this book, the development of positive social relationships and the provision of appropriate school experiences must be seen as a vital contribution to formal learning outcomes. Such conditions complement curriculum provision and underpin both classroom order and personal fulfilment for pupils and teachers. Experience and curriculum are not opposed, as Alan Blyth (1984) and Maurice Galton (1995) have also argued. Thus we might try to rewrite Hadow, less rhetorically, with something like:

> Children's school education is to be thought of in terms of experiences, social relationships and development in a close interaction with curriculum knowledge, skills and understandings.

Certainly national curricula and structures for educational accountability are necessary, but they are not sufficient for high-quality learning. To think otherwise is an unnecessary and damaging delusion and we must hope that the 21st century will see the development of a more balanced appreciation of the complementary roles of child development, experience, social processes, curriculum and educational structures.

References

Alexander, R. (1984) *Primary Teaching*. London: Cassell.

Alexander, R. (1992) *Policy and Practice in Primary Education*. London: Routledge.

Alexander, R., Rose, J. and Woodhead, C. (1992) *Curriculum Organisation and Classroom Practice in Primary Schools: A Discussion Paper*. London: DES.

Apple, M. (1986) *Teachers and Texts*. London: Routledge.

Armstrong, M. (1981) *Closely Observed Children*. London: Readers and Writers.

Ashton, P., Kneen, P., Davies, F. and Holley, B. J. (1975) *The Aims of Primary Education: A Study of Teachers' Opinions*. London: Macmillan.

Athey, C. (1990) *Extending Thought in Young Children: A Parent-teacher Partnership*. London: Paul Chapman.

Atkinson, P. (1990) *The Ethnographic Imagination*. London: Routledge.

Ball, S. (1990) *Politics and Policy Making in Education*. London: Routledge.

Ball, S. and Goodson, I. (1985) *Teachers' Lives and Careers*. London: Falmer.

Barker Lunn, J. (1982) Junior schools and their organisational practices, *Educational Research*. **24**(4), 250-61.

Becker, H. and Geer, B. (1975) Participant observation and interviewing: a comparison, *Human Organisation*. **16**, 28-34.

Bennett, N. (1976) *Teaching Styles and Pupil Progress*. London: Open Books.

Bennett, N. (1987) The search for the effective primary school teacher, in S. Delamont (ed.) *The Primary School Teacher*. London: Falmer.

Bennett, N., Desforges, C., Cockburn, A. and Wilkinson, B. (1984) *The Quality of Pupil Learning Experiences*. London: Lawrence Erlbaum.

Bennett, N. and Kell, J. (1989) *A Good Start? Four Year Olds in Infant Schools*. Oxford: Blackwell

Bennett, N. and Dunne, E. (1992) *Managing Classroom Groups*. London: Simon and Schuster.

Bennett. N., Wragg, E. C., Carré, C. and Carter, D. S. G. (1992) A longitudinal study of primary teachers' perceived competences in, and concerns about, National Curriculum implementation, *Research Papers in Education*. **7**(1), 53-78.

Bennett, N. and Carré, C. (1993) *Learning to Teach*. London: Routledge.

Bernstein, B. (1975) Class and pedagogies: visible and invisible, in *Class, Codes and Control*, Vol. 3. London: Routledge.

Blenkin, G. and Kelly, A. V. (eds) (1992) *Assessment in Early Childhood Education*. London: Paul Chapman.

Blyth, W. A. L. (1984) *Development, Experience and Curriculum in Primary Education*. London: Croom Helm.

Board of Education (1931) *Report of the Consultative Committee on the Primary School*. (The Hadow Report). London: HMSO.

Bourdieu, P. and Passeron, J. C. (1977) *Reproduction in Education, Society and Culture*. London: Sage.

Broadfoot, P. and Osborn, M. (1988) What professional responsibility means to teachers: national contexts and classroom constants, *British Journal of Sociology of Education*, **7**(3), 265-87.

Bruner, J. (1986) *Actual Minds, Possible Worlds*. London: Harvard University Press.

Bruner, J. (1990) *Acts of Meaning*. Cambridge, MA: Harvard University Press.

Bruner, J. and Haste, H. (eds) (1986) *Making Sense: The Child's Construction of the World*. London: Methuen.

Burgess, R. G. (1984) *In the Field: An Introduction to Field Research*. London: Batsford.

Campbell, J. and Neill, S. (1994) *Curriculum Reform at Key Stage*. London: Longman.

Campbell, J. and Emery, H. (1994) Curriculum policy for Key Stage 2: possibilities, contradictions and constraints, in Pollard, A. (ed.) *Look Before You Leap? Research Evidence for the Curriculum at Key Stage 2*. London: Tufnell.

Central Advisory Council for Education (CACE) (1967) *Children and their Primary Schools* (Plowden Report). London: HMSO.

Central Statistical Office (1994) Social Trends. London: Statistical Office.

Clarke, K. (1991a) *Primary Education: A Statement by the Secretary of State for Education*. London: Department of Education and Science.

Clarke, K. (1991b) Transcript of interview with Kenneth Clarke, *World this Weekend*, broadcast on the BBC, 15 December.

Clarricoates, K. (1987) Child culture at school: a clash between gendered worlds?, in Pollard, A. (ed.), *Children and Their Primary Schools*. London: Falmer.

Croll, P. and Moses, D. (1985) *One in Five*. London: Routledge.

Dale, R. (1989) *The State and Education Formation*. Buckingham: Open University Press.

Daniels, H. (ed.) (1993) *Charting the Agenda: Educational Activity after Vygotsky*. London: Routledge.

Davies, B. (1989) *Frogs and Snails and Feminist Tales: Pre-school Children and Gender*. Sydney: Allen and Unwin.

Davies, B. (1993) *Shards of Glass: Children Reading and Writing Beyond Gendered Identities*. Sydney: Allen and Unwin.

Dearing, R. (1994) *The National Curriculum and its Assessment: Final Report*. London: School Curriculum and Assessment Authority.

Delamont, S. (1992) *Fieldwork in Educational Settings*. London: Falmer.

Department of Education and Science (1978) *Primary Education in England: A Survey by HMI*. London: HMSO.

Department of Education and Science (1982) *Education 5-9: An Illustrative Survey*. London: HMSO.

Department of Education and Science (1985) *Education 8-12 in Middle and Combined Schools*. London: HMSO.

Department of Education and Science (1992) *The Parents' Charter*. London: DES.

Department of Education and Science/Welsh Office (1987) *The National Curriculum 5-16: A Consultation Document*. London: DES/WO.

Donaldson, M. (1978) *Children's Minds*. London, Fontana.

Doyle, W. (1986) Classroom organisation and management, in M. Wittrock (ed.), *Third Handbook of Research on Teaching*. New York: Macmillan.

Doyle, W. and Carter, K. (1984) Academic tasks in classrooms, *Curriculum Inquiry* **14**(2), 129-49.

Dreeben, R. (1968) *On What is Learned in School*. London: Harvard University Press.

Dunn, J. (1988) *The Beginnings of Social Understanding*. Oxford: Blackwell

Edwards, D. and Mercer, N. (1987) *Common Knowledge*, London: Methuen.

Ernest, P. (1991) *The Philosophy of Maths Education*. London: Falmer.

Evans, T. (1988) *A Gender Agenda*. Sydney: Allen & Unwin.

Filer, A. and Pollard, A. (forthcoming) *The Social World of Pupil Assessment*. London: Cassell.

Finch, J. (1986) *Research and Policy*. London: Falmer.

Galton, M. (1989) *Teaching in the Primary School*. London: David Fulton.

Galton, M. (1995) *Crisis in the Primary Classroom*. London: David Fulton.

Galton, M. and Williamson, J. (1992) *Groupwork in the Primary Classroom*. London: Routledge.

Galton, M., Simon, B. and Croll, P. (1980) *Inside Primary Schools*. London: Routledge.

Glaser, B. and Strauss, A. (1967) *The Discovery of Grounded Theory.* Chicago: Aldine.

Goffman, E. (1959) *The Presentation of Self in Everyday Life.* Garden City, NY: Doubleday.

Goodnow, J. and Burns, A. (1985) *Home and School: A Child's Eye View.* Sydney: Allen & Unwin.

Grant, D. (1989) *Learning Relations.* London: Routledge.

Green, A. (1990) *Education and State Formation.* London: Macmillan.

Hammersley, M. and Atkinson, P. (1983) *Ethnography: Principles into Practice.* London: Tavistock.

Hammersley, M., Gomm, R. and Woods, P. (1994) Study Guide, MA in Educational Research Methods. Milton Keynes: Open University.

Hargreaves, A. (1978) The significance of classroom coping strategies, in L. Barton and R. Meighan, (eds), *Sociological Interpretations of Schooling and Classrooms,* Driffield: Nafferton

Hargreaves, D. H. (1972) *Interpersonal Relationships and Education.* London: Routledge & Kegan Paul.

Hartley, D. (1985) *Understanding Primary Schools.* London: Croom Helm.

Haste, H. (1984) Morality, social meaning and rhetoric, the social context of moral reasoning, in W. Kurtines and J. Gewitz (eds), *Morality, Moral Behaviour and Moral Development.* New York: Wiley.

Haste, H. (1987) Growing into rules, in J. Bruner and H. Haste, (eds), *Making Sense.* London: Methuen & Co.

Heath, S. B. (1983) *Ways with Words.* Cambridge: Cambridge University Press.

Hughes, M., Wikeley, F. and Nash, T. (1994) *Parents and their Children's Schools.* Oxford: Blackwell.

Jackson, P. (1969) *Life in Classrooms.* New York: Holt, Rinehart & Winston.

Kelly, A. V. (1994) *The National Curriculum: A Critical Review*, second edition. London: Paul Chapman.

King, R. A. (1978) *All Things Bright and Beautiful.* London: Wiley.

King, R.A. (1989) *The Best of Primary Education? A Sociological Study of Junior and Middle Schools.* London: Falmer.

Lee, V. E. (1985) Intellectual origins of Vygotsky's semiotic analysis, in J. V. Wertsch (ed.), *Culture, Communication and Cognition.* Cambridge: Cambridge University Press.

Lofland, J. (1971) *Analysing Social Settings: A Guide to Qualitative Observation and Analysis.* Belmont, CA: Wadsworth.

Lubeck, S. (1985) *Sandbox Society.* London: Falmer.

Macbeth, A. (1989) *Involving Parents: Effective Parent–teacher Relationships.* London: Heinemann.

Macintyre, A. (1989) *M. E. Post-viral Fatigue Syndrome: How to Live with It.* London: Unwin.

Maitland, S. (1991) *Three Times Table.* London: Virago.

Major, J. (1994) New Year message to Conservative Party activists. London: Conservative Central Office.

Mandell, N. (1984) Children's negotiation of meaning, *Symbolic Interaction* 7(3), 191-211.

Mead, G. H. (1934) *Mind, Self and Society.* Chicago: University of Chicago.

Meadows, S. (1993) *The Child as Thinker: The Development and Acquisition of Cognition in Childhood.* London: Routledge.

Measor, L. and Woods, P. (1984) *Changing Schools: Pupil Perspectives on Transfer to a Comprehensive.* Milton Keynes: Open University Press.

Meyer, J. W., Kamens, D. H. and Benavot, A. (1992) *School Knowledge for the Masses.* London: Falmer.

Moll, L. C. (1990) *Vygotsky and Education: Instructional Implications and Applications of Socio-historical Psychology.* Cambridge: Cambridge University Press.

Muschamp, Y., Pollard, A. and Sharpe, R. (1992) Curriculum management in primary schools, *Curriculum Journal.* 3(1), 21-39.

National Curriculum on Education (1993) *Learning to Succeed.* London: Hamlyn.

Nias, J. (1989) *Primary Teacher's Talking.* London: Routledge.

Nutbrown, C. (1994) *Threads of Thinking.* London: Chapman.

Paley, V. (1990) *The Boy Who Would Be a Helicopter.* Cambridge, MA: Harvard University Press.

Patten, J. (1993) Speech on the reform of teacher education, reported in *The Sunday Times,* 24 May.

Piaget, J. (1926) *The Language and Thought of the Child.* New York: Basic Books.

Piaget, J. (1950) *The Psychology of Intelligence.* London: Routledge & Kegan Paul.

Piaget, J. (1951) *Play, Dreams and Imitation*. New York: Norton.

Polanyi, M. (1958) Personal Knowledge. Chicago: University of Chicago.

Pollard, A. (1982) A model of coping strategies *British Journal of Sociology of Education*, **3**(1), 19-37.

Pollard, A. (1985a) *The Social World of the Primary School*, second edition, in press. London: Cassell.

Pollard, A. (1985b) Opportunities and difficulties of a teacher–ethnographer: a personal account, in R. G. Burgess (ed.), *Field Methods in the Study of Education*. Lewes: Falmer.

Pollard, A. (1987a) *Children and their Primary Schools, A New Perspective*. London, Falmer.

Pollard, A. (1987b) Studying children's perspectives: a collaborative approach, in G. Walford. (ed) *Doing Sociology of Education*. London: Falmer.

Pollard, A. (1990) Towards a Sociology of Learning in Primary Schools, *British Journal of Sociology of Education* **11**(3), 241-56.

Pollard, A. (1992a) Teachers' responses to the reshaping of primary education, in M. Arnot and L. Barton (eds), *Sociological Perspectives on Contemporary Educational Reforms*. Oxford: Triangle.

Pollard, A. (1992b) Balancing priorities: children and curriculum in the nineties, in R. Campbell (ed.), *Breadth and Balance in the Primary Curriculum*. London: Falmer.

Pollard, A. (ed.) (1994) *Look Before You Leap? Research Evidence for the Curriculum at Key Stage 2*. London: Tufnell.

Pollard, A. (in press) *An Introduction to Primary Education*. London: Cassell.

Pollard, A., Broadfoot, P., Croll, P., Osborn, M. and Abbott, D. (1994) *Changing English Primary Schools? The Impact of the Education Reform Act at Key Stage One*. London: Cassell.

Pollard, A. and Tann, S. (1993) *Reflective Teaching in the Primary School*, first edition 1987. London: Cassell.

Pollard, A. and Filer, A. (in press) *The Social World of Pupil Careers*. London: Cassell.

Proctor, N. (ed.) (1990) *The Aims of Primary Education and the National Curriculum*. London: Falmer.

Richards, M. and Light, P. (eds) (1986) *Children of Social Worlds*. Oxford: Blackwell.

Rogers, C. (1969) *Freedom to Learn*. New York: Merrill.

Rogoff, B. and Lave, J. (eds) (1984) *Everyday Cognition: Its Development in Social Context*. Cambridge, MA: Harvard University Press.

Rowland, S. (1985) *The Enquiring Classroom*. London: Falmer.

Rowland, S. (1987) Child in control. in A. Pollard (ed.), *Children and their Primary Schools*. London: Falmer.

Rubin, Z. (1980) *Children's Friendships*. London: Fontana.

Schatzman, L. and Strauss, A. L. (1973) *Strategies for a Naturalistic Sociology*. New York: Prentice Hall.

Shulman, L. S. (1986) Those who understand: knowledge growth in teaching, *Educational Researcher* **15**, 1-14.

Shulman, L. S. (1987) Knowledge and teaching: foundations of the new reforms, *Harvard Educational Review* **57**, 1-22.

Sikes, P., Measor, L. and Woods, P. (1985) *Teacher Careers: Crises and Continuities*. London: Falmer.

Simon, B. (1992) *What Future for Education?* London: Lawrence and Wishart.

Tate, N. (1994) Target vision, *Times Educational Supplement*, 2 December.

Tharpe, R. G. and Gallimore, R. (1988) *Rousing Minds to Life: Teaching, Learning and Schooling in Social Context*. Cambridge: Cambridge University Press.

Thomas, A. (1994) *Third World Atlas*. Buckingham: Open University Press.

Thorne, B. (1993) *Gender Play: Girls and Boys in School*. Buckingham: Open University Press.

Tizard, B. and Hughes, M. (1984) *Young Children Learning*. London: Fontana.

Tizard, B., Blatchford, P., Burke, J., Farquhar, C. and Plewis, I. (1988) *Young Children at School in the Inner City*. Hove: Lawrence Erlbaum.

Topping, K. J. (1986) *Parents as Educators*. London: Croom Helm.

Troyna, B. and Hatcher, R. (1991) *Racism in Children's Lives*. London: Routledge.

Vygotsky, L. S. (1962) *Thought and Language*. New York: Wiley.

Vygotsky, L. S. (1978) *Mind in Society*. London: Harvard University Press.

Walkerdine, V. (1988) *The Mastery of Reason: Cognitive Development and the Production of Rationality*. London: Routledge.

Waller, W. (1932) *The Sociology of Teaching*. New York: Russell & Russell.

Weider, D. (1974) Telling the code, in R. Turner (ed.) *Ethnomethodology*. London: Tavistock.

Wells, G. (1986) *The Meaning Makers*. London: Hodder & Stoughton.

Wertsch J. V. (1991) *Voices of the Mind*. Cambridge, MA: Harvard University Press.

Whiting, B. B. and Edwards, C. P. (eds) (1988) *Children of Different Worlds: The Formation of Social Behaviour*. Cambridge, MA: Harvard University Press.

Wolfendale, S. (1992) *Primary Schools and Special Needs*. London: Cassell.

Wood D. (1988) *How Children Think and Learn*. Oxford: Blackwell.

Woodhead, M., Light, P. and Carr, R. (eds) (1991) *Growing Up in a Changing Society*. London: Routledge.

Woods, P. (1977) Teaching for survival, in P. Woods and M. Hammersley (eds), *School Experience*. London: Croom Helm.

Woods, P. (1983) *Sociology and the School: An Interactionist Viewpoint*. London: Routledge.

Woods, P. (1990) *Teacher Skills and Strategies*. London: Falmer.

Wragg, E., Bennett, N. and Carré, C. (1989) Primary Teachers and the National Curriculum, *Research Papers in Education* **4**(3), 17-37.

Wright, C. (1992) *Race Relations in the Primary School*. London: David Fulton.

Author Index

Abbott, D.   4
Alexander, R. J.   93, 95, 310, 311, 312, 314
Apple, M.   6
Armstrong, M.   88
Ashton, P.   4
Athey, C.   4, 87, 306
Atkinson, P.   289, 298, 300

Ball, S. J.   314
Barker-Lunn, L. J.   310
Becker, H.   296
Bennett, S. N.   93, 309, 311, 312, 314
Bernstein, B.   18
Blenkin, G.   312
Blyth, W. A. L.   317
Bourdieu, P   86
Broadfoot, P   4
Bruner, J.   3, 4, 6, 298, 306, 307
Burgess, R.   287
Burns, A.   5

Campbell, J.   311
Carr, R.   306
Carré, C. G.   314
Carter, K.   309, 311
Clarke, K.   314, 316
Clarricoates, K.   84
Croll, P.   4, 309

Dale, R.   6
Daniels, H.   4, 6
Davies, B.   4
Dearing, Sir Ron   95, 311
Desforges, C.   314
Donaldson, M.   4
Doyle, W   91, 309, 311

Dreeben, R.   4
Dunn, J.   4, 6, 85, 86
Dunne, E.   93,   311

Edwards, D.   306, 310
Emery, H.   312
Ernest, P.   313
Evans, T.   4

Filer, A.   21, 27, 98, 270, 271, 284, 291, 301, 309

Gallimore, R.   296
Galton, M.   4, 90, 91, 93, 309, 310, 311, 312, 317
Geer, B.   298
Glaser, B.   291
Goffman, E.   310
Gomm, R.   302
Goodnow, J.   5
Grant, D.   5, 308
Green, A.   4, 6

Hammersley, M.   289, 298
Hargreaves, D.   90
Hartley, D.   4
Haste, H.   4, 6–7
Hatcher, R.   4
Heath, A. F.   5
Hughes, M.   4, 82, 86, 87, 308, 315

Jackson, P.   305

Kelly, A. V.   312
King, R.   4

Lave, J. 306
Lee, V. 5
Light, P. 306
Lofland, J. 298
Lubeck, S. 4

Macbeth, A. 308
Maitland, S. 306
Mandell, N. 6
Mead, G. H. 5, 8, 83
Meadows, S. 5, 85, 306
Measor, L. 309
Mercer, N. 310
Moses, D. 4
Moll, L. C. 6
Muschamp, Y. 311

Nash, R. 82
Neill, S. R. St J. 309
Nias, J. 312
Nutbrown, C. 4

Osborn, M. 4

Paley, V. G. 88
Passeron, J. C. 86
Patten, J. 314
Piaget, J. 4
Polanyi, M. 13
Pollard, A. 4, 6, 21, 27, 83, 92, 270, 271, 284,
    289, 291, 292, 297, 309, 310, 312, 315
Proctor, N. 312

Richards, M. 306
Rogers, C. 294
Rogoff, B. 306

Rose, J. 93, 311, 313
Rowland, S. 88, 92, 299
Rubin, Z. 307

Schatzman, L. 289
Sharp, R. 4
Shulman, L. S. 314
Simon, D. 4, 309, 312
Strauss, A. 289, 291

Tann, S. 92, 292
Tate, N. 312
Tharp, R. 96
Thomas, A. 305
Thorne, B. 4
Tizard, B. 4, 86, 87, 308, 310
Topping, K. 308
Troyna. B. 4

Vygotsky, L. S. 4, 5, 89, 92, 306

Walkerdine, V. 4
Waller, W. 307
Weider, D. 29
Wells, G. 86, 308
Wertsch, J. V. 5, 306
Whiting, B. B. 306
Wikeley, F. 82
Williamson, J. 93, 309, 311
Wolfendale, S. 4
Wood, D. 92
Woodhead, C. 93, 306, 311, 314
Woods, P. 6, 302, 309, 314
Wragg, E. 314
Wright, C. 4

Case-study Index of Children and Teachers

This is an index of case-study narrative chapters. It has been constructed to:

* facilitate cross-referencing to children who feature in both this book and in successive Social World books;

* support readers in tracking the teachers and classroom contexts across the cases.

Daniel 98, 146 *passim*
   structural position in classes 147
   immediate family tree 147
   Reception year summary matrix 167
   Year 1 summary matrix 174
   Year 2 summary matrix 183
   case-study overview 185

Harriet 73, 123, 135-6, 143, 146, 153-4, 155, 157, 165, 167, 216, 224

Hazel 73, 98, 101 *passim*, 216
   structural position in classes 102
   immediate family tree 103
   Reception year summary matrix 119
   Year 1 summary matrix 133
   Year 2 summary matrix 143
   case-study overview 144

James 98, 136, 213, 216, 225 *passim*
   structural position in classes 226
   immediate family tree 226
   Reception year summary matrix 245
   Year 1 summary matrix 252
   Year 2 summary matrix 263
   case-study overview 264

Mary 39 *passim*, 107-8, 135, 155, 186, 189, 192, 194, 202-3, 205, 208, 210, 212-13, 216, 217, 218, 221
   structural position in classes 39
   immediate family tree 40
   Reception year summary matrix 51

Year 1 summary matrix 64
Year 2 summary matrix 78
case-study overview 80

Miss George 26-31, 69-74, 137-40, 214-18, 255-9

Miss Sage 26, 176-80

Miss Scott 23-6, 55-61, 124-30, 171-73, 206-8, 248-50

Mrs Davison, headteacher 19-21, 291-2

Mrs Powell 21-3, 44-6, 108-17, 155-63, 193-200, 234-40

Robert 123, 154, 176, 182, 183, 194, 206, 224

Sally 40, 43-5, 51, 53-5, 58-9, 62, 64, 67-9, 70, 72, 74, 78, 84, 98, 135, 154, 186 *passim*, 216, 254, 263, 264
   structural position in classes 187
   immediate family tree 188
   Reception year summary matrix 203
   Year 1 summary matrix 210
   Year 2 summary matrix 221
   case-study overview 223

Sarah 53-5, 58, 64, 107, 154, 192, 205, 210, 224

William 170, 182, 206, 224

Analytic Subject Index

This is an index of the analytic chapters. It has been constructed to:

* assist engagement with the concepts and theoretical models contained in the book;

* direct readers to the research design, data gathering methods and forms of analysis;

* highlight issues of policy relevance.

access, negotiation 291–4

career 97, 284
child culture 87
child psychology 4
classroom
  effectiveness 314
  settings 12, 87, 279
coping strategies xiii, 3, 89, 270–1, 309–11
cultural variations 307–8
curriculum 10, 12, 88, 95, 274, 281
  attainment 12, 95, 281–2
  National *see* National Curriculum
  'negotiated' 19
cycle
  of learning 14, 96–8, 281–4, 299, 306
  of teaching 314
  of teaching and learning 315

data collection 294–8
  annual schedule 294–5
  methods 295–8

data analysis 298–9
  coding 298
  descriptive analysis 299
  interpretation 298
  theoretical modelling 299
  theoretical inference 304
  'tool kit' 3
  units of analysis 299

Easthampton
  city 16
  local education authority 14–7
Education Reform Act, 1988 16, 311

ethics
  agreement with parents and teachers 292
  writing up 301
ethnicity 6, 10
ethnography 289, 291, 298, 300

family 6, 17, 82–6, 267–73, 278, 307

gender 6, 10, 86, 269–70, 272
government, national 15–6, 311–13, 316
Greenside Primary School 16, 18–21, 82, 95, 268
  families 17–18
  headteachers 18–21
  change 19
  suburb 16–17, 81, 268
home setting 13, 83–4, 277
How supportive is the specific learning context?
  11–12, 89–95, 277–81

identity 9, 82–7, 268–73, 309–11
  relationships between self and others 83–4,
    269–71
  potential 9, 85, 271, 306
    intellectual 85, 271
    physical 85, 271
    resources 85, 272
    cultural 86, 272
    linguistic 86, 273
    material 85, 272
interests-at-hand 90
intra-individual factors 5, 6, 9, 85, 271–2, 306
inter-personal factors 5, 7, 83–4, 269–71, 306–11

learning
  achievements 12, 96, 281
  ambiguity 309, 311

challenges   10, 87–8, 94, 274–5, 307
control   91, 94, 279
cycle   14, 96–8, 281–3
experiences of   87, 94, 274
motivation   88, 274
opportunities to learn   11, 90–1, 94, 277–9, 309–10
outcomes   12, 95, 281
quality of teaching and assistance   12, 91–3, 279
risks   11, 91, 94, 279, 309
self-confidence   88, 91, 275
stance   10, 11, 88–9, 275–6
strategies   87, 89, 274–6, 309–11
tasks   88, 274, 309

'making sense' as a reader   14, 97, 283, 304
media   272

narrative   298
National Curriculum   16–20, 92, 95, 311–13, 316
negotiation   11, 87, 90, 92, 310
neuro-biology   5, 85, 271

parents   13, 19–20, 82, 267–8, 273, 307
   relationships with teachers   308
peers   13, 83, 270, 278
playground setting   87, 278
power   11, 90, 94, 279, 309
praxis   3, 307
primary schooling
   complementary factors   315
   sociology   4

questions for enquiry   3, 8, 307

'reflective agent'   2, 310
   parents   93
   teachers   93
relationships between self and others   83–4, 269–71, 280, 307
relevance of study   307–17
research identity   291–3
   with children   294
   with parents   293
   with teachers   292
research process   289–91
rule-frame 11, 91

sample
   Greenside Primary School   291
   pupils   292–3
'scaffolding'   12, 92, 279, 310
self   5, 83–6, 306, 310
self-esteem   12, 96, 281–2
siblings   83, 269, 272
significant others   13, 82
social class   6, 10, 11, 85–6, 268, 272
social constructivism   3, 4, 7, 12, 92, 297
social differentiation   4, 280–1
social status   12, 96, 281–2
socio-historical factors   6, 8–9, 81–2, 267–8 , 307–8
Social World of the Primary School   11, 83, 89, 90, 271, 309
Social World of Pupil Careers   97, 284, 300, 309
spiral of learning and career   283–4
strategies   87, 89, 90, 270–1, 311
structural position   90, 280
subject knowledge   313
symbolic interactionism   5, 83

teachers   87, 93, 279–80
teaching, quality   12, 91–3, 279–80

validity, assessment   302–3
   respondent validation   303
   triangulation   303
   unobtrusive data gathering   302

What are the outcomes?   12–13, 95–6, 281–3
What is to be learned?   10–11, 87–9, 274–6
Where and when is learning taking place?   8, 81–2, 267–8
Who is learning?   9, 82–6, 268–73
Why do social factors influence children's approach to learning?   13, 97–8, 283–5
working consensus   90, 279, 309–10
writing up   299–301
   ethics   301
   narrative   300
   respondent validation   301
   strategy   300

zone of proximal development (ZPD)   89, 92, 279